BAKING WITH DORIE

# DORIE GREENSPAN

SWEET,

SALTY

# BAKING
## *with* DORIE

& SIMPLE

For information about permission to reproduce
selections from this book, write to trade
.permissions@hmhco.com or to Permissions,
Houghton Mifflin Harcourt Publishing Company,
3 Park Avenue, 19th Floor, New York, New York
10016.

hmhbooks.com

Book design by Mia Johnson
Food styling by Samantha Seneviratne
Prop styling by Brooke Dionarine

Library of Congress Cataloging-in-Publication Data

Names: Greenspan, Dorie, author. |
    Weinberg, Mark, other.
Title: Baking with Dorie : sweet, salty &
    simple / Dorie Greenspan ; photographs by
    Mark Weinberg.
Description: Boston : Houghton Mifflin
    Harcourt, 2021. | Includes index.
Identifiers: LCCN 2021013014 (print) | LCCN
    2021013015 (ebook) | ISBN 9780358223580
    (hardback) | ISBN 9780358613336
    (hardback) | ISBN 9780358212416 (ebook)
Subjects: LCSH: Baking. | LCGFT: Cookbooks.
Classification: LCC TX763 .G6539 2021 (print) |
    LCC TX763  (ebook) | DDC 641.81/5—dc23

FOR GEMMA, OF COURSE.

# CONTENTS

# *Acknowledgments*

When the printers bind the covers to this book, I'll celebrate thirty years of cookbookery, as Julia Child used to call what we do. And, yes, there'll be cake. And there'll be toasts to all the people who've encouraged and inspired me and made my work better over the decades, and to the group that did so much to bring this book to life.

I'm fortunate beyond measure to be surrounded, once again, by people whose talents are matched only by their willingness to share them with me. For years now, Rux Martin, my editor; David Black, my agent; Mary Dodd, my recipe tester; Judith Sutton, who has copyedited thirteen of my fourteen books; and Carrie Bachman, publicist, and I have been together. It's rare to have a great team, rarer to have one that endures, and I'm grateful to each of you. And I'm delighted to now count Sarah Kwak among us. Sarah, who worked with Rux on my last two books, has now taken the reins on this one.

I loved working with the extraordinary artists who made the images for this book: Mark Weinberg, photographer; Samantha Seneviratne, food stylist; Brooke Deonarine, prop stylist; and Laura Manzano, assistant food stylist. I loved their commitment to the book and to each other—every voice was heard, every idea considered, then reconsidered and then looked at once more to be sure each photograph was the best it could possibly be. Thank you for being so open, so eager and so generous.

And how wonderful it was to once again have Melissa Lotfy as the art director on my book. She and designer Mia Johnson created a book that made the spirit of my recipes real. They're both geniuses and mindreaders.

When you work on a cookbook, especially when you're lucky enough to be published by Houghton Mifflin Harcourt, you're never alone—there is a battalion of experts behind you. Thank you, Deb Brody and Karen Murgolo, for believing in me and my ideas. Thank you to Marina Padakis Lowry, for being the ghostbuster of errors. To Crystal Paquette, for keeping the production wheels rolling. To Andrea DeWerd, for marketing, and Bridget Nocera, for publicity.

Creating recipes, baking them and writing about them is pretty sweet, but it's not without a bump here and there. It touches me deeply that my friends have stuck with me whether the times were as smooth as chocolate glaze, as knotty as Twist Bread or as bumpy as a Chunklet. A bundle of bisous to my friend, the writer Nina Brickman, whose timing is impeccable—just when you need counsel most, she appears like a good fairy offering equal parts wisdom and hilarity. Love and wonder to Louise Penny, whose gift for friendship is as great as her gift for writing—I'm not sure how she managed to write two stunningly good novels while sending hundreds of smart, funny, insightful and perfectly punctuated emails to me, but I'm so glad that she did. And bushels of hugs to my generous friends Leslie Gill, Ellen Madere, Priscilla Martel and Meg Zimbeck—it means everything to me to have you in my life. Special thanks to my friend Ann Mah, who casually suggested I write a cookbook with some savories in it—your short message was the seed.

My endless thanks to the countless home bakers who find happiness in the kitchen. Special thanks to the members of Tuesdays with Dorie, who have baked through many of my cookbooks—what you do is remarkable. Hugs to Laurie Woodward, who started the group so long ago, and to Stephanie Whitten and Julie Schaeffer, who keep it going. And an extra cookie to Mardi Michels, who hasn't missed a recipe in over a decade, and to Mary "French Fridays with Dorie" Hirsch.

As always—and for always—it's my family that sustains me. They are my world. First there was Michael, my husband. Then Joshua, our son. And Linling Tao, our daughter-in-law. And now, there's Gemma, sparkling Gemma, the sweetest sweet ever.

# *Introduction*

The idea for this book was born on a family trip to Santa Barbara. The first morning I was there, I got up early, drove to a nearby café and got a cappuccino and a wedge-shaped cheddar scone, studded with bits of scallion and fragrant from butter and warm cheese. That was more than three years and 150 recipes ago, the first of which was my version of that scone, followed by a band of breads and muffins, biscuits, more scones and some morning cakes to keep it company.

Over those years, I worked on the kinds of recipes I love most, recipes that are simple, rely on basic techniques and have deep flavors and complex textures. I created recipes that are flexible, that allow you to play with them, swap ingredients, fancy them up with icing or leave them bare, their natural color their own decoration. And, since I love surprises, I built them into lots of the recipes. I'm happiest when a recipe that looks familiar harbors something unexpected, which is why, for example, I tucked the sassy brightness of fresh cranberries into spice bars reminiscent of gingerbread. And if almost everything about a recipe is surprising, so much the better. That's the story with the S'mores Ice Cream Cake. It's big, tall, ready for a crowd and birthday candles; it has three flavors of ice cream and the usual graham crackers, but it also has frozen hot fudge sauce and a peanut butter and marshmallow fluff that would steal the show if the rest of the cake weren't so spectacular.

As I worked, one recipe inspired another, or one brought back a memory of another, and a few sparked questions that sent me skittering down paths that often led to revelations. Can there really be something new when it comes to chocolate chip cookies? Yes! Try Moko's cookies with chocolate and poppy seeds or my take on the latest trend in Paris: cookies with

1

extravagant toppings. Must babka, that rich yeasted loaf usually swirled around a chocolaty filling, be sweet? No! It can be made with cheese and a salty streusel that's so good it can be a snack on its own. Can you bake muesli into a Bundt cake? Yes—it's great! Can the dough that we use for cream puffs, éclairs and profiteroles—one of my favorite doughs—be stretched out long and thin, like breadsticks? And can they be sweet or salty? And will they look and taste like something completely new? Yes, yes and yes.

I made recipes inspired by my travels, like the glossy-topped almond cake that a Swedish pastry chef taught me—she also taught me about the custom of *fika,* the daily breaks for coffee, conversation and something sweet that are cherished throughout her country. And the Lisbon Chocolate Cake, a dense, almost brownie-like layer topped with a whipped dark chocolate ganache. I had it at a café where the coffee-and-tea menu was long and the dessert menu short—it was just this cake.

Once I'd decided to fold some savories into the mix, it was great to finally write down the recipes for the vegetable tarts and pies, quiches and quick breads that I serve often. Like the Vegetable Ribbon Tart that I think of as "fridge fancy," because it looks so elegant, even though the crust and filling (sometimes hummus, sometimes tzatziki or guacamole) are supermarket ready-mades and the topping, a riot of raw vegetables, can be anything you want; for me, it's usually odds and ends from the crisper.

Of course there are cookies. There are bars and brownies and squares, cookies for holidays and for every day. Fill a jar with hermits; pack Glenorchy Flapjacks, a New Zealand treat like granola bars, into a lunchbox; make Copenhagen Rye Cookies and have them with coffee; and try Tenderest Shortbread, slice-and-bake cookies you can make four different ways.

There are pies and tarts to take you through the year. Start with my friend Rosa Jackson's French Riviera Lemon Tart—it's the one she teaches in her cooking studio in Nice. Make the Chocolate-Rhubarb Tart in the spring, and then make it in every other season with bananas and Nutella. Make the Maple-Walnut Pie for Thanksgiving, the Cocoa-Cranberry Linzer Tart for Christmas, and when June rolls around, make the Father's Day Blueberry-Cherry Pie, a mix of cherries and blueberries, and top it with homemade berry ice cream.

It wasn't until I was deep into baking for this book, putting hearts next to the recipes I was sure I'd include, that I realized that I was playing favorites. Within almost every chapter, there was a kind of recipe, or a family of recipes, that was getting extra attention. I hadn't done it knowingly, but there they were, clustered together, small collections of my pet recipes. When I saw them, I knew immediately how right they were, and I dubbed them my "Sweethearts." I was glad to make a special place for those recipes that use brioche dough and those based on cream puff dough, to highlight chocolate chip cookies, meringues, layer cakes for celebrations big and small and pies, pandowdies, crisps and pastries made with apples, including a splendid tarte Tatin that's foolproof, even for first-timers.

It may have taken me longer than it should have to see the mini collections, but one thing I never lost sight of was the pleasure of being in the kitchen every day, of baking every day. This is my fourteenth cookbook, and it arrives exactly thirty years after my first. A lot has changed over those decades, but not the joy I get from baking. That's constant and unfailing.

If you're a baker, you know exactly how I feel. If you're not, the sweetest thing I can wish you is that you become one. Bake something and share it. It might change your life. It changed mine.

# *Just So You Know*

## WEIGHTS AND MEASURES, DOS, DON'TS AND PREFERENCES

MY HUSBAND'S FIRST JOB out of graduate school was as a research engineer. He'd work on something for what seemed like forever, test it, retest it, send it off to someone else to test and then, after he was sure it was right, he'd turn it in and, without fail, his boss would come back to him and say, "Yeah, yeah, yeah, it works under conditions a, b, c through q, but does it work under peanut butter?" It was his way of saying, "Are you sure it's bulletproof?"

Like Michael, I test my recipes and send them out to be tested again. And, like his boss, when they come back, I ask: "Will they work under peanut butter?" Here's what I know: They did work under peanut butter and they should work under peanut butter again.

Here's something else I know: Once my recipes go into the world—into your kitchen—different kinds of variables sneak in. Different ovens. Different mixers and blenders and processors and pans. Many different kinds of pans. Different brands. Different ingredients. Different climates. Different measurement systems. I can't control for everything, and neither can you. But if we start off as equal as possible—using the same systems, following the same methods—we should all finish with food we love, we take pleasure in making and we're proud to share.

MEASURING. I use two systems of measurement: volume, meaning cups and spoons, and metric weights. All of the recipes include both measurements and they've been tested with both, but my preference is to weigh the ingredients using metric measurements. Yes, weighing is more accurate and consistent, but that's not the only reason why I urge you to get a scale if you don't have one and to use it. Weighing ingredients is faster and easier, and it often dirties fewer bowls. You don't have to learn the metric system—your digital scale already knows it. But if you get the hang of it, you'll get a bonus: You can divide and multiply recipes in a flash with the metric system. Try it. Please.

FLOUR. You can use bleached or unbleached all-purpose flour for these recipes. My preference is for unbleached, and my house flour is King Arthur.
- *Measuring flour:* For all of the recipes, my standard is 1 cup all-purpose flour=136 grams.
- If you are measuring by volume, use a big fork or a whisk to loosen the flour in the bin (please don't store flour in its bag and certainly don't measure flour out of it—it will be too compressed), scoop your cup into the bin, getting enough flour so that it mounds over the cup, and then sweep it level with the back of a table knife. It's important not to shake the measure or to press down on the flour, either of which would give you a heavy cup.

**BUTTER.** All of the recipes were tested with unsalted butter. I love salted butter—it's my daily bread-and-butter butter—but I don't recommend it for baking because the amount of salt can vary. For example, European brands might have more salt than American brands. If you want to use salted butter, taste the butter to get an idea of how salty it is and then cut down the salt in the recipe as needed. If you're using American salted butter, you may not have to change the recipe. It all depends on your taste.

**EGGS.** I use large eggs and, when I have to figure their weight, I go with 1 egg = 50 grams; 1 white = 30 grams; 1 yolk = 20 grams.

- *Some recipes call for raw eggs.* If you make these recipes, please use fresh eggs, preferably organic and/or local. And know your audience—most people will not have a problem with wholesome raw eggs, but pregnant women and anyone with a compromised immune system should avoid raw eggs.

**SUGAR.** Granulated sugar is my basic.

**BROWN SUGAR.** I don't specify either light or dark brown sugar, because my recipes are neither fussy nor demanding in this regard. That said, while I always have dark brown sugar in my pantry, it's light brown that I reach for most often.

**SALT.** My kitchen salt is fine sea salt. I use flaky sea salt, such as Maldon, when I want a sprinkle on top of cookies or tarts, and fleur de sel, a French sea salt, when I want a salt that might hold a little of its texture in baking. I also like the mineral flavor of fleur de sel and the fact that it's a little less salty than fine sea salt. Taste a few salts and see what you like.

**MILK AND OTHER DAIRY PRODUCTS.** My preference is always for whole milk, yogurt, sour cream, cream cheese and ricotta. Buttermilk's the exception—it's usually a non- or low-fat ingredient. But if the choice is between lower-fat dairy or not baking, always bake! The only time I'd tell you to hold off is when it comes to cream—heavy (or whipping) cream must be full-fat. And, while some of the recipes specify Greek yogurt (because of its thicker texture), you can use regular and Greek yogurt interchangeably. No matter what kind you use, if there's liquid in the container, pour it off (and do the same with ricotta).

**DRIED FRUIT.** It may sound oxymoronic, but dried fruit needs to be moist and plump. If your fruit is hard and shriveled, plump it before adding it to whatever you're baking: Put the fruit in a bowl and cover with very hot water—water from the tap is usually hot enough. Let the fruit sit for a minute, then drain and pat it dry.

**PREHEATING THE OVEN.** Always, always preheat your oven. Turn your oven on as soon as you start on a recipe, so you can be sure that it's at temperature when you're ready to bake. In fact, it's best if the oven is at the proper temperature for at least 10 minutes before you're ready for it. It's good to keep a thermometer in your oven. Often, even in very expensive ovens, the ready-light goes out before the oven has actually reached the temperature you set it for.

**ROTATING BAKING PANS.** Your oven may or may not have hot spots—most do, so it's good to know whether yours does and, if it does, where they are. You can't make hot spots disappear, but you can get an even bake if you rotate your pans during baking. Unless I have a couple of baking pans on the rack, when I'm baking on one rack, I usually don't turn the pan. The exception is a baking sheet. Baking sheets are big and so

air doesn't circulate around them the way it does with, let's say, a cake pan, and because of that, I'll turn them. If I'm baking on two racks, I'll rotate the sheets front to back and top to bottom halfway through the baking period. In general, though, I try not to open the oven while I'm baking and so, if the hot spots are not going to damage whatever I've got in the oven, I skip the rotating part. Get to know your oven and figure out what works best for you.

TESTING FOR DONENESS. I've tried to give you as many clues as possible to judge when what you've got in the oven is ready to come out. Color is usually a good indicator, especially with crusts. Firmness reveals a lot. Does the

top of a cake spring back when you press it gently? Sometimes checking to see if a cake is starting to pull away from the sides of the pan will tell you the time is nigh. When it comes to cakes, the most reliable test is often the one where you poke a tester into the center of the cake—if it comes out clean, the cake is done. To get an accurate reading, you need a tester that's long enough to reach the center of the cake. A toothpick is traditional, but I like to use a bamboo skewer: It's long and slender, and it doesn't get lost in the tall jar I keep on the counter, the one crammed with spatulas for stirring and spreading and frosting, spoons, whisks and a couple of rulers.

GREAT STARTS

# BREAKFAST

TO EVERY DAY

# The Daily Bread: White Bread Edition

*Makes 1 loaf*

½ stick (4 tablespoons; 2 ounces; 57 grams) unsalted butter, cut into small pieces, softened, plus extra for the top of the dough

3 cups (408 grams) all-purpose flour, plus a few tablespoons more if needed

3 tablespoons powdered milk

2 teaspoons sugar

1¼ teaspoons fine sea salt

2¼ teaspoons instant yeast (such as Saf, Fleischmann's or Red Star; see page 12)

1 large egg, at room temperature

1 cup (240 ml) milk, at room temperature

Melted butter or 1 egg, lightly beaten with a splash of cold water, for glazing (optional)

**A WORD ON MIXING AND PATIENCE:** Like all yeast breads, this one takes patience. The dough must be mixed for a while—this is a job for a stand mixer with a dough hook (although you could tackle it with a wooden spoon and stamina). And it must rise three times. At each step, the dough progresses at its own rate and you mustn't rush it—a verity of yeast and a particular pleasure of baking.

IF YOU'RE NEW TO BREAD BAKING, start here—you'll be so happy with what you get and so proud of yourself for getting it. The Daily Bread is richer than most white breads—it's got butter, egg and milk, both whole and powdered, which makes the taste and texture even more luxurious. This is the bread I use for morning toast, weekend French toast and sandwiches as simple as peanut butter and jelly and as swanky as smoked salmon and crème fraîche. Leftovers from the loaf can be whirred in a food processor or cut up to make crumbs or croutons. And when you're looking for something a little sweeter and a lot more dramatic, you can use the dough to make the beautiful Twist Bread (page 21).

Butter a container with a capacity of at least 3 quarts or a large bowl. Have a tablespoon or so of softened butter at hand.

Put the flour, powdered milk, sugar and salt in the bowl of a stand mixer and stir to blend. Stir in the yeast. Drop in the pieces of butter and stir until they're coated with flour. Beat the egg into the milk and pour the mixture into the bowl. Attach the bowl to the mixer stand and fit it with the dough hook.

Start mixing the ingredients together at low-medium speed. It will only take a couple of minutes for the hook to pick up everything and pull it together into a messy mass. Give the bowl a scrape and then turn the speed up to medium to begin kneading the dough. Knead until the dough is smooth and cleans the sides of the bowl, 8 to 10 minutes. Scrape the hook and bowl a few times while you're working. When the dough is properly kneaded, it will be smooth and have a lovely sheen; it will also be a bit tacky.

Turn the dough out onto a work surface and knead it by hand to bring it together—sprinkle it with a spoonful or two of flour if it's sticking. Shape the dough into a ball, place the ball seam side down in the buttered container or bowl and rub a little butter over the top of the dough.

FOR THE FIRST RISE: Drape a clean kitchen towel over the container. Put the dough in a warm place (75 degrees F is ideal; see page 16) and let it rise until it doubles in volume, about 1 hour.

FOR THE SECOND RISE: Press the dough down, fold it over on itself and shape it into a ball again. Turn it seam side down, cover and allow the dough to double in volume again, 45 to 60 minutes. To test that it's properly risen, gently press it—if the indent from your fingerprint doesn't rebound, you're good to go.

Butter an 8- to 8½-inch loaf pan.

FOR THE THIRD RISE: Turn the dough out onto the work surface, fold it over on itself to deflate it and then press it into an approximately 8-x-6-inch rectangle. Starting from a long side, roll it up as tightly as you can; seal the seam by pinching it.

Place the dough seam side down in the loaf pan, tucking in the ends to fit if necessary. Rub the top of the dough with a little butter, cover the pan with the kitchen towel and return the dough to its warm spot to rise until it comes above the edges of the pan by about 2 inches, 45 to 60 minutes.

GETTING READY TO BAKE: When the dough is almost fully risen, center a rack in the oven and preheat it to 375 degrees F.

If you'd like to glaze the loaf, gently brush some melted butter over the top; this will give you a soft crust. Or, for a firmer top crust, brush with the beaten egg, taking care not to let the glaze drip down between the bread and the sides of the pan, or the egg will glue the dough to the pan and impede your bread's triumphant rise.

Bake the loaf for 35 to 40 minutes, or until it is golden brown. To test for doneness, turn the bread out and tap the bottom—if it sounds hollow, it's done. Alternatively, use an instant-read thermometer to check that the bread is about 200 degrees F at its center. Transfer the pan to a rack and let rest for 5 minutes, then turn the bread out onto the rack, invert again and let it cool to room temperature.

STORING: Wrapped well, the bread will keep for up to 3 days at room temperature or for up to 2 months in the freezer; defrost in its wrapper.

## Yeast

Once I discovered instant yeast, it became my go-to. There's no need to "proof" instant yeast, meaning you don't have to dissolve it in warm water and let it stand before incorporating it into your dough. Instead, the yeast goes in with the flour, no special treatment needed. All of the recipes in this book that use yeast were tested with Saf, Fleischmann's or Red Star instant yeast. If you want to use active dry yeast instead of instant yeast, you can make a direct one-to-one substitution; follow the proofing directions on the packet.

# Whole Wheat and Flax Edition

*Makes 1 loaf*

BECAUSE THIS LOAF has whole wheat flour, wheat germ and flax, the wholesome, nutty down-to-earth flavor of wheat is very present. Comforting too. Like its sister, the White Bread Edition (page 11), this is rich in dairy—it's got milk, whole and powdered, and some butter too. It cuts nicely, toasts beautifully and is good for sandwiches. It's the loaf I reach for when I'm making grilled cheese sandwiches, especially when the cheese is sharp.

Softened unsalted butter for the top of the dough

1 cup (240 ml) warm water, at room temperature

½ cup (120 ml) milk, at room temperature

2 tablespoons unsalted butter, melted and cooled

2 tablespoons honey

2 cups (272 grams) all-purpose flour, plus a little more if needed

1¾ cups (238 grams) whole wheat flour

¼ cup (20 grams) wheat germ

2 tablespoons powdered milk

1½ teaspoons sugar

1 teaspoon fine sea salt

2¼ teaspoons instant yeast (such as Saf, Fleischmann's or Red Star; see page 12)

¼ cup (40 grams) flaxseeds (see below)

A WORD ON MIXING: This is a sticky dough that's most easily mixed and kneaded in a stand mixer. However, if you feel up to it, you can do the work in a large bowl with a sturdy wooden spoon. Once the dough comes together, knead it in the bowl or on a floured work surface.

A WORD ON THE FLAXSEEDS: I'm partial to flax here, but you can use sunflower, poppy or sesame seeds. If you use poppy or sesame, start with 2 tablespoons and then see how much more you might want.

Butter a container with a capacity of at least 3 quarts or a large bowl. Have a tablespoon or a little more of softened butter at hand.

Whisk the water, milk, melted butter and honey together in a bowl.

Put both flours, the wheat germ, powdered milk, sugar and salt in the bowl of a stand mixer and stir to blend. (If you've got the muscle, you can make the bread in a large bowl with a sturdy spoon.) Stir in the yeast. Attach the bowl to the mixer stand and fit it with the dough hook.

With the mixer on low-medium, slowly and steadily pour in the liquid ingredients. Keep mixing until all the dry ingredients are moistened, then increase the speed to medium and beat for 4 minutes. If the dough doesn't come together and clean the sides of the bowl, add more flour a tablespoon at a time until it does. Add the flax and spin to incorporate the seeds. When the dough is whirling around on the dough hook and feels smooth, remove it from the bowl and pull it together into a ball.

FOR THE FIRST RISE: Drop the dough into the buttered container or bowl, cover with a kitchen towel and set aside in a warm place (75 degrees F is ideal; see page 16). Let the dough rise until it doubles in volume, about 90 minutes.

While the dough is rising, lightly butter a 9-inch loaf pan.

**FOR THE SECOND RISE:** Turn the dough out onto a work surface and fold it over on itself to deflate it. Press it out into a rectangle that's about 9 × 6 inches. Starting from a long side, roll it up very tightly, pinching the seam to seal it. Place the dough seam side down in the pan and tuck in the ends if necessary. Cover lightly with the kitchen towel and return the dough to its warm place to rise until it comes just a little above the edges of the pan, about 45 minutes.

**GETTING READY TO BAKE:** When the dough is almost fully risen, center a rack in the oven and preheat it to 375 degrees F.

When the dough has risen, lightly rub the top with softened butter.

Bake the bread for about 45 minutes, or until it is golden brown. To test for doneness, turn the bread out and tap the bottom—if it sounds hollow, it's done. Alternatively, use an instant-read thermometer to check that the bread is about 200 degrees F at its center. Unmold the bread onto a rack, invert again and allow it cool completely before slicing.

**STORING:** Wrapped well, the bread will keep for up to 3 days at room temperature or for up to 2 months in the freezer; defrost in its wrapper.

## A Cozy Spot for Bread

If you're a seasoned bread baker, you probably have a favorite place to let your bread rise. Some people put the dough in a turned-off oven with the light on. Some wrap the container or bowl in bath towels and leave it on the counter (I'm this kind of cocooner). And some have oven settings made specifically for proofing (which is the pro word for letting the dough rest and rise). For yeast breads like the ones I make, a temperature that hovers at or a little above 75 degrees F is good. If the room is cooler, the rise will be fine, but it will take a bit longer. Judge the rise by volume, not minutes.

# Cinnamon-Raisin Bread

*Makes 1 loaf*

Softened butter for the top of the dough

1 cup (160 grams) raisins (or more, if you'd like)

Hot water or black tea

3¾ cups (510 grams) all-purpose flour

¼ cup (50 grams) sugar

2 teaspoons ground cinnamon

1 teaspoon fine sea salt

2¼ teaspoons instant yeast (such as Saf, Fleischmann's or Red Star; see page 12)

2 tablespoons unsalted butter, melted and cooled

1 large egg, at room temperature

1 teaspoon pure vanilla extract

1¼ cups (300 ml) milk, at room temperature

Melted butter or 1 egg, lightly beaten with a splash of cold water, for glazing (optional)

Cinnamon sugar for dusting (optional)

I CAN'T REMEMBER A TIME where there wasn't something cinnamon-raisin in the kitchen. There were always cinnamon-raisin loaves from the bakery and the supermarket in my mother's bread box, and then cinnamon-raisin bagels, muffins and breads in my own kitchen—my husband and son both love the combination. And they both love this bread. Because it has more sugar than most loaves, it toasts beautifully. It's great for breakfast, of course, but it's also very good for sandwiches. If you're a cinnamon-raisin fan, then you'll already be thinking of a day-after-Thanksgiving sandwich with turkey and cranberry sauce.

If your raisins are soft, you can skip the step of soaking them in water or tea, but I think that soaked raisins make a better bread.

For a richer and dressier-looking cinnamon-raisin loaf, take a look at the Twist Bread (page 21).

Butter a container with a capacity of at least 3 quarts or a large bowl. Have a tablespoon or so of softened butter at hand.

Put the raisins in a bowl and pour over hot water or tea to cover generously. Let soak for a couple of minutes, then drain and pat the raisins dry between sheets of paper towels—no need to be too thorough; set aside.

Put the flour, sugar, cinnamon and salt in the bowl of a stand mixer and stir to blend. Stir in the yeast. Beat the butter, egg and vanilla into the milk and pour the milk into the bowl. Attach the bowl to the mixer stand and fit it with the dough hook.

Start mixing the ingredients together on low-medium speed. When you've got a messy mass, scrape the bowl and hook, turn the speed up to medium and begin kneading the dough. Knead for 6 to 8 minutes, or until you've got a smooth dough that cleans the sides of the bowl. Drop in the raisins and spin to incorporate them.

Turn the dough out onto a work surface and knead it a few times to bring it together. If it's sticking, add a little more flour, a bit at a time. Shape the dough into a ball, drop it into the buttered container,

*Breakfast*

seam side down, and lightly butter the top of the dough. Drape a kitchen towel over the container.

Put the dough in a warm place (see page 16) and let it rest until it doubles in volume, 60 to 90 minutes. To test that it's there, gently press it—if your fingerprint doesn't rebound, you're good to go.

Butter a 9- to 9½-inch loaf pan.

Turn the dough out onto the work surface and fold it over on itself a few times to deflate it. Press the dough out into a rectangle that's about 9 × 6 inches and, starting from a long side, roll it up very tightly, then seal the seam by pinching the dough together. Place the dough in the pan, seam side down—tuck in the ends if necessary—cover lightly with a kitchen towel and allow it to rest in a warm place until it comes just a little above the sides of the pan, about 45 minutes.

GETTING READY TO BAKE: When the dough is almost fully risen, center a rack in the oven and preheat it to 375 degrees F.

If you'd like to glaze the loaf, gently brush some melted butter over the top, which will give you a soft top crust, or, for a firmer top crust, brush with the egg, taking care not to let the egg drip between the bread and the sides of the pan—the egg would glue the dough to the sides of the pan and hamper your bread's lovely rise. Dust the top with cinnamon sugar, if you'd like.

Bake the loaf for about 45 minutes, or until it is golden brown. To test for doneness, turn the bread out and tap the bottom—it sounds hollow, it's done. Alternatively, use an instant-read thermometer to check that the bread is around 200 degrees F at its center. Transfer the pan to a rack and let rest for 5 minutes, then turn the bread out onto the rack, invert again and let it cool to room temperature.

STORING: Wrapped well, the bread will keep for up to 3 days at room temperature or for up to 2 months in the freezer; defrost in its wrapper.

# *Twist Bread*

*Makes 1 round loaf*

3 tablespoons sugar

1 teaspoon ground cinnamon

1 teaspoon unsweetened cocoa powder (optional)

¼ teaspoon fine sea salt

2 tablespoons very soft unsalted butter

1 recipe dough for Daily Bread (page 11), ready to shape (see below)

½ cup (80 grams) moist, plump raisins or dried cranberries

1 egg, beaten with a splash of cold water, for glazing

Sanding or granulated sugar for sprinkling

**PLAN AHEAD:** To make the twist, you've first got to make the dough for The Daily Bread (page 11) up to the point where it's ready to be shaped. In other words, it must rise twice before you roll it out and fill it in this recipe.

**BASED ON THE DAILY LOAF: WHITE BREAD EDITION** (page 11), my favorite white bread, the twist is filled with a mix of butter, cinnamon, sugar and raisins, then braided and baked until it's so tall and brown and beautiful that you might not believe that you made it so easily. I never can. Because it looks fancy, the bread is a perfect centerpiece for a brunch, but I often make it during the week to have for breakfast, fresh with butter when it's just made, toasted when it's a day or three old. And it makes the best French toast! If you love bread pudding, swap cubes of this loaf for the scones in the Scones Pudding (page 60).

Butter an 8-inch round cake or springform pan.

Mix the sugar, cinnamon, cocoa, if you're using it, and salt together in a small bowl.

Working on a floured surface, roll the dough into a rectangle that's about 8 × 16 inches. Dust the dough with flour as needed and flip it over a few times so that you roll it on both sides. Using your fingers (my first choice) or a brush, gently spread the butter evenly over the surface of the dough. Sprinkle the dough with the sugar mixture and then scatter over the raisins or cranberries; pat the fruit gently to help it settle into the dough.

Starting with a long side of the dough, roll it up snugly, finishing with the seam on the bottom; the log should be perpendicular to you. Using a chef's knife, and starting an inch or so from the top, so that the small top piece remains intact, slice the log lengthwise into 3 strips (see the photos on pages 22–23). You're going to braid the strips, but to get the prettiest loaf and to distribute the filling evenly throughout the loaf, it's best to twist them first: Twist each strand, so you have three corkscrews of dough attached at the top, and then braid them. Form the braid into a coil, pinch the ends together and tuck them under the dough. Carefully lift the coil up and into the buttered pan. ⟶

Cover the dough with parchment or a kitchen towel and let it rise in a warm place for 45 to 60 minutes, or until it's soft and puffy and comes about 2 inches above the sides of the pan.

**GETTING READY TO BAKE:** When the dough is almost fully risen, center a rack in the oven and preheat it to 375 degrees F.

Brush the top of the risen twist with the beaten egg, taking care not to let it drip between the bread and the sides of the pan, then sprinkle the top with sanding sugar.

Bake the loaf for 35 to 40 minutes, or until it is golden brown. To test for doneness, turn the bread out and tap the bottom—if it sounds hollow, it's done. Alternatively, use an instant-read thermometer to check that the bread is about 200 degrees F at its center. Transfer the pan to a rack and let the bread rest for 5 minutes, then turn it out onto the rack (or remove the sides and bottom of the springform). Invert again and let cool to room temperature.

**STORING:** Wrapped well, the bread will keep for up to 3 days at room temperature or for up to 2 months in the freezer; defrost it in its wrapper.

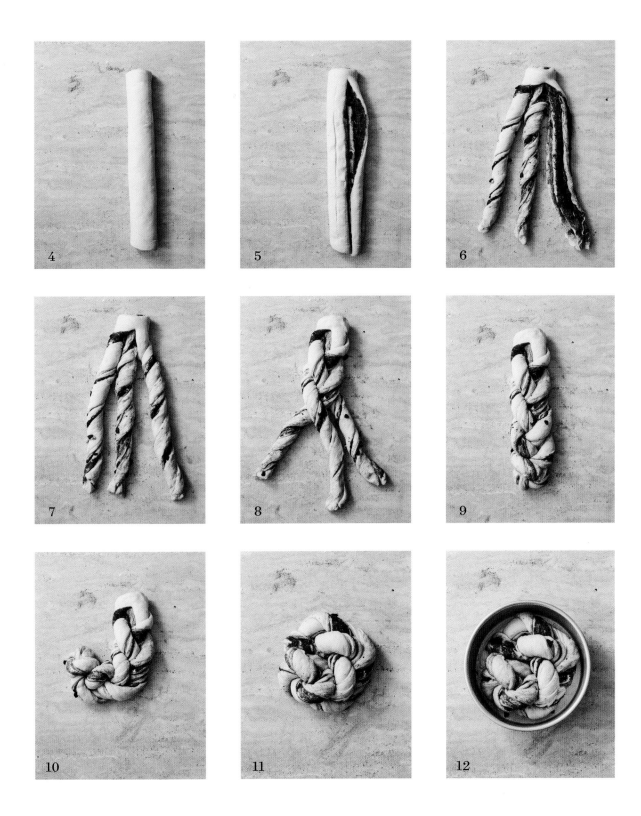

# English Muffins

*Makes 12 muffins*

1 cup (240 ml) warm water

½ cup (120 ml) milk, at room temperature

2 tablespoons flavorless oil, such as canola

3¾ cups (510 grams) all-purpose flour, plus more for dusting

2 tablespoons sugar

1¼ teaspoons fine sea salt

1¼ teaspoons instant dry yeast (such as Saf, Fleischmann's or Red Star; see page 12)

Cornmeal for dusting

Butter for griddling

Butter and/or jam for serving

YOU CAN BUY good English muffins at just about any supermarket, so there's no imperative to make them at home—unless you count superior taste and texture and the pleasure of crafting something by hand. Homemade English muffins, especially those made with a dough that's had time to rest, have a fully developed wheat flavor that hints gently of sourdough. They have the muffins' characteristic crags—they toast beautifully—and a little extra chew, which is satisfying. While I take pride in everything that I bake, there's a particular delight that comes from making a better version of something I'd normally buy. And this is a much better version.

English muffins are a kind of flatbread. They're made with yeast, so they rise like regular breads—I usually give the dough an overnight rest—but then they're cooked on a griddle. Cooked, not baked. The muffins never go into the oven, but they should go into the toaster. The griddle only partially cooks the muffins; it's the toaster that finishes them—it's the muffins' oven.

Butter a large container or bowl—3 to 4 quarts is about right.

Stir the water, milk and oil together in a bowl.

Put the flour, sugar and salt in the bowl of a stand mixer fitted with the dough hook and spin a few times to mix the ingredients. Add the yeast and mix it in. With the mixer on low, slowly and steadily pour the liquid into the bowl. Keep the mixer on low, and in a couple of minutes, the ingredients will come together in a shaggy mass. When they do, mix for another minute or two, or until the dough loops around the hook. Increase the speed to medium-high and beat for 7 to 8 minutes, until the dough is smooth and creamy—it will still be sticky, and that's fine. A word of warning: Don't turn your back on the mixer while it's kneading the dough—the mixer is bound to jiggle and creep from the rollicking spin and it can jump right off the counter (a very expensive mishap).

Scrape the dough into the buttered container or bowl. Turn it over (so that the top is now lightly buttered) and cover the container with a clean kitchen towel.

Set the container aside in a warm place (see page 16) and allow the dough to double in volume—it'll take about 60 minutes.

Reach into the container and fold the dough over on itself a few times to deflate it. Cover again and refrigerate for at least 3 hours, or for as long as overnight. The dough will more than double if you leave it overnight—not a problem.

When you're an hour or so away from wanting your muffins, line a baking sheet with parchment and dust it with cornmeal. Dust a work surface with flour, and keep out some extra.

Remove the container from the fridge and once again, fold the dough over on itself to deflate it. Turn the dough out onto the work surface and, using a dough scraper or a chef's knife, divide it into 12 pieces.

Flour your hands and one by one, roll each piece of dough against the work surface, pressing it under your cupped hand to make a ball (and using a bit more flour if needed). Place the ball on the lined baking sheet and pat it down lightly. Cover the baking sheet with a kitchen towel or a piece of parchment, set in a warm place and allow to rest and rise for about 40 minutes, until puffed.

Lightly butter a griddle or large frying pan and set it over low-medium heat. You want it to reach 350 degrees F. Measure the temperature with a thermometer gun or test it by holding your hand about 5 inches above the griddle—if you can keep it there comfortably for 3 to 4 seconds, you should be good. Working in batches, place as many balls of dough as you can fit on the griddle, cornmeal side down and at least 1 inch apart. Give each muffin a couple of slaps with a pancake turner or another metal spatula and leave them to cook for 7 minutes, or until their bottoms are golden. Turn them over, slap them again and cook for another 7 minutes or so. Transfer them to a rack.

You could eat the muffins while they're hot, but I don't think you should. The insides are purposely not fully baked: These muffins should be toasted. When the muffins are just warm or, better yet, at room temperature, use the tines of a fork to deeply prick each one around its middle and then use your hands to pry the halves apart. Toast and serve with butter or jam, or both.

STORING: The muffins will keep in a sealed container at room temperature for about 2 days, or they can be packed airtight and frozen for up to 2 months. If you freeze them, prick them in half before you freeze them—it will make early-morning muffining faster and easier.

# Brioche

*Makes 2 loaves*

2 sticks (8 ounces; 226 grams) unsalted butter, taken out of the refrigerator 15 minutes ahead of time, plus softened butter for the top of the dough

3½ cups (476 grams) all-purpose flour

¼ cup (50 grams) sugar

1½ teaspoons fine sea salt

4 teaspoons instant yeast (such as Saf, Fleischmann's or Red Star; see page 12)

⅓ cup (80 ml) milk, at room temperature

⅓ cup (80 ml) water, at room temperature

3 large eggs, at room temperature, lightly beaten

1 large egg, beaten with a splash of cold water, for glazing

**A WORD ON QUANTITY:** This recipe makes 2 loaves. Because you get better texture and rise when you're working with a generous amount of dough, it's best not to cut the recipe down. Prepare the full recipe whether you're making brioche or using the dough for babka, sticky buns or another brioche-based bread. If you've got a loaf left over, freeze it.

**PLAN AHEAD:** The dough needs to be made at least 1 day ahead.

**IF I WERE PRESSED** to choose a favorite bread, it would be brioche. The dough for it is rich—it includes both eggs and butter—and once baked, the loaf is golden, it's flavorful, its crumb soft and just a bit stretchy. Brioches can be loaves or buns. They can be filled or iced. They can be studded with something sweet or filled with something savory. But no matter how they're shaped, filled or flavored, they are elegant.

Brioche is a treat that takes time, patience and a heavy-duty mixer: The texture that makes brioche so alluring requires long, strong beating. (A hand mixer is not powerful enough.) You can do this by hand—it's the way it was done for hundreds of years—but it's strenuous. Once the dough is mixed, it has to rise and then chill overnight. On baking day, you'll need to allow for rising time as well. Yes, it's worth the effort and the wait.

This loaf is good for sandwiches, great for toast, regular or French—but the dough can also be used to make sandwich buns (page 34), sticky buns (page 31) and babka, sweet (page 35) or savory (page 38). If you'd like a loaf that pulls apart into buns, see Playing Around.

**ONE DAY AHEAD:** Butter a container with a capacity of at least 3 quarts or a large bowl. Have a tablespoon or so more of softened butter at hand.

Put the flour, sugar and salt in the bowl of a stand mixer and, using a spoon or flexible spatula, stir to blend. Stir in the yeast. Attach the bowl to the mixer stand and fit it with the dough hook.

Stir the milk and water together in a bowl and, with the mixer on medium-low, gradually add the liquid to the flour mixture. When it's all in, scrape the bowl and then mix on medium for 2 to 3 minutes, until you've got a bowl of shaggy bits of dough. It won't look good, but things will improve.

Working on medium-low, gradually pour in the eggs. When they're in, increase the speed to medium (or a notch higher) and beat for about 5 minutes, scraping the bowl now and then. For a few minutes, the mixture will slosh around and you'll think it's a failure—just keep mixing! When the eggs are fully incorporated, the dough still

won't be pretty, but it will spin around on the hook and although it will pool at the bottom of the bowl, it will clean the sides.

Keep the mixer at medium and start adding the butter a small piece at a time. I usually squish the butter between my fingers as I add it. Add it slowly, so that you don't have more than 2 pieces visible at the same time. This can take a while, maybe 10 minutes or so. When all the butter is in, increase the mixer speed to a bit higher than medium and beat for about 10 minutes: Stay close to the mixer—it might crawl or jump while it's beating! Scrape the bowl and hook occasionally, beating until the dough comes together in a soft, smooth, glossy mass; when you reach into the bowl and pull the dough, it will stretch, not break.

Scrape the dough into the buttered container or bowl and press it down so that it's smooth; rub a little softened butter over the top of the dough. Cover with a kitchen towel, put it in a warm place (see page 16) and let the dough rise until it's doubled in size, 45 minutes to 1 hour (it might take more or less time, depending on the temperature of the room and the dough—go by volume, not time).

When the dough has risen, lift up four corners one at a time and let the dough fall back into the container, or fold the dough over on itself; smooth the top. Cover the container and put it in the fridge.

After 30 minutes, lift the dough with your fingers—work around the dough so that you get to all of it—and let it fall. Do this every 30 minutes until it is cold, firm and no longer rising significantly, about 2 hours. Cover the dough with plastic wrap, pressing it directly against the dough, then cover the container and leave the dough in the refrigerator overnight. (*The dough can be refrigerated for up to 2 days.*)

After the dough has had its big chill, it's ready to be used to make the 2 loaves or for any of the other recipes that call for brioche dough (see headnote).

**TO SHAPE AND BAKE THE LOAVES:** Generously butter two 8- or 8½-inch loaf pans.

Remove the dough from the fridge, unwrap it and cut it in half. Working with one piece of dough at a time, press it down and shape it into a tight sausage that's as long as the loaf pans. Drop each piece into a pan and cover the top with a piece of plastic.

Place the pans in a warm place and let the dough rise until it peeks over the rims of the pans, about 2 hours (again, it might be more—as much as an hour more—or less; go by volume).

**GETTING READY TO BAKE:** When the loaves are just about fully risen, center a rack in the oven and preheat it to 400 degrees F.

Gently brush the egg glaze over the top of the dough, taking care not to let it drip down the sides—it'll hamper the dough's rise. Slide the loaves into the oven and turn the heat down to 375 degrees F. Bake for about 35 minutes, or until the loaves have risen and are deeply golden. To test for doneness, take the breads out of the pans and tap on their bottoms—if they sound hollow, they're done. Alternatively, an instant-read thermometer inserted into the center of the breads should read about 200 degrees F.

Transfer the pans to a rack and wait 5 minutes, then turn the loaves out. Turn them right side up on the rack and allow them to cool to room temperature.

**STORING:** Wrapped well, the loaves will keep for a day or so at room temperature or for up to 2 months in the freezer; thaw in the wrappers.

## Playing Around

### PULL-APART BRIOCHE

To shape the loaf, divide the dough into 6 or 8 equal pieces. Roll each piece into a tight ball and place the balls seam side down in the pan in 2 rows. If you'd like, after you've glazed the balls, you can use scissors to snip a small X in the top of each one.

# Brioche Sticky Buns

*Makes 8 buns*

## FOR THE STICKY GLAZE

¾ stick (6 tablespoons; 3 ounces; 85 grams) unsalted butter

¾ cup (150 grams) packed brown sugar

½ cup (120 ml) heavy cream

2 tablespoons honey

½ teaspoon ground cinnamon

¼ teaspoon fine sea salt

## FOR THE FILLING

¼ cup (50 grams) sugar

2 tablespoons brown sugar

1 teaspoon ground cinnamon

1 teaspoon unsweetened cocoa powder

Pinch of fine sea salt

## FOR THE BUNS

½ recipe dough for Brioche (page 28), chilled and ready to shape

**PLAN AHEAD:** It's foolish to pretend that these buns are anything but a project, because you must make the dough a day ahead (you can make it farther in advance and freeze it until ready to thaw and bake, if you'd like). But because the filling and caramel can be made in advance, they're a project easily worked into a weekend or another at-home stretch.

IT MIGHT BE the gooey filling that makes us crave sticky buns, but I'm convinced that the true greatness of these pastries depends on the dough—it's got to be remarkable on its own. I use my favorite brioche dough (page 28), rich, tender and flavorful, and I keep the filling simple—a mix of brown and white sugars with cinnamon and a touch of cocoa. The buns rise and bake in a not-too-sweet caramel sauce; because it's made with honey and salt, it has a slight, pleasantly bitter edge.

Generously butter a 9-x-13-inch baking pan.

**TO MAKE THE GLAZE:** Put all the ingredients in a medium heavy-bottomed saucepan and cook over medium heat, stirring, until the butter melts and all the ingredients are blended. Turn up the heat and let the glaze boil for 2 to 3 minutes.

Pour the glaze into the pan and jiggle it to get as even a layer as you can. (*The glaze can be made up to 1 day ahead. Let it cool, cover the pan and leave at room temperature until needed.*)

**TO MAKE THE FILLING:** Mix all of the ingredients together and keep at hand. (*Covered and stored at room temperature, the filling will keep for up to 1 week, so you can make it whenever it's convenient.*)

**TO MAKE THE BUNS:** Lightly flour a work surface. Shape the cold dough into a rectangle and dust the top with flour. Roll into a 12-x-14-inch rectangle, flipping the dough so that you work on both sides, flouring the surfaces as needed. Sprinkle the filling over the dough and use your fingers to spread it evenly.

Starting with a long side, roll the dough up as snugly as you can, ending with the seam on the bottom. If the ends of the log look ragged and perhaps a little low on filling, cut them away. Using a chef's knife, slice the log into 8 buns, about 1½ inches wide. Place the buns spiral side up in the pan with the glaze. You'll have a lot of space between the buns, and that's just fine.

Lightly cover the pan with a piece of parchment and put it in a warm place (see page 16). You want the buns to double in volume,

*Breakfast*

feel soft and light and touch one another here and there. Be patient—depending on the warmth of your room, this can take up to 2 hours, or maybe a little more.

GETTING READY TO BAKE: When the buns are verging on full-puff, center a rack in the oven and preheat it to 375 degrees F.

Remove the parchment and bake the buns for 25 to 30 minutes, or until they're golden brown and puffed—they'll have cozied up to one another in the oven, and the glaze will be bubbling. Transfer the pan to a rack.

You need to unmold the buns now, while the glaze is still molten. And you need to do this very carefully! Turn the buns out onto a platter or, if you don't have one large enough, a baking sheet lined with a baking mat or even a cutting board.

The buns are ready to serve when the danger of burning your fingers or tongue has passed. These are good warm, but they're also delicious at room temperature, so there's no rush.

STORING: The buns are at their peak the day they're made, but you can wrap them and keep them overnight—reheat them in a 350-degree-F oven (or microwave them for about 20 seconds), if you like. You can't freeze the glazed baked buns, but you can freeze the filled and rolled dough, before or after or it's been sliced into buns—just be sure to wrap it airtight. Defrost overnight in the fridge, then make the glaze, slice the dough into buns, if necessary, pop the buns into the pan, let them rise (which will take longer) and bake.

*Baking with Dorie*

# Brioche Sandwich Buns

*Makes 12 buns*

1 recipe dough for Brioche (page 28), chilled and ready to shape

1 large egg, lightly beaten with 1 teaspoon cold water, for glazing

**PLAN AHEAD:** You need brioche dough for these, which you'll have to make a day ahead.

**WHETHER YOU SPLIT THESE BUNS** for a breakfast sandwich—eggs, bacon, tomato, lettuce and cheese, avocado optional—or save them for a burger or a tuna-salad sandwich later in the day, they're an upgrader: They'll turn even the simplest filling into a luxury. And if you want to serve them as dinner rolls, warm and with butter on the side, that's okay too.

One full recipe of brioche (page 28) will make a dozen buns; of course you can use less dough and make fewer. If you make a dozen but won't be using them all quickly, split them after they cool and pack them for the freezer. Defrost them in their wrappers and warm them, toast them, heat them cut side down in a buttered skillet or give them a little time on the grill.

Line a baking sheet with parchment paper or a baking mat. Lightly flour a work surface, and have extra flour on hand.

Divide the cold dough into 12 portions. Flour your palms and, working with one piece at a time, cup your hand over the dough and roll it around on the work surface under your cupped palm until you've got a nice ball. It helps to press down lightly on the ball while you're rolling it. (Use a bit more flour on your hands or the surface, if needed.) As you finish each ball, place it on the baking sheet, leaving room between the balls.

Cover the buns with a sheet of parchment or a kitchen towel and put the baking sheet in a warm place (see page 16). Let the buns rise until they double in size, 1 to 2 hours, depending on the warmth of the room and the dough (go by volume, not time).

**GETTING READY TO BAKE:** Just before the buns are fully risen, center a rack in the oven and preheat it to 400 degrees F.

When the buns are ready for the oven, lightly brush the tops with the beaten egg. Try not to let the glaze dribble down the sides (it can glue the buns to the baking sheet and impede their rise) and be gentle—the dough is now beautifully risen, and it would be sad to deflate it.

Bake for 23 to 28 minutes, or until the buns are puffed and deeply golden; an instant-read thermometer inserted into the center of a bun (I poke it through the side) should read about 200 degrees F. Let the buns sit for a couple of minutes, then transfer them to a rack and cool to room temperature.

**STORING:** Wrapped well, the buns will keep at room temperature for 2 days or more. They can be frozen for up to 2 months; thaw in their wrapping (see headnote for rewarming instructions).

# Chocolate Babka

*Makes 1 loaf*

## FOR THE FILLING

7½ tablespoons (3¾ ounces; 106 grams) unsalted butter, melted

⅔ cup (133 grams) packed brown sugar

3 tablespoons all-purpose flour

1½ tablespoons ground cinnamon

1½ tablespoons unsweetened cocoa powder

½ teaspoon fine sea salt

½ recipe dough for Brioche (page 28), chilled and ready to shape

## FOR THE TOPPING

1 egg white, lightly beaten

½ recipe Streusel (page 366)

**PLAN AHEAD:** The babka starts with brioche dough, which you'll need to make a day ahead.

BABKA BRINGS BACK a hundred memories of my childhood—all of them happy. The babkas my mom brought home from the bakery were sweet yeasted loaves dappled, swirled or otherwise twisted around a cinnamon filling. I think there were raisins inside, and perhaps bits of chocolate were tucked in there as well. The top, my favorite part, was bumpy and generously crusted with nubbly streusel.

My babka is made from luxurious brioche dough (page 28), filled with a mixture of brown sugar, cinnamon and just a little cocoa—you can add a smattering of chopped chocolate, if you'd like. The filled dough is rolled up into a log, then split so that you've got two long strands to wrap over and under one another in a thick plait. When the babka has risen and is ready to go into the oven, it's showered with as much streusel as it can hold. My husband, whose mother shopped at the same bakery as mine did, says that this babka reminds him of the loaf that he too loved as a child. I'll take it.

**TO MAKE THE FILLING:** Stir all the ingredients together in a bowl. The mixture will not be smooth and it may look as though you've got too much butter, but you don't. Set it aside for at least 15 minutes to allow the butter to cool and be absorbed by the other ingredients. (*You can make the filling up to 1 week ahead and keep it well covered in the refrigerator. Bring to room temperature before using—it doesn't spread well when it's cold.*)

**TO FILL AND SHAPE THE LOAF:** Generously butter a 9- to 9-½ inch loaf pan and line it with parchment paper, leaving an overhang on two opposite sides that you can use as handles to lift the babka out of the pan once it's baked.

Lightly flour a work surface. Shape the cold dough into a square and dust the top with flour. Roll into a 16-inch square, flipping the dough so that you work on both sides, and sprinkling it with more flour as needed. Don't make yourself crazy—if the square's a little smaller or if it's uneven, you're still going to have a delicious babka.

Spoon dabs of the filling all over the dough and, using a small offset spatula (or a butter knife or the back of a spoon), gently spread it over the dough. If you can completely cover the surface of the dough, great! But if you end up with bare spots, that's okay.

Starting from the side of the dough closest to you, roll the dough up snugly, ending with the seam on the bottom. Turn the log so that it's perpendicular to you and, using a chef's knife, starting about 2 inches from the top, slice it lengthwise in half. You're going to braid the strips, and you will get the ⟶

prettiest loaf if you turn the strips so that the cut sides face up. Keep those sides up as you braid the strands. Pinch the ends together, lift the braid and lay it in the lined pan, tucking the ends under the loaf if necessary.

Lightly cover the pan with a piece of parchment and put it in a warm place to rise (see page 16) until the dough has doubled in volume—it should crest the rim of the pan and fill the pan. (If you've got an empty spot or two, as sometimes happens with a braid, ignore it—it will even out in the oven.) It can take about 2 hours for the babka to double.

TO TOP AND BAKE THE BABKA: When the babka is almost fully risen, center a rack in the oven and preheat it to 350 degrees F. Have a baking sheet at hand.

Remove the parchment from the loaf and use it to line the baking sheet, then put the pan on the baking sheet. Lightly brush some egg white over the top of the babka. Try not to let the white drip down the sides of the loaf—it can glue the dough to the pan and hamper its rise. Top with the streusel—I like to squeeze the streusel into small

chunks as I sprinkle it over the babka—pressing it ever so lightly onto the soft dough.

Bake the babka for about 50 minutes, loosely tenting the pan with foil after 35 minutes if the streusel is browning too quickly. The topping should be deeply golden and an instant-read thermometer inserted into the center of the loaf should read around 200 degrees F.

Transfer the pan to a rack and let it sit for 5 minutes, then use the parchment handles to lift the babka out of the pan and onto the rack; peel away the paper and allow the babka to cool to room temperature right side up. The temptation to eat it warm is great, but the loaf is difficult to cut when it's warm and you get the nice contrast between the crunchy streusel and the soft, stretchy brioche only after the loaf has cooled.

STORING: Wrapped well, the babka will keep for about 2 days at room temperature. If it stales a bit, toast it—it makes fabulous toast. Wrapped airtight, it can be frozen for up to 2 months. Let come to room temperature in its wrapping, then reheat briefly in a 350-degree-F oven, or slice and toast it.

# Cheese-Swirl Babka Buns

*Makes 8 buns*

## FOR THE FILLING

½ cup (125 grams) ricotta

2 ounces (65 grams) cream cheese, softened

2 tablespoons finely chopped shallots or onion, rinsed and patted dry

2 tablespoons minced fresh chives or scallion greens

1 tablespoon finely grated Parmesan

¼ teaspoon fine sea salt, or to taste

Pinch of freshly ground pepper

5 tablespoons (60 grams) tiny-cubed Comté, Gruyère or cheddar

½ recipe dough for Brioche (page 28), chilled and ready to shape

## FOR THE TOPPING

1 large egg, lightly beaten with 1 teaspoon cold water, for glazing

¼ cup (30 grams) chopped almonds or walnuts (optional)

1 tablespoon finely grated Parmesan (optional)

½ recipe Cheddar Streusel (page 378)

**PLAN AHEAD:** The babka buns start with brioche dough, which you'll need to make a day ahead.

MADE WITH BRIOCHE DOUGH, rolled up and cut like sticky buns and reminiscent of cheese Danish, these are sweet babka's flip side. The filling is a mix of ricotta and cream cheese, shallots and chives. You can play around with the flavorings, but make sure to add the cubes of hard sharp cheese—they're there for both taste and texture. Just before the buns are slid into the oven, they're covered with streusel, a crunchy crown. But here the streusel is salty and cheesy, a crisp echo of the filling.

Make these for a special brunch or serve them when lunch is a salad. And while they're best just baked, they make a really good breakfast the next day.

TO MAKE THE FILLING: Mix everything except the cubed cheese together. Taste for salt and pepper, then stir in the cheese. Cover and refrigerate until needed. (*The filling can be refrigerated for up to 2 days.*)

TO MAKE THE BUNS: Generously butter a 9-x-13 inch baking pan.

Lightly flour a work surface. Shape the cold dough into a rectangle and dust the top with flour. Roll into a 12-x-14-inch rectangle, flipping the dough so that you work on both sides and sprinkling the dough or work surface with more flour as needed. Dab the filling over the dough and, using an offset spatula (or a butter knife or the back of a spoon), spread it evenly over the dough, leaving an inch or so bare on one long side.

Starting with the long side that has filling, roll the dough up as compactly as you can, ending with the seam on the bottom. (If the dough is soft and difficult to work with, you may want to chill it for a bit before cutting it.) Cut away the ends of the log if they look ragged and perhaps a little low on filling. Then, using a chef's knife, slice the log into 8 buns, about 1½ inches wide (it's fine if they're slightly bigger or smaller). Place them spiral side up in the baking pan. You'll have a lot of space between the buns, and that's just as it should be.

Lightly cover the pan with a piece of parchment and put it in a warm place (see page 16). You want the buns to double in volume, feel soft and light and touch one another here and there. Be patient—depending on the warmth of your room, this can take up to 2 hours, maybe a little more.

GETTING READY TO BAKE: When the buns are almost fully puffed, center a rack in the oven and preheat it to 375 degrees F.

Remove the parchment and gently brush the top of each bun with beaten egg white. If you'd like to add the nuts and/or Parmesan to the streusel topping, now's the time. Scatter the streusel over the buns—if you think it needs it, pinch the streusel as you scatter so that you've got little nuggets.

Bake for 30 to 35 minutes, or until the buns are golden brown and puffed—they may bake into one another, and that's nice. Transfer the pan to a rack and let rest for 5 minutes or so before lifting the buns onto the rack. They're ready to eat when they're warm or at room temperature.

STORING: The buns are best the day they're baked, but they'll be good the following morning; wrap them well. If you'd like, reheat them in a 350-degree-F oven (or microwave them for about 20 seconds). You can freeze the baked buns, well wrapped, for up to 2 months (rewarm them when they defrost), but it's better to freeze the filled and rolled dough or the cut buns. Defrost overnight in the fridge, slice into buns, if necessary, place in the buttered pan and let rise, which will take longer; glaze and cover with the topping, then bake.

# BISCUITS AND SCONES: A HOW-TO

Biscuits and scones are made the same way, so if you can make one, you can make the other. While they are closely related, biscuits usually skew saltier than scones, which usually have egg in the dough. If there's a secret to making characteristically flaky biscuits and scones, it might be nonchalance. An easy-going attitude wins over diligence. Here are a few things to keep in mind:

• Always start with very cold ingredients. Be sure that your butter is cold and firm—if you've got time, cut it into bits and then refrigerate it while you set yourself up to work. You also want the cream, milk or whatever liquid you're using to be cold; ditto the eggs.

• Get your tools in order: a big bowl—a wide one is nice; a fork; a surface you can pat or roll the dough out on; and something to cut the dough with. Because the dough will be thick after you roll it out, it's good to have a true biscuit cutter, a cutter that's much taller than a cookie cutter. If you don't have one, you can use a glass. Scones can be cut into wedges, squares or rectangles with a chef's knife or a bench or dough scraper.

• Add the bits of cold butter to the dry ingredients in the bowl and use your hands to toss them around and coat them with flour. Then, using your fingers, mash and press and smush the ingredients together until you have pieces of butter that are as small as oatmeal flakes and as chubby as peas. Don't overdo anything, just squeeze and check on what you've got after a couple of minutes.

• Whisk the wet ingredients together and mix them into the dough with a fork. Save your energy: Less is more. Drier is better than wet. Flour that's left at the bottom of the bowl is fine. Get your already-messy hands back in the bowl and lightly knead the dough to bring it together—"lightly" is more important than "together."

• Turn the dough out onto a floured surface and flour the top—again, let moderation be your guide. Pat and slap the dough into the shape and thickness you want, or use a rolling pin.

• Follow the recipe's directions for cutting out the biscuits or scones. No matter what you use to cut, cut with determination, conviction and a crisp up-and-down movement. While it's tempting to twist the cutter or slide the knife after making the cut, don't! If you drag or smear the dough, you won't get the beautiful layers that are the hallmark of the best biscuits and scones.

• Gently gather any scraps together, press them together and cut some more biscuits or scones. The second and third rounds never look as pretty as those from the first pat-and-cut, but they always taste as good.

• If you want to freeze the biscuits or scones, put them on a parchment-lined baking sheet, freeze them until solid and then pack them airtight. When you're ready for them, arrange them on a lined baking sheet and let sit while you preheat the oven. If you want to brush their tops or sprinkle anything over them, do it just before you slide them into the oven. Because they were frozen, they might need a couple more minutes of baking time, or they might not—take a look at them.

# Tender Biscuits

*Makes about 8 biscuits*

½ cup (120 ml) cold plain yogurt

¼ cup (60 ml) cold milk or buttermilk (well shaken before measuring)

2 tablespoons minced fresh herbs, such as dill, parsley, chives and/or cilantro (optional)

2 cups (272 grams) all-purpose flour

1 tablespoon baking powder

2 teaspoons sugar

½ teaspoon fine sea salt

¼ teaspoon baking soda

¾ stick (6 tablespoons; 3 ounces; 85 grams) cold unsalted butter, cut into small pieces

Milk for brushing

**THESE BISCUITS CAN STAND** on their own as a breakfast treat or be a go-along for bacon and eggs, a bowl of oatmeal or even a cup of soup. They're made with a combination of yogurt and milk or buttermilk, so they're particularly tender. I've added a little sugar, not so much for sweetness as for balance. If you'd like an even more savory biscuit, add the minced herbs.

**A WORD ON WORKING AHEAD:** The dough can be made, cut and frozen for up to 2 months—make sure to wrap the rounds airtight—and then baked straight from the freezer. As soon as you start to preheat the oven, place the biscuit pucks on a lined baking sheet and let them stand until the oven reaches temperature. You may need to bake them a few minutes longer.

Center a rack in the oven and preheat it to 425 degrees F. Line a baking sheet with parchment paper or a baking mat.

Stir the yogurt and milk or buttermilk together in a small bowl. Add the herbs, if you're using them.

Put the flour, baking powder, sugar, salt and baking soda in a large bowl and whisk to combine. Scatter over the butter pieces, toss so that they're coated with flour and then, using your hands, press, mash and rub the butter and dry ingredients together until you have a bowl full of pieces as small as flakes and as large as peas. (You can do this with a pastry cutter, but it's easier and faster to use your fingers.) Pour the yogurt-milk mixture into the bowl and, using a fork, roughly mix the ingredients together. The dough will be dry, so you'll need to toss it with the fork, squeeze it a few times with your fingers and knead it a couple of times with your hands to bring it together.

Lightly flour a work surface, turn the dough out and pat it into a ½-inch-thick circle, square, rectangle or a raggedy whatever-shape-it-wants-to-be. Cut out as many biscuits as you can using a 2- to 2½-diameter biscuit cutter (or cut other shapes; see page 43) and place them a couple of inches apart on the baking sheet. Your goal is cut the biscuits as close to one another as possible so you get the most you can out of this first round. Gently pat the scraps together and cut out as many more biscuits as possible. The scrap-dough biscuits will be delicious, but they won't rise as high as the others. (*At this point, the biscuits can be frozen for up to 2 months; see headnote.*)

Lightly brush the tops of the biscuits with milk. Bake for 15 to 18 minutes, until they're golden and high. Pile them into a basket and serve while they're hot. Or, if you'd like to use them for shortcakes, let them rest on a rack until they are just warm or at room temperature.

**STORING:** Biscuits are best served soon after they're baked and best on the day that they're made. If you must hold them overnight, cover and keep at room temperature, then rewarm or split and toast them before serving.

# Potato Flake Biscuits

*Makes 8 to 10 biscuits*

1 tablespoon olive oil

½ medium onion, finely chopped

Fine sea salt and freshly ground black pepper

2 cups (272 grams) all-purpose flour

¾ cup (45 grams) potato flakes

1 tablespoon baking powder

1 tablespoon sugar

¼ teaspoon baking soda

3 tablespoons finely grated Parmesan (see headnote)

1 to 2 teaspoons (more or less, to taste) finely minced fresh herbs, such as chives, thyme, rosemary, oregano or parsley

1 stick (8 tablespoons; 4 ounces; 113 grams) cold unsalted butter, cut into small chunks

1 cup (240 ml) cold milk or buttermilk (well shaken before measuring)

Milk or heavy cream for brushing (optional)

**A WORD ON SHAPE:** While I usually make my biscuits round, the shape is really up to you. Once you roll or pat the dough out, you can cut it into squares, rectangles or diamonds, using all the dough in one go; no rerolling, no scraps. Think about it.

**AND A WORD ON WORKING AHEAD:** The dough can be made, cut and frozen up to 2 months ahead—make sure to wrap the rounds airtight—and then baked straight from the freezer. As soon as you start to preheat the oven, place the biscuit pucks on a lined baking sheet and let them stand until the oven reaches temperature. You may need to bake them a few minutes longer.

IF YOU THOUGHT that the word "flake" in the recipe's title referred to the lovely texture of the biscuits, you can be forgiven for falling for my little wordplay. The biscuits do, indeed, flake—as all good biscuits should—but they're also made with instant potato flakes, the kind used to make a side dish. Adding the flakes is an easy way to get the flavor of spuds on the spur of the moment. While the biscuits are fine made with just the flakes, they're much better if you treat them the way you might mashed potatoes, going a little heavy on the salt and pepper and adding sautéed onions, minced herbs and some cheese, as I do here.

I like to cook the onions until they take on some color, but if you're not the type to plan ahead, you can add finely chopped raw onion or scallions or lots of snipped chives. My usual cheese is finely grated Parmesan—I always have some in the fridge—but cheddar, Monterey Jack or Gouda will work as well. These are also nice made with the addition of ½ teaspoon sweet or hot paprika.

Center a rack in the oven and preheat it to 400 degrees F. Line a baking sheet with parchment paper or a baking mat and put it on top of another baking sheet, or use an insulated baking sheet—these biscuits need a double pan to keep their bottoms from getting too dark.

Heat the oil in a small skillet over medium heat. When it's hot, add the onions and cook, stirring, until they are soft and, if you like, take on some color. Season with salt and pepper, then scrape the onions and whatever oil remains onto a plate. Let cool while you start the dough. (*You can make the onions up to 3 days ahead and keep them covered in the refrigerator.*)

Working in a large bowl, whisk together the flour, potato flakes, baking powder, sugar, baking soda, Parmesan, herbs, 1 teaspoon salt and ½ teaspoon pepper. Scatter over the pieces of butter and toss them with your fingers to coat. Press, mash and otherwise squish the butter between your fingertips until you've got flour-covered pieces that are every size from flake to pea. (If you prefer, you can use a

*Breakfast*

43

pastry blender to cut in the butter, but I think doing this by hand is more efficient—and more fun.) Scrape the onions over the mixture and toss a couple of times. Pour over the cold milk, grab a fork and start turning and tossing until the milk is incorporated and you've got clumps of moist dough. Don't mix too much—you want a rough, knobby dough; if there's a little dry flour milling about, that's okay.

Continue working in the bowl or turn the dough out onto a work surface and gently pull the dough together into a ball, rolling it around and gathering it with your hands. You shouldn't have to knead to bring the ingredients into line, but if you find you must, work lightly and quickly. Now, on the work surface, pat the dough out so that it's ¾ inch high—height matters more than shape here.

Using a 2- to 2½-inch biscuit cutter, cut out as many biscuits as you can (or cut other shapes; see page 43)—cut the biscuits as close to one another as possible so that you get the most out of this round—place the pucks on the baking sheet. Press the scraps together, pat them to a thickness of ¾ inch and cut out more biscuits. If you've still got

scraps, press, pat and cut again—the last biscuits will not be as pretty or rise as high as the others, but they'll be just as delicious. (*At this point, the biscuits can be frozen for up to 2 months; see headnote.*)

If you'd like, brush the tops of the biscuits lightly with milk or cream (this will give you a slightly softer top crust with nice color). Bake for 15 to 17 minutes, or until the biscuits are tall and golden and their sides and tops feel firm. Transfer to a rack and cool for at least 5 minutes.

These biscuits are good hot, warm or at room temperature. At room temperature, they might be a bit denser, but they'll be just as tasty as hot biscuits.

STORING: Biscuits are best served soon after they're baked and best on the day that they're made. If you must hold them overnight, cover, keep at room temperature and then rewarm in a 350-degree-F oven or, better, split and toast them before serving.

# Cottage Cheese Biscuits

*Makes 8 to 10 biscuits*

2 cups (272 grams) all-purpose flour

1 tablespoon baking powder

½ teaspoon fine sea salt

¼ teaspoon baking soda

½ cup (113 grams) cottage cheese

½ cup (120 ml) cold milk

¾ stick (6 tablespoons; 3 ounces; 85 grams) very cold unsalted butter, cut into small chunks

TO ADD COTTAGE CHEESE to a biscuit dough is to add tang. It's also to make a dough that's very easy to work with. These are good served finger-burning-hot from the oven, and because they bake up tall, they're ideal split in half and used to make open-face sandwiches—think eggs and bacon or smoked salmon and red onion.

A WORD ON WORKING AHEAD: The dough can be made, cut and frozen up to 2 months ahead—make sure to wrap the rounds airtight—and then baked straight from the freezer. As soon as you start to preheat the oven, place the biscuit pucks on a lined baking sheet and let them stand until the oven reaches temperature. You may need to bake them a few minutes longer.

Center a rack in the oven and preheat it to 425 degrees F. Line a baking sheet with parchment paper or a baking mat.

Whisk the flour, baking powder, salt and baking soda together in a large bowl. In another bowl, whisk together the cottage cheese and milk.

Scatter the butter over the dry ingredients and toss to coat. Using your fingertips, squeeze and cut the butter into the dry ingredients. Aim for a lumpy mix with pieces of every shape and size, from pea to flake. It's fine that it'll look rough.

Pour the cottage cheese and milk mixture over the dry ingredients and, using a fork, gently toss, turn and stir everything around until you've got a soft dough. Squeeze a bit of it, and it should hold together. You might have a few dry spots here and there, but you're about to take care of them. Reach into the bowl and turn, fold and knead the dough—go easy, it's not bread—just enough to bring everything together into a ball.

Lightly dust a work surface with flour and turn out the dough. Dust the top of the dough very lightly and pat the dough out with your hands or roll it with a rolling pin until it is between ½ and ¾ inch high. Don't worry if the dough isn't rolled out evenly—a quick, light touch is more important than precision here.

Using a 2- to 2½-inch biscuit cutter (or cut other shapes; see page 43), cut out as many biscuits as you can. Your goal is cut the biscuits as close to one another as possible so you get the most you can out of this first round. Transfer them to the baking sheet. Gather together the scraps, lightly pat the dough out again, working it as little as possible, and cut as many additional biscuits as you can; transfer these to the sheet. You can go for another round, but they won't rise as dramatically as the others—they'll still be delicious. (*At this point, the biscuits can be frozen for up to 2 months; see headnote.*)

Bake the biscuits for 14 to 18 minutes, or until they are tall, puffed and golden brown. Remove them from the baking sheet and serve immediately.

STORING: The biscuits should be eaten straight from the oven (best) or within 2 hours. You can reheat them in a 350-degree-F oven, but the texture will be denser than just-baked.

# Blueberry Biscuits

*Makes about 10 biscuits*

½ cup (120 ml) cold plain yogurt

¼ cup (60 ml) cold milk or buttermilk (well shaken before measuring)

2 cups (272 grams) all-purpose flour

1 tablespoon baking powder

½ teaspoon fine sea salt

¼ teaspoon baking soda

3 tablespoons sugar

Grated zest of 1 lemon

¾ stick (6 tablespoons; 3 ounces; 85 grams) cold unsalted butter, cut into small pieces

1 cup (240 ml) blueberries

Sugar for sprinkling

**A WORD ON WORKING AHEAD:** The dough can be made, cut and frozen up to 2 months ahead—make sure to wrap the rounds airtight—and then baked straight from the freezer. As soon as you start to preheat the oven, place the biscuit pucks on a lined baking sheet and let them stand until the oven reaches temperature. You may need to bake them a few minutes longer.

THESE YOGURT-BASED BISCUITS border on cake because they've got a little more sugar than most and, more notably, because they've got berries stirred into the dough. When baked, the berries' sweetness and flavor intensify. I like to serve these at breakfast with butter and jam, but they can also make a really good dessert. Sliced and topped with sugared berries and whipped cream, they become a shortcake (see Playing Around).

Center a rack in the oven and preheat it to 425 degrees F. Line a baking sheet with parchment paper or a baking mat.

Stir the yogurt and milk or buttermilk together in a bowl.

Put the flour, baking powder, salt and baking soda in a large bowl and whisk to combine. Push the flour mixture to the side, so you've got a little work space in the bowl, and pour the sugar into the space. Top with the lemon zest and, using your fingers, work in the zest until the sugar is moist and fragrant. Then stir everything together.

Scatter the butter pieces over the dry ingredients, toss so that they're coated with flour and then, using your hands, press, mash and rub the ingredients together into you have a bowl full of pieces as small as flakes and as large as peas. Pour the yogurt-milk mixture into the bowl and, using a fork, roughly mix the ingredients together. Stir in the blueberries. The dough will be dry, so you'll need to toss it with the fork, squeeze it a few times with your fingers and knead it a couple of times with your hands to bring it together. Some berries will bruise and break, but that's fine.

Turn the dough out onto a lightly floured surface and pat it out ½ inch thick into a circle, a square, a rectangle or a raggedy whatever-shape-it-wants-to-be. Cut out as many biscuits as you can using a 2- to 2 ½-inch biscuit cutter (or cut other shapes; see page 43)—cut the biscuits close to one another, so you get as many as possible out of this round—and place them a

*Breakfast*

couple of inches apart on the baking sheet. Gently pat the scraps together and cut out as many more biscuits as possible. The biscuits made with scraps will still be delicious, but they won't rise as high as the others. (*At this point, the biscuits can be frozen for up to 2 months; see headnote.*) Sprinkle the tops lightly with sugar.

Bake the biscuits for about 15 minutes, until they're tall and golden. Pile them into a basket and serve while they're hot. Or, if you'd like to shortcake them, let them rest on a rack until they are just warm or at room temperature.

STORING: Biscuits are best served soon after they're baked and best on the day that they're made. If you must hold them overnight, cover, keep at room temperature and then rewarm them in a 350-degree-F oven or split and toast before serving.

## Playing Around

### BERRY-BISCUIT SHORTCAKE

Biscuits full of berries (use the recipe's blueberries or go for raspberries, if you'd like) make a luscious base for a shortcake. Toss some fresh berries with sugar and let them sit for 10 minutes or so, until there's a little juice. If you'd like, add a little chopped fresh lemon verbena, a pinch of chopped fresh thyme or some grated citrus zest. When the biscuits are only just warm or have reached room temperature, split them, pile on the berries and top with some lightly whipped cream—whether or not you sweeten the cream and add a touch of vanilla is up to you. Cap with the tops of the biscuits and serve with spoons.

# Buttermilk Scones

*Makes 8 scones*

2½ cups (340 grams) all-purpose flour

2 teaspoons sugar

1 tablespoon baking powder

½ teaspoon fine sea salt

¼ teaspoon baking soda

¾ stick (6 tablespoons; 3 ounces; 85 grams) cold unsalted butter, cut into small chunks

1 cold large egg

1 cup (240 ml) cold buttermilk (well shaken before measuring)

Milk for brushing (optional)

**A WORD ON WORKING AHEAD:** The dough can be made, cut and frozen up to 2 months ahead—make sure to wrap the scones airtight—and then baked straight from the freezer. As soon as you start to preheat the oven, place the scones on a lined baking sheet and let them stand until the oven reaches temperature. You may need to bake them a few minutes longer.

NOT SO LONG AGO, scones seemed fancy. And very British. They were a teatime treat, made small and dainty and served with clotted cream and jam. And then, I'm not sure when, scones were everywhere and being eaten at just about every daylight hour. And the great fun was that they were being made every which way. They were big or small, meant for morning or midday. No matter where I'd travel, I'd find scones, some that were sweet, some that had fruit, some that were made with cheese and some that seemed like a biscuitish equivalent of a quiche. I loved them all and cheered their leap into everydayness.

These don't have any add-ins or flourishes, although they could (see Playing Around). And they're easy to make. (Take a look at the how-to for biscuits and scones, page 41, if you're a newcomer to the process.) Their texture is delightfully tender and light, their flavor just a touch tangy, thanks to the buttermilk. Like all scones, these are best shortly after they come out of the oven—that's when their texture is at its peak; they'll be a little firmer and denser later in the day. But later in the day, or the next day, is when scones are good for reheating or toasting or turning into Scones Pudding (page 60).

My preference is for wedge-shaped scones, but you can cut the dough into squares, rectangles or rounds. Unless you decide to go for mini scones, which might bake more quickly, the shape won't affect the baking time.

Center a rack in the oven and preheat it to 400 degrees F. Line a baking sheet with parchment paper or a baking mat.

Working in a large bowl, whisk together the flour, sugar, baking powder, salt and baking soda. Scatter the bits of cold butter over the flour, toss so that they're coated with flour and then use your fingers to mash and press and mush the butter into the flour. (You can do this with a pastry cutter, but it's easier and faster to use your fingers.) Keep tossing the dry ingredients around and smushing the butter until you've broken it into flour-coated pieces as small as cornflakes and as big as peas.

Whisk the egg and buttermilk together, pour the mixture over the dry ingredients and, using a fork, toss, turn and stir everything together until the flour is moistened. With your hands, gently—and sparingly—squeeze and knead the dough just enough to pull it into a ball. It's futile (and unnecessary) to expect a smooth, neat packet of dough, because this dough is sticky.

Turn the dough out onto a lightly floured surface and shape it into a round that's about 6½ inches across and 1 inch high. (Get the diameter, and the height will follow.) Dust the top of the dough with flour. Using a bench scraper or a chef's knife, cut the dough into quarters and then cut each quarter in half, so you have 8 wedges. Carefully transfer them to the baking sheet. (*At this point, the scones can be frozen for up to 2 months; see headnote.*)

If you'd like, brush the tops of the scones lightly with milk. Bake for 18 to 20 minutes, or until they're tall and golden brown on top and bottom. Transfer the baking sheet to a rack and wait a couple of minutes, then lift the scones onto the rack. The scones are ready to eat about 15 minutes out of the oven and at their best within 3 or 4 hours.

STORING: The scones are at their peak the day they're made. After that, they'll be good reheated or toasted, or used for Scones Pudding (page 60). You can keep baked scones in the freezer for up to 2 months, or you can freeze them before you bake them (a better option), as described above.

## *Playing Around*

### MILK SCONES

Replace the buttermilk with milk and omit the baking soda.

### LEMON–POPPY SEED SCONES

Rub the grated zest of 1 lemon into the sugar before adding it to the flour. Mix 2 to 3 tablespoons poppy seeds into the dry ingredients.

### ROSEMARY-ORANGE SCONES

Rub the grated zest of 1 tangerine or ½ orange and 1 or 2 teaspoons minced fresh rosemary into the sugar before adding it to the flour.

### FRUIT SCONES

Mix about ½ cup moist, plump dried fruit, like raisins or cranberries or snipped dried fruit, like prunes or apricots, into the dough. Or try fresh fruit, such as ½ banana, cut into small chunks, or about ½ cup cubed apple or pear.

### OATMEAL SCONES

Use 1¾ cups all-purpose flour and 1 cup oats (not instant or thick-cut).

### WHEATY SCONES

Use 1½ cups all-purpose flour and ½ cup whole wheat flour.

### GLAZED SCONES

Mix ½ cup confectioners' sugar and 1 tablespoon milk together until you have a glaze that falls easily from the tip of a spoon. Drizzle or brush the glaze over the scones while they're still warm.

# Cheddar-Scallion Scones

*Makes about 14 scones*

2½ cups (340 grams) all-purpose flour

1 tablespoon baking powder

2 teaspoons sugar

¾ teaspoon fine sea salt

½ to 1 teaspoon mustard powder
(such as Colman's), to taste

¼ to ½ teaspoon paprika (see headnote;
you may want the smaller amount if
you're using hot or smoked paprika)

¼ teaspoon baking soda

¾ stick (6 tablespoons; 3 ounces;
85 grams) cold unsalted butter,
cut into small chunks

1¼ cups (3½ ounces; 105 grams)
shredded cheddar

¼ cup (20 grams) thinly sliced scallions
(save the dark green parts to top the
scones, if you'd like)

1 cold large egg

1 cup (240 ml) cold milk

Milk for brushing (optional)

Sliced scallion tops for finishing (optional)

A WORD ON WORKING
AHEAD: The dough can be made,
cut and frozen up to 2 months
ahead—make sure to wrap the
scones airtight—and then baked
straight from the freezer. As soon
as you start to preheat the oven,
place the scones on a lined baking
sheet and let them stand until the
oven reaches temperature. You
may need to bake them a few
minutes longer.

THIS IS A GOOD-LOOKING SCONE—it bakes to an inviting golden color—and it has just enough scallion and spice to be perfect for breakfast or brunch (or even dinner). The scallions go into the dough raw and yet once they're baked, they taste just the teensiest bit like caramelized onions. (If you want to bolster that flavor, you can add sautéed onions to the dough; see Playing Around.) I like spiking the dough with mustard powder and paprika. Because I don't use very much, their flavors aren't very strong, but you'd miss them if they weren't there. My preference is for smoked paprika, sweet or hot, but you could go with unsmoked, if you'd like.

Although the texture of these scones is characteristically light and tender, they're substantial in the flavor department, and so I make them small, patting the dough into a rectangle and cutting slender bars. They get a little chubbier and a little more ragtag in the oven, but that's part of their appeal.

Center a rack in the oven and preheat it to 400 degrees F. Line a baking sheet with parchment paper or a baking mat.

Working in a large bowl, whisk together the flour, baking powder, sugar, salt, mustard powder, paprika and baking soda. Scatter the bits of cold butter over the flour, reach in and use your fingers to mash and press and mush the butter into the flour. (You can do this with a pastry cutter, but it's really easier and faster to use your fingers.) Keep tossing the dry ingredients around and smushing the butter until you've broken it into flour-coated pieces as small as cornflakes and as large as peas. Add the cheese and scallions to the bowl and toss them around until they're coated with flour too.

Whisk the egg and milk together in a small bowl, pour the mixture over the dry ingredients and, using a fork, toss, turn and stir everything together until the flour is moistened. With your hands, gently—and sparingly—squeeze and knead the dough just enough to pull it into a ball. It's futile (and unnecessary) to expect a smooth, neat packet of dough, because this dough is sticky.

Turn the dough out onto a lightly floured surface and shape it into a rectangle that's about 6 × 7 inches and 1 inch high. (The height is more important than the exact measurements of the rectangle's sides.) Dust the top of the dough with flour. Using a bench scraper or a chef's knife, cut the dough lengthwise in half and then cut it crosswise into 1-inch-wide bars. Carefully transfer them to the baking sheet. (*At this point, the scones can be frozen for up to 2 months; see headnote.*)

If you'd like, brush the tops of the scones lightly with milk, and, if you've saved them, sprinkle with the sliced scallion greens. Bake the scones for 17 to 20 minutes, or until they're tall and golden brown on top and bottom. Transfer the baking sheet to a rack and wait a couple of minutes, then lift the scones onto the rack. The scones are ready to eat about 15 minutes out of the oven and at their best within 3 or 4 hours.

STORING: The scones are best the day they're made. After that, they'll be good reheated or toasted. You can keep baked scones in the freezer for up to 2 months, or you can freeze them before you bake them (a better option), as directed above.

## Playing Around

If you'd like to accentuate the onion flavor, finely dice or chop a small onion and sauté it in a little olive oil. When it's cool, drain and stir it into the dough along with the cheese and scallions. And it almost goes without saying that these scones would be extra-good with some crisply cooked bacon bits added to the mix; 2 strips is all you'll need.

# Iced Honey-Apple Scones with Spelt

*Makes 12 snowball-shaped or 8 wedge-shaped scones*

2 cups (272 grams) all-purpose flour

½ cup (75 grams) spelt flour

1 tablespoon baking powder

¼ teaspoon baking soda

¼ teaspoon fine sea salt

1 small tangerine, 1 clementine or ½ orange

¾ stick (6 tablespoons; 3 ounces; 85 grams) cold unsalted butter, cut into small chunks

1 medium apple, peeled, cored and finely chopped

¼ cup (60 ml) honey

1 cold large egg

¾ cup (180 ml) cold milk

FOR THE ICING

½ cup (60 grams) confectioners' sugar

About 1 tablespoon milk

About 1 teaspoon bee pollen for finishing (see headnote; optional)

A WORD ON WORKING AHEAD: The dough can be made, cut and frozen up to 2 months ahead—make sure to wrap the scones airtight—and then baked straight from the freezer. As soon as you start to preheat the oven, place the scones on a lined baking sheet and let them stand until the oven reaches temperature. You may need to bake them a few minutes longer.

THESE ARE THE SCONES to make the instant you feel fall in the air. They've got apples, honey and tangerine, flavors of the season, and the surprise addition of some spelt, a wheat flour that speckles their interiors. Their texture is light, and because they are only slightly sweet, they can take a slick of icing. My choice is a simple confectioners' sugar icing, brushed on when the scones come out of the oven. While the icing is still wet, I sometimes sprinkle the tops with a few grains of bee pollen. The pollen is optional, but its light sweetness and chewiness finish the scones nicely.

The dough for these is very sticky, so sticky that you might want to make drop scones rather than patty-cake the dough into a disk and cut wedges. It's a good option. Whatever you do, don't decide that the dough needs more flour—it doesn't! All that stickiness bakes to a light, airy crumb.

Center a rack in the oven and preheat it to 400 degrees F. Line a baking sheet with parchment paper or a baking mat.

Working in a large bowl, whisk together both flours, the baking powder, baking soda and salt. Finely grate the zest of the tangerine, clementine or orange into the bowl and whisk it in—hold onto the fruit. Scatter the bits of cold butter over the flour, reach in and use your fingers to mash and press and mush the butter into the flour. (You can do this with a pastry cutter, but it's really easier and faster to use your fingers.) Keep tossing the dry ingredients around and smushing the butter until you've broken it into flour-coated pieces as small as cornflakes and as big as peas. Add the apple to the bowl and toss until covered in flour. Pour over the honey and, using a fork, give the mixture a couple of turns. There's no need to be thorough now.

Whisk the egg and milk together in a small bowl, squeeze in the juice from the zested citrus and stir to blend. Pour the mixture over the dry ingredients and, using the fork, toss, turn and stir everything together until the flour is moistened. ⟶

With your hands, gently—and sparingly—squeeze and knead the dough just enough to pull it into a ball. It's futile (and unnecessary) to expect a smooth, neat packet of dough, because this dough is wet and very sticky.

Now you've got a choice: If you want to make drop scones, choose an ice cream scoop—one with a capacity of ¼ cup is good, as is a ¼-cup measure or a large spoon—and scoop 12 portions of dough onto the baking sheet. If you want to make wedge-shaped scones, turn the dough out onto a lightly floured surface and shape it into a circle that's about 6½ inches across and 1 inch high (the height's more important than the diameter here). Dust the top with flour. Using a bench scraper or a chef's knife, cut the dough into quarters and then cut each quarter in half, so you have 8 wedges. Carefully transfer them to the baking sheet. (*At this point, the scones can be froze for up to 2 months; see headnote.*)

Bake the scones for 18 to 20 minutes, or until they're tall and golden brown on top and bottom. Transfer the baking sheet to a rack and make the icing.

TO MAKE THE ICING: Put the sugar in a medium bowl and add the milk a little at a time, stirring with a small flexible spatula or a spoon. It's hard to give a precise measurement for the milk—just keep stirring until you get a shiny icing that falls slowly from the tip of your spatula or spoon.

Spread some icing over each scone, using a silicone brush, a small offset spatula or a table knife. If you'd like, sprinkle over a little bee pollen while the icing is still wet.

Serve the scones as soon as the icing dries, or transfer to a rack and serve within the next 3 or 4 hours. You can wait longer, but the scones are best as close to freshly baked as possible.

STORING: These are best the day they're made.

# Scones Pudding

*Makes 8 servings*

5 stale Buttermilk Scones (page 52) or other scones (about 14 ounces)

About ⅓ cup (80 ml) lemon curd, homemade (page 362) or store-bought such as Stonewall Kitchen or Bonne Maman

1 cup (240 ml) milk

1 cup (240 ml) heavy cream

Finely grated zest and juice of ½ lemon

½ teaspoon ground cardamom, cinnamon or allspice, plus more for dusting

2 large eggs

1 large egg yolk

½ cup (100 grams) sugar, plus more for dusting

1 teaspoon pure vanilla extract

3 small apples

2 tablespoons unsalted butter, melted

**A WORD ON WORKING AHEAD:** If you'd like, you can construct the pudding, cover it and keep it in the refrigerator for as long as overnight before baking it. Take it out of the fridge when you turn on the oven.

IF YOU LOVE BREAD PUDDING, I'm betting that you'll love this recipe. Day-old scones are cut into thin slices, fitted into the baking pan jigsaw-style and glossed with lemon curd before the custard is poured over them. The custard is a classic mix of milk, cream and eggs, but it's flavored with cardamom, cinnamon or allspice. To finish, the pudding's topped with apple slices, brushed with melted butter and sprinkled with sugar and more spice. You can mix up the fruit and curd according to what you love and what you've got on hand (see Playing Around). Puddings like this are neither prescriptive nor restrictive—be clever!

Butter a 9-inch square baking pan. (I like a glass, pottery, porcelain or other nonreactive pan.) Have a baking pan large enough to hold the pudding pan at hand.

Cut the scones horizontally into thirds—you want large thin slices. Fit half the slices, cut side up, into the pan, packing them snugly to make an evenish layer. Check the curd—if it's too stiff, stir it vigorously or pop it into the microwave for 10 seconds to soften— and then brush it lightly over the scones. Make a second layer of the remaining sliced scones, again cut side up, and brush the tops with curd. Save the rest of the curd—you'll use it for the topping.

Pour the milk and cream into a small saucepan. Stir in the lemon zest and the spice you've chosen and heat the liquid until there's a ring of small bubbles around the edges of the pan.

Meanwhile, whisk the eggs, yolk, sugar and vanilla together in a medium bowl. When the liquid is hot, whisk it into the egg mixture: Start by just dribbling in some of the hot liquid while whisking constantly and then, once you've got about a quarter of it incorporated, pour in the remainder in a steadier stream, still whisking.

Pour the custard over the scones. Let it seep into the scones (press them down now and then with the back of a spoon) while you work on the apples. (*The pudding can be covered and refrigerated at this point; see at left.*)

Center a rack in the oven and preheat it to 350 degrees F.

Peel the apples. Cut them into quarters, remove the cores and cut each quarter lengthwise into 4 slices. Toss the apples into a bowl, drizzle over the lemon juice and stir to coat.

Arrange the apple slices over the top of the pudding—I usually make 4 rows of slices, keeping the slices close together and pressing them gently into the pudding. Brush the slices with the melted butter and dust them lightly with a little sugar and a very little bit of spice. (You can mix the sugar and spice together and use a strainer to dust the top with the mixture.) Place the pan in the larger pan and fill it with hot water to come about halfway up the sides of the pudding pan.

Bake for about 45 minutes, or until the pudding is puffed all over and a skewer inserted into the center comes out clean. Carefully—very carefully!—lift the pudding pan out of the larger pan and onto a rack. Brush the apples with the remaining curd.

Allow the pudding to cool for about 30 minutes before cutting and serving. The pudding is really at its best warm, but it's nice at room temperature too.

STORING: Once the pudding is cool, you can cover it and keep it in the refrigerator for up to 2 days. While you can nibble at it when it's cold, I think it's better gently reheated (a microwave works well) or allowed to come to room temperature.

## *Playing Around*

Instead of lemon curd, you can brush the scones with marmalade, jam or a fruit butter—apple butter is great. And you can easily swap the apples for pears or bananas. If you want to, scatter some raisins or snipped dried apricots over the first layer of scones.

# Lemony Yogurt Muffins

*Makes 12 muffins*

2 cups (272 grams) all-purpose flour

2¼ teaspoons baking powder

¼ teaspoon baking soda

¼ teaspoon fine sea salt

⅔ cup (133 grams) sugar

Finely grated zest of 1 lemon

¾ cup (180 ml) plain yogurt, not straight from the fridge

2 large eggs, at room temperature

1 stick (8 tablespoons; 4 ounces; 113 grams) unsalted butter, melted and cooled

1½ cups (360 ml) blueberries (optional)

### FOR FINISHING—CHOOSE ONE OR NONE

Lemon curd, homemade (page 362) or store-bought, such as Stonewall Kitchen or Bonne Maman

Lemon (or other) marmalade, warmed to liquefy

Confectioners' Sugar Icing (page 372)

**A WORD ON TEXTURE AND TEMPERATURE:** To get the cakey texture that makes these muffins so lovely, your ingredients should be at room temperature, or as close to room temperature as your patience allows. Pull the yogurt and eggs out of the refrigerator as soon as you decide to make the muffins and melt the butter before you do anything else, so that it will have time to cool.

**HERE'S MY CHOICE** for a house muffin, a recipe you can turn to daily knowing that whether you make the muffins plain, fold in some add-ins or decide to finish them fancifully, they'll be just right. The backbone ingredients are yogurt, which adds sharp flavor even as it tenderizes the batter, and its boon companion, lemon zest. Simple and comforting soon after they come from the oven, the muffins can also be prettied up with a little confectioners' sugar and lemon juice icing or—my favorite—lemon curd or marmalade brushed on while they're hot.

Not surprisingly, the muffins are particularly good when you fold berries into them. Blueberries are my go-to, but think of this recipe as a template for fruit muffins. Take a look at Playing Around for some ideas to get you started.

Center a rack in the oven and preheat it to 400 degrees F. Line a regular-size muffin tin with cupcake papers (first choice, especially if you're including the blueberries) or coat the cups with baker's spray.

Whisk the flour, baking powder, baking soda and salt together in a large bowl. Put the sugar and lemon zest in a medium bowl and, using your fingers, press and mash them together until the sugar is moist and fragrant. Whisk the sugar into the flour mixture.

Scrape the yogurt into the bowl you used for the sugar, add the eggs and whisk to blend. Whisk in the melted butter—the mixture may look slightly curdled, but it will be fine.

Pour the wet ingredients over the dry and, using a flexible spatula and a few brisk strokes, stir and fold until most of the flour is moistened. You might have a few patches of dry flour here and there, and that's okay. Add the berries, if you're using them, and stir to incorporate. Don't overmix—a bit of negligence yields a nicer texture. Divide the batter evenly among the muffin cups.

Bake for 18 to 20 minutes, or until the muffins are golden brown and a tester inserted into the center of one comes out clean. Transfer the tin to a rack and let the muffins rest for 5 minutes, then lift them out of the tin and onto the rack.

**TO FINISH THE MUFFINS (OR NOT):** If you're going to add curd or marmalade, now's the moment, while the muffins are still hot. Brush them lightly with the curd or marmalade and allow them to sit for at least 15 minutes before serving. Or, if you'd like to ice them, wait until they reach room temperature and then drizzle over as much icing as you'd like—I usually use the tip of a spoon to do this.

**STORING:** Muffins are best eaten soon after they're made. However, you can keep them covered at room temperature overnight; if you keep them longer, split and toast them (provided you haven't topped them). Do that, and you might want to butter them. If you haven't topped the muffins with curd, marmalade or icing, you can freeze them in an airtight container for up to 2 months.

## Playing Around

### RASPBERRY-LAVENDER MUFFINS

About 30 minutes before you start making the muffins, put the butter in whatever pan you'll be melting it in and add 1 tablespoon culinary lavender. Melt the butter, cover the pan and let the butter steep until you're ready for it—strain out the lavender before adding the butter to the batter. Omit the lemon zest—or don't; lemon, raspberries and lavender are good together—and use 1½ cups (about 250 grams) raspberries. These can be finished with curd, marmalade or icing, if you like.

### STRAWBERRY-GINGER MUFFINS

Whisk ¼ to ½ teaspoon ground ginger into the dry ingredients. Finely chop a few pieces of crystallized ginger—you need a total of about 2 tablespoons—and have some strawberry jam handy. Half-fill the muffin cups, then put a teaspoon of jam in each cup and about ½ teaspoon chopped ginger. Finish filling the cups and sprinkle a little granulated or sanding sugar over the tops. These are fine without a topping.

### BLACKBERRY-LIME MUFFINS

Use 1½ cups (about 250 grams) blackberries and replace the lemon with lime. Finish with the curd, marmalade or icing, or simply sprinkle sanding or granulated sugar over the tops before or after the muffins are baked.

# Carrot Muffins

*Makes 12 muffins*

2 cups (272 grams) all-purpose flour

⅔ cup (133 grams) sugar

1 tablespoon baking powder

1½ teaspoons ground ginger

½ teaspoon fine sea salt

¼ teaspoon baking soda

¾ cup (180 ml) milk

⅔ cup (160 ml) flavorless oil,
  such as canola

1 tablespoon pomegranate molasses,
  or a little more to taste (optional)

2 large eggs

1 teaspoon pure vanilla extract

⅓ cup (67 grams) packed brown sugar

Grated zest of 1 tangerine or small orange

1½ cups (150 ml) grated carrots (about
  3 carrots; see below)

⅓ cup (about 50 grams) raisins, dried
  cranberries or chopped dried fruit
  (see below)

Sunflower seeds for topping (optional)

**A WORD ON THE CARROTS:**
I always have packaged grated
carrots in the house—I use them
for a quick salad or slaw. If you've
got them, you can certainly use
them, but chop them—the strands
are too long for muffins. They're
also a little drier than freshly
grated carrots. If you grate your
own and they seem wet, press
them between paper towels to dry
them a bit.

**A WORD ON THE DRIED
FRUIT:** I like raisins, dark or
golden, in these, but they're also
excellent with dried cranberries or
small pieces of dried dates or figs.
If you'd like, you can add chopped
nuts too.

**THE SURPRISING THING ABOUT** these exceedingly good
muffins is that they're neither what you expect them to be nor
even what they seem. They are not carrot cake made as muffins,
although they share many of the cake's ingredients. And they're
not very sweet or particularly rich. Brown sugar and vanilla
give the muffins their warmth, ginger and tangerine zest give
them their high notes and oil gives them their unusual lightness.
They can include dried fruit or chopped nuts or even a spoonful
of pomegranate molasses, an ingredient that is sweet and sour,
unexpected in a muffin and very at home in these.

Center a rack in the oven and preheat it to 375 degrees F. Line a
regular-size muffin tin with cupcake papers. For these, papers work
better than baker's spray, although it's a good idea to spray the top
of the tin, since the batter can spread over the tops of the cups.

In a large bowl, whisk together the flour, sugar, baking powder,
ginger, salt and baking soda.

In a medium bowl, whisk together the milk, oil, pomegranate
molasses, if you're using it, eggs and vanilla. Pour the liquid
ingredients into the bowl with the dry ingredients and scatter over
the brown sugar (if there are any lumps in the sugar, mash them or
pick them out and discard) and zest. Using a flexible spatula, stir
until most of the flour is moistened—make sure to get to the bottom
of the bowl. Add the carrots and raisins or other dried fruit and stir
to blend. Divide the batter evenly among the muffin cups—it will fill
them. Scatter over some sunflower seeds—go light here—if you're
using them.

Bake for 20 to 22 minutes, or until the muffins are golden brown
and a tester inserted into the center of a muffin comes out clean.
Transfer the tin to a rack and leave the muffins for 10 minutes, then
turn the tin over and gently shake them out. Serve the muffins
warm, or wait until they reach room temperature.

**STORING:** These muffins, like most, are best eaten soon after they
come from the oven, but they hold surprisingly well overnight—
keep them in a covered container. You can also pack the muffins
airtight and freeze them for up to 2 months.

*Breakfast*

# Grain and Seed Muffins

*Makes 12 muffins*

1 cup (136 grams) whole wheat flour

½ cup (68 grams) all-purpose flour

2 teaspoons baking powder

½ teaspoon fine sea salt

½ teaspoon ground cinnamon

¼ teaspoon baking soda

½ cup (50 grams) oats (*not* instant)

½ cup (30 grams) wheat bran

½ cup (100 grams) packed brown sugar

2 large eggs, at room temperature

1 large yolk, at room temperature

1 cup (240 ml) milk, not very cold

⅔ cup (160 ml) flavorless oil, such as canola

⅓ cup (80 ml) maple syrup

⅓ cup (40 grams) sunflower seeds, preferably raw

2 tablespoons flaxseeds

2 tablespoons sesame seeds

½ cup (80 grams) moist, plump dried cranberries or raisins

GOLDEN BROWN AND POINTY-TOPPED, these muffins are hearty, sturdy and pleasantly rough, the kind you'd pack for a hike or a picnic. The batter is made with whole wheat flour, oats and wheat bran—small flakes with big flavor—and sweetened with brown sugar and maple syrup. Using oil rather than butter provides a little spring in the crumb. Good plain, they're extra-good with butter or jam, cream cheese, a slice of cheddar or alongside an apple. I'm also partial to them with apple butter.

Center a rack in the oven and preheat it to 400 degrees F. Line a regular-size muffin tin with cupcake papers or coat the cups with baker's spray.

Whisk together both flours, the baking powder, salt, cinnamon, baking soda, oats and bran in a large bowl. Stir in the brown sugar, making sure there aren't any lumps.

In a large measuring cup or a medium bowl, whisk together the eggs, yolk, milk, oil and maple syrup.

Pour the liquid ingredients over the dry and, using a flexible spatula, stir until most of the flour is moistened, making sure to get to the bottom of the bowl; you might have a few patches of dry flour, and that's okay. Add all the seeds and the dried cranberries and stir to incorporate. Divide the batter evenly among the muffin cups—it will fill them.

Bake for 15 to 18 minutes, or until the muffins are peaked (their tops may crack, and that's nice) and deeply golden; a tester inserted into the center of a muffin should come out clean. Transfer the tin to a rack and wait for 5 minutes, then pop the muffins out onto the rack.

Serve the muffins warm, or wait until they reach room temperature.

STORING: Muffins are best eaten soon after they're baked and certainly on the day that they're made. However, you can keep them covered at room temperature overnight—then, if you think they need it, split and toast them. Or freeze the muffins in an airtight container for up to 2 months.

# Mochaccino Muffins

*Makes 12 muffins*

2 cups (272 grams) all-purpose flour

¼ cup (21 grams) unsweetened cocoa powder

2½ teaspoons baking powder

½ teaspoon ground cinnamon

½ teaspoon fine sea salt

¼ teaspoon baking soda

⅔ cup (133 grams) sugar

2 tablespoons ground coffee (*not* instant)

¾ cup (180 ml) milk, at room temperature

2 large eggs, at room temperature

2 teaspoons Coffee Extract (page 371)

1 stick (8 tablespoons; 4 ounces; 113 grams) unsalted butter, melted and cooled

⅓ cup (69 grams) mini chocolate chips or finely chopped semisweet or milk chocolate

Turbinado or sanding sugar for sprinkling (optional)

**A WORD ON TEXTURE AND TEMPERATURE:** If you can make sure that your ingredients are at room temperature, or close to it, the muffins' texture will be better. Take the milk and eggs out of the refrigerator as soon as you decide to make the muffins, and melt the butter before you do anything else, so that it will have time to cool.

**THESE ARE STRADDLERS**—they're muffins for the morning, but they might as rightly be cupcakes for the afternoon. As their name announces, they have both chocolate and coffee in them, and milk and sugar too, just like the drink. I added a little cinnamon, because that's what I like with my mochaccino. Their texture is tender, particularly soon after they're baked, when they're most cake-like; later they're more muffiny. And their flavor is full and not really sweet—they're made for grown-ups, even if they are really nice with a glass of milk.

Center a rack in the oven and preheat it to 400 degrees F. Line a regular-size muffin tin with cupcake papers or coat the cups with baker's spray.

Sift the flour, cocoa, baking powder, cinnamon, salt and baking soda together into a large bowl. Add the sugar and ground coffee and whisk to combine.

In a medium bowl, whisk the milk, eggs and coffee extract together to blend, then whisk in the melted butter.

Pour the wet ingredients over the dry and, using a flexible spatula, stir until most of the flour is incorporated. You'll have a thick, brownie-like mixture. Stir in the chips or chopped chocolate and gently finish mixing. Divide the batter evenly among the muffin cups and sprinkle the tops with sugar, if you're using it.

Bake for 18 to 20 minutes, or until the muffins have risen and their tops are firm and cracked; a tester inserted into the center of a muffin should come out clean. Transfer the tin to a rack and let the muffins rest for 5 minutes, then lift them out of the cups and onto the rack. Allow the muffins to sit for at least 15 minutes before serving.

These are good warm, but you really get the coffee and chocolate flavors after they've reached room temperature—and the texture's better then too.

**STORING:** Muffins are best eaten soon after they're baked and certainly on the day that they're made. However, you can keep them covered at room temperature overnight. If you want to hold them for a longer time, freeze them—they'll keep for up to 2 months.

*Baking with Dorie*

# Miso-Maple Loaf

*Makes about 10 servings*

1¾ cups (238 grams) all-purpose flour

1¾ teaspoons baking powder

¼ teaspoon baking soda

¾ cup (150 grams) sugar

¼ teaspoon fine sea salt

Finely grated zest of 1 orange or tangerine

1 stick (8 tablespoons; 4 ounces; 113 grams) unsalted butter, at room temperature

¼ cup (70 grams) white miso

¼ cup (60 ml) pure maple syrup

2 large eggs, at room temperature

1½ teaspoons pure vanilla extract

⅓ cup (80 ml) buttermilk (well shaken before measuring)

### FOR THE GLAZE (OPTIONAL)

About ¼ cup (80 grams) orange marmalade or apricot jam

1 tablespoon water

**IF I OWNED A BED-AND-BREAKFAST,** I'd make this my signature treat. Sturdy, coarse-crumbed (I say this with admiration) and on the brink of savory, the loaf is reminiscent of many crowd-pleasers. It may make you think of honey cake, but in the end, it will never be anything other than itself—it's an original.

The miso and maple are less stand-out individual players than they are a team working together to create flavors that are robust, warm and mysterious. And, along with the recipe's buttermilk, their moistness contributes to the cake's lovely crumb.

I prefer white (shiro) miso here, but if you're looking for a stronger flavor, you can use red. You can also switch the orange or tangerine zest for lemon, if you'd like.

Center a rack in the oven and preheat it to 350 degrees F. Butter an 8½-inch loaf pan and dust with flour, or use baker's spray.

Whisk together the flour, baking powder and baking soda.

Put the sugar, salt and zest in the bowl of a stand mixer or a large bowl that you can use with a hand mixer. Reach in and rub the ingredients together until the sugar is moist and fragrant; it may even turn orange. Add the butter, miso and maple syrup to the bowl. If using a stand mixer, attach the bowl and fit it with the paddle attachment.

Beat on medium speed for about 3 minutes, scraping down the bowl and beater(s) as needed, until you've got a smooth, creamy mixture. One by one, add the eggs, beating for a minute after each goes in. Beat in the vanilla. The mixture might curdle, but this is a temporary condition. Turn off the mixer, add the dry ingredients all at once and then pulse to begin the blending. Beat on low speed until the dry ingredients are almost incorporated. With the mixer still on low, pour in the buttermilk and blend well. Scrape the batter into the pan, working it into the corners and smoothing the top.

Bake for 50 to 55 minutes, checking the loaf after 40 minutes and covering the top loosely with a foil or parchment tent if it's browning too fast. The loaf is properly baked when it pulls away from the sides of the pan and a tester inserted into the center comes out clean. The top will be flat and most likely cracked down the middle. Transfer the pan to a rack and let the bread rest for 5 minutes, then run a table knife around the edges of the loaf and unmold onto the rack; turn it right side up.

**IF YOU'D LIKE TO GLAZE THE LOAF**: Stir the marmalade or jam and water together and heat the mixture in the microwave or over low heat until it comes just to a boil. Using a pastry brush (or a spoon), cover the top of the loaf with the glaze.

Allow the loaf to cool to room temperature before slicing.

**STORING**: Wrapped well, the cake will keep for about 4 days at room temperature. If it stales—or maybe even if it doesn't—toast it lightly before serving. If you haven't glazed it, you can wrap it airtight and freeze it for up to 2 months; defrost, still wrapped, at room temperature.

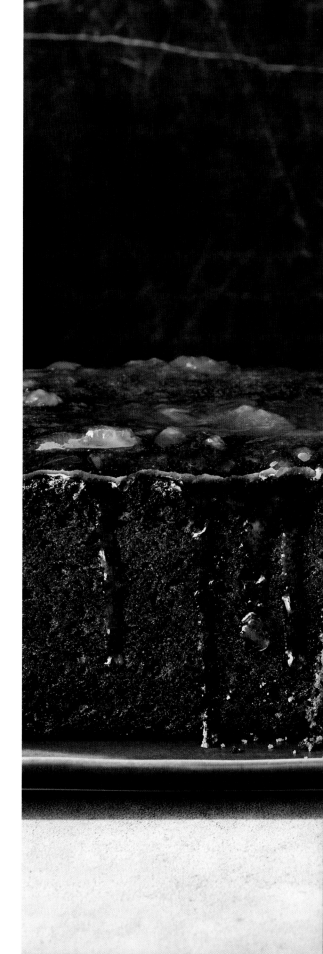

# Pecan-Cranberry Loaf

*Makes 8 servings*

1½ cups (204 grams) all-purpose flour

1½ teaspoons baking powder

½ teaspoon ground coriander

¼ teaspoon baking soda

¼ teaspoon fine sea salt

⅔ cup (134 grams) sugar

Finely grated zest of 1 orange or tangerine

¼ cup (50 grams) packed brown sugar

3 large eggs, at room temperature

½ cup (120 ml) buttermilk (well shaken before measuring), at room temperature

½ cup (120 ml) flavorless oil, such as canola

⅔ cup (80 grams) finely chopped lightly toasted pecans

½ cup (55 grams) fresh or frozen cranberries, coarsely chopped (don't thaw if frozen)

IT WOULD BE EASY to underestimate this cake, and it would be a shame if you did. Plain but appealing in every way, it bakes up nutshell brown and crowns with a rugged crack at its center; in other words, it's beautiful. Its crumb is compact and speckled, as though it were made with coarsely milled whole wheat flour, and its texture is somewhere between that of a sponge cake and a pound cake (it's the oil in the batter that does that). Because it's got finely chopped pecans (the speckles), brown sugar and ground coriander, the flavor is warm; because it's got buttermilk and fresh cranberries, it's also got pep. Make the cake to serve for breakfast or brunch and then enjoy it over the next few days. Whenever you serve it, cut thick slices to showcase the cake's texture and taste. It's a good keeper, a good packer, a good traveler and a good go-along with your favorite jam or marmalade.

Center a rack in the oven and preheat it to 350 degrees F. Butter an 8½-inch loaf pan and dust with flour, or use baker's spray.

Whisk together the flour, baking powder, coriander, baking soda and salt.

In a large bowl, rub the granulated sugar and zest together with your hands until the sugar is moist and fragrant. Add the brown sugar and stir to blend. One by one, whisk in the eggs, beating for a minute after each goes in. Whisk in the buttermilk.

Switch to a flexible spatula, add half the flour mixture, stir and fold until it's almost combined, then mix in the remainder. Gradually fold in the oil, mixing until you have a smooth batter. Stir in the nuts and cranberries and scrape the batter into the pan.

Bake the cake for 58 to 65 minutes, or until the top rises and cracks and, most important, a tester inserted deep into the center of the cake comes out clean. Transfer the pan to a rack and wait for 5 minutes, then unmold the cake, turn it right side up and let cool until it is only just warm or reaches room temperature.

STORING: Well wrapped, the cake will keep for at least 4 days—in fact, I think it tastes better the day after it's baked. Slices of stale cake are a treat toasted and topped with ice cream. Or, if you wrap it airtight, you can freeze the cake for up to 2 months; defrost in the wrapper.

# Morning Bundt Cake

*Makes about 12 servings*

## FOR THE CAKE

2¼ cups (306 grams) all-purpose flour

2 teaspoons baking powder

½ teaspoon baking soda

½ teaspoon fine sea salt

¼ teaspoon ground cinnamon

¼ teaspoon ground cardamom (or more cinnamon)

A tiny pinch of ground allspice or cloves

1½ cups (300 grams) sugar

2 tangerines or clementines or 1 large orange

⅔ cup (160 ml) flavorless oil, such as canola

4 large eggs, at room temperature

3 tablespoons honey

2 teaspoons pure vanilla extract

⅔ cup (160 ml) plain yogurt

1 cup (about 115 grams) muesli

½ cup (about 75 grams) moist, plump raisins cranberries or other dried fruit, such as chopped cherries or figs, or a combination (optional)

½ cup (about 60 grams) coarsely chopped nuts, such as almonds, walnuts or hazelnuts, toasted or not (optional)

## FOR THE SYRUP

½ cup (100 grams) sugar

⅓ cup (80 ml) freshly squeezed citrus juice, preferably a mix of orange and lemon

IN NAMING THIS MORNING BUNDT, I leave it to you to decide just how early in the morning you'd like to have it. The cake includes lots of the things that might be part of breakfast: yogurt, oranges—the pieces of chopped orange scattered throughout the cake are delightfully unexpected—orange juice, eggs, honey and muesli, the dry cereal based on oats. Muesli's texture tips toward chewy when it is baked and its softness adds moisture to the cake.

As soon as the Bundt comes out of the oven, it gets drenched with an orange-lemon syrup. The soak picks up the citrus flavors in the cake and gives the crust an extra bit of very appealing tang. It also makes the color of the cake darker and the look glossier, both nice.

TO MAKE THE CAKE: Center a rack in the oven and preheat it to 350 degrees F. Butter a large Bundt pan and dust with flour, or use baker's spray.

Whisk the flour, baking powder, baking soda, salt and spices together.

Put the sugar in the bowl of a stand mixer or in a large bowl that you can work in with a hand mixer. Grate the tangerine, clementine or orange zest over the sugar, then use your fingers to rub the ingredients together until the sugar is moist, fragrant and tinted orange.

Using a sharp paring knife, cut off the top and bottom of the citrus fruit, then stand it on its end and cut away the peel and white pith to reveal the flesh. Cut the fruit into rounds about ½ inch thick, remove the pits and chop into small chunks. Scrape the fruit and whatever juice there might be into a small bowl and set aside.

Add the oil and eggs to the bowl with the sugar. If using a stand mixer, attach the bowl and fit it with the paddle attachment. Mix on medium speed for about 2 minutes, until homogeneous. Add the honey and vanilla and beat for 1 minute. Scrape in the yogurt and beat on low to incorporate.

Turn off the mixer, add half the flour mixture and pulse to start blending it in, then beat on low until the dry ingredients disappear. Add the remainder of the flour and pulse to start the mixing, then add the citrus pieces and whatever juice you have and mix on low for a minute. Add the muesli and the dried fruit and/or nuts, if you're using them. Mix on low for 1 minute more, then remove the bowl from the mixer stand if using and use a sturdy spatula to finish the mixing by hand. Scrape the batter into the Bundt; use the spatula to nudge it into the pan's crannies and to even the top.

Bake the cake for 55 to 60 minutes, or until it is browned on top and a skewer plunged deep into it comes out clean. If the cake looks like it's getting too brown at the 35-minute mark, tent it loosely with foil or parchment.

**MEANWHILE, AS SOON AS THE CAKE GOES INTO THE OVEN, MAKE THE SYRUP:** Mix the sugar and juice together in a bowl and set aside, stirring occasionally. If the sugar hasn't dissolved by the time the cake is ready, warm the mixture in the microwave for a few seconds.

When the cake is done, transfer the pan to a rack, leave for 5 minutes and then unmold.

**TO SOAK THE CAKE:** Place the hot cake, still on the rack, on a foil-lined baking sheet—the drip-catcher. Using a pastry brush—a silicone brush works nicely here—brush the cake with the syrup, working slowly and continuing until all of the syrup has been absorbed. Be patient—the cake needs time to absorb all the syrup. Let cool to room temperature.

**STORING:** Tightly covered, the cake will hold for about 5 days at room temperature. It can be frozen for up to 2 months, but if you're going to freeze the cake, it's best not to soak it.

# Breakfast-in-Rome Lemon Cake

*Makes 12 servings*

1½ cups (204 grams) all-purpose flour

2 teaspoons baking powder

½ teaspoon fine sea salt

6 large eggs, separated, at room temperature

1½ cups (300 grams) sugar

Finely grated zest of 2 lemons

½ cup (120 ml) flavorless oil, such as canola

Juice of 1 lemon

2 teaspoons pure vanilla extract

¼ teaspoon pure lemon extract or oil (optional)

About 1½ cups (about 250 grams) blueberries, raspberries and/or blackberries (optional)

Confectioners' sugar for dusting (optional)

IN ROME FOR A LONG WEEKEND one early spring, Michael and I had breakfast at the Roscioli Caffè the first morning and then every day thereafter. The cappuccino was excellent and the pastries, both sweet and savory, were equally good, but it was a yellow cake set on a counter above all the buns, tarts and *cornetti* that became my daily treat. It was full of lemon flavor and had the lightness and textbook-perfect spring and stretch of the best sponge cakes—tug on a slice gently, and it pulls itself back into shape. It was spare—no whipped cream, no sugar icing, no candied fruit. I didn't get the recipe, but I devised one that captures all the pleasures of that cake. The batter is made with oil and uses whipped egg whites (along with leavener) to get the airiness I loved in the original.

In summer, I fold berries into the cake, but most of the year I make it just the way I remember it: plain. At Roscioli, the cake is made in a tube pan, and so it is part of a family of *ciambelle,* or ring cakes.

Center a rack in the oven and preheat it to 350 degrees F. Generously butter a 10-inch tube pan (or use a Bundt pan with as few curves and crannies as possible) and dust with flour. Be assiduous—this cake is a sticker. Alternatively, use baker's spray.

Whisk the flour, baking powder and salt together.

Working in the bowl of a stand mixer fitted with the whisk attachment, or in a large bowl with a hand mixer, beat the egg whites on medium-high speed until they form firm, glossy peaks.

If you're using a stand mixer, scrape the whites into another bowl—there's no need to rinse the mixer bowl. Switch the whisk for the paddle attachment.

Put the sugar and lemon zest in the mixer bowl, or in another large bowl if using a hand mixer, and rub them together until the sugar is moist and fragrant. Attach the bowl to the mixer stand, if using. Add the yolks and beat on medium speed for about 3 minutes,

scraping the bowl as needed, until the batter is thick, pale and shiny. With the mixer still on medium, drizzle in the oil, pouring it down the side of the bowl, and continue to beat for another 3 minutes. Working on low speed, mix in the lemon juice, vanilla and lemon oil, if you're using it, then scrape the bowl well. Turn off the mixer, add all the dry ingredients and pulse a few times to start incorporating them. Then mix on low until the flour is blended into the batter and it is smooth and thick. Remove the bowl from the mixer stand, if using.

Give the whites a couple of brisk turns with a whisk to re-stiffen them and incorporate any liquid that may have seeped to the bottom of the bowl, then scrape a few spoonfuls of them over the batter. Use a flexible spatula to stir them in and lighten the batter. Turn the rest of the whites into the bowl and fold them in gingerly; if you're using the berries, gently fold them in just before the whites are fully incorporated. Scrape the batter into the pan and level the top.

Bake the cake for 45 to 50 minutes, until the top is lightly browned and perhaps cracked. A tester inserted deep into the cake should come out clean. Transfer to a rack and wait for 5 minutes. If you've used a tube pan, run a table knife around the edges of the pan to loosen the cake (this won't be as easily done if you used a Bundt). Invert the pan onto the rack and unmold the cake. If you used a tube pan, decide whether you like the top or the bottom of the cake best and turn that side up to cool to room temperature. If you've used a Bundt, just unmold it onto the rack to cool.

Dust the cake with confectioners' sugar at serving time, if you'd like.

STORING: Well covered, the cake will keep for a couple of days. It's delicious lightly toasted if it gets a bit stale. (If the cake has berries, it may not keep as well or as long.) It can also be wrapped airtight and frozen for up to 2 months; defrost in the wrapping.

# Crumb-Topped Ricotta Coffee Cake

*Makes about 16 servings*

## FOR THE CRUMBS

¾ cup (102 grams) all-purpose flour

½ cup (100 grams) sugar

½ cup (100 grams) packed brown sugar

⅓ cup (57 grams) cornmeal

¼ teaspoon fine sea salt

7 tablespoons (3½ ounces; 100 grams) cold unsalted butter, cut into small chunks

½ teaspoon pure vanilla extract

## FOR THE CAKE

1½ cups (204 grams) all-purpose flour

1 teaspoon baking powder

¼ teaspoon baking soda

¾ cup (150 grams) sugar

¼ teaspoon fine sea salt

¾ cup (187 grams) ricotta, drained if necessary

3 large eggs, at room temperature

1 stick (8 tablespoons; 4 ounces; 113 grams) unsalted butter, melted and cooled

1½ to 2 cups (about 250 to 335 grams) berries (see right)

**WHENEVER I SERVE THIS CAKE,** someone compares it to a favorite bakery or boxed cake from their childhood. That's not what I'd set out to do when I first made the cake, but it's been my goal ever since because I too have good memories of a store-bought cake like this one. The cake is tight-grained but tender. It's made with ricotta, which is part of why it's tender and part of why its flavor is so distinctive. I like to sprinkle berries over the batter as a middle layer—they add color, another taste and a nice surprise—and then go heavy on the sweet, crunchy crumbs. The secret to the crumbs' crunch is the cornmeal.

**A WORD ON THE FRUIT:** You can use blueberries, raspberries and/or blackberries, but avoid strawberries—they're a little too watery and their vibrancy diminishes in the oven.

**A WORD ON THE CRUMBS:** You can make the crumbs by hand—work all the ingredients together between your fingertips—or use a mixer. A stand mixer with the paddle attachment is fastest and easiest.

**PLAN AHEAD:** While the crumb topping is good to go after an hour in the fridge, it's better after 2 or 3 or more hours, so see if you can build this chill time into your schedule. Colder crumbs hold their shape better. To save time, you can pinch the crumbs into nuggets and freeze them for 30 minutes or more.

**TO MAKE THE CRUMBS:** Put all of the ingredients *except* the butter and vanilla in the bowl of a stand mixer fitted with the paddle attachment (see headnote for other options) and mix on low just to combine. Add the pieces of cold butter, toss them around until they're coated and then beat on medium-low until the ingredients form moist clumps. Squeeze some, and the crumbs should hold together. Getting to this stage can take a few minutes, so don't rush it. Add the vanilla and mix until incorporated.

Remove the bowl from the mixer stand, reach in and grab a spoonful or two of the mixture at a time between your fingers and squeeze, so that you get little balls of crumbs. Cover (in the bowl or in another container) and chill until needed. If you can give the crumbs at least an hour, that would be great; 2 to 3 hours or more (or 30 minutes or more in the freezer) would be ideal. (*You can make the crumbs up to 3 days ahead; keep tightly wrapped in the refrigerator.*)

TO MAKE THE CAKE: Center a rack in the oven and preheat it to 350 degrees F. Butter a 9-inch square baking pan, or use bakers' spray.

Whisk the flour, baking powder and baking soda together.

Working in a large bowl, whisk the sugar and salt together. Add the ricotta and whisk to blend well. One by one, add the eggs, whisk until each is incorporated. Whisk in the melted butter. When the mixture is blended, switch to a flexible spatula and gently fold and stir in the dry ingredients until you've got a heavy, smooth batter. Scrape the batter into the pan, spreading it evenly and taking care to nudge some into the corners. Scatter the fruit over the batter.

Remove the crumbs from the refrigerator (or freezer) and top the cake with them, grabbing a little of the mixture each time and squeezing it so that you end up with a really bumpy layer.

Bake the cake for about 50 minutes, or until the top is golden brown, whatever fruit you can see is bubbling up through the crumbs and, most important, a tester inserted into the center of the cake comes out clean. Transfer the pan to a rack and let rest for 3 minutes, then run a table knife between the cake and the sides of the pan. Let the cake settle for about 10 minutes and then unmold it onto the rack; invert and cool right side up. The cake is ready to enjoy when it is only just warm or after it has reached room temperature.

I usually cut the cake into 16 squares, but cut for your crowd.

STORING: Wrapped well, the cake will keep for up to 4 days at room temperature or for up to 2 months in the freezer; defrost, still wrapped, at room temperature.

# Buttermilk-Molasses Quick Bread

*Makes 8 servings*

1¼ cups (170 grams) all-purpose flour

¾ cup (90 grams) rye flour

½ cup (68 grams) whole wheat flour

¼ cup (15 grams) wheat bran

2 tablespoons wheat germ

2¼ teaspoons baking soda

1 teaspoon fine sea salt

2 teaspoons ground anise
(see headnote)

1½ teaspoons ground caraway

1½ teaspoons ground fennel

2⅓ cups (560 ml) buttermilk
(well shaken before measuring)

½ cup (120 ml) unsulfured molasses

MY HUSBAND, MICHAEL, AND I loved staying at the Ett Hem Guesthouse in Stockholm, but I blame their luxurious breakfasts, which we lingered over, for the fact that we ran out of time and left the city without seeing half of what was on our list. A highlight of those leisurely meals was this loaf, traditional throughout Sweden. Very dark and fragrant, it's a one-bowl quick bread, slightly cake-like but not fragile, made with a blend of rye, whole wheat and all-purpose flours, as well as wheat bran and germ. Molasses is the sweetener and ground caraway, anise and fennel the spices. Having made it often since adapting the recipe they gave me at the guesthouse, I can say with assurance that it's good with butter, with jam, with hard cheese, with smoked salmon, with ham, with soft goat cheese—and more.

A NOTE ON THE SPICE MEASUREMENTS: If you're using whole spices, start with just a smidge less than the ground amount specified. Grind each spice separately in a spice or coffee grinder and then measure to make sure you've got what you need.

Center a rack in the oven and preheat it to 300 degrees F. Butter a 9-inch loaf pan.

Put all of the dry ingredients in a large bowl and whisk them together to blend. Whisk together the buttermilk and molasses, pour the liquid ingredients over the dry and stir until the dry ingredients are completely moistened. The mixture will bubble a little—it's supposed to. Scrape the batter into the pan and jiggle the pan to settle it.

Bake for 55 to 65 minutes, or until a tester inserted into the center of the loaf comes out clean; the temperature at the center of the loaf should be between 195 and 210 degrees F. Run a table knife around the edges of the pan, if needed, to release the loaf, and turn it out onto a rack. Invert again and let it cool to room temperature.

Depending on how you're serving the bread, you might want to first cut the loaf in half the long way and then cut it into slices. Also, the loaf has more flavor when you let it "ripen" for a few hours or even a day, so—wrap it and keep it at room temperature if you can.

STORING: Wrapped well, the loaf will keep at room temperature for about 4 days; it can be frozen for up to 2 months. Stale bread is delicious toasted.

## Playing Around

The spices in the loaf go well with fruit and nuts, so think about adding currants or raisins and chopped almonds, hazelnuts or walnuts. And you can replace the buttermilk with yogurt or sour cream.

# Banana Breakfast Squares

*Makes 16 squares*

2¼ cups (306 grams) all-purpose flour

⅔ cup (90 grams) whole wheat flour

2 teaspoons instant espresso or ground coffee (optional but good)

1½ teaspoons baking soda

¾ teaspoon baking powder

½ teaspoon fine sea salt

1 cup (200 grams) sugar

¾ cup (150 grams) packed brown sugar

1 stick (8 tablespoons; 4 ounces; 113 grams) unsalted butter, at room temperature

½ cup (120 ml) flavorless oil, such as canola, or coconut oil (nice with banana)

3 large eggs, at room temperature

2 teaspoons pure vanilla extract

3 large or 4 medium mushy, overripe bananas, cut into chunks

⅔ cup (160 ml) buttermilk (well shaken before measuring) or sour cream

¾ cup (60 grams) oats (*not* instant)

½ cup (60 grams) finely chopped walnuts or pecans (optional)

⅓ cup (50 grams) moist, plump raisins or an equal amount of chopped or diced soft dates

¼ cup (40 grams) flaxseeds

OPTIONAL GO-ALONGS

Plain yogurt

Softened butter

Peanut butter

Jam or marmalade

Sugared berries

CUT INTO SQUARES that can be eaten out of hand—I love its nab-it-on-the-go character—this cake is warm, inviting and appealingly plain. There are stir-ins for flavor and texture, including oats (they lighten the cake); raisins or chopped dates; nuts, if you want them; and flax seeds, which I hope you'll embrace. They give the cake a speckled crumb, a little crunch and an earthy edge. The cake is big, so make it for a crowd. Or don't—it keeps well and can be frozen.

Center a rack in the oven and preheat it to 350 degrees F. Butter a 9-x-13-inch baking pan, preferably one with 2-inch-high sides, and dust it with flour, or use baker's spray. Line the bottom of the pan with parchment paper.

Whisk both flours, the coffee, if you're using it, baking soda, baking powder and salt together.

Working in the bowl of a stand mixer fitted with the paddle attachment, or in a large bowl with a hand mixer, beat both sugars and the butter together at medium speed for about 2 minutes; you'll have a pasty mixture. Pour in the oil and beat for another 2 minutes, or until smooth, scraping the bowl as needed. One by one, add the eggs, beating for a minute after each goes in. With the mixer on medium, drop in the pieces of banana, beating until they are blended into the batter. You'll have a very light, almost fluffy mixture; if you still have chunklets of banana here and there, that's fine.

Turn off the mixer, add half of the flour mixture and pulse to begin the blending. Then mix on low speed only until most of the flour disappears. Pour in the buttermilk or sour cream and mix until it's almost all in, then turn off the mixer, add the remaining flour mixture and pulse and mix only until the flour is almost incorporated.

One by one—still on low speed—add the oats, nuts, if using, raisins or dates and flax. Remove the bowl from the mixer stand, if using, and finish the blending by hand with a flexible spatula. Scrape the batter into the pan, smoothing the top.

Bake for 45 to 50 minutes, or until the cake is deeply golden brown (if you think it is getting too dark, tent it loosely with foil or parchment) and starting to pull away from the sides of the pan; a tester inserted into the center should come out clean. Transfer the pan to a rack and let sit for 5 minutes, then run a table knife around the edges of the pan, if needed, to loosen the cake. Turn it out onto the rack, peel away the paper and turn it right side up. Let cool until just warm or at room temperature.

Cut the cake into 16 squares and serve as is or with some or all of the suggested go-alongs.

STORING: Wrapped well, the cake will keep for about 4 days at room temperature or for up to 2 months in the freezer; defrost it in its wrapper.

BIG AND SMALL,

# CAKES

FANCY AND SIMPLE

# CAKES: A HOW-TO

"A party without a cake is just a meeting." It was Julia Child who famously said that, and it's something I think of often. I'm the type who bakes simple cakes for meetings of all kinds, but when there's a party, I always fuss a bit, maybe make a few layers, add some cream, whip up a frosting. I think of dressy cakes as a present for everyone around the table—flourishes are the ribbons and bows.

Whether you're making a plain cake to cut into squares or a cake with layers, frosting and maybe even sprinkles, there are a few basics that hold.

• Pay attention to the temperature of your ingredients. You'll get the best volume and texture when your ingredients are at room temperature, so take the butter, eggs, milk and any other cold ingredients out of the refrigerator the instant the urge to bake strikes.

• Keep an eye on your batter and scrape down the bowl and beater(s) as needed.

• If you're making layers, try to get the same amount of batter in each pan. Level the top of the batter with a flexible spatula or swivel the pan back and forth to even the batter.

• Once the cake is in the oven, check on it a few minutes before the recipe tells you to—even though these recipes have been thoroughly tested, ovens vary.

• Let the cake cool to room temperature before cutting it and/or frosting it. Cooling is actually an important part of the baking process with cakes—their texture doesn't knit together fully until they're cool.

• If you're making a layer cake and the layers have domed, it's best to even them before you stack them. I like to use a gently serrated knife—a bread knife—for this job. Using an easy sawing motion, cut away the crowned part of the layer. Depending on the kind of cake you're making, you might want to crumble these bits and press them into the frosting as decoration. Or you just might want to nibble them.

• Once you've put the first layer on your cake plate, slip strips of parchment or wax paper all the way around the cake (you only have to tuck them under the cake a smidge) to protect the plate from errant frosting.

• Sandwich the layers together with filling or frosting. If the filling is very soft—as is true of curd and creams—you might want to slide the first layer into the refrigerator for about 15 minutes after adding the filling or frosting before topping it with the next layer and carrying on.

• When frosting, it's easy to start with the sides, smoothing or swooping the frosting with an offset icing spatula or a table knife to cover them and allowing it to rise just a little above the top of the cake. Then dollop the remaining frosting onto the top and spread it across the surface, drawing in the excess frosting from the sides as you go.

• If you've got time, once you've frosted the cake, put it in the refrigerator for an hour or so. This is not so much to chill the cake as it is to set the frosting.

• Most fancy cakes can be made in stages: The layers can usually be baked ahead, wrapped and kept overnight or frozen for a couple of months; the filled and frosted cakes can be set aside for a day and sometimes longer; and often even the finished cake can be frozen (the recipe will tell you everything).

With a little planning, you can turn more meetings into parties.

# Devil's Food Party Cake

*Makes 10 servings*

## FOR THE CAKE

1¾ cups (238 grams) all-purpose flour

⅔ cup (56 grams) unsweetened cocoa powder

1½ teaspoons baking powder

1 stick (8 tablespoons; 4 ounces; 113 grams) unsalted butter, at room temperature

1¼ cups (250 grams) sugar

½ teaspoon fine sea salt

¼ cup (60 ml) flavorless oil, such as canola

3 large eggs, at room temperature

2 teaspoons pure vanilla extract

1 cup (240 ml) milk, at room temperature

½ cup (120 ml) boiling water

## FOR THE FROSTING

3⅓ cups (405 grams) confectioners' sugar

½ cup (42 grams) unsweetened cocoa powder

½ teaspoon fine sea salt

2¼ sticks (9 ounces; 254 grams) unsalted butter, cut into small chunks and well softened

⅓ cup (80 ml) milk, at room temperature

Sprinkles, dragées, chocolate shavings or other decorations (optional)

**A WORD ON LAYERS:** Once you've baked the two layers, you've got a choice: You can stack them as is, or you can split each one in half to make a four-layer cake. It's all about how much frosting you want with each bite. Four layers means more frosting. It also means more height. You've got plenty of frosting to work with here, so you can be generous no matter which option you choose.

**HERE'S A CHOCOLATE CAKE** friends and family will ask for, the one for birthdays and holidays, a good-to-celebrate-everything cake. The first time I made it, my son, who had wanted the same chocolate birthday cake for years, said, "This is my new favorite!" I understood. Anyone who loves chocolate would have the same reaction. Because the layers are made with cocoa, their flavor is decisively, profoundly chocolate. And if you choose a cocoa with deep color (I use Valrhona), the layers will be as dark as a devil's heart. I purposefully dialed back the cake's sweetness so I could lavish it with a frosting that's unabashedly sweet, rich and creamy.

**TO MAKE THE CAKE:** Center a rack in the oven and preheat it to 350 degrees F. Butter two 8-inch round cake pans and dust with flour, or use baker's spray. Line the bottoms of the pans with parchment.

Sift the flour, cocoa and baking powder together.

Working in the bowl of a stand mixer fitted with the paddle attachment, or in a large bowl with a hand mixer, beat the butter, sugar and salt together on medium speed until smooth, about 4 minutes (the mixture will be pasty). Drizzle in the oil, pouring it against the side of the bowl, and beat until you've got a light, creamy mixture, about 3 minutes. One by one, add the eggs, beating for a minute after each goes in. Beat in the vanilla.

Working on low, add the dry ingredients alternately with the milk—begin and end with the dry, so that you've got 3 additions of dry ingredients and 2 of milk. The batter will be dark and look a little like frosting. Still on low speed, add the boiling water, drizzling it down the side of the bowl and mixing until the batter is smooth. Divide the batter evenly between the two pans, swiveling the pans from side to side to even them.

Bake the cakes for 27 to 30 minutes. A tester inserted into the cakes might come out clean earlier, but you want to wait until the cakes start to pull away from the sides of the pans. Transfer the pans to racks and let rest for 10 minutes, then run a table knife around the edges of the pans to loosen the cakes, if needed, and ⟶

*Cakes*

turn them out onto the racks. Turn the cakes right side up and allow them to cool to room temperature. (*You can make the layers up to 2 days ahead, wrap them well and keep them in the refrigerator, or freeze them for up to 2 months; thaw in the wrappers.*)

**TO MAKE THE FROSTING:** Sift the confectioners' sugar and cocoa into the bowl of a stand mixer fitted with the paddle attachment or a large bowl that you can use with a hand mixer. Add the salt and butter and pulse the mixer on and off to begin the blending and to avoid a shower of sugar and cocoa. (Draping a kitchen towel over the mixer isn't a bad idea.) When it's safe, mix on medium speed until you have a thick, homogenous mixture. Reduce the speed to low and drizzle in the milk, then beat to complete the blending—you should have a lovely frosting that will spread and swirl easily. It's best to use it now, although you can refrigerate it for a few hours or for up to 1 day (if you do, bring it to room temperature and stir until it's spreadable before using).

**TO FINISH THE CAKE:** These cake layers usually bake flat, but if the tops have domed, slice away the crowns to even them. You can make a two-layer cake or cut each layer in half to make four layers— the cake is great both ways and there's plenty of frosting for a taller cake. Put a dab of frosting in the middle of a serving platter, center one layer on it,

right side up, and slip strips of parchment or wax paper just under the edges of the cake all around to protect the plate from errant frosting. Cover the layer evenly and generously with frosting. Top with a second layer, top side down—if you're using four layers, frost it and just keep going, leaving the fourth layer unfrosted for the moment. Frost the sides and top of the cake. (You can leave the sides bare, but I think this cake is best frosted with a full heart. You have plenty of frosting.) If you'd like, decorate the cake with sprinkles or whatever you fancy,—but this cake is good and good-looking plain. Run a table knife around the bottom edges of the cake and remove the paper strips.

The cake can be served now—I love it fresh and soft—but it's easier to slice if you give it a couple of hours in the refrigerator. The cake is good cold, but it's nicer when it's not served directly from the fridge. I usually chill the cake thoroughly, then set it on the counter for half an hour before cutting and serving.

**STORING:** Filled and frosted, the cake can be refrigerated for up to 2 days. You can also freeze the frosted cake on a baking sheet until it's solid, then wrap it airtight and keep it in the freezer for up to 2 months. Defrost it, still wrapped, in the refrigerator overnight.

# A Big Banana Cake

*Makes 12 servings*

## FOR THE CAKE

2 cups (272 grams) all-purpose flour

1 cup (136 grams) whole wheat flour

2 teaspoons ground allspice

½ teaspoon fine sea salt

½ teaspoon baking soda

2 sticks (8 ounces; 226 grams) unsalted butter, at room temperature

1 cup (200 grams) packed brown sugar

½ cup (100 grams) sugar

2 large eggs, at room temperature

2 teaspoons pure vanilla extract

1¾ cups (420 ml) mashed bananas (from 3 to 4 overripe bananas)

1 cup (240 ml) sour cream or full-fat Greek yogurt

## FOR THE FILLING AND FROSTING

About ¾ cup (6 ounces; 170 grams) cookie spread, such as Lotus Biscoff

3 ounces (85 grams) cream cheese, softened

1 stick plus 1 tablespoon (9 tablespoons; 4½ ounces; 127 grams) unsalted butter, at cool room temperature

4½ cups (540 grams) confectioners' sugar

2 tablespoons milk, plus a little more if needed

½ teaspoon fine sea salt

Chocolate shavings, chocolate pearls or any kind of sprinkles for decoration (optional)

THIS IS A CAKE for a time when the house is filled with people, when its arrival at the table will be met with cheers. It's a three-layer cake, filled and frosted with a billowy mix of cream cheese and spiced cookie spread—a splendid match—and topped with chocolate shavings or pearls, colorful sprinkles or even sparklers, if you like. I've grounded the cake with some whole wheat flour and more brown sugar than white, given it a touch of sharpness by using sour cream and gone deep on allspice. Allspice is a warm spice and so good with banana. Allspice is a little peppery (it's also known as Jamaican pepper) and calls to mind cloves, nutmeg and cinnamon. Save your soft, speckled bananas for this—you need 3 or 4 of them. If they are ready before you are, pop them into the freezer to hold them until cake day.

I like this cake plain, but it lends itself to add-ins; see Playing Around.

TO MAKE THE CAKE: If your oven is large enough to hold three 9-inch round cake pans on one rack, center the oven rack; if not, position the racks to divide the oven into thirds. Preheat the oven to 350 degrees F. Butter and flour the three cake pans, or use baker's spray. Line the bottoms of the pans with parchment paper.

Whisk both flours, the allspice, salt and baking soda together.

Working in the bowl of a stand mixer fitted with the paddle attachment, or in a large bowl with a hand mixer, beat the butter and both sugars together on medium speed until light, smooth and creamy, about 3 minutes, scraping the bowl as needed. One at a time, add the eggs, beating for a minute after each goes in. Reduce the mixer speed to low and beat in the vanilla, then the bananas.

Turn off the mixer, add half of the dry ingredients and pulse to begin blending them in. Add the sour cream or yogurt and, working on low speed, mix to combine. Turn off the mixer again, add the remaining dry ingredients and then beat on low to finish mixing the batter. Divide the batter evenly among the three pans and smooth the tops.

Bake for 20 to 22 minutes, until the cakes are lightly golden around the edges (they'll remain rather pale in the middle) and just starting to pull away from the sides of the pans; a tester inserted into their centers will come out clean. (If you're baking on two racks, rotate the pans top to bottom and front to back after 10 minutes. If you're baking on one rack, you still might want to rotate the pans to get a more even bake.) Transfer the pans to racks and leave for 5 minutes, then run a table knife around the edges of the pans to loosen the cakes, if needed. Invert the cakes onto the racks, carefully peel away the paper and turn them right side up to cool to room temperature. (*The cooled layers can be wrapped well and refrigerated overnight or frozen for up to 2 months; thaw in the wrappers.*)

TO MAKE THE FILLING AND FROSTING: Working in the bowl of the stand mixer fitted with the paddle attachment, or in a large bowl with the hand mixer, beat all of the ingredients together on medium speed, scraping the bowl and beater(s) often, until smooth and light. If the frosting looks a bit too thick to spread in swirls (unlikely, but possible), add more milk by the droplet. (*You can cover and refrigerate the frosting for up to 3 days; beat before using to restore its spreadability.*)

TO FINISH THE CAKE: If any of the layers has crowned, use a long serrated knife and a gentle sawing motion to even the top. Put a tiny dab of frosting in the center of a serving platter, center one layer right side up on it and slip strips of parchment or wax paper just under the edges of the cake all around to protect the plate from any wayward frosting. Cover the top of the layer evenly with frosting. Top with another layer, this time upside down, and frost. Finish with the last layer, again upside down. Frost the sides of the cake (I like the sides frosted, but they can be left bare) and then the top. If you'd like, decorate the cake with chocolate shavings, pearls or sprinkles. Run a table knife around the bottom edges of the cake and remove the paper strips.

The cake can be served now, but it's easier to slice if you give it a couple of hours in the refrigerator. The cake is good cold, but it's nicer when it's not served directly from the fridge. I usually chill the cake thoroughly, then set it on the counter for half an hour before cutting and serving.

STORING: The filled and frosted cake can be refrigerated for up to 2 days. You can also freeze it on a baking sheet until it's solid, then wrap it airtight and keep it in the freezer for up to 2 months. Defrost it, still wrapped, in the refrigerator overnight.

## Playing Around

If you want, add chopped chocolate or chocolate chips (dark or milk), chopped toasted nuts (walnuts or peanuts) or even very soft, moist raisins or dried cranberries to the batter just before scraping it into the pans. Instead of this filling and frosting, you can use a more traditional cream cheese frosting; quadruple the recipe on page 109.

# Lemon Meringue Layer Cake

*Makes 8 servings*

## FOR THE CAKE

1¾ cups (238 grams) all-purpose flour

2 teaspoons baking powder

¼ teaspoon baking soda

1 cup (200 grams) sugar

¼ teaspoon fine sea salt

Finely grated zest of 2 lemons (reserve the lemons for the syrup)

1¼ sticks (10 tablespoons; 5 ounces; 141 grams) unsalted butter, at room temperature

3 large eggs, at room temperature

1 large egg yolk, at room temperature

1½ teaspoons pure vanilla extract

¾ cup (180 ml) buttermilk (well shaken before measuring), at room temperature

## FOR THE SYRUP

¼ cup (60 ml) freshly squeezed lemon juice (from 2 lemons)

¼ cup (50 grams) sugar

## FOR THE LEMON CREAM

½ cup (120 ml) freshly squeezed lemon juice (from 4 lemons)

½ cup (100 grams) sugar

¼ cup (32 grams) cornstarch

3 large egg yolks

1⅓ cups (320 ml) milk

## FOR THE BUTTERCREAM FROSTING

¾ cup (150 grams) sugar

3 large egg whites

2¼ sticks (18 tablespoons; 9 ounces; 255 grams) unsalted butter, at cool room temperature

¼ cup (60 ml) freshly squeezed lemon juice (from 2 lemons)

1½ teaspoons pure vanilla extract

## FOR DECORATION (OPTIONAL)

Candied lemon peel or slices, homemade (see Playing Around) or store-bought

**EVERY ELEMENT OF THIS CAKE** is worthy of adoration. It starts with a pair of delicious buttermilk layers, flavored with lemon and soaked in a lemon syrup. These are sandwiched with a creamy lemon filling that's in a class by itself, rich, velvety and tart as can be; that it also seems light is inexplicable but lovely. Once put together, the layers are swathed in a meringue buttercream frosting and finished with a skim of that sunshine-bright puckery lemon cream. For an even more fanciful decoration, think about scattering candied lemon peel or slices over the cake; see Playing Around.

**TO MAKE THE CAKE:** Center a rack in the oven and preheat it to 350 degrees F. Butter two 8-inch round cake pans and dust with flour, or use baker's spray.

Whisk the flour, baking powder and baking soda together.

Stir the sugar and salt together in the bowl of a stand mixer or in a large bowl that you can use with a hand mixer. Add the lemon zest and rub the ingredients together with your fingers until moist and fragrant. Attach the mixer bowl to the mixer stand, if using, and fit it with the paddle attachment. Drop the butter into the bowl and beat on medium speed for about 3 minutes, until smooth. One by one, beat in the eggs followed by the yolk, beating for a minute after each goes in. Beat in the vanilla. Beat on medium-high speed for 2 minutes; don't be discouraged if the batter looks curdled.

Turn off the mixer, add one third of the flour mixture and pulse to begin blending, then mix on low speed until the flour is incorporated. Blend in half of the buttermilk. Mix in half of the remaining flour, followed by the rest of the buttermilk and then the last of the dry ingredients. Give everything a good stir by hand, then divide the batter between the pans, leveling the tops.

Bake for 28 to 30 minutes, or until the cakes are golden and starting to come away from the sides of the pans; a tester inserted into their centers will come out clean. Transfer the pans to a rack and let rest for 5 minutes, then run a table knife around the edges of the

*Cakes*

pans to loosen the cakes, if needed; unmold onto the rack and turn right side up.

**AS SOON AS YOU SLIDE THE PANS INTO THE OVEN, MAKE THE SYRUP:** Stir the lemon juice and sugar together in a bowl. Stir now and then while the mixture sits to dissolve the sugar.

The instant the layers are right side up on racks, begin brushing their tops with the syrup. If you'd like, you can poke some holes in the layers with a tester or skewer so that the syrup seeps in further. Work slowly—you want to give the cakes a chance to drink up the syrup. Then allow the cakes to cool to room temperature. (*When the cakes are cool, you can wrap them well and hold them at room temperature overnight.*)

**TO MAKE THE LEMON CREAM:** Working in a medium heavy-bottomed saucepan, whisk together the juice, sugar and cornstarch until smooth. Whisk in the yolks, followed by the milk. Place the pan over medium-high heat and, whisking nonstop and making sure you're getting into the corners of the pan, cook until the cream starts to thicken and the whisk leaves tracks. You'll see a bubble or two pop at the surface—that's your sign to lower the heat, then keep cooking and whisking diligently for another 2 minutes. The whole process will take about 10 minutes; the exact time depends on your pan and the heat you give it.

Scrape the cream into a bowl and press a piece of plastic directly against the surface to keep a skin from forming. Refrigerate until chilled. If you're in a hurry, you can put the bowl of lemon cream into a larger bowl filled with ice cubes and cold water and whisk now and then until the cream is cold. (*The cream can be refrigerated, tightly covered, for up to 3 days.*)

**TO MAKE THE FROSTING:** Put the sugar and egg whites in the bowl of a stand mixer or in another large heatproof bowl that you can use with a hand mixer. Set the bowl over a pan of steadily simmering water and whisk energetically until the mixture feels hot to the touch—it will be white and shiny and the sugar will have dissolved. Remove the bowl from the heat.

Attach the bowl to the mixer stand, if using, and fit it with the whisk attachment. Beat on medium-high speed until the meringue is cool, about 5 minutes (the bottom of the bowl will no longer feel hot). Switch to the paddle attachment if using a stand mixer and, beating on medium speed, add the butter one third at a time. Increase the speed to medium-high and beat until the buttercream is thick and smooth, 6 to 10 minutes. If the buttercream breaks, don't worry—keep beating, and it will come together. Reduce the mixer speed to medium and gradually beat in the lemon juice, followed by the vanilla. You can use the frosting now or cover and refrigerate until needed. (*The frosting is best made the day you're going to use it, but you can hold it for a day in the fridge; return it to room temperature and beat it to bring back its spreadability.*)

**TO ASSEMBLE THE CAKE:** Place one layer syrup side up on a serving plate and slip strips of parchment or wax paper just under the edges of the cake all around to protect the plate from errant frosting. Stir the lemon cream to smooth it and then spread a generous amount over the cake layer. (You'll have plenty of cream for the layer and the topping—you may even have some left over.) Freeze the cake for 15 minutes to set the cream enough to support the next layer.

When the cream is firm, position the second layer over it, soaked side down. Stir the frosting, if necessary, and frost the sides and top of the cake. Swirl the frosting, if you'd like, or, if you want a sleek finish, run a metal spatula or knife under hot water, dry it and smooth the frosting; repeat the rinsing and drying as needed. Spread a thin layer of lemon cream over the top of the cake.

The cake needs to chill for at least 3 hours before serving. Take it out of the fridge 15 to 20 minutes before cutting and serving.

If you'd like, top the cake with candied lemon peel (cut into small pieces) or slices. Just before serving, drain and pat dry as many pieces or slices as you'd like and arrange them over the cake.

STORING: Wrapped well, the cake, without the candied lemon decoration, can be refrigerated for up to a day.

## Playing Around

### CANDIED LEMON PEEL OR SLICES

For candied peel, cut away the tops and bottoms of 2 large lemons, then cut away bands of peel, each about 1 inch wide, working your way around the lemons and making sure to include the white pith and a bit of fruit in each band. For slices, cut the lemons into slices—peel and all—about ⅛ inch thick.

Bring a pot of water to a boil, drop in the peel or slices, and boil for 1 minute; drain, rinse and repeat. Rinse out the pot and bring 2 cups (475 ml) water, 1 cup (200 grams) sugar and the juice of 1 lemon to a boil. Add the peel or slices, cover, reduce the heat to low and cook until the lemon is soft and translucent. The peel can take about 90 minutes; check the slices after 30 minutes. Cool to room temperature before packing the fruit and syrup into a clean jar. Refrigerate until needed, or for up to 2 weeks.

# Double-Decker Salted Caramel Cake

*Makes 10 servings*

## FOR THE CAKE

2¼ cups (306 grams) all-purpose flour

1½ teaspoons baking powder

½ teaspoon ground cinnamon

¼ teaspoon baking soda

2 large egg whites, at room temperature

1 large egg, at room temperature

1½ sticks (12 tablespoons; 6 ounces; 170 grams) unsalted butter, at room temperature

¼ cup (60 ml) flavorless oil, such as canola

1 cup (200 grams) packed brown sugar

¾ cup (150 grams) sugar

½ teaspoon fine sea salt

2 teaspoons pure vanilla extract

1 cup (240 ml) buttermilk (well shaken before measuring)

1 recipe Caramel Sauce (page 370), at room temperature, or just warm, and pourable

## FOR THE FROSTING

2 cups (240 grams) confectioners' sugar, or a little more if needed

1 cup (240 ml) Caramel Sauce (from above)

A few tablespoons of heavy cream if necessary

## FOR FINISHING (OPTIONAL)

Caramel Sauce (from above)

About 1 cup (2 handfuls) toffee bits, chopped chocolate or chips, chopped toasted nuts or cocoa nibs

MY FRIEND JOHN BENNETT used to say that anything worth doing is worth overdoing, and I thought of him as I kept adding more caramel flavor to this cake. Baked in a springform pan and then sliced into two layers, the soft brown-sugar cake looks plain, but don't be fooled: It's got swirls of caramel sauce running through it. It's covered with caramel frosting, made in seconds by beating confectioners' sugar and some caramel sauce together. It's ready to go once it's frosted, but I usually drizzle a little of the caramel sauce over the top or press a bunch of crunchy bits into the soft frosting. If you're worried that all this sugar will make the dessert too sweet, don't. The magic of burnt sugar, which is what caramel is, is its tinge of bitterness—that's what makes it so intriguing. I know that if John were serving the cake, each slice would get a big ball of vanilla ice cream and even more caramel sauce. It would be overdoing it, but it would also be great.

**A WORD ON TEXTURE:** This is a tender cake, the kind that cuts easily with the side of your fork, and it's smooth all the way through. If you'd like to add a touch of crunch here or there, you've got a couple of choices. Since caramel is such an easygoing companion, you can fold some toasted nuts, toffee bits, chopped chocolate (or chips) or cocoa nibs into the batter and bake in the crunch (about 1 cup does the trick). Or, if you'd like, sprinkle these same kinds of crunchy bits over the top or press them into the sides of the cake.

**TO MAKE THE CAKE:** Center a rack in the oven and preheat it to 350 degrees F. Butter and flour a 9- or 9½-inch springform pan, or use baker's spray.

Whisk the flour, baking powder, cinnamon and baking soda together.

Lightly stir together the egg whites and whole egg in a small bowl.

Working in the bowl of a stand mixer fitted with the paddle attachment, or in a large bowl with a hand mixer, beat the

*Cakes*

99

butter, oil, both sugars and the salt together on medium speed until smooth and creamy, about 4 minutes. Still beating on medium, add the egg mixture a little at a time, then continue beating for another minute or two. Beat in the vanilla. You'll have a shiny batter that forms pretty peaks when the beater is lifted.

Turn off the mixer, add one third of the flour mixture and pulse to begin incorporating it. Then, mixing on low, beat until the flour almost disappears. Still beating, pour in half of the buttermilk. Don't be discouraged when your beautiful batter curdles—it's ugly, but harmless. Mix in half of the remaining flour mixture, the rest of the buttermilk and then the last of the dry ingredients. Do the final bit of mixing by hand with a flexible spatula. (If you're adding any candy, nuts or chocolate to the batter, do it now; see headnote.)

Scrape the batter into the pan and smooth the top. Polka-dot 3 tablespoons of the caramel sauce on top and swirl it through the batter with a table knife.

Bake for 40 to 44 minutes, or until the cake is deeply golden and starting to pull away from the sides of the pan. A tester inserted into the center of the cake should come out clean. Transfer the pan to a rack and allow it rest for 5 minutes, then run a table knife around the edges of the pan to loosen the cake, if needed, and remove the sides. You can leave the cake on the pan bottom or wait a few more minutes and remove it. Let the cake cool to room temperature. (If it's more convenient, you can wrap the cake and leave it at room temperature overnight.)

TO MAKE THE FROSTING: Put the confectioners' sugar in the bowl of a stand mixer fitted with the paddle attachment, or in a large bowl you can use with a hand mixer. Pour in the 1 cup caramel sauce. (You can reserve the remaining few spoonfuls of sauce for the top of the cake.) Beat the sugar and sauce together on medium-high speed until you have a smooth, creamy frosting—a matter of seconds. If the frosting seems too thick to spread easily (because caramelizing sugar isn't a precise art, the sauce's consistency can vary), stir in a little heavy cream. If, on the other hand, it seems too thin, add a little more confectioners' sugar and stir until smooth. (The frosting is best used soon after it's made, but it will hold in the fridge overnight; let it warm up a bit and then stir it until it's easy to spread.)

TO ASSEMBLE THE CAKE: Split the cake in half using a long slicing knife—a gently serrated one is good here. Place the bottom layer cut side up on a serving plate and slip strips of parchment or wax paper just under the edges of the cake all around to protect the plate from errant frosting. Spread the cake layer evenly with frosting and then top with the second layer, cut side down. Frost the sides and top of the cake and remove the strips of paper.

If you'd like to finish the cake with a little more caramel sauce, spoon the reserved sauce onto the top in whatever pattern you like: random polka dots, drips, squiggles, spirals. Have fun. If you want to decorate it with anything more, sprinkle whatever crunchy bits you've chosen over the top and/or press them into the sides of the cake.

The cake is ready to serve as soon as it's finished—I love it when it's very soft—but it can be refrigerated for a couple of hours before cutting and serving. It slices more easily when it's cold, but it tastes better when it's had the chance sit at room temperature for about 15 minutes.

STORING: The cake is best within 2 days of being assembled. Leftovers should be wrapped well and refrigerated.

# Curd, Cream and Berry Cake

*Makes 10 servings*

## FOR THE CAKE

1 cup (136 grams) all-purpose flour

1 teaspoon baking powder

1 cup (200 grams) sugar

¼ teaspoon fine sea salt

1 clementine or ½ orange

1 lemon

½ cup (120 ml) milk

2 tablespoons unsalted butter

2 large eggs, at room temperature

1½ teaspoons pure vanilla extract

## FOR THE SYRUP

¼ cup (50 grams) sugar

¼ cup (60 ml) water

Reserved strip of clementine or orange zest (from above)

Reserved strip of lemon zest (from above)

Juice of ½ lemon (from above)

## FOR THE CREAM

1 cup (226 grams) mascarpone

1 cup (240 ml) very cold heavy cream

2 large egg whites, at room temperature

½ cup (100 grams) sugar

## FOR THE FRUIT AND CURD

About 1 pound (453 grams) berries, such as strawberries, hulled and cut into bite-size pieces, blueberries or raspberries, or a mix

About ¼ cup (60 ml) lemon curd, homemade (page 362) or store-bought, such as Stonewall Kitchen or Bonne Maman

**THERE IS A CACHE OF SURPRISES,** little twists of taste and texture, that make this dessert singular, starting with the cake itself, a simple old-fashioned hot-milk sponge cake that manages to be both soft and sturdy at the same time. Baked as one layer and then split, it's flavored with orange and lemon zest and brushed with orange-lemon syrup. Then the layers are covered with whipped cream mixed with mascarpone, which tastes rich and sharp, its texture all the more sublime because you fold in meringue. There are berries, lots of them, in the middle of the cake and crowning the top in a tumble. Finally, there's lemon curd, dabs of it between the layers and on the top of the cake, doing double duty: adding pops of big flavor and making a beautiful cake even more beguiling.

**TO MAKE THE CAKE:** Center a rack in the oven and preheat it to 350 degrees F. You can use a 9-inch round cake pan, one with 2-inch-high sides, or a 9-inch springform. Butter and flour the pan, or use baker's spray.

Whisk together the flour and baking powder.

Put the sugar and salt in the bowl of a stand mixer or in a large bowl that you can use with a hand mixer. Remove a strip of zest from the clementine or orange and one from the lemon and set aside for the syrup. Working over the bowl, finely grate the remaining zest from the clementine or orange and the zest from half of the lemon (set the lemon aside for the syrup). Using your hands, rub the ingredients together until moist and fragrant. Attach the bowl to the mixer stand, if using, and fit with the whisk attachment.

Put the milk and butter in a small saucepan and bring just to a boil, or do this in the microwave. Set aside for the moment—when you're ready for it, you're going to want it very hot, so don't transfer it into another pan or container.

Add the eggs to the sugar and beat on medium-high speed for 5 minutes—the mixture will be pale and light. Beat in the vanilla. With the mixer on low, add the flour mixture in 3 additions, mixing only until the flour disappears before adding more. Scrape the bowl really well—get down to the bottom to make sure there are no clumps. Check that the milk-butter mixture is still very hot—if it's not, give it more heat—and, with the mixer on low, slowly and steadily pour it into the bowl. When it appears to be incorporated, give the batter a last turn by hand and scrape it into the pan. Swivel the pan to even the batter.

Bake for 23 to 25 minutes, or until the cake is golden, springs back when gently prodded and is starting to come away from the sides of the pan; a tester inserted into the center of the cake will come out clean. Transfer the cake to a rack and let rest for 5 minutes, then run a table knife around the edges of the pan to loosen the cake, if needed, and unmold onto the rack; invert the cake and allow it to cool to room temperature right side up. (*At this point, the cake can be wrapped well and kept at room temperature overnight.*)

TO MAKE THE SYRUP: Bring the sugar, water and reserved strips of clementine and lemon zest to a boil in a saucepan, stirring to dissolve the sugar (or use the microwave). Stir in the lemon juice, and set the syrup aside until it is just warm or at room temperature. (*You can make the syrup up to a week ahead; remove the zest and refrigerate the syrup in a covered jar.*)

TO MAKE THE CREAM: Scrape the mascarpone into a large bowl and, using a flexible spatula, stir until it's creamy and spreadable. Don't beat it—it will tighten rather than smooth.

Working in the bowl of a stand mixer fitted with the whisk attachment, or in a large bowl with a hand mixer, beat the cream until it holds medium peaks. Using the spatula, fold the whipped cream into the mascarpone. There's no need to be thorough—you'll be folding again in a minute.

Wash and dry the bowl and beater(s) and start beating the egg whites at medium-high speed. When the whites are foamy and opaque, begin adding the sugar 1 tablespoon at a time, waiting until each spoonful is incorporated before adding the next. When all the sugar is in, the whites should be glossy and hold firm peaks. Scrape the whites onto the mascarpone and fold everything together with a light touch.

TO ASSEMBLE THE CAKE: Using a long slicing knife—I like one that's gently serrated—split the cake in half. Place the bottom half cut side up on a serving platter. (If you've got a footed cake stand, this is a good time to pull it out.) Brush the layer with half of the syrup. Cover it with one quarter of the cream, scatter over half the berries and dot with lemon curd. Then top the fruit with one third of the remaining cream, spreading it gently. Place the top layer cut side down on the filling. Brush the cake with the remaining syrup, spread the rest of the cream over the cake—swirl extravagantly—and top with the remaining berries. Dot with the remaining curd.

You can serve the cake now, but it will taste better and slice more easily if you refrigerate it for at least 1 hour; 3 hours would be even better.

STORING: The cake is best served the day it is made.

# Swirled, Spiced
# Sour Cream Bundt Cake

*Makes 12 servings*

## FOR THE SWIRL

½ cup (100 grams) sugar

½ cup (about 100 grams) mini chocolate chips, milk or semisweet, or finely chopped chocolate

½ cup (60 grams) chopped nuts, such as walnuts or pecans, toasted or not

1 tablespoon unsweetened cocoa powder

¼ teaspoon ground cinnamon

¼ teaspoon ground allspice

Pinch of fine sea salt

## FOR THE CAKE

2 cups (272 grams) all-purpose flour

½ cup (68 grams) whole wheat flour

1½ teaspoons ground allspice

1¼ teaspoons baking powder

½ teaspoon baking soda

½ teaspoon ground cinnamon

2 sticks (8 ounces; 226 grams) unsalted butter, at room temperature

1 cup (200 grams) sugar

1 cup (200 grams) packed brown sugar

¾ teaspoon fine sea salt

3 large eggs, at room temperature

2 teaspoons pure vanilla extract

1 cup (240 ml) sour cream, at room temperature

Confectioners' sugar for dusting if you're not icing the cake

## FOR FINISHING (OPTIONAL)

Confectioners' Sugar Icing (page 372)

Chopped toasted nuts

**A CLASSIC REBORN.** Tweaking my sour cream Bundt cake, I fiddled with the flour, adding some whole wheat, sneaked in brown sugar, went strong on allspice and put in some cinnamon too. Finally, I double-swirled my new cake with a mix of sugar and cocoa, nuts, chocolate and spice. My husband, after polishing off every bit of it, gave the cake his highest compliment: He begged me not to make it again unless I was planning to have a crowd over.

While the cake is great on its own, the patterns of a Bundt pan invite icing. If you agree, drizzle or spread a little confectioners' sugar icing over the cake so that it runs down the nooks and crannies and sprinkle toasted nuts over the top as well.

Center a rack in the oven and preheat it to 325 degrees F. Butter and flour a large Bundt pan, or use baker's spray.

**TO MAKE THE SWIRL:** Put all the ingredients in a bowl and stir to blend. *(The swirl can be covered and kept at room temperature for up to a week.)*

**TO MAKE THE CAKE:** Whisk both flours, the allspice, baking powder, baking soda and cinnamon together.

Working in the bowl of a stand mixer fitted with the paddle attachment, or in a large bowl with a hand mixer, beat the butter, both sugars and the salt together on medium speed for about 3 minutes, scraping the bowl as needed, until the mixture is well blended. One at a time, add the eggs, beating for a minute after each egg goes in and then beating for an extra minute after they're all incorporated. Mix in the vanilla. Scrape the sour cream into the bowl and mix on low until blended—it might look curdled, but that's fine.

Turn the mixer off, scrape the bowl and add half the dry ingredients. Mix on low until the flour mixture is almost blended, then stop the mixer, add the remainder of the flour mixture and mix on low until almost incorporated. Do the last bit of blending by hand with a flexible spatula.

Spoon a thin layer of batter (use a quarter to a third of it) into the pan, smoothing it with the back of the spoon or a spatula. Sprinkle over half of the swirl mixture, trying to keep it away from the sides of the pan. Spoon half of the remaining batter over the swirl, smooth it and then sprinkle on the rest of the swirl. Cover the swirl with the last of the batter and smooth it as best as you can.

Bake for 68 to 72 minutes, or until the cake has started to pull away from the sides of the pan and, most important, a skewer inserted deep into the cake comes out clean. Transfer the pan to a rack and let rest for 5 to 10 minutes, then turn the cake out onto the rack and let cool to room temperature.

If you're not going to use the icing, dust the cake with confectioners' sugar before serving.

TO ICE THE CAKE: If you decide to use the icing, the pattern of your Bundt pan will determine the pattern of the icing. Get some icing along the top and then let it drip down some or all of the curves or crannies. This is the kind of finish that's best when it's least fussed with. Scatter over the nuts.

STORING: Wrapped well, the cake will keep for up to 1 week at room temperature. If it's not iced, it can be frozen for up to 2 months; thaw in its wrapper.

## Playing Around

### CLASSIC SOUR CREAM BUNDT CAKE

Use 2 cups (272 grams ) all-purpose flour, omitting the whole wheat, and 1¾ cups (350 grams) sugar, omitting the brown sugar. Omit the allspice and cinnamon as well, but do add some grated lemon zest, if you'd like.

# Coconut–Milk-Chocolate Marble Cake

*Makes 8 servings*

2 cups (272 grams) all-purpose flour

1¼ teaspoons baking powder

¼ teaspoon baking soda

4 ounces (113 grams) milk chocolate, chopped

1 stick plus 2 tablespoons (10 tablespoons; 5 ounces; 141 grams) unsalted butter, at room temperature

1 cup (200 grams) sugar

½ teaspoon fine sea salt

3 large eggs, at room temperature

1½ teaspoons pure vanilla extract

½ cup (120 ml) full-fat canned coconut milk (shaken and stirred before measuring)

⅓ cup (33 grams) shredded unsweetened coconut

HATS OFF TO WHOEVER INVENTED marble cakes—they're a brilliant twofer: one cake, two flavors. In addition, it's almost impossible to make a marble cake that isn't beautiful. In this one, the base cake, an excellent yellow cake, is made with rich coconut milk. I added finely shredded coconut to one half of the batter and milk chocolate to the other. They're perfect together, look pretty when marbled and give the cake terrific texture and flavor.

A WORD ON MARBLING: I like to portion out the batters with a cookie scoop, alternating dark and light batters in the pan and then swirling the two with a table knife. Of course, you can use a spoon. Or you can lay down a layer of the dark batter, then a layer of the white and do the squiggle. You can make bigger dollops of one batter and smaller but more numerous dollops of the other. You can make half a dozen zigs and zags in the batter or you can make more. Whatever you do, the cake will look great.

Center a rack in the oven and preheat it to 325 degrees F. Butter a 9-inch loaf pan and dust with flour, or use baker's spray.

Whisk the flour, baking powder and soda together.

Melt the chocolate and 2 tablespoons of the butter together on the stovetop or in the microwave, and set aside in a warmish place (you don't want the mixture to get firm).

Working in the bowl of a stand fitted mixer with the paddle attachment, or in a large bowl with a hand mixer, beat the remaining stick of butter, the sugar and salt together on medium speed for 3 minutes. One by one, add the eggs, beating for a minute after each egg goes in. (The batter might curdle a bit, but it will be silken after the last egg is incorporated.) Mix in the vanilla. Turn the mixer off, add half the dry ingredients and mix on low until almost blended. Still on low, mix in the coconut milk, and when it's almost incorporated, add the rest of the dry ingredients, mixing until they disappear into the batter.

Scoop half of the batter into a bowl and stir in the melted chocolate and butter, mixing until no streaks of chocolate are visible. Stir the shredded coconut into the remaining batter.

Using a cookie scoop or a spoon, drop dollops of the batter into the pan, alternating dark and light batters (see headnote). Grab a table knife, plunge it into the pan and zig and zag a few times to marble the two batters.

Bake the cake for 68 to 72 minutes, or until it is deep golden brown and has started to pull away from the sides of the pan; a tester inserted into the center of the cake should come out clean. Transfer the pan to a rack and wait for 5 minutes, then run a table knife around the edges of the pan to loosen the cake, if needed. Unmold the cake onto the rack, then turn it right side up and let cool to room temperature.

STORING: Well wrapped, the cake will keep for about 4 days at room temperature or for up to 2 months in the freezer; defrost in the wrapper.

# Cranberry Spice Squares

*Makes 16 squares*

## FOR THE CAKE

½ cup (68 grams) all-purpose flour

½ cup (68 grams) whole wheat flour

½ cup (50 grams) rye flour

½ teaspoon baking soda

½ teaspoon fine sea salt

½ teaspoon ground cinnamon

½ teaspoon ground ginger

¼ teaspoon ground allspice

¼ teaspoon ground cloves

½ cup (100 grams) sugar

⅓ cup (80 ml) unsulfured molasses

¼ cup (60 ml) flavorless oil, such as canola

1 large egg, at room temperature

3 tablespoons buttermilk (well shaken before measuring)

¾ cup (75 grams) halved or coarsely chopped fresh or frozen cranberries (don't thaw if frozen)

## FOR THE FROSTING

4 ounces (113 grams) cream cheese, softened

½ stick (4 tablespoons; 2 ounces; 56 grams) unsalted butter, at cool room temperature

About 1⅓ cups (267 grams) confectioners' sugar

**A WORD ON MEASURING MOLASSES:** To make getting the molasses out of the measuring cup easy, measure the oil in the (glass) measuring cup first and then measure the molasses—the slick from the oil will help the molasses slide out of the cup.

WARM AND COZY, the way gingerbread is, but with the ping of fresh cranberries, these cake squares taste a bit earthy too, because they're made with three flours: all-purpose, whole wheat and rye. They look sweet, plain and old-fashioned, but their flavor turns out bright, sassy and tough to pin down. They're good with the cream cheese frosting or, for something a bit more offbeat, cranberry curd (page 364) or lemon curd, homemade (page 362) or store-bought.

**TO MAKE THE CAKE:** Center a rack in the oven and preheat it to 350 degrees F. Generously butter an 8-inch square baking pan, or coat it with baker's spray. Line the bottom with parchment paper.

Whisk the three flours, baking soda, salt and spices together.

Working in the bowl of a stand mixer fitted with the paddle attachment, or in a large bowl with a hand mixer, beat the sugar, molasses, oil and egg together on medium speed until smooth. Add the dry ingredients all at once and pulse the mixer to start blending them in. Then beat on low speed only until the flour disappears into the batter. Pour in the buttermilk and mix until it's incorporated; you'll have a heavy, sticky batter. Stir in the cranberries by hand.

Scrape the batter into the pan, pushing it into the corners and leveling the top.

Bake for 26 to 30 minutes, or until the cake is starting to come away from the sides of the pan and a tester inserted into the center comes out clean. Transfer the pan to a rack and wait 10 minutes, then run a table knife around the edges of the pan and unmold the cake onto the rack; peel away the paper. Turn the cake right side up and let cool to room temperature.

**TO MAKE THE FROSTING:** Beat the cream cheese and butter together—you can do this in the bowl of a stand mixer fitted with the paddle attachment, in a bowl with a hand mixer or by hand (if you'll be working by hand, let the cream cheese and butter soften a bit more before you beat them). When the mixture is very smooth. gradually beat in the sugar, starting with about 1¼ cups (250 grams) and stopping when the frosting is the consistency you want and just as sweet as you'd like it to be.

Spread the frosting over the top of the cake, swirling and swooping or smoothing it as you go.

You can cut and serve the cake now or wait—spice cakes are nice after they've had a day to rest.

STORING: This cake is a good keeper. Wrapped and refrigerated, it will hold for at least 4 days. Unfrosted and wrapped airtight, it can be frozen for up to 2 months; thaw in the wrapping.

# Strawberry-Rhubarb Squares

*Makes 16 squares*

1½ cups (204 grams) all-purpose flour

1 teaspoon baking powder

¼ teaspoon baking soda

1 stick (8 tablespoons; 4 ounces; 113 grams) unsalted butter, at room temperature

½ cup (100 grams) sugar

½ teaspoon fine sea salt

¼ cup (60 ml) honey

2 teaspoons pure vanilla extract

1 large egg, at room temperature

⅓ cup (80 ml) buttermilk (well shaken before measuring)

2 cups (200 grams) sliced rhubarb (from 3 to 4 trimmed stalks)

2 cups (200 grams) sliced strawberries

AS MODEST AS THIS CAKE IS, it beckons you back. It's a low, simple cake—soft, tender and hinting of honey—topped with a classic combination, strawberries and rhubarb. The rhubarb and strawberries are naturally tart, which is why I chose them, and the reason I don't sugar them before scattering them over the cake: They're just right with the cake's honey-and-buttermilk tang. For other fruits that make good toppings, see Playing Around.

Center a rack in the oven and preheat it to 350 degrees F. Spray a 9-inch square baking pan with baker's spray (for this cake, baker's spray works better than butter and flour; if you don't have it, butter the pan, dust with flour and line the bottom with parchment paper).

Whisk together the flour, baking powder and baking soda.

Put the butter, sugar and salt in the bowl of a stand mixer fitted with the paddle attachment, or in a large bowl that you can use with a hand mixer. Beat on medium speed, scraping the bowl as needed, until the mixture is smooth, about 3 minutes. Add the honey and beat for another minute or so to blend. Pour in the vanilla extract, add the egg and beat for 2 minutes—don't be concerned when the mixture curdles.

Turn off the mixer, add half of the dry ingredients and pulse the mixer to begin the blending. Then beat on low until the flour almost disappears into the batter. Still working on low, pour in the buttermilk. When almost all the liquid is incorporated, turn off the mixer, add the rest of the dry ingredients and beat on low until you have a fully blended, very thick batter.

Scrape the batter into the pan. It will take a little nudging to get it into the corners and to smooth the top—do your best to get it even. Scatter over the rhubarb and strawberries.

Bake for 35 to 40 minutes, until the cake, which will be pale in the center and golden at the edges, is starting to come away from the sides of the pan; a tester inserted into the center should come out clean. Transfer the pan to a rack and let rest for 5 minutes, then run a table knife around the edges of the pan. Unmold the cake onto a rack, peel away the paper, if you used it, invert again and let cool to room temperature on the rack.

Cut the cake into squares at serving time. With this, a cut-as-you-go strategy is best.

STORING: The cake is best soon after it's made. You can wrap and keep it overnight, but it won't be as good as it is when just made.

## Playing Around

When rhubarb is no longer in season, you can top the cake with a mix of summer berries. And when fall and winter roll in, switch to sliced plums, apples, pears or mangoes or segments of oranges, tangerines and/or even grapefruit. Nuts are a welcome addition in any season.

# Chunky Lemon Cornmeal Cake

*Makes 8 servings*

2 medium lemons (plus ½ medium lemon if not using sumac)

1¼ cups (170 grams) all-purpose flour

½ cup (86 grams) cornmeal

1½ teaspoons baking powder

½ teaspoon salt

¼ teaspoon baking soda

½ stick (4 tablespoons; 2 ounces; 57 grams) unsalted butter, melted

¼ cup (60 ml) flavorless oil, such as canola

1 cup (200 grams) sugar

2 teaspoons ground sumac (or another ½ lemon; see headnote)

½ cup (120 ml) plain yogurt

3 large eggs, at room temperature

½ teaspoon pure vanilla extract

THE TEXTURE OF THIS CAKE is so winning that it might take you a beat to appreciate all the flavor that's packed into it. The loaf is substantial yet tender, slightly chewy and, because it's made with cornmeal, the texture is a bit gritty, in the nicest way. After the pleasure of that nice graininess, you're into lemon—lots of lemon. Zest, of course, and pulp too, chopped into little pieces and mixed into the batter. Finally, there's sumac, a beautiful rust-red spice often found in savory Mediterranean dishes—and not often enough in desserts. In ancient times, sumac was used in place of lemon. Here the ground spice adds a touch of tartness and another level of citrus flavor and zing. If there's no sumac in your cupboard when the urge to bake this loaf hits you, add another half lemon to the mix.

You can serve the cake fresh or sliced and toasted, either as is, or spread with marmalade or topped with sugared berries. For a few ideas on tinkering with the cake, see Playing Around.

You'll need both the zest and the pulp of the lemons. You can finely grate the zest, but if you want even more flavor and textural interest, remove the zest with a vegetable peeler or knife (cut away any bitter white pith) and very finely chop it. For the lemon segments, cut off the top and bottom of each lemon, then stand the fruit on end and trim away the remaining pith. Using a small paring knife, slice between each lemon segment and the membranes that hold it to release it. When you've liberated all the segments (discard the membrane), spread a kitchen towel or a double thickness of paper towels on a plate or cutting board, lay the segments out on it, cover with another towel (or towels) and let drain and dry while you measure out the ingredients for the cake (letting them dry for a couple of hours is even better).

Center a rack in the oven and preheat it to 350 degrees F. Butter an 8- to 8½-inch loaf pan, or use baker's spray.

Whisk together the flour, cornmeal, baking powder, salt and baking soda.

Stir the butter and oil together in a small bowl and keep at hand.

Finely chop the lemon segments; set aside. Put the grated or chopped zest in a large bowl and cover with the sugar. Using your fingertips, rub the sugar and zest together until the mixture is moist and fragrant. Add the sumac, if you've got it, and massage it into the sugar. Working with a flexible spatula, blend in the yogurt, then add the eggs one at a time, beating for a minute after each egg goes in. Beat in the vanilla.

Add the dry ingredients in 2 additions, gently stirring and folding until all of the flour is blended into the batter. Stir in the butter-oil mixture—the batter will be thick and have a lovely sheen. Stir in the chopped lemon. Scrape the batter into the pan and smooth the top.

Bake the cake for 50 to 60 minutes, or until a tester inserted into the center comes out clean. The cake should be golden brown and have started to pull away from the sides of the pan; it may or may not crack down the center—it will be beautiful whether it does or doesn't. Let the cake rest in the pan for 5 minutes on a rack, then run a table knife around the sides of the pan and unmold the cake onto the rack. Turn right side up and let cool to room temperature.

STORING: Well wrapped, the cake can be kept for at least 5 days at room temperature. If you think it's a little stale, toast it. Wrapped airtight, it can be frozen for up to 2 months; thaw in the wrapper.

## *Playing Around*

You can swap the lemons for an orange or 1 or 2 limes, and if you do, use just 1½ teaspoons sumac. You can also add some fruit—sweet cherries are really nice with sumac. For a less sweet, tad more savory loaf, reduce the sugar to ¾ cup (150 grams) and replace the sumac with za'atar or herbes de Provence, or some finely chopped fresh rosemary or thyme.

# Apricot and Pistachio–Olive Oil Cake

*Makes 8 servings*

1¾ cups (240 grams) all-purpose flour

1 teaspoon baking powder

¼ teaspoon baking soda

¼ teaspoon fine sea salt

1⅓ cups (166 grams) sugar

1 tablespoon tea leaves, preferably loose-leaf, finely chopped if necessary (see below), or a pinch of saffron

Finely grated zest of 1 orange or tangerine

2 large eggs, at room temperature

1 stick (8 tablespoons; 4 ounces; 113 grams) unsalted butter, melted and cooled

⅔ cup (180 ml) plain Greek yogurt (*not* cold)

6 tablespoons olive oil

6 (75 grams) large soft, plump dried apricots, cut into small cubes

½ cup (70 grams) shelled pistachios (salted or not), coarsely chopped

**FOR FINISHING**

⅔ (160 ml) apricot preserves

About ½ cup (70 grams) shelled pistachios (salted or not), coarsely chopped

Strained Yogurt (see page 379) for serving (optional)

**A WORD ON THE TEA:** I usually use black tea, but the cake's ingredients are also good with a green leaf tea (matcha powder is not right here), so choose a tea you love. If you've got loose tea (my preference), spoon it out onto a cutting board and chop it before rubbing it into the sugar.

**WITH THIS CAKE,** what you see is only half of the pleasures you get. Crowned with chopped pistachios pressed into a slick of apricot jam, it pulls off the trick of looking simultaneously plain and posh. Even the bare golden-brown sides, which show just a trace of the jam that's between the layers, are an invitation to discover what's inside. The cake itself is moist and a bit tangy—that's the yogurt and olive oil—and chockablock with small pieces of plump dried apricots and more pistachios, their flavors highlighted by orange zest. Although the mélange of flavors swings Mediterranean, the cake's charms are universal. But if you love the flavors of that region and want to accentuate them, think about replacing the tea with a pinch of saffron. And, whether you opt for tea or saffron, consider serving the cake with spoonfuls of strained yogurt.

Center a rack in the oven and preheat it to 350 degrees F. Butter an 8-inch round cake pan, one with 2-inch-high sides, and dust with flour, or use baker's spray. (You can also use a springform pan—the sides of the cake may not bake as straight as in a cake pan, but the height will be good.)

Whisk the flour, baking powder, baking soda and salt together.

Put the sugar in the bowl of a stand mixer or in a large bowl that you can use with a hand mixer. Add the tea or saffron and use your fingers to rub it into the sugar. Add the grated orange zest and continue to rub the ingredients together until the sugar is fragrant and moist from the zest.

If you're using a stand mixer, attach the bowl to the mixer stand and fit it with the paddle attachment. With the mixer on medium, one at a time, add the eggs, beating for a minute after each egg goes in. Reduce the speed to low and beat in the melted butter. Add the yogurt and mix until thoroughly blended.

Add the flour in 2 additions, mixing just until incorporated and scraping the bowl with a flexible spatula as necessary. With the mixer still on low, blend in the olive oil, then add the apricots and pistachios. Give the batter a few last turns by hand with the spatula to finish mixing everything together. Scrape the batter into the pan and level the top.

Bake for 38 to 42 minutes, or until the cake is golden and is starting to pull away from the sides of the pan; a tester inserted into the center of the cake should come out clean. Transfer the cake to a rack and wait for 5 minutes, then run a table knife around the edges of the pan to loosen the cake, if needed. Unmold it onto the rack, turn right side up, and let cool to room temperature.

**TO FINISH THE CAKE:** Split the cake horizontally in half. Place the bottom layer cut side up on a serving platter.

Put the jam in a microwave-safe container, stir in a couple of teaspoons of water and bring to a boil in the microwave. (Or do this on the stovetop, if you prefer.) Spread half the jam over the bottom cake layer. Place the second layer on top, cut side down. Brush the top of the cake with the rest of the jam and then sprinkle the chopped pistachios over the top and press them lightly into the jam. You can serve the cake now or allow it to stand uncovered until the jam sets.

If you'd like to serve the cake with yogurt, you can either top it with the yogurt or offer a spoonful with each slice.

**STORING:** Wrapped well, the cake will keep for up to 3 days at room temperature.

# Orange Spice Cake

*Makes 10 servings*

1½ cups (204 grams) all-purpose flour

1¼ teaspoons baking powder

1 teaspoon ground cardamom

½ teaspoon ground ginger

½ teaspoon fine sea salt

1¼ cups (250 grams) sugar

1 large orange or 2 tangerines or clementines

4 large eggs, at room temperature

½ cup (120 ml) heavy cream, at room temperature

1½ teaspoons pure vanilla extract

5½ tablespoons (2¾ ounces; 77 grams) unsalted butter, melted and cooled

### FOR THE GLAZE (OPTIONAL)

⅓ cup (80 ml) marmalade

½ teaspoon water

EVERYTHING ABOUT THIS CAKE conspires to bring happiness: the way it's mixed—in one bowl and by hand; the way it looks—familiar and inviting, plain, but glossed with a glimmer of jam; and the way it tastes—wholesome, lightly spiced, warm and comforting, yet, almost paradoxically, fresh and bright. And then there's its texture—moist, firm, easily sliceable, like your favorite pound cake. Because it's sturdy, it's perfect for picnics and road trips, packing up for friends or keeping out on the counter over the weekend, there to be enjoyed in slices thin or thick.

I flavor the cake with orange, cardamom and ginger, but each of these ingredients can be varied. Swap the cardamom for pinches of cloves and allspice and make this a holiday cake; replace the orange with lemon and add a little coriander to the mix; or run some candied peel or toasted nuts through the batter. Oh, I almost forgot to mention another of its virtues: It keeps for days. Actually, it's even better after it settles for a day—the spices will be more flavorful then.

Center a rack in the oven and preheat it to 350 degrees F. Butter an 8½-inch loaf pan, dust with flour and tap out the excess. (For this cake, baker's spray isn't as good as butter and flour.) Place on a baking sheet.

Whisk the flour, baking powder, cardamom, ginger and salt together.

Put the sugar in a large bowl and grate the orange (or tangerine or clementine) zest over it. Squeeze 3 tablespoons juice from the fruit; set aside.

Using your fingers, rub the sugar and zest together until the mixture is moist and aromatic. One at a time, add the eggs, whisking well after each egg goes in. Whisk in the juice, followed by the heavy cream. Still using the whisk, gently stir the dry ingredients into the batter in 2 additions. Stir the vanilla into the melted butter and then gradually blend the butter into the batter. The batter will be thick and have a beautiful sheen. Scrape it into the pan.

Bake for 70 to 75 minutes (if the cake looks like it's getting too dark too quickly, tent it loosely with foil or parchment), or until the cake is deeply golden and a tester inserted deep into its center comes out clean; the top of the cake will have probably cracked, and that's lovely. Transfer the pan to a rack and let rest for 5 minutes, then carefully run a table knife between the sides of the cake and the pan, invert the cake onto the rack and turn right side up. If you want to glaze the cake, do it now; if not, let it cool to room temperature.

TO MAKE THE OPTIONAL GLAZE: Bring the marmalade and water to a boil on the stovetop or in a microwave. Brush the glaze over the top of the warm cake and allow it to set at room temperature for 2 hours. The glaze will remain slightly tacky.

STORING: Well wrapped, the cake will keep for about 4 days at room temperature. If you haven't glazed the cake, you can freeze it for up to 2 months; defrost in its wrapper.

*Cakes*

# Swedish Fika Cake

*Makes 8 servings*

## FOR THE CAKE

1¾ cups (240 grams) all-purpose flour

1 teaspoon baking powder

¼ teaspoon fine sea salt

1¼ cups (250 grams) sugar

2 large eggs, at room temperature

1¾ sticks (14 tablespoons; 7 ounces; 200 grams) unsalted butter, melted and cooled to lukewarm

⅔ cup (160 ml) lukewarm milk (if necessary, heat it gently)

2 teaspoons pure vanilla extract

## FOR THE TOPPING

7 tablespoons (3½ ounces; 100 grams) unsalted butter, cut into small chunks

¾ cup (75 grams) sliced almonds

½ cup (100 grams) sugar

2 tablespoons all-purpose flour

2 tablespoons milk

**A WORD ON TEMPERATURE AND TIMING:** Be sure to use eggs that are at room temperature; the butter and milk should be lukewarm. You need to start making the topping after the cake has been in the oven for 30 minutes or so.

**THIS RECIPE COMES FROM** Mia Öhrn, the Swedish pastry chef and author who introduced me to the custom of *fika*. *Fika* (the word was created by flipping the two syllables in *kaffe*) is the moment during the day when everything stops so that people can get together to have coffee and a snack, usually something sweet. It is less a coffee break as we know it than a brief get-together. It is so much a part of Swedish life that even companies, large or small, have *fika* twice a day. For children, there's often a *fika* before bed, a time for a glass of milk and a small sandwich or a cookie. Of course I fell in love with the tradition in a flash.

I also fell in love with this cake. The cake is a moist, tender butter cake, but it's the topping that steals the spotlight: a mix of sweet, buttery sliced almonds that bakes to a crackle and sheen.

**TO MAKE THE CAKE:** Center a rack in the oven and preheat it to 350 degrees F. Butter a 9- to 9½-inch springform pan and dust with flour (baker's spray isn't a good option here). Place the pan on a baking sheet lined with parchment paper or a baking mat.

Whisk the flour, baking powder and salt together.

Working in the bowl of a stand mixer fitted with the paddle attachment, or in a large bowl with a hand mixer, beat the sugar and eggs together on medium-high speed until light and slightly thickened, about 3 minutes. Reduce the speed to medium and gradually add the melted butter, followed by the milk and vanilla, and mix until the batter is smooth and shiny. Reduce the speed to low and gradually add the dry ingredients, mixing until they're almost fully incorporated., Using a flexible spatula, give the batter a few last turns to finish the blending. Scrape it into the pan.

Slide the cake into the oven and set your timer for 30 minutes.

As soon as the timer dings, look at the cake: If it seems set and firm enough for you to be able to spread the topping over it, start making the topping; if it doesn't, bake it for a few minutes more and then make the topping.

TO MAKE THE TOPPING: Combine all of the ingredients in a medium saucepan. Place over medium-high heat and cook, stirring constantly with a heatproof spatula, until you see a couple of bubbles around the edges. Lower the heat to medium and cook, stirring nonstop, for 3 minutes. The mixture will thicken a little and your spatula will leave tracks as you stir. Remove the pan from the heat.

When the top of the cake is firm, take it out of the oven (leave the oven on) and carefully pour the topping over the cake, nudging it gently with a spatula so it covers the top completely.

Return the cake to the oven and bake for another 15 minutes (the total baking time for the cake is about 50 minutes), or until the topping—which will bubble and seethe—is a beautiful golden brown and a tester inserted into the center of the cake comes out clean. Transfer the pan on the baking sheet to a rack and let rest for 5 minutes. Carefully work a table knife between the sides of the pan and the cake, gently pushing the cake away from the sides (it's a delicate job, because the sticky topping won't have set yet). Remove the side of the pan and let the cake cool to room temperature on the base.

When you're ready to serve, lift the cake off the springform base and onto a platter.

STORING: The cake may look delicate, but it will keep well for up to 3 days if your kitchen isn't humid. The easiest way to keep it is to return it to the (clean) springform pan and cover the top of the pan.

*Baking with Dorie*

# Mocha-Walnut Torte

*Makes 10 to 12 servings*

## FOR THE CAKE

1½ cups (200 grams) walnuts (whole or pieces)

1 cup (200 grams) plus 2 tablespoons sugar

4 ounces (113 grams) semisweet or bittersweet chocolate, coarsely chopped

2 tablespoons ground coffee, preferably espresso

1 teaspoon ground cinnamon

4 large eggs

1½ teaspoons pure vanilla extract

½ teaspoon fine sea salt

½ recipe Chocolate Ganache (page 363) for finishing (optional)

Toasted walnuts for sprinkling (optional)

Whipped cream, crème fraîche and/ or confectioners' sugar for serving (optional)

THIS IS THE KIND OF CAKE served in Italian caffès, French bistros and Austrian coffeehouses. You can find renditions of it, usually made with almonds, around the Mediterranean and on Passover tables all over the world (there's no leavening, so it's perfect for the holiday). It's a simple, unfussy and unfussed-over cake, a slim torte made with just three ingredients: eggs, sugar and nuts (there's no wheat, so it's gluten-free). Here I use walnuts, which have a pleasantly bitter side to them. Playing to the nuts' strengths, I've included a few other flavorful ingredients—most important, chocolate and ground coffee (preferably espresso), as well as a touch of cinnamon and vanilla.

The cake is an excellent keeper and, because it's sturdy, a good traveler—make it for a friend or take it to a potluck. It's good plain and good with whipped cream or crème fraîche. And if you want to dress it up, it takes nicely to a drizzle of chocolate ganache.

TO MAKE THE CAKE: Center a rack in the oven and preheat it to 350 degrees F. Butter a 9- or 9½-inch springform pan, or use baker's spray. Line the bottom with parchment and butter or spray the parchment, then dust the pan with cocoa powder. Place the pan on a baking sheet lined with parchment or a baking mat.

Put the nuts, 2 tablespoons of the sugar, the chocolate, coffee and cinnamon in a food processor and pulse, scraping the sides and bottom of the bowl often and taking care that you don't process for so long that the walnuts become a paste and the chocolate melts. You want to end up with a bread-crumb–like mixture—it's better to have some discernible morsels than to overdo it. Set aside.

Separate the eggs, putting the yolks in a large bowl and the whites in the bowl of a stand mixer or a large bowl that you can use with a hand mixer.

*Cakes*

123

Working with a whisk, beat the yolks until they're homogeneous. Gradually whisk in ¾ cup (150 grams) of the sugar and then beat for a couple of minutes, until the mixture is pale and your whisk leaves tracks. Beat in the vanilla. Switch to a flexible spatula and stir in the walnut mixture.

Add the salt to the whites. Attach the bowl to the mixer stand, if using, and fit it with the whisk attachment. Beat the whites until they are foamy, opaque and just a bit thick. Beat in the remaining ¼ cup (50 grams) sugar, adding it a tablespoon at a time. Once all the sugar is in, the whites should be thick and glossy—lift the beater(s), and the meringue should hold a pretty peak.

Using a flexible spatula, scoop out about a quarter of the meringue and add it to the bowl with the egg yolk mixture. Stir everything together energetically so that the whites lighten the thick mixture. Scrape the rest of the meringue into the bowl and, being gentle, stir and fold it in. Without overdoing it, you want to get as much of the meringue into the nut mixture as quickly as possible. If there are a few white streaks, it's fine (better to have streaks than to knock all the air out of the meringue). Scrape the batter into the pan, swiveling the pan from side to side to settle the batter evenly.

Bake for 43 to 48 minutes, or until the cake feels firm to the touch and has risen. The rise might be higher around the edges, but the middle should lift too; a tester inserted into the center of the cake should come out clean. Transfer the pan to a rack and let rest for 5 to 10 minutes, then run a table knife between the cake and the sides of the pan to release the cake; remove the sides of the springform and allow the cake to cool to room temperature on the rack.

When the cake is cool, invert it, remove the base of the pan and the parchment and turn the cake right side up onto the rack. If you want to glaze the cake, now's the time. Put a piece of foil or other drip-catcher under the rack, pour the ganache over the cake and use an offset spatula or knife to smooth it over the top. Alternatively, you can drizzle the ganache over the cake. And if you're using toasted walnuts, sprinkle them over the glaze while it's still warm. Refrigerate the cake until chilled, wrapping it well once it's cold.

The cake is good at room temperature, but I prefer it straight from the fridge. It also cuts better when it's cold. Serve with whipped cream or crème fraîche or, if you prefer, dust the top with confectioners' sugar. Or don't—it's fine just the way it is.

STORING: Wrapped well, the cake will keep for about a week in the refrigerator or for up to 2 months in the freezer; thaw in the wrapper.

# Lamingtons

*Makes 16 cubes*

## FOR THE CAKE

6 large eggs, at room temperature

1⅓ cups (181 grams) all-purpose flour

1 teaspoon baking powder

¼ teaspoon fine sea salt

½ stick (4 tablespoons; 2 ounces; 56 grams) unsalted butter, melted

1 cup (200 grams) sugar

## FOR THE COATING

About 2 cups (160 grams) shredded unsweetened coconut

## FOR THE CHOCOLATE SAUCE

1 tablespoon plus 1 teaspoon unsalted butter

½ cup (120 ml) water

2¼ cups (254 grams) confectioners' sugar

3½ tablespoons unsweetened cocoa powder

**PLAN AHEAD:** The cake needs to be made at least 1 day ahead.

THE LAMINGTON, which may or may not have been named for Lord or Lady Lamington of Queensland at the turn of the twentieth century, is a national treasure in Australia. It's cubes of cake covered in chocolate and coated with unsweetened coconut. It's as simple as it sounds, but something about it makes it irresistible. I think it's the chocolate.

The cake itself is a yellow sponge, often a génoise, which is what I make. A génoise is a whole-egg sponge cake that's easy to work with—it's got great texture, cuts cleanly and holds its shape when dipped. The secret to a great Lamington is to let the cake sit overnight so it stales a bit—the dry cake will soak up more chocolate, and that's a fine thing. That chocolate is neither a frosting nor an icing; it's a hot cocoa sauce that seeps into the cake just enough to create a soft, sweet outer layer. It's completely delightful. Don't be tempted to make the sauce ahead—wait until you've cut the cake and are ready to dip the cubes.

TO MAKE THE CAKE: Center a rack in the oven and preheat it to 350 degrees F. Butter a 9- inch square cake pan and dust with flour, or use baker's spray. Line the bottom of the pan with parchment paper. Have a sifter or strainer at hand.

If your eggs are still cool to the touch, put them in a bowl of hot water for 5 minutes—warmed eggs beat more voluminously than cold eggs and you want volume.

Whisk the flour, baking powder and salt together. Put the melted butter in a small bowl.

Working in the bowl of a stand mixer fitted with a whisk attachment, or in a large bowl with a hand mixer, beat the sugar and eggs together on medium-high speed until they triple in volume, about 4 minutes; when you lift the whisk, the batter should form a ribbon as it falls into the bowl. If you're using a stand mixer, remove the bowl. Grab a big flexible spatula, sift or strain one third of the flour mixture over the eggs and sugar and gently fold it in. Repeat twice more, until all of the flour is in. No matter how gentle you are, the batter will deflate—it's the nature of the cake. ⟶

*Cakes*

Stir two or three spoonfuls of the batter into the melted butter and then gradually fold the butter mixture into the batter in the bowl. As you fold, check the bottom of the bowl—the butter has a tendency to lurk there: Find it and fold it in. Scrape the batter into the pan and jiggle the pan to level it.

Bake for 26 to 29 minutes, or until the cake is golden, is starting to come away from the sides of the pan and springs back when gently prodded; a tester inserted into the center of the cake will come out clean. Transfer the pan to a rack and wait for 5 minutes, then run a table knife around the edges of the pan to loosen the cake. Unmold the cake onto the rack, carefully peel away the paper and let cool to room temperature. Lightly cover the cake—you can put a kitchen towel over it—and leave it out overnight. (*The cake can be wrapped in plastic and kept at room temperature for up to 2 days.*)

**TO CUT THE CAKE AND GET READY TO FINISH IT:** Unwrap the cake if necessary and place it right side up on a cutting board. The top will have crowned in baking, so use a long serrated knife and a gentle sawing motion to level the cake. Cut the cake into 16 squares, each about 2¼ inches on a side. Place the cubes on a rack set over a piece of parchment or a baking sheet—the sauce will drip—and prepare your dipping and coating station: Put some of the coconut in a shallow bowl—work with a little at a time, so that if you get chocolate sauce in it (almost inevitable), you've got backup. Have four table forks at hand—two for dipping and two for turning the chocolate-coated cake cubes in the coconut.

**TO MAKE THE SAUCE:** Bring the butter and water to a boil—I do this in the microwave. Sift or strain the confectioners' sugar and cocoa together into a bowl—a deep narrow one is best. Pour the boiling water–butter mixture into the bowl and stir with a flexible spatula to blend.

**TO DIP AND COAT THE CAKE:** One by one, drop the cubes of cake into the sauce, turning each one around with two forks until it's coated on all sides. Lift up the cube, letting any excess sauce drip back into the bowl, and return the cube to the rack. After you've dipped two or three cubes, one by one, coat each of the dipped cubes with coconut, using two clean forks to turn the cubes around in the coconut. Continue working in batches until all of the cubes are dipped and coated. If the sauce thickens as you work, thin it with drops of very hot tap or boiling water.

Leave the Lamingtons on the rack to set for an hour or so before serving.

**STORING:** You can wrap the Lamingtons well and keep them at room temperature for 3 days or so. Yes, they'll be drier, but they'll still be so good.

# The Everything Cake

*Makes 8 servings*

## FOR THE CAKE

1½ cups (204 grams) all-purpose flour

¾ teaspoon baking powder

1 cup (200 grams) sugar

3 large eggs, at room temperature

½ teaspoon fine sea salt

1½ teaspoons pure vanilla extract

⅓ cup (80 ml) milk, at room temperature

1½ sticks (12 tablespoons; 6 ounces; 170 grams) unsalted butter, melted and cooled

Confectioners' Sugar Icing (page 372) or Chocolate Icing (page 372) (optional)

Sliced toasted almonds for sprinkling (optional)

**I HAD TROUBLE** deciding on a name for this easy one-bowl cake that you mix by hand. It's like a sponge cake, but moist and a smidge chewy; you taste the butter, but you wouldn't call the cake rich, just good. Its beauty lies in its possibilities. You can flavor it by adding other ingredients to the batter or by infusing spices, herbs or tea into the melted butter that goes into it. It can welcome fruit, fresh or dried, either in the batter or on top of it (the fruit usually sinks, but that's fine). It can be frosted—I like it with a confectioners' sugar icing—or brushed with warm jam, or just sprinkled with sugar. It can be sliced and filled, and it's nice with a topping of poached fruit, whipped cream or even hot fudge sauce (page 371). I've suggested a few ideas (see Playing Around), but there are many more possibilities for you to discover on your own.

**TO MAKE THE CAKE:** Center a rack in the oven and preheat it to 350 degrees F. Butter a 9-inch round cake pan, or use baker's spray.

Whisk the flour and baking powder together.

Put the sugar in a large bowl and add the eggs and salt, whisking for a minute or two to get a homogenous mixture. Whisk in the vanilla and milk. Switch to a flexible spatula and stir in the dry ingredients. When they're fully incorporated, gradually fold in the butter. Scrape the batter into the pan.

Bake the cake for 28 to 32 minutes, or until the top is set and golden, the cake is starting to pull away from the sides of the pan and a tester inserted into the center comes out clean. Transfer to a rack and let rest for 5 minutes, then run a table knife around the edges of the cake and unmold it onto the rack. Turn it right side up and let cool to room temperature.

If you want to ice the cake, do this when the cake is cool. If you're using almonds, sprinkle them over the cake while the icing is still wet. Let the icing set at room temperature before serving.

**STORING:** Wrapped well, the cake will keep at room temperature for up to 4 days. If you haven't iced the cake, it can be frozen, well wrapped, for up to 2 months; thaw in the wrapper.

## Playing Around

### LEMON, LIME, ORANGE AND/OR TANGERINE CAKE

Grate 2 to 3 tablespoons of citrus zest (use one kind or several) over the sugar and use your fingers to rub the ingredients together until the sugar is moist and fragrant. Use just ½ teaspoon vanilla (or omit it) and add 2 tablespoons citrus juice to the batter along with the milk. If you'd like, arrange pieces of fruit (either segments or thin slices) over the top of the batter and sprinkle with sugar before baking.

*variations continue* ⟶

*Cakes*

### APPLE OR PEAR CAKE

Add up to 1 tablespoon dark rum to the batter along with the vanilla. Arrange slices of peeled apple or pear on top of the batter and sprinkle with cinnamon sugar.

### BERRY CAKE

Grate 2 to 3 tablespoons lemon or lime zest over the sugar and use your fingers to rub the ingredients together until the sugar is moist and fragrant. Stir 1 to 1½ cups (about 165 to 250 grams ) berries into the finished batter or scatter them over the top of the batter just before baking.

### TEA CAKE

Rub 2 teaspoons loose tea (finely chop the tea if it's coarse) into the sugar or add the leaves to the butter before you melt it; don't strain.

### SPICE CAKE

Add a cinnamon stick, some cracked cardamom pods, a few slices of fresh ginger, a spoonful of peppercorns and some grated citrus zest to the butter before you melt it. Remove from the heat and let infuse for about 20 minutes; strain.

### HERB CAKE

Add 2 teaspoons culinary-grade dried lavender or rosemary to the butter before melting it; strain the butter before proceeding. Or rub a smaller amount of minced fresh lavender or rosemary into the sugar. If using lavender, think about topping the cake with berries; if using rosemary, consider orange segments.

### BOOZY CAKE

Add 2 tablespoons dark rum, Grand Marnier, amaretto or bourbon along with the vanilla.

### NUT CAKE

Replace ¼ cup (34 grams) of the all-purpose flour with ⅓ cup (about 25 grams) ground nuts or nut flour. If you'd like, add some toasted chopped nuts to the batter at the end or scatter chopped nuts and sugar over the top of the batter.

# Lisbon Chocolate Cake

*Makes 10 servings*

## FOR THE CAKE

⅓ cup (28 grams) unsweetened cocoa
   powder

1½ tablespoons cornstarch

¼ teaspoon baking powder

¼ teaspoon fine sea salt

1 stick (8 tablespoons; 4 ounces;
   113 grams) unsalted butter,
   cut into chunks

5 ounces (142 grams) semisweet
   or bittersweet chocolate,
   coarsely chopped

½ cup (100 grams) sugar

3 cold large eggs

## FOR THE GANACHE

1¾ cups (420 ml) heavy cream

6 ounces (170 grams) semisweet
   or bittersweet chocolate,
   finely chopped

## TO FINISH

About 3 tablespoons unsweetened
   cocoa powder

Ice cream, whipped cream or crème
   fraîche for serving (optional)

ON OUR LAST DAY in Lisbon, my husband and I had the
cake at Landeau Chocolate, a beautiful café. I say *the* cake,
because it is the only cake, indeed the only thing other than
coffee and tea, on the menu. The cake is remarkable in that
it is intense but not overwhelming. It has three layers—a
dense-but-not-heavy brownie-like cake; a whipped chocolate
ganache, very much like a mousse; and a dusting of cocoa
that is its own important component. The day I returned
home, I set to work making my own version of it.

As impressive as this cake looks, it's not difficult or
tricky to make. The batter for the dark cake layer is mixed
on top of the stove—just make sure you beat in the cold eggs
until the mixture is thick, shiny and puddingish. The ganache
is a cinch—get it cold, give it a quick whisking and then fold in
some whipped cream. And the whole cake can be made days
ahead—it can even be frozen. All that, and it's gluten-free too.

TO MAKE THE CAKE: Center a rack in the oven and preheat it to
325 degrees F. Butter a 9-inch cake pan, or use baker's spray. Line
the bottom of the pan with a piece of parchment paper and butter
or spray the paper.

Sift together the cocoa powder, cornstarch, baking powder and salt
into a bowl; whisk to blend.

Put the butter in a heatproof bowl set over a pan of simmering water
(make sure the water isn't touching the bottom of the bowl) and scatter
the chopped chocolate over it. Heat, stirring often, until the chocolate
and butter have melted and the mixture is smooth and glossy.

Remove the bowl from the pan and, working with a flexible spatula,
stir in the sugar. The mixture will turn grainy. One by one, add the cold
eggs, stirring energetically after each egg goes in. Once the third egg
has been added, beat with the spatula for another minute or so. You
really must stir with vigor and you really must beat for a while. The
mixture will be slippery and may seem on the verge of separating,
but that's just the sign that you're not done yet. Keep stirring, and
it will thicken considerably, look more coherent and remind you of
pudding. When it's just right, the mixture will form a little ribbon

if you lift up a bit of it and let it fall back into the bowl. Add the dry ingredients all at once and stir them in. Scrape the batter into the pan and give the pan a couple of good raps against the counter to settle it.

Bake the cake for 18 to 20 minutes, or until the top feels set to the touch and a tester inserted into the center comes out clean. (If you've got a tiny streak of chocolate on the tester, that's fine—it's better to underbake this cake than to overbake it.) Transfer the pan to a rack and let rest for 5 minutes, then run a table knife around the edges of the pan to loosen the cake, if needed, and turn it out onto the rack. Peel off the paper, invert the cake again and let cool right side up on the rack. Wash and dry the baking pan.

TO MAKE THE GANACHE: Put 1¼ cups (300 ml) of the cream in a small saucepan; keep the remaining ½ cup (120 ml) cream in the refrigerator. Heat the cream over medium heat until you see little bubbles around the perimeter, then turn off the heat, add the chopped chocolate and stir until it's melted and fully incorporated. Transfer the ganache to a heatproof bowl and refrigerate for 10 minutes.

Gently stir the ganache with a whisk and put it back in the refrigerator. Repeat this chilling and gentle whisking every 10 minutes until the ganache is thick enough that the whisk makes tracks when you stir; it should feel cool to the touch. It usually takes 50 to 60 minutes to reach this point, so don't plan any outings.

Cut two long pieces of parchment or foil and crisscross them in the baking pan, leaving enough excess to securely grab the ends—these will be your cake lifters. Return the cake to the pan, right side up.

Whip the remaining ½ cup (120 ml) heavy cream in a medium bowl until it holds soft to medium peaks.

Using a whisk, give the ganache a few firm beats—it should be soft and easily spreadable, like a frosting.

Scrape the whipped cream over the ganache and use a flexible spatula to fold it in until the mixture is smooth.

Spread the ganache in an even layer over the top of the cake, then slide the cake into the refrigerator for at least 2 hours. If you want to keep it longer, cover it once the ganache is firm.

Although the cake is good when it's cold, I think it's best served at cool room temperature, so pull it out of the fridge at least 30 minutes before you're ready for it.

TO FINISH THE CAKE: Put the cocoa powder in a fine-mesh strainer and shake it over the top of the cake, covering the top completely and evenly.

TO SERVE: The ganache may extend beyond the edges of the cake and even be stuck to the sides of the pan, so run a table knife between the cake and the sides of pan to loosen it, as well as to even the edges of the topping. Then, using the parchment or foil handles, carefully lift the cake out of the pan and onto a serving plate. Slide a cake lifter or the bottom of a tart pan under the cake and raise the cake so that you can remove the parchment or foil.

To slice the cake, treat it like a cheesecake—cut it with a thin knife run under hot water and wiped dry between each cut. If you're offering ice cream, whipped cream or crème fraîche as a go-along, put it on top of each slice of cake or just alongside.

STORING: Once topped with cocoa, the cake can be kept covered in the refrigerator for up to 2 days. If the cocoa powder sinks into the ganache, give it a fresh dusting. Miraculously, this cake can be frozen for up to 2 months (best to hold off on topping it with the cocoa, though, or re-cocoa it before serving). Put it in the freezer uncovered and then wrap it airtight once it is firm; defrost it, still wrapped, in the refrigerator.

# Jelly Roll Cake

*Makes 8 to 10 servings*

## FOR THE CAKE

½ cup (68 grams) all-purpose flour

¼ cup (32 grams) cornstarch

6 large eggs, separated, at room temperature

Finely grated zest of ½ lemon, plus a squirt of the juice

1½ teaspoons pure vanilla extract

¼ teaspoon fine sea salt

⅔ cup (133 grams) sugar

Confectioners' sugar for dusting

## FOR THE FILLING

About 1 cup (240 ml) jelly or jam, stirred to loosen (it needs to be easily spreadable)

About 1½ cups (360 ml) cold firmly whipped cream (optional)

Confectioners' sugar or cocoa powder for dusting

**A WORD ON ROLLING:** If you'd like a taller, chubbier cake with more spirals, roll up the sponge cake from a short side.

THERE'S NOTHING ABOUT THIS CLASSIC, a light sponge cake rolled around a filling, that isn't surprisingly doable. Even getting it to look spectacular is simple. The spirals—so dramatic—shape themselves as you roll up the pliable cake. The hardest thing you have to do is decide what filling you want. To start you on the path to jelly-rolling, naturally I'm suggesting jelly here (or jam); you can add a cushion of whipped cream, if you'd like. You can switch things up and go with a swath of Vanilla Pastry Cream (page 360), Lemon Curd (page 362) or Cranberry Curd (page 364). Or turn this clever construction into an extravagant ice cream cake—fill the sponge with your favorite ice cream, cover it with whipped cream, decorate it with cherries and sprinkles and pass the hot fudge sauce; take a look at Playing Around.

**TO MAKE THE CAKE:** Center a rack in the oven and preheat the oven to 400 degrees F. Line a rimmed baking sheet that's about 12 × 17 inches with parchment paper. Lightly coat the parchment and the edges of the baking sheet with baker's spray (spray works better than butter here). Have a clean kitchen towel and a strainer at hand.

Sift the flour and cornstarch together.

Whisk the egg yolks, lemon zest, vanilla and salt together in a large bowl.

Put the whites in the bowl of a stand mixer fitted with the whisk attachment, or in a large bowl you can use with a hand mixer. Add the squirt of lemon juice and beat the whites at medium-high speed until they turn opaque and just start to hold a shape. With the mixer running, add the sugar a tablespoon at a time—take your time, patience makes a good meringue. Then continue beating until the meringue holds firm, glossy peaks.

Spoon about a quarter of the whites over the yolk mixture and whisk to blend—you're using these whites to lighten the yolks, so there's no need to be gentle. Scrape the remainder of the whites into the bowl, top with the dry ingredients and, working with a flexible spatula, gingerly fold everything together, turning the bowl as you fold and being on the lookout for pockets of flour—they have a way of hiding out at the bottom of the bowl. No matter how mindful you are, the mixture will deflate a little, just carry on. Scrape the batter onto the baking sheet and spread it evenly across the entire surface.

Bake for 8 to 10 minutes, until the cake has puffed and feels dry to the touch. Transfer the baking sheet to a rack and immediately, while the cake is still hot, lay the kitchen towel out on the counter and dust it with confectioners' sugar, shaking it onto the towel through the strainer. Run a table knife around the edges of the baking sheet to loosen the cake and turn it out onto the towel. Lift off the baking sheet and very carefully peel away the parchment.

If necessary, turn the towel so that a long side of the cake is parallel to you, and roll the cake up snugly in the towel. Roll it as tightly as possible and then twist the ends of the towel to compress the cake. Allow to cool to room temperature. (*The cake can be made ahead and left rolled up on the counter overnight.*)

**TO FILL AND ROLL THE CAKE:** Unroll the cake—leave it on the towel—and spread the jam or jelly evenly over it, leaving just a thin strip bare at the far end. If you're going with a layer of whipped cream, cover the jam with it. Using the towel and your hands, roll the cake up as neatly and carefully as you can, finishing with the seam on the bottom (or as close to it as you can manage). If you used whipped cream and you've got the time, chill the cake for an hour or so. (If the jelly roll is just jelly, it's good cold too.)

Just before serving, trim the ends of the jelly roll—it's nice to see a neat spiral—and dust the top with confectioners' sugar or cocoa.

**STORING:** Wrapped well, the cake will keep in the refrigerator for a day.

## Playing Around

### CREAM-SWIRLED ROLL

Instead of putting whipped cream inside the cake, fill the cake with jelly or jam, curd, fruit butter, Nutella or Lotus Biscoff Cookie Butter and use the cream to frost the cake. Do that, and you can decorate the cake with chopped toasted nuts, sprinkles, dragées, cookie crumbs or chopped cookies, toasted coconut, chocolate shavings or birthday candles.

### ICE CREAM ROLL

Because this cake is so thin and light, if you freeze it, it can be eaten straight from the freezer, making it perfect for an ice cream roll. Cover the cake with a generous layer of softened ice cream, add chocolate bits or chopped toasted nuts, if that's your fancy, roll it up and freeze it well wrapped, (*you can keep it in the freezer for up to 1 week*). When you're ready to serve, frost the roll with whipped cream. If you'd like, decorate the cake with sprinkles. Putting a little pitcher of hot fudge sauce (page 371) on the table adds to the fun.

### SPICE ROLL

When you're sifting the flour and cornstarch together, add 1 teaspoon ground cinnamon, 1 teaspoon ground ginger and a pinch of ground allspice. This is a good cake to fill with Lotus Biscoff or apple butter.

### COCOA ROLL

Reduce the flour to 6 tablespoons (8 grams) and the cornstarch to 3 tablespoons. Before sifting them together, add ¼ cup (21 grams) cocoa powder. Think about filling this cake with Nutella and finishing it with a dusting of cocoa powder. If you want, you can add some chopped nuts to the filling.

# Marbled Cheesecake

*Makes 16 servings*

## FOR THE CRUST

1¾ cups (about 200 grams) graham cracker crumbs (from about 12 crackers)

2 tablespoons sugar

1 teaspoon instant espresso or instant coffee

Pinch of ground cinnamon

5 tablespoons (70 grams) unsalted butter, melted

## FOR THE SYRUP

2 teaspoons instant espresso or 1 tablespoon instant coffee

1½ tablespoons sugar

¼ teaspoon ground cinnamon

2 tablespoons boiling water

## FOR THE CAKE

4 ounces (113 grams) chocolate—semisweet, bittersweet or fine-quality milk—finely chopped

2 pounds (907 grams) cream cheese, softened

1¼ cups (250 grams) sugar

¾ teaspoon fine sea salt

4 large eggs, at room temperature

2 teaspoons pure vanilla extract

1⅓ cups (320 ml) heavy cream, not very cold

**A WORD ON TENTING THE CAKE:** As the cheesecake bakes and the top browns, the contrast between the dark and light marbling weakens. If you want a stronger contrast, you can loosely tent the cake—the trade-off is that you might get condensation spots. You can blot them dry when the cake comes out of the oven, but they might persist. I don't find this tragic.

**PLAN AHEAD:** The cheesecake needs to chill for at least 6 hours.

**CHEESECAKE IS EASY AND IMPRESSIVE**, a dessert that delivers delight. This one is mostly classic—a graham cracker crust (you could use cookies instead; see Playing Around) and a filling made by whipping together cream cheese, heavy cream and eggs. And the preparation is classic: The cheesecake is baked in a water bath, rested in the turned-off oven and then given a long chill. The leisurely bake produces a meltingly creamy texture, and the marbling creates the distinctive look, with chocolate, coffee and cinnamon giving the dark streaks their good flavor. Like all cheesecakes, this one must be refrigerated before serving, making it ideal for celebrations.

Butter a 9½- to 10-inch springform pan and wrap the bottom in a double thickness of foil—it's easiest and most effective if you make an X with two long pieces. Draw the foil up as high as you can and wrap it tightly around the pan. Line a baking sheet with parchment paper or a baking mat.

**TO MAKE THE CRUST:** Put all the ingredients *except* the melted butter in a large bowl and toss to blend. Add the butter and, using a fork or your fingers, toss and mash everything together until the crumbs are thoroughly moistened and hold together when pinched. Turn the crumbs into the pan and press them evenly over the bottom and as far up the sides as you can go, which may only be about ½ inch. Slide the pan into the freezer while you preheat the oven. (*Wrapped airtight, the crust can be frozen for up to 2 months.*)

Center a rack in the oven and preheat it to 350 degrees F.

Put the springform on the baking sheet and bake the crust for 10 minutes. Transfer to a rack and let cool while you make the syrup and cake. Turn the oven down to 325 degrees F.

Have a roasting pan that's large enough to hold the springform at hand.

**TO MAKE THE SYRUP:** Put all the ingredients in a bowl and mix until the coffee dissolves and the syrup is smooth. (*You can make the syrup up to 2 weeks ahead and keep it in a sealed jar in the refrigerator. Shake before using.*)

*Cakes*

TO MAKE THE CAKE: Put the chocolate and syrup in a heatproof bowl set over a pan of simmering water (don't let the bottom of the bowl touch the water) and heat, stirring often, until the chocolate is melted and the mixture is smooth. Alternatively, you can do this in the microwave. Set aside.

Working in the bowl of a stand mixer fitted with the paddle attachment, or in a large bowl with a hand mixer, beat the cream cheese, sugar and salt together on medium speed, scraping the bowl often, until the mixture is smooth, about 4 minutes. One by one, add the eggs, beating for a minute after each egg goes in, again scraping the bowl as needed. Beat in the vanilla. With the mixer on low speed, pour in the cream, then turn up the speed to medium and beat until the batter is billowy and velvety smooth. Scrape the bowl and make sure that there aren't any lumps at the bottom.

Pour one third of the batter into a bowl, add the melted chocolate and stir to blend evenly.

Spoon some of the white batter into the springform pan and spoon over polka dots of chocolate batter, then continue, alternating vanilla and chocolate batters and remembering that you've got twice as much white as black batter. Plunge a table knife deep into the pan and drag it in swirls to marble the batters. Don't overdo it—eight or so swirls are usually enough to produce a pretty pattern.

Fill a pitcher with very hot tap water. Put the pan in the roaster, slide the setup into the oven, and pour enough hot water into the roasting pan to come halfway up the sides of the springform. (If you want to loosely cover the top, make a tent with a piece of foil or parchment and put it on top of the cake; see headnote.) Close the oven, set a timer for 90 minutes and walk away. The cheesecake must bake undisturbed, so don't open the door.

When you hit the 90-minute mark, turn off the oven and open the oven door just enough to slip in a wooden spoon that will keep it slightly ajar. Allow the cheesecake to rest undisturbed for 1 hour.

Pull the roasting pan out of the oven. Very carefully lift the springform out of the roaster and onto a rack, leaving the foil wrap behind. No matter how tightly you've wrapped the pan, there's always hot water in the foil, so pay attention as you do this.

Let the cake cool to room temperature, then transfer it to the refrigerator. Chill the cake for at least 6 hours. (*The cake can be refrigerated for up to 4 days; cover it once it's cold.*)

When you're ready to serve the cake, warm the outside of the pan: I do this with a hairdryer, but you can use a kitchen torch, if you have one, or you can wrap the pan in warm, damp kitchen towels. If necessary, run a table knife between the cake and the sides of the pan, and release the sides of the pan. If you can lift the cake off the pan's base, great; if not, leave the cake on the base—in either case, transfer it to a serving platter.

TO CUT THE CAKE: The best way to cut a cheesecake is to run a long slicing knife under hot water (or dip it in hot water), wipe the blade dry, cut a slice and repeat. Alternatively, you can use dental floss to cut the cake—not very elegant, but very effective.

STORING: Wrapped well, the cake will keep for about 4 days in the refrigerator. It can be wrapped airtight and frozen for up to 2 months—thaw, still wrapped, in the refrigerator overnight.

## *Playing Around*

The crust is really good made with crumbs of chocolate wafer cookies, Lotus Biscoff cookies (speculoos) or spice cookies.

# S'Mores Ice Cream Cake

*Makes 16 servings*

## FOR THE CRUST

2 cups (about 220 grams) graham cracker crumbs (from about 13 crackers)

¼ teaspoon fine sea salt

1 stick (8 tablespoons; 4 ounces; 113 grams) unsalted butter, melted

½ cup (75 grams) salted peanuts, finely chopped

## FOR THE HOT FUDGE SAUCE

12 ounces (340 grams) semisweet or bittersweet chocolate (not chips), finely chopped

1½ cups (360 ml) heavy cream

6 tablespoons light corn syrup

¼ cup (50 grams) sugar

## FOR THE PEANUT BUTTER FLUFF FILLING

1 cup (125 grams) marshmallow crème

1 cup (260 grams) chunky peanut butter (*not* natural)

¼ cup (60 ml) milk, warmed

1½ quarts (about 1½ liters) premium ice cream (see right)

2 cups (about 57 grams) mini marshmallows for topping

THIS CAKE IS BIG AND BEAUTIFUL. I went with the name "s'mores" for concision. If I'd wanted to be truly descriptive, I'd have had to add something about the salted peanuts in the graham-cracker crust, the three different flavors of ice cream, the hot fudge sauce that becomes velvety in the freezer, the layer of peanut-butter marshmallow crème and, oh yes, the toasted marshmallows. The cake is very easy to make, but it takes time. You have to let each layer firm in the freezer before you can move on to the next.

Choose any flavors for the ice cream that you'd like, or use just a single flavor. I'm partial to vanilla, chocolate and coffee for this, but you needn't be as conservative as that. The only thing that's important about the ice cream is that it be a premium brand—a thick, slow-melting kind is best for beating and refreezing.

A WORD ON SOFTENING ICE CREAM: There are a few ways to get the ice cream soft enough to spread. You can put it in the bowl of a stand mixer and give it a few beats with the paddle attachment. Or you can do the job in a food processor. In either case, you're taking frozen ice cream, digging it out of the container in chunks and spinning it around for as little time as possible just to get it soft enough to spoon into the cake pan and spread it to the edges. Alternatively, you can put the ice cream in the fridge for 20 minutes to soften, or you can give it a few spurts in the microwave or some bashes with a wooden spoon. Go with your favorite method. They're all messy—soft ice cream is inevitably drippy—but fine in the end.

PLAN AHEAD: The assembled cake needs to be frozen for at least 6 hours.

*steps continue* ⟶

**TO MAKE THE CRUST:** Butter the bottom and sides of a 9- or 9½-inch springform pan. Have a baking sheet lined with parchment paper or a baking mat handy.

Put the crumbs and salt in a large bowl and, using a fork, toss to blend. Pour in the melted butter and stir until the crumbs are moistened. Squeeze some crumbs, and they should hold together. Stir in the peanuts. Pat the crumbs evenly over the bottom of the springform and as far up the sides of the pan as possible. Stow the pan in the freezer for at least 30 minutes. (*The crust can be covered and frozen for up to 2 months; bake directly from the freezer.*)

(You can make the hot fudge sauce and filling while the crust is firming.)

**WHEN YOU'RE READY TO BAKE:** Center a rack in the oven and preheat it to 375 degrees F.

Put the crust on the baking sheet and bake for 7 to 9 minutes, or until the crumbs are lightly browned. Cool on a rack.

**TO MAKE THE HOT FUDGE SAUCE:** Put all the ingredients in a medium pan and cook over medium-low heat, stirring constantly, until the chocolate melts and the mixture comes to a light simmer, about 5 minutes. Still stirring, let it simmer for a minute or two, then scrape it into a heatproof container. Let cool to room temperature. (*You can make the sauce up to 2 weeks ahead and keep it tightly covered in the refrigerator.*)

**TO MAKE THE FILLING:** Put the marshmallow crème and peanut butter in the bowl of a stand mixer fitted with the paddle attachment or in a large bowl that you can use with a hand mixer and beat on low to blend—the ingredients will ball up around the beater. Still mixing, slowly pour in the warm milk. As soon as you have a homogeneous mixture, scrape it into a bowl, cover and set aside until needed. (*The filling can be made up to 2 days ahead and kept covered at room temperature.*)

**TO ASSEMBLE THE CAKE:** Soften one pint (one third) of the ice cream (see headnote), then very quickly scrape it into the crust and, using an offset icing spatula, spread it into an even layer. Put the pan in the freezer and leave it there until the ice cream is firm, 30 to 60 minutes, depending on your ice cream and your freezer.

For the next layer, pour over half of the cooled hot fudge sauce. Jiggle the pan from side to side to even the sauce and slide the pan back into the freezer; freeze until the sauce is set, 45 to 60 minutes.

Soften another pint (third) of the ice cream, spread it evenly over the fudge sauce and freeze again.

When the ice cream is firm, spread over the peanut butter fluff filling; freeze until cold and set.

Repeat with the last of the ice cream and then, when it's set, pour over the rest of the hot fudge sauce and smooth the top.

Freeze the cake for at least 5 hours; overnight is better. Once the cake is solid, cover the pan. (*The cake can be wrapped well and frozen for up to 1 month.*)

**TO FINISH AND SERVE THE CAKE:** If you've got a hairdryer, blow a little warm air over the top of the cake to soften it a bit so that the marshmallows will stick to it. If you don't, run a broad spatula under hot water, dry it and use it to soften the top layer. Top the cake with the marshmallows, pressing them down lightly.

You can toast the marshmallows using a kitchen torch or your broiler. If you're using the broiler, set it to high and position the rack a few inches beneath it; put the pan on the baking sheet you used before (make sure to remove the parchment—it can burn under the broiler). Toast the marshmallows with the torch or under the broiler until golden brown. Remove the sides of the springform and, if you've got time, pop the cake back into the freezer briefly.

To slice the cake, use a long slicing knife, running the knife under hot water and wiping the blade dry between cuts.

STORING: If you've got leftover cake, press a piece of plastic or foil against the cut surfaces, wrap the cake well and return it to the freezer.

ALL KINDS

# COOKIES

FOR ALL TIMES

# CHOCOLATE CHIP COOKIES: A FEW POINTERS

We all have Ruth Wakefield and her Toll House Inn in Massachusetts to thank for the chocolate chip cookie. Hers was the first recipe, and the one most of us probably started with. One can only wonder what she'd think about the huge extended family that has grown up around her creation. I'm pretty sure that all of us have riffed on her back-of-the-bag recipe. I know I have. And I still do.

Years ago, I made a "chipper" that was a little crisper than the original. Like all my chocolate chip cookies, it used hand-chopped good-quality chocolate rather than packaged chips. I liked it so much that I called it My Classic Best Chocolate Chip Cookie. But then, restless and seduced by endless possibilities, I began to play around with the recipe again. I recalibrated the sugars and sometimes jiggered the proportion of white to brown; I melted the butter for some cookies and browned it for others; I added nuts, occasionally chopped, sometimes ground; I put in whole-grain flours and, once, oatmeal. Later there was the World Peace Cookie, not really a chocolate-chipper, but inspired by one—a cocoa sablé with a lot of chopped chocolate and the lingering flavor of fleur de sel.

While there are some chocolate chip cookies that I like less than others—I don't really like super-large cookies with underbaked centers—there are too many that I like enormously, and so I no longer search for the perfect cookie. The fun for me is in the variety. The pleasure is in the possibilities.

I don't think I'll ever stop playing around, but for now, here are a clutch of chocolate chip cookies recipes—some new, some treasured old-timers—and some pointers.

**BUTTER:** Pull the butter out of the refrigerator about 10 minutes before you begin mixing the dough. With chocolate chip cookies, you want the butter to be just a tad cool and never so soft that it's oily.

**CHOCOLATE:** All of the recipes can be made with packaged chocolate chips, but every cookie is better made with good chocolate. Choose a bar chocolate that you like—my preference is for semisweet or bittersweet, but milk chocolate always works in a cookie—and chop it into bite-size pieces. Don't worry about uniformity—it's better when you've got both bits and chunklets—and if you like tweedy cookies, as I do, scrape the chocolate dust into the dough.

**DRY INGREDIENTS:** Whisk the flour(s), leaveners (baking powder and/or baking soda) and spices together. You can add the salt to this mixture, but I usually mix the salt in with the butter and sugar, because I think it blends into the dough more uniformly.

**COCOA AND CONFECTIONERS' SUGAR:** Both of these ingredients have a tendency to form clumps that won't pulverize during mixing, so you should press them through a sieve or sift them before using. (I know this is annoying.)

**SALT:** I like to use fine sea salt in the cookies and fleur de sel or a flaky sea salt like Maldon as a sprinkle on top of some of the cookies.

**MIXING:** It's important to mix the butter, sugar and eggs together well (a creamy mixture is

usually better than a fluffy one for cookies) and just as important not to mix too much once the dry ingredients go in. It's best to beat the dry ingredients into the dough only until they are almost—not completely—incorporated and then to add the chocolate and any other add-ins. When you mix in the chunky bits, you'll automatically finish blending in the dry ingredients.

CHILLING: You can bake the cookies as soon as the dough is mixed, or you can wait a few hours or even a day or two. In general, if you bake the cookies as soon as they're mixed, they'll spread more than they will after they've had some fridge time. However, the cookies have more flavor after they've chilled. Try them both ways, and see which you prefer.

FREEZING: If you know you won't be using an entire batch of cookies within a day or two, the best thing to do is to scoop out the dough and freeze the balls. When they're solid, wrap them airtight and then, when you're ready for one cookie or for a batch, put the frozen dough balls on a lined baking sheet, let sit on the counter while you preheat the oven and then bake them. If they're still frozen when they go into the oven, they might need a minute or two more baking time—or they might not: Check early and then check again.

# Classic Chocolate Chip Cookies

*Makes about 45 cookies*

2 cups (272 grams) all-purpose flour

¾ teaspoon baking soda

2 sticks (8 ounces; 226 grams) unsalted butter, at room temperature

1 cup (200 grams) sugar

⅔ cup (133 grams) packed brown sugar

1 teaspoon fine sea salt

2 teaspoons pure vanilla extract

2 large eggs, at room temperature

12 ounces (340 grams) bittersweet chocolate, chopped (chip-size pieces), or 2 cups (340 grams) chocolate chips

1 cup (120 grams) finely chopped walnuts or pecans, preferably toasted (optional)

**I'VE BEEN MAKING** these for decades. If they look like Toll House Cookies, it's because that recipe, the mother of so many chocolate-chippers, was my starting point. These spread more than Toll House cookies, and I like that about them. They've got a bit more salt and more vanilla too, and they've got chunks of real chocolate instead of chips. Of course, you can use chips, but chopping bar chocolate and including all the slivers, fly-away shards and dust makes the cookies look more interesting and certainly makes them taste more interesting—each bite has a different chocolate-to-dough balance. Sometimes I add nuts and sometimes I don't. Sometimes I add a little cinnamon or cardamom or allspice or instant espresso and sometimes I don't. And yes, I've been known to stir in raisins or bits of dried apricot. And there are times when I toss in some toasted coconut. The sign of a true classic is its ability to accept change yet keep its character. This one can do that, so play away.

Center a rack in the oven and preheat the oven to 375 degrees F. Line two baking sheets with parchment paper or baking mats.

Whisk together the flour and baking soda.

Working in the bowl of a stand mixer fitted with the paddle attachment, or in a large bowl with a hand mixer, beat the butter, both sugars and the salt together until smooth, about 3 minutes. Beat in the vanilla. One by one, add the eggs, beating for a minute after each egg goes in.

Turn off the mixer, add the dry ingredients all at once and pulse the mixer to begin blending. When the risk of a flour shower has passed, work on low speed, mixing only until the dry ingredients are almost incorporated. Continuing with the mixer or working by hand with a sturdy spatula, stir in the chocolate and nuts. (*The dough can be covered and refrigerated for up to 3 days.*)

Use a medium cookie scoop (one with a capacity of 1½ tablespoons) to shape the cookies and arrange on a lined baking sheet, leaving about 2 inches between the mounds; or portion the dough out by slightly rounded tablespoonfuls. (*You can freeze the scooped balls for up to 2 months; see page 149.*)

Bake the cookies, one sheet at a time, for 10 to 12 minutes, or until they are brown at the edges and golden in the center; they may still be a little soft in the middle, and that's just fine. Let the cookies rest for a minute on the baking sheet, then carefully lift them onto racks to cool until they are just warm or have come to room temperature. Repeat with the remaining dough, always using a cool baking sheet.

**STORING:** The cookies can be kept in an airtight container for about 4 days at room temperature or for up to 2 months in the freezer.

# One Big Break-Apart Chipper

*Makes about 8 servings*

1¼ cups (170 grams) all-purpose flour

½ cup (68 grams) whole wheat flour

1½ teaspoons ground espresso (optional)

1 teaspoon ground cinnamon

1 teaspoon ground cardamom

1 stick plus 1 tablespoon (9 tablespoons; 4½ ounces; 128 grams) cold unsalted butter, cut into small pieces

½ cup (100 grams) packed brown sugar

¼ cup (50 grams) sugar

¼ teaspoon fine sea salt

1 large egg

1 tablespoon honey

4 ounces (113 grams) dark, milk or white chocolate, or a combination, finely chopped

½ cup (60 grams) finely chopped nuts

Sanding or turbinado sugar for sprinkling (optional)

**COOKIES ARE ALWAYS A TREAT,** but one giant cookie to share is a party. This is a party cookie: You put it in the center of the table and let everyone reach in, break off a piece and then go back for more. It sounds like a kids' dessert, and it is, but I like it after a long dinner with friends—its "nibble a little and then nibble a bit more" quality seems to keep the conversation going. Serve it with an after-dinner whiskey, and you'll have everyone at the table even longer. The cookie is crispy around the edges, softer in the belly, intermittently crunchy and tasty no matter which morsel you get. The flavorings are espresso, cinnamon and cardamom; the sweeteners are more brown sugar than white and some honey; the add-ins are chopped chocolate and nuts; and the result is a cookie that teeters between old-fashioned and surprising.

Like all good chocolate chip cookies, this one invites variations. You can change the spices, add more or different crunchy bits or leave them out. True, if you left out the chocolate it wouldn't be a chipper, but the dough makes a great spice cookie. The cookie is also good drizzled with melted chocolate or served with hot fudge (page 371) or caramel sauce (page 370) for dipping. For another way of finishing the cookie, see Playing Around.

Whisk together both flours, the coffee and spices.

Working in the bowl of a mixer fitted with the paddle attachment, or in a large bowl with a hand mixer, mix the cold butter, both sugars and the salt on low speed for about 3 minutes, until the mixture forms clumps and then comes together. You'll see pieces of butter here and there—you're supposed to. Add the dry ingredients all at once and pulse the mixer just until the risk of flying flour has passed. Then mix on low-medium speed until you've got a bowl of crumbs, about 3 minutes.

Lightly whisk the egg and honey together in a small bowl and, with the mixer on low, gradually add the egg mixture, then continue to mix until the dough forms clumps. Squeeze a bit of the dough, and it will hold together. Mix in the chocolate and nuts. Reach into the bowl and press the dough into a ball.

Turn the dough out onto a sheet of parchment paper. Press it down, cover it with another sheet of paper and roll the dough until it's about ⅛ inch thick. It can be any shape—round, oval, rectangular, raggedy-edged or pristine. The thickness is more important than the dimensions—being neat doesn't buy you anything with this cookie. Slide the sandwiched dough onto a baking sheet and refrigerate it for at least 1 hour. (*You can refrigerate the dough, wrapped airtight, for up to 3 days or freeze it for up to 2 months; let it sit on the counter while you preheat the oven.*)

**WHEN YOU'RE READY TO BAKE:** Center a rack in the oven and preheat it to 350 degrees F.

Remove the top piece of paper. Peel away the bottom piece (the cookie bakes better if you've loosen it from the paper) and use it to line the baking sheet; put the cookie on the baking sheet. If you're using sugar, sprinkle the dough with about 2 tablespoons of it.

Bake for 20 to 24 minutes—the edges of the cookie will be darker than the middle. If you press the center of the cookie, it should be firm with just a tiny bit of give; it will feel firmer as you work your way out to the edges. Transfer the baking sheet to a rack and allow the cookie to cool to room temperature.

You can serve the cookie whole, letting everyone break off pieces (of course there will be crumbs—they're part of the cookie's appeal), or you can break or cut it in the kitchen and serve the pieces as you would any cookie.

**STORING:** Well wrapped, the cookie will keep for up to 4 days at room temperature.

## *Playing Around*

### PRALINE-TOPPED BREAK-APART COOKIE

This is an extravagant but wonderful idea: Top the cookie with Praline Spread (page 368) and then dust it with Praline Sprinkle (page 368). Make it peanut, if you'd like, or choose a different nut.

# Peanut-Butter Chocolate Chip Cookies, Paris Style

*Makes 18 cookies*

## FOR THE COOKIES

2¼ cups (306 grams) all-purpose flour

1 teaspoon baking powder

¼ teaspoon baking soda

1 stick (8 tablespoons; 4 ounces; 113 grams) unsalted butter, at room temperature

1 cup (200 grams) packed brown sugar

½ cup (100 grams) sugar

⅓ cup (85 grams) smooth peanut butter (*not* natural)

⅓ cup (85 grams) Praline Spread (page 368)

1¼ teaspoons fine sea salt

2 large eggs, at room temperature

About 1 cup (135 grams) coarsely chopped peanuts

Sugar for flattening the cookies

## FOR THE TOPPING

About ½ cup (128 grams) Praline Spread (page 368)

About ½ cup (68 grams) coarsely chopped peanuts

About ¼ cup (40 grams) chopped chocolate or chocolate chips

About ¼ cup (33 grams) Praline Sprinkle (page 368)

Fleur de sel, Maldon or other sea salt

**PLAN AHEAD:** The dough needs an overnight rest in the fridge, but you can shape the cookies and top them with peanuts in advance and freeze them, ready to bake.

A FEW YEARS AGO, I started seeing great-looking cookies in Parisian shops that hadn't seemed to care much about cookies before. These new-wave creations had something in common—there was a lot happening on their tops. Their surfaces were paved with nuts, candied and chopped; there were swishes or spots of praline, caramelized nut butter; and sometimes bits of chocolate or dried fruit. It was as though a rocky-road cookie had been turned inside out. I loved them!

My homage to these cookies is decidedly Franco-American. The cookie is a very American peanut butter cookie, chewy at the center and a little crisp around the edges. For extra crunch, I scoop the dough and roll the balls in chopped peanuts before baking. The topping is the French part—a mishmash of chopped chocolate, chopped peanuts and peanut praline two ways. The praline is fun to make—you cook peanuts in caramelized sugar to make a brittle, then you crush the brittle into a sprinkle to dust over the cookies; the remaining sprinkle is whirred into a spread. Make the sprinkle and spread once, and they'll become house standards.

If you don't have time to make the praline, you can use store-bought Lotus Biscoff Cookie Butter (see Playing Around) instead. Even without the praline, the peanut butter cookies are awfully good.

TO MAKE THE COOKIES: Whisk the flour, baking powder and baking soda together.

Working in the bowl of a stand mixer fitted with the paddle attachment, or in a large bowl with a hand mixer, beat the butter, both sugars, the peanut butter, praline spread and salt together on medium speed until smooth and creamy, about 3 minutes, scraping the bowl and beater(s) as needed. One by one, add the eggs, beating for a minute after each egg goes in. ⟶

*Cookies*

Turn off the mixer, add the flour all at once and pulse to start mixing in the dry ingredients. When the risk of runaway flour has passed, mix on low until you have a homogenous dough. Scrape it out of the bowl, shape it into a ball and wrap it well. Refrigerate overnight. (*The dough can be refrigerated for up to 5 days.*)

**TO BAKE THE COOKIES:** Position the racks to divide the oven into thirds and preheat it to 325 degrees F. Line two baking sheets with parchment paper or baking mats.

You want 18 cookies, so either divide the dough into 18 pieces or use a large cookie scoop, one with a capacity of 3 tablespoons, to portion out the dough. Roll each piece of dough between your hands to make a ball and then roll each ball in the chopped peanuts. Put the balls on the baking sheets, leaving about 2 inches of spread space between them. Slightly dampen the bottom of a glass, dip it in sugar and lightly press down on each ball with the glass until you have a puck with a 2-inch diameter. (*You can freeze the cookie pucks for up to 2 months; see page 149.*)

Bake the cookies, rotating the sheets top to bottom and front to back after 6 minutes, for 14 to 16 minutes, or until they're golden brown, firm around the edges and only just barely set in the center. Transfer the baking sheets to racks and leave the cookies on the sheets for about 5 minutes, then transfer them to the racks. Let cool for at least 10 minutes before topping them.

**TO TOP THE COOKIES:** Use an offset spatula or a table knife to cover the top of each cookie with a thin layer of praline spread. (I usually leave a little border of cookie bare, but there are really no rules here.) Scatter some chopped peanuts and bits of chocolate or chips over the top and press them down lightly. Speckle the top of each cookie with 3 or 4 dabs of praline spread, then finish with a few (very few) grains or flakes of salt. Serve the cookies now or let them dry for about 30 minutes at room temperature.

**STORING:** If you don't top the cookies with the spread and sprinkle, they'll keep for 3 to 4 days in an airtight container at room temperature. Topped, they're best eaten the day they're made or the next day. Of course, you can always top the cookies on demand.

## Playing Around

### BISCOFF-PEANUT PARIS COOKIES

Substitute Lotus Biscoff Cookie Butter or another cookie spread for the praline spread. You can either skip the sprinkle on the tops of the cookies or replace it with crushed store-bought speculoos or spice cookies. Graham cracker crumbs work too.

# Mary Dodd's Maple-Bacon Chocolate Chip Cookies

*Makes 15 cookies*

2 cups (272 grams) all-purpose flour

¾ teaspoon baking soda

1 stick plus 5 tablespoons (6½ ounces; 187 grams) unsalted butter, at room temperature

2 tablespoons bacon fat, cold or at room temperature

1 teaspoon fine sea salt

1 cup (200 grams) sugar

⅓ cup (67 grams) packed light brown sugar

⅓ cup (67 grams) packed dark brown sugar

2 teaspoons pure vanilla extract

2 tablespoons maple syrup

2 large eggs, at room temperature

12 ounces (340 grams) semisweet chocolate, coarsely chopped

4 strips crisp cooked bacon, chopped, at room temperature

About ¼ cup (60 ml) maple syrup for finishing

Maldon or other flaky sea salt for finishing

**A WORD ON BATCHES:** In order to get the wrinkle and spread that she wants, Mary makes these in mini batches, baking one sheet at a time with just three cookies on a sheet. To get a jump on the batches, you can prep two baking sheets so that another batch will be ready to go into the oven as soon as the previous batch comes out.

SINCE MARY DODD AND I have worked together for fifteen years—Mary tests all my recipes—when she says she's come up with a recipe she thinks I might like, I'm always grateful for the gift. This gift from Mary is a cookie that hits all the notes we love in chocolate-chippers, but it uses a different mix of ingredients to get that range of sweet and salty and almost caramel. There's bacon fat mixed with the usual butter; maple syrup mixed with vanilla; bits of bacon mixed with the chips; and brown sugar both light and dark. The cookie bakes thin and wrinkly; Mary says it's "bendy."

Center a rack in the oven and preheat it to 375 degrees F. Line two baking sheets with parchment paper or baking mats.

Whisk together the flour and baking soda.

Working in the bowl of a stand mixer fitted with the paddle attachment, or in a large bowl with a hand mixer, beat the butter, bacon fat and salt together on medium speed until smooth, about 2 minutes. Add the three sugars and beat for another 2 minutes, or until well blended. Beat in the vanilla and maple syrup. One by one, add the eggs, beating for a minute after each egg goes in.

Turn the mixer off, add the dry ingredients all at once and pulse the mixer to get the blending started. When the risk of fly-away flour has passed, mix on low speed only until the dry ingredients are incorporated. Working on low, or by hand with a sturdy spatula, mix in the chopped chocolate and bacon bits.

These cookies are meant to be large—you need a scoop with a capacity of ¼ cup, or you can use a measuring cup. Scoop 3 cookies onto each baking sheet, arranging them far apart. Brush the tops with maple syrup; try to avoid letting the syrup drip onto the baking sheet—it burns easily. Sprinkle a few flakes of salt over each scoop. (*The balls of dough, without the syrup and flaky salt, can be frozen for up to 2 months; see page 149. Let the frozen cookies sit on the counter while you preheat the oven. Brush them with maple syrup and sprinkle with salt just before baking.*)

Bake the cookies, one sheet at a time, for 13 to 15 minutes, or until they have spread and are wrinkled almost to the centers. The edges will be crispy and uneven and the middles soft. Transfer the baking sheet to a rack and cool for 5 minutes, then lift the cookies off the sheet and onto the rack to cool to room temperature.

Continue baking the cookies 3 at a time, always starting with a cool baking sheet.

STORING: The cookies will keep for about 3 days in an airtight container at room temperature or for up to 2 months in the freezer.

# World Peace Cookies 2.0

*Makes about 30 cookies*

1 cup (136 grams) all-purpose flour

½ cup (60 grams) rye flour

⅓ cup (30 grams) Dutch-processed cocoa (I prefer Valrhona)

½ teaspoon baking soda

1 stick plus 3 tablespoons (11 tablespoons; 5½ ounces; 155 grams) unsalted butter, cut into chunks, at cool room temperature

⅔ cup (135 grams) packed brown sugar

¼ cup (50 grams) sugar

½ teaspoon fleur de sel or ¼ teaspoon fine sea salt

Pinch of piment d'Espelette or a smaller pinch of cayenne

1 teaspoon pure vanilla extract

5 ounces (140 grams) semisweet or bittersweet chocolate, chopped (chip-size pieces)

⅓ cup (45 grams) cocoa nibs

½ cup (15 grams) freeze-dried raspberries, coarsely chopped or broken

Maldon or other flaky sea salt for sprinkling (optional)

PIERRE HERMÉ, the famous Paris pastry chef, gave me his recipe for chocolate sablés, a recipe I renamed World Peace Cookies, more than twenty years ago. Over the years, I've made little tweaks that were fine, but none better than the original.

Then my friend the author Charlotte Druckman asked if I'd rethink the cookie for her book, *Women on Food,* and so I thought about the qualities that I admire in women, looked for ingredients that would highlight them and mixed them into the cookie. I added rye flour for groundedness; cocoa nibs to represent strength; pepper for a touch of unpredictability; and raspberries for sharpness and verve. The raspberries are freeze-dried and their flavor takes a little time to reveal itself. While you taste them soon after the cookies cool, they really come into their own a day later.

If you've never had the original World Peace Cookies, please make them too; see Playing Around.

A WORD ON THE DOUGH: Although making these cookies is easy, each batch seems to have its own quirks. It's always easy, it's just not always the same. Sometimes the differences have to do with the cocoa. (I usually use Valrhona Dutch-processed cocoa because I love its flavor and color, but I've made WPCs with many kinds of cocoa—they're always good, not always the same.) Sometimes the differences have to do with the butter, and often the temperature of the butter—it's best if it's at cool room temperature, but sometimes I miss the moment when it's just right. My advice is to mix the dough for as long as it takes to get big, moist curds that hold together when pressed. Often this happens quickly; just as often, it takes more time than you think it should. Go with it. Also, when you roll the dough into logs, check that they're solid—squeeze the logs to see if there are hollow spots. If there are, ball up the dough and roll into logs again.

PLAN AHEAD: The logs of dough need to be frozen for at least 2 hours or refrigerated for at least 3 hours.

*steps continue*

Sift both flours, the cocoa and baking soda together into a bowl; whisk to blend.

Working in the bowl of a stand mixer fitted with the paddle attachment, or in a large bowl with a hand mixer, beat the butter and both sugars together on medium speed until smooth, about 3 minutes. Beat in the salt, piment d'Espelette or cayenne and vanilla. Turn off the mixer, add the dry ingredients all at once and pulse to start the blending. When the risk of a flour storm has passed, beat on low speed until the dough forms big, moist curds—this can take a couple of minutes, so don't be afraid to keep mixing. Toss in the chocolate pieces, nibs and raspberries and mix to incorporate. Sometimes the dough comes together and cleans the sides of the bowl and sometimes it crumbles—it'll be fine no matter what.

Turn the dough out, gather it together and, if necessary, knead it a bit to bring it together. Divide the dough in half. Shape each half into a log that is 1½ inches in diameter. The length will be between 7 and 8 inches, but don't worry about it—it's the diameter that counts here. If you get a hollow in either of the logs, just start over. Wrap the logs and freeze them for at least 2 hours, or refrigerate for at least 3 hours. (*If you'd like, you can freeze the logs for up to 2 months; let stand at room temperature for about 15 minutes before slicing and baking.*)

WHEN YOU'RE READY TO BAKE: Center a rack in the oven and preheat it to 325 degrees F. Line a baking sheet with parchment paper or a baking mat.

Using a chef's knife, slice one log of dough into ½-inch-thick rounds. (Don't worry if they crack, just pinch and squeeze the bits back into the cookie.) Arrange the rounds on the baking sheet, leaving about 2 inches between them. If you'd like, sprinkle the tops sparingly with flaky salt.

Bake the cookies for 12 minutes—don't open the oven door to check, just let them bake. They won't look fully baked and they won't be firm, but that's the way they're supposed to be. Transfer the sheet to a rack and let the cookies cool until they're only just warm or at room temperature.

Repeat with the remaining log of dough, using a cool baking sheet.

STORING: Packed airtight, the cookies will keep for 5 days at room temperature (they will get a little drier, but they're still good) or for up to 2 months in the freezer.

## *Playing Around*

THE ORIGINAL WORLD PEACE COOKIES

Use 1¼ cups (170 grams) all-purpose flour and omit the rye flour. Omit the piment d'Espelette, cocoa nibs and raspberries. Sprinkle the tops of the cookies with flaky salt—or not.

# Mokonuts' Rye-Cranberry Chocolate Chunk Cookies

*Makes 15 cookies*

1 cup plus 1½ tablespoons (130 grams) rye flour (if you can find medium rye, use it)

½ cup plus 2 tablespoons (85 grams) all-purpose flour

1 teaspoon baking powder

½ teaspoon baking soda

1 stick plus 2 tablespoons (10 tablespoons; 5 ounces; 140 grams) unsalted butter, at cool room temperature

½ cup (100 grams) sugar

½ cup (100 grams) packed brown sugar

¾ teaspoon fine sea salt

1 large egg, at room temperature

⅔ cup (80 grams) moist, plump dried cranberries

⅓ cup (50 grams ) poppy seeds

4 ounces (113 grams) bittersweet chocolate, chopped into small chunks

Maldon or other flaky sea salt for sprinkling

**PLAN AHEAD:** The shaped cookies need to be refrigerated overnight.

**PEOPLE COME FROM** around the world to eat at Mokonuts, a small restaurant in Paris that is always full, and everyone wants the same thing for dessert: one of Moko Hirayama's cookies. Moko makes only a few varieties, but they all share a similar chubbiness, great texture, an offbeat choice of flavor combinations and a signature indentation in the center that looks like Moko's handprint but is actually made by tapping each cookie with a spatula. This cookie is one of my favorites. Its texture, soft and chewy in the middle, is perfect, and its flavor is a surprise—sweet, but only just sweet enough; edgy, because the chocolate is always bittersweet and there are tangy cranberries in the mix; and earthy, because it has more rye than all-purpose flour, and some poppy seeds too. To describe it as extraordinarily good is to understate its merits.

Whisk together both flours, the baking powder and baking soda.

Working in the bowl of a stand mixer fitted with the paddle attachment, or in a large bowl with a hand mixer, beat the butter, both sugars and the salt together on medium speed for 3 minutes, or until thoroughly blended; scrape the bowl as needed. Add the egg and beat for 2 minutes more.

Turn off the mixer, add the dry ingredients all at once and pulse a few times to begin blending. Then beat on low just until the flour almost disappears. Add the cranberries, poppy seeds and chocolate and mix only until incorporated. Scrape the bowl to bring the dough together.

Line a baking sheet with parchment. Divide the dough into 15 pieces, roll each piece into a ball between your palms and place on the baking sheet. Cover the balls and refrigerate overnight. Or, if you're short on space, wrap and refrigerate the dough, then divide and shape it when you're ready to bake. *(The balls can be refrigerated for up to 3 days. You can also wrap them airtight and freeze them; see page 149.)*

*Cookies*

**WHEN YOU'RE READY TO BAKE:** Center a rack in the oven and preheat it to 425 degrees F. Line a baking sheet with parchment paper or a baking mat.

Keeping the remaining balls of dough in the refrigerator until needed, arrange 8 cookies on the sheet, leaving 2 inches between them. Sprinkle each cookie with a little flaky salt, crushing it between your fingers as you do.

Bake the cookies for 10 minutes, then pull the baking sheet from the oven and, using a metal spatula, a pancake turner or the bottom of a glass, tap each cookie lightly but smartly—you want to deflate a bit of the cookie and leave an indentation. Let the cookies rest on the sheet for 3 minutes, then carefully transfer them to a rack.

Repeat with the remaining dough, using a cool baking sheet.

The cookies are ready for munching after they've cooled for about 10 minutes, or you can wait until they reach room temperature.

**STORING:** These are best the day they're baked and really best shortly after they come from the oven. But they're still way above average even 3 days later; keep them in an airtight container.

# Copenhagen Rye Cookies with Chocolate, Spice and Seeds

*Makes about 40 cookies*

1¾ cups (238 grams) all-purpose flour

½ cup (60 grams) rye flour

1½ tablespoons ground coffee, preferably espresso

2 teaspoons ground cardamom (or to taste)

1½ teaspoons ground cinnamon

½ teaspoon baking powder

½ teaspoon baking soda

2 sticks (8 ounces; 226 grams) unsalted butter, at room temperature

¾ cup (150 grams) sugar

¾ cup (150 grams) packed brown sugar

1 teaspoon fine sea salt

2 large eggs, at room temperature

1½ teaspoons pure vanilla extract

8 ounces (227 grams) chocolate (dark or milk), chopped (chip-size pieces)

½ cup (about 80 grams) mixed seeds (see headnote), plus a few tablespoons for sprinkling

Maldon or other flaky sea salt for sprinkling

THESE COOKIES WERE INSPIRED by a brief but delicious trip I made to Copenhagen, where rye is a commonly used grain and many breads, muffins and loaf cakes are studded or topped with a mix of seeds and nuts. Made like traditional chocolate chip cookies, these have a tender texture and stay soft because of the seeds. I use a mix of small seeds and grains—sunflower, flax, sesame and poppy seeds and millet. Often I'll add some buckwheat in the form of kasha. The sunflower seeds are important, and I like the sesame and flax, but really, what's in the mix is up to you. What's nonnegotiable are the rye; the addition of espresso, cardamom and cinnamon; and a good chocolate. My preference is always for dark chocolate, but the spices in these also go well with milk chocolate.

If you bake the cookies immediately after making the dough, they will be larger; the dough doesn't spread as much if it's refrigerated. Try them both ways. I like the way they look when they're baked just after mixing, but their flavors are more pronounced after the dough has had some time in the fridge.

If you're going to bake the cookies as soon as you've mixed the dough, position the racks to divide the oven into thirds and preheat it to 350 degrees F. Line two baking sheets with parchment paper or baking mats.

Whisk together both flours, the coffee, spices, baking powder and baking soda.

Working in the bowl of a stand mixer fitted with the paddle attachment, or in a large bowl with a hand mixer, beat the butter, both sugars and the salt together on medium speed until soft and creamy, about 3 minutes. Add the eggs one at time, beating for a minute after each goes in, then beat in the vanilla extract. The mixture may look curdled, but it'll be fine.

Turn off the mixer, add the dry ingredients all at once and pulse to start blending in the flour. Then mix on low speed, scraping the bowl as necessary, until the flour is almost incorporated. With the mixer off, add the chocolate, then pulse to blend. Do the same with the seeds. Then give the mixer a few spins on low to finish pulling the dough together, or do this by hand with a flexible spatula. If you want to let the dough rest (see headnote), wrap and refrigerate it. (*The dough can be refrigerated for up to 3 days.*)

Use a medium-size cookie scoop (one with a capacity of about 1½ tablespoons) to portion out balls of dough and arrange on the baking sheets, leaving a couple of inches between them; or use a rounded tablespoon of dough for each cookie. Sprinkle a little of the seed mixture and a few flakes of salt on top of each. (*You can freeze the balls airtight for up to 2 months; see page 149. Sprinkle with the seeds and salt just before baking.*)

Bake the cookies for 10 to 12 minutes, rotating the pans from top to bottom and front to back after 6 minutes. They're done when they're deep golden brown, only just firm at the edges and not really set at the center. Remove the baking sheets from the oven and let the cookies sit on the sheets for 2 minutes, then carefully transfer them to racks using a broad spatula. Resist eating the cookies for at least 15 minutes, but then have at them.

Repeat with the remainder of the dough, always using a cool baking sheet.

STORING: Packed in an airtight container, the cookies will keep for about 4 days at room temperature. You can freeze the cookies for up to 2 months, but really the best thing to do is to freeze the balls of dough (see above).

# Oatmeal Cookies with Nuts and Chocolate

*Makes about 45 cookies*

2 cups (272 grams) all-purpose flour

1½ teaspoons ground cinnamon

1 teaspoon baking soda

2½ cups (300 grams) old-fashioned oats (*not* instant)

2 sticks (8 ounces; 226 grams) unsalted butter, at room temperature

¾ cup (150 grams) packed brown sugar

⅓ cup (67 grams) sugar

1 teaspoon fine sea salt

2 large eggs, at room temperature

2 teaspoons pure vanilla extract

¼ cup (60 ml) honey

4½ ounces (127 grams) dark or milk chocolate, finely chopped, or ¾ cup (127 grams) chocolate chips

⅓ cup (40 grams) coarsely chopped walnuts, toasted or not

¼ cup (40 grams) plump, moist raisins or other dried fruit (optional; see headnote)

Granulated or turbinado sugar for flattening the cookies

**A WORD ON SIZE:** If you bake the cookies as soon as the dough is made, the cookies will spread. If you bake them after the dough has chilled—my preference in terms of flavor—the cookies will be smaller. No matter what you do, the cookies will taste great, so choose what's most convenient for you.

IF YOU LOVE OATMEAL COOKIES, I'm betting you'll love these. I'm making this wager based on the fact that I put a sack of the pebbly-topped cookies on the counter when I had weekend guests and the cookies didn't last through Sunday breakfast. I like them with a lot of chopped chocolate, a middling amount of chopped walnuts and a small amount of raisins. Skip the raisins, if you like, or swap them for snipped dried apricots, dates or dried cranberries. Whatever dried fruit you use, just make sure it's moist and plump.

Position the racks to divide the oven into thirds and preheat it to 350 degrees F. Line two baking sheets with parchment paper or baking mats.

Whisk together the flour, cinnamon and baking soda in a bowl, then whisk in the oats.

Working in the bowl of a stand mixer fitted with the paddle attachment, or in a large bowl with a hand mixer, beat the butter, both sugars and the salt together on medium speed for 3 minutes, until well blended, scraping the bowl as needed. Reduce the mixer speed to low and add the eggs one at a time, beating for a minute after each goes in—the mixture will curdle a bit. Beat in the vanilla and then the honey, which will smooth the mixture out beautifully.

Turn off the mixer, add one third of the dry ingredients and pulse to start the blending. Then mix on low until the flour is almost incorporated. Repeat with the remaining flour in 2 additions. When the last of the dry ingredients is almost blended in, start adding the chocolate, walnuts and raisins, if you're using them, mixing just enough to get the chunky bits into the heavy, sticky dough. (*The dough can be refrigerated for up to 5 days; scoop and bake straight from the fridge.*)

Using a medium cookie scoop, one with a capacity of about 1½ tablespoons, scoop the dough, roll each piece into a ball between your palms and place about 1 inch apart on the baking sheets; or portion the dough out by slightly rounded tablespoonfuls. (*You can freeze the balls for up to 2 months; see page 149.*)

Moisten the bottom of a glass, dip it into sugar and give each ball a quick firm tap to round and flatten it slightly.

Bake the cookies for 11 to 13 minutes, or until they are golden brown and feel soft and springy around the edges—they'll get firmer as they cool. (If your oven has hot spots, rotate the sheets from top to bottom and front to back after 6 minutes.) Let the cookies sit on the sheets for about 3 minutes, then use a spatula to lift them onto racks to cool.

Repeat with the remaining dough, always using cool baking sheets.

STORING: The cookies will keep in a covered container for about 5 days. They might get a little drier or harder, but they'll still be tasty.

# *Caramel Crunch–Chocolate Chunklet Cookies*

*Makes 24 cookies*

2 sticks (8 ounces; 226 grams) unsalted butter, cut into chunks, at room temperature

½ cup (100 grams) sugar

½ cup (60 grams) confectioners' sugar

½ teaspoon fine sea salt

1 teaspoon pure vanilla extract

2 cups (272 grams) all-purpose flour

3 ounces (85 grams) dark or milk chocolate chopped into small chunks

About ½ cup (60 grams) coarsely chopped walnuts, toasted or not (or more chocolate chunks)

A NOTE ON MUFFIN-TIN BAKING: You might be tempted to use a baking sheet, but I hope you won't—the texture is really best in the muffin tins.

PLAN AHEAD: The dough needs to be refrigerated for 2 hours.

YOU WON'T FIND CARAMEL in the ingredient list, yet it's the flavor you catch with the first bite. The alchemy happens in the oven. Because these slice-and-bake cookies are baked in muffin tins until their bottoms and sides are deeply golden, the butter and sugar brown so completely that they produce the full, nutty, edgily sweet flavor of caramel. A treat! But not the cookies' only treat. Their texture is a delightful mix of crisp and tender, the sign that they're shortbread at heart. And the addition of chopped walnuts and small chunks of chocolate means that they could rightly be called chocolate chip cookies, though perhaps ones that lived briefly in France.

Working in the bowl of a stand mixer fitted with the paddle attachment. or in a large bowl with a hand mixer, beat the butter, both sugars and the salt together on medium speed until creamy, about 2 minutes. Beat in the vanilla.

Turn off the mixer, scrape down the bowl and add the flour all at once. Pulse the mixer a few times, just until the risk of flying flour has passed, and then, working on low speed, beat until the flour is almost completely incorporated, a couple of minutes. Don't beat too much—you want the mixture to be more clumpy than smooth. Still working on low speed, mix in the chocolate and nuts. Then finish incorporating the chunky ingredients with a flexible spatula.

Turn the dough out onto the work surface and knead it to bring it together. Divide the dough in half and shape each hunk into a 6-inch-long log (the rolls will be a scant 2 inches in diameter). Wrap each log well and refrigerate until firm, at least 2 hours. (*You can refrigerate the logs for up to 3 days. Or you can freeze them, wrapped airtight, for up to 2 months; let stand at room temperature for about an hour before slicing and baking, or defrost in the fridge overnight.*)

**WHEN YOU'RE READY TO BAKE:** Center a rack in the oven and preheat it to 350 degrees F. (If you can't fit two muffin tins on one rack in your oven, position the racks to divide the oven into thirds.) Butter two regular-size muffin tins—you can use bakers' spray, but butter is really nicer for these.

One at a time, mark each log at ½-inch intervals and, working with a chef's knife, cut into rounds. Place each puck in a muffin cup.

Bake for 20 to 22 minutes, rotating the pans if necessary, or until the cookies are golden on top, browned around the edges and slightly soft in the center; they'll firm as they cool. Transfer the pans to racks and let rest for 3 minutes, then gently pry each cookie out with the tip of a table knife and place on the racks to cool. You can serve the cookies warm, but their texture shines brighter at room temperature.

**STORING:** Kept in an airtight container at room temperature, the cookies will be good for at least 5 days.

# Devil's Thumbprints

*Makes about 38 cookies*

¾ cup (102 grams) all-purpose flour

½ teaspoon fine sea salt

½ teaspoon ground cinnamon

5 tablespoons (71 grams) unsalted butter, cut into pieces

8 ounces (226 grams) semisweet or bittersweet chocolate, coarsely chopped

⅔ cup (132 grams) sugar

2 cold large eggs

1 teaspoon pure vanilla extract

Sanding, turbinado or granulated sugar for finishing

About ⅓ cup (80 ml) raspberry (or other) jam

**I'M OFTEN ASKED** if I ever make a mistake in a recipe and end up with something good. These cookies were that kind of a lucky accident. I must not have paid attention while I was mixing the dough, because I put in too much chocolate and got cookies as dark and rich as devil's food. I thought I'd sandwich them with jam, but then I had a better idea: thumbprints. I pressed the center of each little ball of dough down with a cork, baked the cookies and then pressed the imprints again when they came out of the oven. The double pressing not only gave me a place for the jam, it also made the cookies fudgy. These are also really good filled with more chocolate; see Playing Around.

**PLAN AHEAD:** The dough needs to be refrigerated for at least 2 hours.

Whisk the flour, salt and cinnamon together.

Place a medium heatproof bowl over a pan of gently simmering water (don't let the water touch the bottom of the bowl). Drop in the chunks of butter and scatter over the chocolate. Heat, stirring now and then, until the butter and chocolate are melted but not so hot that they separate.

Remove the bowl from the pan and whisk in the sugar—don't be alarmed when the mixture turns grainy. One by one, add the cold eggs, beating vigorously until the mixture is thick and smooth. Beat in the vanilla, then switch to a flexible spatula and add the flour, stirring gently until it disappears into the thick dough. Cover the dough well and refrigerate for at least 2 hours. (*The dough can be refrigerated for up to 4 days.*)

**WHEN YOU'RE READY TO BAKE:** Center a rack in the oven and preheat it to 350 degrees F. Line a baking sheet with parchment paper or a baking mat.

Put some sanding, turbinado or granulated sugar in a small bowl and have a cork from a wine bottle, if you've got one, at hand.

Using a small cookie scoop (one with a capacity of 2 teaspoons) or a teaspoon, scoop the dough (you want a rounded teaspoon of dough for each cookie). Roll the dough into balls between your palms and then roll the balls around in the sugar to coat. Place the balls on the baking sheet, giving them 1½ inches or so of space to spread. Hold each cookie between two fingers to steady it and press the cork into the center of it (or use your thumb) to make an indentation.

Bake for 10 minutes, or until the cookies feel firmish. It's hard to give a bunch of clues for doneness with these; if your oven is accurate, 10 minutes will be perfect. Transfer the baking sheet to a rack. The indentations will have puffed in the oven, so press them down again. ⟶

Repeat with the remaining dough, always using a cool baking sheet.

To fill the prints, put the jam in a microwave-safe bowl, add a splash of water and heat for about 20 seconds, or until it has melted. (Or do this in a saucepan over low heat.) Using a small spoon, fill each indentation to the brim with jam.

The cookies are ready to eat as soon as the jam has cooled and set. They are good just warm or at room temperature.

STORING: The cookies will keep for about 5 days in a covered container at room temperature.

## *Playing Around*

### CHOCOLATE-FILLED THUMBPRINTS

The cookies are so good filled with melted chocolate. I'm particularly fond of ruby chocolate here. Ruby chocolate is naturally a beautiful shade of pink—like a rose—and its flavor is a bit acidic. It's a fine match for this cookie's richness.

To fill the prints with chocolate, melt 3 ounces (85 grams) coarsely chopped chocolate of any type and let it fall from the tip of a spoon into the cookies' indentations. Slide the cookies into the refrigerator for about 10 minutes to set the filling.

# Coffee-Anise Stars

*Makes about 50 cookies*

**FOR THE COOKIES**

1¼ cups (170 grams) all-purpose flour

1 cup (120 grams) spelt flour

2 teaspoons instant espresso powder

1½ teaspoons ground cinnamon

½ teaspoon ground star anise (see below)

1 stick butter (8 tablespoons; 4 ounces; 113 grams), at room temperature

⅓ cup (67 grams) packed light brown sugar

¼ cup (50 grams) turbinado sugar

½ teaspoon fine sea salt

1 large egg, at room temperature

1½ tablespoons unsulfured molasses

1 teaspoon pure vanilla extract

**FOR THE GLAZE**

1½ tablespoons egg white (beat 1 white and measure out 1½ tablespoons, or use liquid whites)

1¼ cups (150 grams) confectioners' sugar, sifted

2½ teaspoons unsalted butter, melted

Warm water if needed

Chocolate pearls, chopped candy coffee beans, sprinkles, dragées or instant espresso powder for finishing (optional)

**A WORD ON THE STAR ANISE:** Ground star anise is not always easy to find, but you can put whole star anise in a coffee or spice grinder and whir away. Or you can make a swap: Cardamom is terrific with the instant espresso and cinnamon, as is ginger or allspice, and none is a compromise.

**PLAN AHEAD:** The dough must be refrigerated for 3 hours or frozen for 1 hour.

**I FIRST MADE THESE** as Christmas cookies and then never stopped making them. It's the spices—cinnamon and star anise powder—that make them so enticing, but pay attention to their texture—a mix of firm and chewy—and the glaze, which is sweet and plain, yet essential to the cookies' appeal. These are delicious and beautiful slicked with glaze, but if all you do is finish them with sprinkles or dust them with colored sugar, they'll still have the look of a quintessential holiday sweet. As with most things that you make with spice, these are better a day after they're baked—it's good to give the spices time to take root and blossom.

**TO MAKE THE COOKIES:** Whisk both flours, the espresso powder, cinnamon and star anise together.

Working in the bowl of a stand mixer fitted with the paddle attachment, or in a large bowl with a hand mixer, beat the butter, both sugars and the salt together on medium speed, scraping the bowl as needed, until smooth and creamy, about 3 minutes. Add the egg and beat for a minute (don't be concerned if the mixture curdles). On low speed, beat in the molasses and vanilla.

Turn off the mixer, add the dry ingredients and pulse just until the risk of flying flour has passed, then mix on low speed until the dough comes together. Scrape the bowl and turn out the dough. Divide it in half and pat each half into a disk.

Working with one disk at a time, place the dough between sheets of parchment and roll it to a thickness of ⅛ inch. Refrigerate the disks for 3 hours or freeze them for 1 hour. (*You can refrigerate the dough for a couple of days or freeze it for up to 2 months.*)

**WHEN YOU'RE READY TO BAKE:** Center a rack in the oven and preheat it to 350 degrees F. Line two baking sheets with parchment paper or baking mats.

Keep one piece of dough in the fridge while you work on the other. Peel off the top sheet of parchment and, using a 2-inch-diameter star-shaped cookie cutter, cut out as many cookies as you can.

Place the cookies about an inch apart on the baking sheet. Gather the scraps and save them to combine with the scraps you'll get from the second piece of dough; then roll, chill, cut and bake the scraps.

Bake the cookies for 8 to 9 minutes, or until they are golden and only just firm—poke one in the center, and it will give a bit. Let the cookies sit on the baking sheet for 2 minutes, then transfer them to a rack to cool.

Bake the remaining cookies, always using a cool baking sheet.

TO MAKE THE GLAZE: Working in a medium bowl, whisk the egg white until it's frothy. Add the confectioners' sugar and, using a flexible spatula, stir until it's incorporated—this takes a little work. Stir in the melted butter and keep mixing until you have a smooth glaze that spreads easily. If you think it needs it, add warm water by the droplet.

TO FINISH THE COOKIES: Using a small offset spatula or a butter knife, spread some glaze over each cookie. If you'd like to add a little chocolate pearl or three, some sprinkles or anything else, do it while the glaze is still wet. Leave the cookies out for an hour or so to allow the glaze to dry.

STORING: Unglazed, the cookies can be frozen, well wrapped, for up to 2 months. Once glazed, they can be kept at room temperature for about 5 days.

## Playing Around

As you'll see when you roll it out, this dough is delightfully workable—it holds its form nicely—so you can vary the shape and size of the cookies. These cookies go well with chocolate, so if you wanted to skip the sugar glaze, you could finish them with melted chocolate—dark, milk or white.

# Trufflish Nuggets

*Makes about 30 cookies*

4½ ounces (125 grams; about 1 cup whole or about 1¼ cups slivered or sliced) almonds (see headnote)

1¼ cups (100 grams) shredded unsweetened coconut

½ cup (100 grams) sugar

2 tablespoons unsweetened cocoa powder

¼ to ½ teaspoon ground cinnamon, to taste (optional)

¼ teaspoon fine sea salt

2 ounces (60 grams) semisweet or bittersweet chocolate, coarsely chopped

3 large egg whites, stirred just enough to break them up

SMALL, NUBBLY AND INVITING, these cookies are a little like truffles and similar to old-fashioned macaroons, but with a lot more flavor and a much more interesting texture. The dough is made in a food processor and includes almonds—you get the best flavor with whole skin-on almonds—coconut, chopped dark chocolate, cinnamon (if you'd like) and some sugar. When the mixture is sandy, you pulse in egg whites—they're what give the cookies a slight crust—and scoop the dough out onto baking sheets. You get a lot of pleasure for what amounts to about 5 minutes of work.

Center a rack in the oven and preheat it to 350 degrees F. Line a baking sheet with parchment paper or a baking mat.

Put all of the ingredients *except* the chocolate and egg whites in a food processor and pulse until the mixture is sandy—it's okay if you've got a few larger bits. Drop in the chocolate and pulse a few times to chop. Gradually add the egg whites, pulsing after each addition, until the dough, which will look like a paste, holds together.

Use a small cookie scoop, one with a capacity of about 2 teaspoons, or a spoon to drop rounded teaspoonfuls of dough onto the baking sheet, leaving an inch between them.

Bake the cookies for 22 to 25 minutes, rotating the pan after 12 minutes, until they feel just firm when gently pressed and, most important, can be peeled away from the paper or mat. Place the baking sheet on a rack and let the cookies cool to room temperature.

STORING: The cookies will keep for up to 4 days in a covered container at room temperature.

# Coffee Shortbread

*Makes 12 cookies*

**FOR THE COOKIES**

⅓ cup (67 grams) sugar

Finely grated zest of ½ lemon

1 stick (8 tablespoons; 4 ounces; 113 grams) unsalted butter, at room temperature

1 teaspoon instant espresso

½ teaspoon ground cardamom

½ teaspoon fine sea salt

1 teaspoon pure vanilla extract

1 cup plus 2 tablespoons (151 grams) all-purpose flour

**FOR THE OPTIONAL ICING**

1 tablespoon egg white (lightly beat 1 white and then measure it, or use 1 tablespoon liquid whites)

¾ cup (90 grams) confectioners' sugar, sifted

1½ teaspoons unsalted butter, melted

½ to 2 teaspoons warm water if needed

Ground coffee or instant espresso for sprinkling (optional)

THIS SHORTBREAD HAS a tantalizing flavor, not quickly recognizable. The coffee is hard to miss, but the lemon zest and cardamon add a slightly offbeat citrusy taste too. The cookies are intrinsically pretty—the dough is pressed into a round cake pan and then cut into wedges that always look elegant. For even more panache, you can swipe the shortbreads with a simple confectioners' sugar icing and dust with ground coffee.

TO MAKE THE COOKIES: Center a rack in the oven and preheat it to 350 degrees F. Generously butter an 8-inch round cake pan and dust with flour, or use baker's spray.

Put the sugar and zest in a small bowl and rub the ingredients together with your hands until the mixture is fragrant.

Working in the bowl of a stand mixer fitted with the paddle attachment, or in a large bowl with a hand mixer, beat the butter at medium speed just until creamy. Add the espresso, cardamom and salt and beat until blended. Drop in the lemon-sugar and beat until the mixture is smooth, about 2 minutes. Beat in the vanilla.

Turn off the mixer, add the flour all at once and mix on low just until you've got moist crumbs and curds that hold together when pressed, about a minute. Don't overdo it—stop before the dough balls up.

Turn the curds of dough into the pan and use your fingertips to press them down. To compress and smooth the dough, roll a spice jar over the curds, or tamp them down with the bottom of a glass or measuring cup. Don't press too forcefully, though—you just want to knit the crumbs together.

Using the tines of a fork, prick holes in the dough to mark 12 triangles: Poke the tines down to the bottom of the pan—you should hear them hit the metal pan. Finish by pressing the back of the tines around the edges of the dough, as though you were crimping a piecrust.

Bake the shortbread for about 25 minutes, or until the top feels firm to the touch and the edges are light brown. Transfer the pan to a rack and wait 3 minutes, then use the fork to re-prick the wedge lines—they might have closed during baking.

Carefully run a table knife around the edges of the shortbread and then invert it onto the rack. Invert the shortbread once again onto a cutting board and use a long knife or a dough scraper to cut along the dotted lines. Return the cookies to the rack and let cool to room temperature.

TO MAKE THE OPTIONAL ICING: Working in a medium bowl, whisk the egg white until foamy. Add the confectioners' sugar and, using the whisk or a small spatula, mash, mix and stir until the sugar is moistened. It's not the easiest job, but keep going, and you'll end up with a thick mass. Add the melted butter and stir, stir, stir. If the glaze looks too thick to spread, add warm water a drop at a time. When you've got a workable consistency—glaze the cookies: Don't wait!

Use a small icing spatula to spread the icing over the cookies—I usually leave an unglazed border. If you'd like, sprinkle over just a few grains of coffee. Let the glaze dry for about 15 minutes before serving or storing the cookies.

STORING: Packed in a covered container, the shortbread will keep for at least 1 week at room temperature. If you've iced the cookies, you might want to put parchment or waxed paper between the layers. If you haven't iced them, you can hold them in the freezer for up to 2 months.

# Tenderest Shortbread
# Four Ways

*Makes about 24 cookies*

**FOR THE ORIGINAL SHORTBREAD**

2 sticks (8 ounces; 226 grams) unsalted butter, at room temperature

⅔ cup (80 grams) confectioners' sugar

¼ teaspoon fine sea salt

Grated zest of 1 lemon (optional)

2 large egg yolks, at room temperature

2 teaspoons pure vanilla extract

2 cups (272 grams) all-purpose flour

**FOR THE WHOLE WHEAT SHORTBREAD**

1 cup (136 grams) all-purpose flour

1 cup (136 grams) whole wheat flour

2 sticks (8 ounces; 226 grams) unsalted butter, at room temperature

⅔ cup (80 grams) confectioners' sugar

¼ teaspoon fine sea salt

Grated zest of 1 lemon

2 large egg yolks, at room temperature

2 teaspoons pure vanilla extract

3 tablespoons wheat germ

**FOR THE RYE-CHOCOLATE SHORTBREAD**

1¼ cups (170 grams) all-purpose flour

1 cup (120 grams) rye flour

2 sticks (8 ounces; 226 grams) unsalted butter, at room temperature

⅔ cup (80 grams) confectioners' sugar

¼ teaspoon fine sea salt

2 large egg yolks, at room temperature

2 teaspoons pure vanilla extract

½ cup (113 grams) mini chocolate chips or 4 ounces (113 grams) semisweet or bittersweet chocolate, finely chopped

**SHORTBREAD'S TEXTURE CAN BE CRACKLY** or melt-in-your-mouth, depending on how much butter you use, which sugar you choose (confectioners' sugar gives tenderness, granulated sugar, crunch) and whether or not you add eggs. This tender, fragile shortbread came about when I made a mistake in a recipe that a Parisian pastry chef gave me decades ago. The chef had used an egg yolk in the cookie dough and another to brush the logs of dough. I inadvertently added both yolks to the dough and have been making the cookies that way ever since. They don't hold their shape as prettily as most other shortbreads, but they're so tasty.

The shortbreads made with whole wheat flour are a great morning cookie; the rye and chocolate cookies are an unexpected mix of earthy and indulgent; and the ones made with spelt are especially good with fruit or ice cream.

**FOR THE SPELT-FLAX SHORTBREAD**

1¼ cups (170 grams) all-purpose flour

1 cup (120 grams) spelt flour

2 sticks (8 ounces; 226 grams) unsalted butter, at room temperature

⅔ cup (80 grams) confectioners' sugar

¼ teaspoon fine sea salt

Finely grated zest of 1 orange or tangerine

2 large egg yolks, at room temperature

2 teaspoons pure vanilla extract

3 tablespoons flaxseeds or chopped toasted walnuts

**PLAN AHEAD:** The dough needs to be refrigerated for a minimum of 3 hours (overnight is better) or frozen for at least 2 hours.

All of the shortbreads are made in the same manner. If you're making a shortbread with two kinds of flour, whisk the flours together.

Working in the bowl of a stand mixer fitted with the paddle attachment, or in a large bowl with a hand mixer, beat the butter, confectioners' sugar, salt and zest, if using, together on medium speed until soft, creamy and homogenous, scraping the bowl as needed. One by one, beat in the yolks, followed by the vanilla.

Turn off the mixer, add the flour(s) all at once and mix on low speed only until incorporated. If you've got wheat germ, chocolate or flax seeds or nuts, mix them in now.

Scrape the dough out onto the work surface and divide it in two; the dough will be soft and sticky. Put each piece on a sheet of parchment and cajole it into a log that's 6 to 6½ inches long, tightening the log with the paper and twisting the ends. Refrigerate the logs for at least 3 hours (overnight is better) or freeze them for 2 hours. (*The logs can be frozen for up to 2 months; slice when they're still frozen. You might need to add a minute to the oven time.*)

WHEN YOU'RE READY TO BAKE: Center a rack in the oven and preheat it to 350 degrees F. Line a baking sheet with parchment paper or a baking mat.

Using a chef's knife, cut each log into ½-inch-thick rounds. Lay them out on the baking sheet, leaving about an inch between them.

Bake, rotating the sheet after 10 minutes, for 21 to 23 minutes, or until the cookies are golden and set. The cookies will still be soft, so leave them on the sheet for 5 minutes before transferring them to a rack and allowing them to cool to room temperature.

STORING: The cookies can be packed in an airtight container and kept at room temperature for at least 5 days.

# Biscuits Rose

*Makes about 16 cookies*

⅔ cup (90 grams) all-purpose flour

⅓ cup (45 grams) cornstarch

¼ teaspoon baking powder

¼ teaspoon baking soda

Pinch of fine sea salt

2 large eggs, separated, at room temperature

½ cup (100 grams) sugar

1 teaspoon pure vanilla extract

Red food coloring

About ½ cup (60 grams) confectioners' sugar for dusting

**A WORD ON PIPING THE COOKIES:** If you'd like, you can make yourself a piping template for these. Draw 16 rectangles or ovals, each 4 inches long and 1 inch wide, on a sheet of parchment paper. Flip the paper over and use it to line the baking sheet.

**EVER SINCE THE SEVENTEENTH CENTURY,** the Fossier company in Reims, the spiritual home of France's Champagne region, has been making elegant rectangular-shaped cookies the color of tea roses. Called *biscuits rose,* or pink cookies, they're like crunchy ladyfingers. They're hardly sweet, very crackly, simple, beautiful and legendary in their homeland. To get the formidable crunch that I love in the Fossier cookies, I "dry" both the egg whites and yolks with sugar and then take the word *biscuit* at face value: like *biscotti,* it means twice-baked. So I bake the cookies and then leave them in the oven for a half hour or so to get them even crisper. Originally the meringue-based cookies were meant to be served with Champagne, and sometimes I do that. But usually I put them out with coffee, tea or a kid's after-school hot chocolate and encourage dunking and double-dipping.

Center a rack in the oven and preheat it to 350 degrees F. Line a baking sheet with parchment paper (with or without a template drawing; see at left) or a baking mat. If you want to pipe the cookies, use a piping bag with a 1-inch-diameter opening if you have one; or snip an opening in the tip of a disposable piping bag or from the bottom corner of a ziplock bag.

Whisk the flour, cornstarch, baking powder, baking soda and salt together.

Working in the bowl of a stand mixer fitted with the whisk attachment, or in a bowl with a hand mixer, beat the egg whites at medium speed until opaque. Increase the speed to high and add half of the sugar about 1 tablespoon at a time, beating until you have a glossy meringue that holds stiff peaks. Transfer to another bowl (unless you have a second mixer bowl ) and put the yolks in the original bowl (no need to wash it). Beat the yolks, the remaining sugar and the vanilla on medium-high speed for 5 minutes, scraping the bowl as needed, or until pale and thick. Add enough food coloring to tint the mixture a deep pink.

*Cookies*

Check the meringue—if it's sagged a bit as it sat, give it a few brisk beats with a whisk to bring it back to stiffness. Scrape the meringue out over the yolks and, working with a flexible spatula and a gentle hand, fold the two mixtures together until almost combined. Fold in half of the dry ingredients, and when they are almost blended, add the rest and finish incorporating—check the bottom of the bowl for lurking flour.

If you're using parchment paper, use a little of the batter to "glue" the four corners to the baking sheet. Spoon the batter into the piping or plastic bag and pipe out fingers about 4 inches long and 1 inch wide, keeping them about an inch apart. (If you're not a piper, spoon the batter out into 16 portions and use a small icing spatula or a table knife to spread it into shape.) Dust the cookies generously with confectioners' sugar, let them rest for 5 minutes and then dust again.

Bake the cookies for 6 minutes, then rotate the pan and bake for 6 minutes more. Turn off the oven, prop the door open a crack—just wiggle a wooden spoon into the door as a wedge—and let the biscuits dry for 30 minutes (or for up to 2 hours).

The cookies are ready to serve as soon as they're cool.

STORING: Packed in an airtight container, the cookies will keep for about 1 week at room temperature.

# Rugelach with Four Fillings

*Makes about 40 rugelach*

## FOR THE DOUGH

1 recipe Cream Cheese Dough (page 352), divided in half and chilled

## FOR THE CLASSIC FILLING

⅔ cup (160 ml) raspberry jam, apricot jam or marmalade

2 tablespoons sugar, mixed with ½ teaspoon ground cinnamon

¼ cup (40 grams) moist, plump raisins or dried cranberries, chopped

¼ cup (30 grams) finely chopped nuts

4 ounces (113 grams) bittersweet or semisweet chocolate, finely chopped, or ⅔ cup (113 grams) mini chocolate chips

## FOR THE COCONUT-FRUIT FILLING

¾ cup (90 grams) shredded sweetened coconut

½ cup (60 grams) lightly toasted pecans, finely chopped

3 ounces (85 grams) milk or semisweet chocolate, finely chopped

⅓ cup (about 55 grams) moist, plump dried cherries or raisins, snipped or chopped

2 tablespoons unsalted butter, melted and cooled

3 tablespoons sugar, mixed with ¼ teaspoon cinnamon

## FOR THE BABKA FILLING

5 tablespoons (2½ ounces; 70 grams) unsalted butter, melted

½ cup (100 grams) packed brown sugar

1 tablespoon ground cinnamon

1 tablespoon unsweetened cocoa powder

2 tablespoons all-purpose flour

¼ teaspoon fine sea salt

## FOR THE CREAM-CHEESE FILLING

6 tablespoons raspberry jam, apricot jam or marmalade

3 ounces (85 grams) cream cheese

¼ cup (30 grams) confectioners' sugar

1 teaspoon pure vanilla extract

½ teaspoon fine sea salt

3 ounces (85 grams) chocolate, finely chopped, or ½ cup (85 grams) mini chocolate chips

1 egg, mixed with 1 teaspoon cold water, for glazing

Sanding or granulated sugar for sprinkling

**A WORD ON AMOUNTS:** Each filling makes enough to spread over a full batch of the cream cheese dough. If you'd like, the dough can be doubled, or the filling recipes can be halved, so you can have more variety.

RUGELACH, A COOKIE with cream-cheese-dough spiraled around a sweet filling, was one of the first things I learned to bake. The recipe came from my mother-in-law, and because the dough was so forgiving, I made it often, confident that each outing would produce delicious cookies. What's changed over the years is what I fill the rugelach with. I still love my basic filling, with jam, cinnamon-sugar, raisins, nuts and chocolate, and my other trusty combination of coconut,

pecans, chocolate and cherries. But recently, playing around, I discovered that the cinnamon-cocoa filling from babka (page 35; it's the filling in the photograph) is terrific with the dough, as is an even richer filling of cream cheese and jam that, when baked, turns custardy.

And while I was playing around, I changed the shape. Instead of the traditional crescents, which were fussy to form, I now roll the dough up and treat it like a slice-and-bake cookie (this makes shaping so easy, which is one reason you often find barrel-shaped rugelach in bakeries). Once you've mastered the dough (easy!) and made your first batch, you can start coming up with your own fillings. Think of this recipe as the first step to your own repertoire.

TO ROLL OUT THE DOUGH: Working with one piece at a time, roll the dough out on a floured surface or between sheets of parchment paper into a 12-inch square. The dough will be very thin and the edges might be ragged. If the dough is not sandwiched between parchment, slide it onto a sheet of parchment and cover with another sheet. Transfer the dough to baking sheets and refrigerate until needed. (*You can refrigerate the dough for up to 3 days or freeze it, wrapped airtight, for up to 2 months. If it's been frozen, don't try to work with the dough until it's pliable.*)

TO SHAPE THE RUGELACH: Follow these basic directions for filling and shaping the dough squares. Work with one square at a time, leaving the second one in the refrigerator until you are ready for it. Spread the filling over the dough, leaving a slim border bare at the top and bottom of the square of dough. Cut the dough crosswise in half, so that you've got two 12-x-6 inch rectangles. Starting from the center edge, where you cut the dough, roll up one rectangle of dough into a log, making the roll as tight as you can and finishing with the bare border. Repeat with the second rectangle. Wrap both logs and refrigerate or freeze them (I usually freeze them; I think they bake better) until they are chilled, or you are ready for them. (*The logs can be refrigerated for about 8 hours or wrapped airtight and frozen for up to 1 month.*)

TO MAKE AND SPREAD THE CLASSIC FILLING: Warm the jam with a splash of water (I do this in the microwave) until it liquefies; let cool. Working with one piece of dough at a time, spread the dough with half the jam, sprinkle with half the cinnamon sugar and scatter over half the raisins, nuts and chocolate. Roll and chill as above.

TO MAKE AND SPREAD THE COCONUT-FRUIT FILLING: Mix together the coconut, pecans and dried fruit. Working with one piece of dough at a time, spread the dough with half the melted butter, sprinkle with half the cinnamon sugar and scatter over half the coconut mixture. Roll and chill as above.

TO MAKE AND SPREAD THE BABKA FILLING: Mix all the filling ingredients together—the mixture will look a little lumpy and maybe even a bit curdly. Let it sit for 15 minutes, and it will be fine. Working with one piece of dough at a time, spread half the filling over the dough with a small offset spatula or the back of a spoon—you might have a few bare spots here and there, but you should be able to get a nice coating over all of the dough. Roll and chill as above.

TO MAKE AND SPREAD THE CREAM-CHEESE FILLING: Warm the jam with a splash of water (I do this in the microwave) until it liquefies; let cool. Mix the cream cheese, confectioners' sugar, vanilla and salt together in a bowl until smooth and spreadable. Working with one piece of dough at a time, spread the dough with half the cream cheese mixture and then half the jam. Scatter over half the chocolate. Roll and chill as above.

TO BAKE THE RUGELACH: Center a rack in the oven and preheat it to 375 degrees F. Line a baking sheet (or two) with parchment paper or a baking mat.

Working with one log at a time, unwrap the log and place it on a cutting board, keeping the seam on the side, not the bottom, if you can. Trim the ends and cut the log into 1-inch-wide cookies. Place them on the baking sheet about an inch apart, again trying to keep the seam to the side. If the seam is on the bottom, it's not fatal, but filling always bubbles out and burns, and it's better if it doesn't burn on the bottom of the cookies. (*The shaped cookies can be frozen, well wrapped, for up to 2 months and then baked from frozen—you might have to add an extra minute to the baking time.*)

Lightly brush the top of each cookie with egg wash and sprinkle with sugar. Bake the rugelach for 21 to 26 minutes; you're looking for a lovely deep golden-brown color; the babka rugelach take less time than the others. There'll be bubbled-up and maybe burned filling around the cookies, but don't worry, it won't spoil them—especially if you lift them off the baking sheet as soon as they come out of the oven.

Use a small offset spatula to very carefully transfer the rugelach to a rack. Cool to room temperature.

STORING: Rugelach are best the day they're made, but they can be refreshed briefly in a 350-degree-F oven.

# Pistachio-Matcha Financiers

*Makes about 28 cookies*

FINANCIERS ARE CAKE-LIKE COOKIES, usually made with hazelnut or almond flour. Named for the stockbrokers, *financiers,* of Paris and originally shaped like gold ingots, they were meant to be a rich treat for the rich men. My rendition—a treat for everyone—is made with ground pistachios, has matcha and whole wheat flour and is baked in mini muffin tins. Matcha, the brilliant green tea powder, adds gorgeous color and a very soft note of bitterness, while the whole wheat adds sweetness. I love these plain, as a snack, but they take to being fancied up. Try them with a white chocolate dip, which can be tinted with matcha. And if you sprinkle them with matcha and/or a little freeze-dried raspberry powder, they'll be ready for Christmas. (For the classic version of financiers, see Playing Around.)

## FOR THE FINANCIERS

1½ sticks (12 tablespoons; 6 ounces; 170 grams) unsalted butter

¾ cup (150 grams) sugar

¾ cup (100 grams) shelled unsalted pistachios

⅓ cup (45 grams) all-purpose flour

⅓ cup (45 grams) whole wheat flour

1½ teaspoons matcha powder

¼ teaspoon fine sea salt

6 large egg whites, at room temperature, lightly beaten

## FOR THE GLAZE (OPTIONAL)

8 ounces (226 grams) white chocolate, coarsely chopped

1½ teaspoons canola oil

Matcha powder for the drizzle and for sprinkling (optional)

Freeze-dried raspberry powder for the drizzle and for sprinkling (optional)

**A WORD ON THE MATCHA:** Choose an affordable culinary- or lower-grade tea; baking destroys the nuance of high-quality matchas.

**PLAN AHEAD:** The batter must be chilled for at least 3 hours.

**TO MAKE THE COOKIES:** Cook the butter in a small saucepan over medium heat until it just comes to a boil. Turn off the heat and keep the butter warm while you make the batter.

Put the sugar and pistachios in a food processor and pulse until the nuts are finely ground. It's okay if you have a few discernible pieces here and there—in fact, it's better than overprocessing the nuts and ending up with paste. Add both flours, the matcha and salt and pulse a few times to blend. Turn everything into a medium bowl.

Pour the egg whites into the bowl and stir gently with a flexible spatula until thoroughly blended. Gradually and gently incorporate the butter—it will take a little while to get all the butter into the batter, but when you do, the batter will be thick, shiny and beautiful. Cover and refrigerate for at least 3 hours. (*The batter can be refrigerated for up to 3 days*.)

**WHEN YOU'RE READY TO BAKE:** Center a rack in the oven and preheat it to 400 degrees F. You'll need mini muffin tins with cups that hold 2 tablespoons. Coat them with baker's spray or butter and flour them.

Spoon the batter into the tins, filling the cups almost to the top. (If you have more batter than tins, bake in batches, always starting with cool tins.)

Bake the cookies for 13 to 15 minutes, or until the sides are deeply golden and the tops have crowned—they'll feel springy to the touch. Remove the tins from the oven and wait 4 or 5 minutes, then flip the cookies out onto a rack. Let sit until they are only just warm or have reached room temperature. If you're going to glaze them, let cool completely.

TO MAKE THE OPTIONAL GLAZE AND FINISH THE COOKIES: Mix the white chocolate and oil together in a microwave-safe bowl and microwave at 50-percent power in short bursts to melt the chocolate. (White chocolate can be finicky, so it's best to keep the power low and to check often; you can also do this in a double boiler.) If necessary, transfer the glaze to a small bowl—deep is better than shallow here.

If you want to drizzle the cookies with color, immediately mix a little of the chocolate with a little matcha (don't use too much, or the color will get too dark and the taste too bitter) in a small bowl and/or a little more chocolate with freeze-dried raspberry powder in another.

Dip the tops of the cookies in the glaze, letting the excess drip back into the bowl; set the cookies on a rack. If you're using colored drizzle, drizzle one or both of them over the glazed financiers. If you'd like to sprinkle the glaze (or the glaze and drizzle) with matcha or raspberry powder, do it now, before the chocolate dries. Refrigerate the cookies for about 30 minutes to set the glaze.

STORING: Undecorated, the cookies will keep in an airtight container for about 4 days at room temperature or for up to 2 months in the freezer. Decorated, they will keep for about 2 days at room temperature.

## Playing Around

### CLASSIC FINANCIERS

Omit the whole wheat flour and use ⅔ cup (90 grams) all-purpose flour; omit the matcha too. Replace the pistachios with 1 cup (100 grams) almond or hazelnut flour or an equal weight of (about 100 grams) almonds or hazelnuts. If you're using nut flour, you can mix the batter in a bowl—no need for a food processor.

# Tea and Honey Madeleines

*Makes 12 madeleines*

7½ tablespoons (3¾ ounces; 106 grams) unsalted butter

2 teaspoons loose Earl Grey tea (the equivalent of 2 tea bags), plus (optional) 1 teaspoon

⅔ cup (91 grams) all-purpose flour

1 teaspoon baking powder

¼ teaspoon fine sea salt

⅓ cup (67 grams) sugar

Finely grated zest of 1 clementine or Meyer lemon

2 large eggs, at room temperature

1 tablespoon honey

1 tablespoon milk, at room temperature

**A WORD ON SHAPE:** No matter the flavor or the texture, an authentic madeleine is baked in a shell-shaped mold and known by its looks: ridged and deeply golden on one side, slightly paler and noticeably humped on the other. The shape echoes the scallop shells that French religious pilgrims wore around their necks. While the look will be different, you can get all the flavor and texture by baking these in mini muffin tins; see Playing Around.

**PLAN AHEAD:** The batter must be chilled for at least 5 hours.

**MADELEINES ARE OFTEN DIPPED IN TEA,** but I've always liked the idea of baking tea into the little cookies or cakes themselves. For these, my most recent riff on the classic (for the classic, see Playing Around), I keep the recipe's melted butter—a must for madeleines—but add Earl Grey tea to it, cook the butter to a light caramel brown and then let it steep. I also add honey and some orange zest. If you'd like, you can add a bit more tea to the batter—just rub it into the sugar along with the zest. The combination is more subtle than it sounds and more intriguing than you might imagine. As with all madeleines, these change texture over time—they're lightest soon after they're baked and become more substantial hours later. In the case of madeleines, a little more substance equals better dunkability.

Put the butter and the 2 teaspoons tea in a small saucepan and cook over medium heat until the butter melts and comes to a boil. Lower the heat and let the butter boil gently for about 4 minutes, until you catch the aroma of caramel tea; the butter will be lightly browned and there may be darker bits on the bottom and sides of the pan. Strain the butter into a bowl (discard the tea); cover to keep warm.

Whisk the flour, baking powder and salt together.

Working in a medium bowl, rub the sugar and zest, and the extra teaspoon of tea, if you're using it, together until the sugar is moist and fragrant. Whisk in the eggs and beat for about 2 minutes—you want the mixture to lighten in color and to thicken a bit. Whisk in the honey, followed by the milk.

Switch to a flexible spatula and gently stir in the flour mixture. When it is fully incorporated, use a light touch to blend in 6 tablespoons of the tea-flavored butter. (This will probably be exactly the amount you've got; measure it just to be sure.) The batter will have a lovely sheen. Press a piece of plastic against the surface and refrigerate for at least 5 hours. (*The batter can be refrigerated for up to 3 days. Or, if you'd like, you can fill the madeleine molds now, cover with a sheet of parchment or plastic and keep the setup in the fridge for up to 6 hours.*)

**WHEN YOU'RE READY TO BAKE:** Center a rack in the oven and preheat it to 400 degrees F. Generously butter a madeleine pan (you'll get the best crust with a metal pan), dust with flour and tap out the excess. Alternatively, use baker's spray.

Divide the batter among the molds. Don't worry if the batter isn't level—everything will work out just right in the oven.

Bake the cookies for 10 to 12 minutes, or until they're golden brown and, most important, humped in the center; they'll feel springy to the touch. As soon as you take the pan out of the oven, rap it against the counter to loosen the madeleines. If any stick, gently pry them out with a table knife. Serve now, when they're still warm, or let cool on a rack and serve at room temperature.

**STORING:** The madeleines can be kept covered for a day at room temperature, but while their taste will hold, their texture will get denser. No matter, they'll still be delicious.

## *Playing Around*

### MINI MUFFIN MADELEINES

If you don't have madeleine pans, bake these in mini muffin tins; the recipe makes 24 mini muffins. Butter and flour the tins or use baker's spray. Bake the minis for 10 to 12 minutes, until they're golden and springy.

### CLASSIC MADELEINES

Use ¾ stick (6 tablespoons; 3 ounces; 85 grams) butter; melt it and let it cool. Omit the tea and use lemon zest in place of the clementine or Meyer lemon zest. Add 1 teaspoon pure vanilla extract to the batter after you've beaten in the eggs. Everything else is the same. This recipe makes 12 full-size or 24 mini madeleines

# Iced Spiced Hermits

*Makes 24 cookies*

## FOR THE COOKIES

2 cups (272 grams) all-purpose flour

¾ teaspoon baking soda

½ teaspoon fine sea salt

¼ teaspoon baking powder

1½ teaspoons ground cinnamon

1½ teaspoons ground ginger

½ teaspoon freshly grated nutmeg

¼ teaspoon freshly ground black pepper

1 stick (8 tablespoons; 4 ounces; 113 grams) unsalted butter, at room temperature

1 cup (200 grams) packed brown sugar

¼ cup (60 ml) unsulfured molasses

1 large egg, at room temperature

½ cup (80 grams) moist, plump raisins (see headnote)

## FOR THE ICING

1 cup (120 grams) confectioners' sugar, sifted

About 2 tablespoons milk, water, lemon juice, brandy or rum

**I'M NOT SURE** how I managed to live in New England for decades, write an entire book on cookies and eat at least a cookie a day for most of my life, yet never bake or eat a hermit, a New England native that's been around since the late 1800s. And then, after weeks of seeing boxes of them stacked up at the end of the bakery section of my local Connecticut supermarket, they were all I could think about.

Hermits are soft and chewy, more dense cake than crisp cookie, and spicy. They've also got some dried fruit—often raisins—but you can use dates or figs, cranberries, currants, even candied ginger. Use what you've got, just be sure that the fruit is plump and moist.

My hermits are spiced with cinnamon, ginger, nutmeg, freshly ground black pepper and sea salt. Play around with their proportions, if you'd like, or include other spices, maybe those that you'd use for Christmas cookies, pumpkin pie or fruitcake.

**TO MAKE THE COOKIES:** Whisk the flour, baking soda, salt, baking powder and spices together.

Working in the bowl of a stand mixer fitted with the paddle attachment, or in a large bowl with a hand mixer, beat the butter and brown sugar together on medium speed until creamy, about 3 minutes. Beat in the molasses and then the egg and beat for a few minutes more, scraping the bowl and beater(s) as needed. The dough will be light and fluffy, like whipped peanut butter.

Turn off the mixer, add the flour all at once and pulse to start blending in the dry ingredients. When the risk of flying flour has passed, turn the mixer to low and beat only until the ingredients are almost incorporated. Add the raisins and continue to mix on low until there are no traces of flour. Turn the dough out, gather it together, wrap and refrigerate it for at least 30 minutes. (*The dough can be refrigerated overnight.*)

**WHEN YOU'RE READY TO BAKE:** Center a rack in the oven and preheat it to 350 degrees F. Line a baking sheet with parchment paper or a baking mat. ⟶

Divide the dough in half. Place one piece 2 to 3 inches away from a long side of the baking sheet and shape into a log about 12 inches long; don't worry about the width. Repeat with the second piece of dough on the other side of the sheet. Flatten the dough a bit with your hands.

Bake the logs for 23 to 26 minutes, or until the edges feel just firm to the touch; the tops will still be soft. The logs will have spread and cracked, and that's just what they're supposed to do. Transfer the baking sheet to a rack and let the logs rest for 15 minutes or so while you make the icing.

**TO MAKE THE ICING:** Put the confectioners' sugar in a medium bowl and pour in 1½ tablespoons of the milk (or whatever liquid you've chosen). Use a spoon to stir the milk into the sugar. Add more milk as needed—you might need more than 2 tablespoons—until you've got an opaque icing that falls easily from the tip of the spoon.

**TO ICE AND SLICE THE COOKIES:** Drizzle the icing over the still-warm logs. Don't worry about being neat or creating a museum-worthy design—just have fun.

When the icing has set and the logs are cool, trim the ends (or don't) and decide how you want to cut the cookies—you can either slice them crosswise into 1-inch-wide pieces or cut them into 2-inch-wide pieces and then cut them crosswise in half to make squarish cookies.

**STORING:** These are good keepers—packed in a tightly covered container, they'll be good for at least 4 days. I think they're still good when they get a bit drier and less chewy. At that point, they make good dunkers—dip them in coffee, tea, cold milk or warm cider.

# *Java Mini Mads*

*Makes 24 mini madeleines*

⅔ cup (91 grams) all-purpose flour

1½ teaspoons instant espresso (or
    2 teaspoons ground espresso, ground
    coffee or instant coffee)

1 teaspoon baking powder

½ teaspoon ground cinnamon

¼ teaspoon fine sea salt

½ cup (100 grams) sugar

2 large eggs, at room temperature

1 teaspoon pure vanilla extract

1 stick (8 tablespoons; 4 ounces; 113 grams)
    unsalted butter, melted and still warm

**PLAN AHEAD:** The batter must
be chilled for at least 5 hours.

MADELEINES, RICH COOKIES masquerading as tiny tea cakes, are usually recognized by their scalloped-shell shape—it's traditional (see Tea-and-Honey Madeleines, page 195)—and beloved for their texture, which is light; tight-grained; a bit springy, the way the best sponge cakes are; and exceptionally well suited to dunking. In this version, I've given the normally plain cookie a memorable new flavor and an even lovelier texture. The madeleines are made with coffee and cinnamon (like cappuccino) and baked in mini muffin tins (if you'd like, you can use classic madeleine pans; see Playing Around). The tins up the ratio of well browned, lightly crunchy crust to glorious crumb, increasing their irresistibility and their dunkability too.

Whisk the flour, espresso or coffee, baking powder, cinnamon and salt together.

Working in a medium bowl, whisk the sugar and eggs together energetically, beating for about 2 minutes—the mixture should thicken a bit. Whisk in the vanilla. Switch to a flexible spatula and gently stir in the flour mixture. When it's fully incorporated, fold and lightly stir in the melted butter. Press a piece of plastic against the surface of the batter and refrigerate for at least 5 hours. (*The batter can be refrigerated for up to 3 days.*)

**WHEN YOU'RE READY TO BAKE:** Center a rack in the oven and preheat it to 400 degrees F. Generously butter two mini muffin tins. (If you've got just one, work in batches.) Or use baker's spray.

Divide the batter evenly among the cups—I use a small cookie scoop (with a capacity of about 2 teaspoons) to do this.

Bake the minis for 11 to 13 minutes, or until they're golden brown and feel springy when gently prodded—they'll have beautiful round humps in the center. As soon as you take the pan out of the oven, rap it against the counter to loosen the madeleines. If any stick, gently pry them out with a table knife. Serve now, when they're still warm and at their lightest, or let cool on a rack and serve at room temperature.

**STORING:** The mads are best soon after they are baked. They can be kept covered at room temperature for up to 1 day, but their texture will get a bit denser.

## *Playing Around*

**JAVA MADS**

The batter will make a dozen full-size madeleines. Butter and flour the madeleine pan or use baker's spray, divide the batter among the molds and bake for 12 to 13 minutes.

# Cocoa-Cornmeal Biscotti

*Makes about 46 biscotti*

1½ cups (204 grams) all-purpose flour

½ cup (42 grams) unsweetened cocoa powder

½ teaspoon baking powder

½ teaspoon baking soda

¼ cup (44 grams) cornmeal (not coarse-grain or polenta)

1 stick (8 tablespoons; 4 ounces; 113 grams) unsalted butter, at room temperature

1 cup (200 grams) sugar

½ teaspoon fine sea salt

2 large eggs, at room temperature

1 teaspoon pure vanilla extract

½ cup (87 grams) mini semisweet chocolate chips or 3 ounces (87 grams) chocolate, chopped

½ cup (50 grams) sliced almonds

LOTS OF COOKIES CALL themselves crunchy, but the king of crunch, the cookies that always deliver crackle, are biscotti. A double bake sets the crunch—logs of dough are baked, sliced and the cookies baked again—and cornmeal, almonds and chocolate chips add flavor and even more crunch to this version. I love these because they're chocolaty and because each bite is different—chocolate chips and chopped nuts are fall-where-they-may add-ins.

Center a rack in the oven and preheat it to 350 degrees F. Line a baking sheet with parchment paper or a baking mat.

Sift the flour, cocoa, baking powder and baking soda together into a bowl, then whisk in the cornmeal.

Working in the bowl of a stand mixer fitted with the paddle attachment, or in a large bowl with a hand mixer, beat the butter, sugar and salt together on medium speed until creamy and smooth, about 3 minutes. Add the eggs one at a time, beating for a minute after each goes in, then beat in the vanilla.

Turn off the mixer and add the flour-cornmeal mixture all at once. Pulse a few times to begin incorporating the ingredients, then mix on low until they disappear into the dough. Mix in the chips and almonds. The dough will be thick and heavy.

Scrape half the dough onto one long side of the baking sheet. (The dough spreads a lot during baking, so you want to leave some space between it and the edge of the baking sheet.) Using your hands and a spatula, cajole the dough into a log about 12 or 13 inches long and 1½ inches wide—perfection is impossible, so just get close. It will be bumpy and rough, and that's fine. Form a second log on the other side of the sheet; leave plenty of space between the two logs.

Bake for 25 minutes, rotating the sheet after 15 minutes. The logs will have spread; they'll give when squeezed and won't be fully baked at this point. Transfer the baking sheet to a rack and allow the logs to rest for 20 minutes. (Leave the oven on.)

One at a time, carefully move the logs to a cutting board. (If the parchment on the baking sheet is sticky, turn it over or replace it.) Using a serrated knife, trim the ends of each log and then cut crosswise into ½-inch-thick slices. Stand the slices up on the baking sheet—you don't have to leave much room between them.

Bake the cookies for another 15 minutes or so—they should be firmer but not completely dry; they firm, dry and come into their own as they cool. Transfer the baking sheet to a rack and let the biscotti cool to room temperature.

STORING: Kept covered and away from humidity, the biscotti can be kept for at least a week at room temperature.

## Playing Around

If you'd like, you can dip one or both ends of each cookie in melted chocolate (page 373). Or lay the cookies on their sides and drizzle with chocolate. You can also change the add-ins: Try chopped dried cherries, apricots or figs,—making certain the fruit you use is moist and plump (see page 6).

# Park Avenue Brownies

*Makes at least 16 bars*

⅓ cup (45 grams) all-purpose flour

2 tablespoons unsweetened cocoa powder

½ teaspoon fine sea salt

5 tablespoons (2½ ounces; 71 grams) unsalted butter, cut into chunks

6 ounces (170 grams) bittersweet or semisweet chocolate, coarsely chopped

⅓ cup (67 grams) sugar

⅓ cup (67 grams) packed brown sugar

2 cold large eggs

1 teaspoon pure vanilla extract

⅓ cup (40 grams) chopped walnuts (or other nuts) for topping (optional)

Maldon or other flaky sea salt for sprinkling (optional)

**A WORD ON SIZE:** I usually cut an 8-inch square pan of brownies into 16 pieces, but these are so chocolaty that you might want to cut smaller bars. Nibble a corner, and then decide.

MY HUSBAND NAMED these Park Avenue Brownies because they're rich and slim, very like so many of the chic denizens of Manhattan's most expensive stretch of real estate. They're quick and easy enough to make every day and good enough to want them that often. They're also a kind of all-things-to-all-people brownie, since they're mostly fudgy, just a little cakey, deeply chocolaty and chewier than traditional brownies (that's the brown sugar at work). In a moment that should be filed under "why didn't I do this sooner," I decided not to fold the nuts into the batter, but to scatter them over it instead. Because the nuts are on the outside, they toast in the oven, adding a bit of crispness to the bars. (If you're not fond of nuts, just omit them.)

Center a rack in the oven and preheat it to 325 degrees F. Coat an 8-inch square baking pan with baker's spray, then line the bottom and two opposite sides of the pan with parchment paper, leaving enough overhang on the two sides that the parchment can later serve as a sling. Lightly spray the parchment. (Because these brownies are so thin and rich, they're hard to flip out of the pan—spray-and-sling is the way to go.)

Whisk the flour, cocoa and salt together—make sure there are no lumps in the cocoa (sift if you must).

Set a large heatproof bowl over a pan of simmering water—the water shouldn't touch the bowl—drop in the butter and top with the chopped chocolate. Heat, stirring frequently, until the butter and chocolate are only just melted, thick and shiny—you don't want to heat the mixture so much that it separates. Transfer the bowl to a work surface.

Add both sugars and whisk them in thoroughly. The mixture will get grainy—it's temporary. One by one, add the cold eggs, beating each one in vigorously. Beat—really beat—for a minute or two after the second egg goes in. The batter will be heavy and glossy and the whisk should leave tracks as you mix. Stir in the vanilla. Switch to a flexible spatula, add the dry ingredients all at once and gently stir them in.

*Cookies*

Scrape the batter into the pan and smooth the top. If you're using the nuts, scatter them over the batter and then, if you'd like, sprinkle sparingly with flaky salt.

Bake for 27 to 30 minutes, or until a tester inserted into the brownies comes out cleanish—you might have a streak of chocolate, and that's fine. Transfer the pan to a rack and allow the brownies to cool until just warm, or until they reach room temperature.

Run a knife around the edges of the brownies that baked against the pan sides, then use the parchment sling to gently lift the square out of the pan and onto a cutting board. Cut into 16 (or more) squares.

STORING: Tightly wrapped, the brownies will keep at room temperature for about 4 days. They can be frozen for up to 2 months; defrost in their wrapper.

# Olive-Oil Brownies

*Makes 16 bars*

½ cup (120 ml) olive oil (fruity
or peppery)

5 ounces (142 grams) semisweet or
bittersweet chocolate, coarsely
chopped

1 cup (136 grams) all-purpose flour

¼ cup (21 grams) unsweetened cocoa
powder

½ teaspoon fine sea salt or ¾ teaspoon
fleur de sel

½ teaspoon freshly ground black
pepper or other pepper
(see headnote)

⅔ cup (133 grams) sugar

3 cold large eggs

1 cold large egg yolk

¾ cup (120 grams) moist,
plump raisins

Maldon or other flaky sea salt for
sprinkling (optional)

IT'S OFTEN THE LAST-MINUTE decisions that nudge a recipe around a culinary corner. These started as all-butter brownies, and they were fine, but not outstanding. Then they were butter-and-olive oil brownies and they were finer, but still not outstanding. When I went all in on the oil, they got interesting. But it wasn't until I added a little more salt and some freshly ground black pepper that I was sure I had a tender, fudgy brownie worth the investment of good chocolate. Adding soft raisins helped too.

Use whatever kind of olive oil you like—my preference is a mild, fruity oil, but peppery oils are also good here. If you want to venture a little further out, you could use ground chile pepper, instead of black pepper—think about a pepper that's a little sweet as well as hot or one that's smoky. The raisins too are up for swapping; see Playing Around.

Center a rack in the oven and preheat it to 325 degrees F. Butter and flour an 8- inch square baking pan, or use baker's spray. Line the bottom with parchment paper.

Set a medium heatproof bowl over a pan of simmering water (make sure the water doesn't touch the bowl), pour in the olive oil and scatter over the chocolate. Heat, stirring now and then, just until the chocolate melts. Don't let it get so hot that the mixture separates.

While the chocolate is melting, sift the flour, cocoa powder, salt and pepper together.

Lift the bowl off the heat and transfer to a work surface. Whisk in the sugar. The mixture may look grainy, but it'll be fine. One by one, whisk in the eggs and yolk, whisking vigorously for a few seconds longer after the yolk goes it—the batter will be thick and shiny.

Grab a flexible spatula, add the dry ingredients all at once and stir until they're almost incorporated. Stir in the raisins and then finish blending in the flour mixture. The dough will be heavy, sticky and a little slippery too. Turn it into the baking pan and press and slide it around until you get it into the corners. The top should be even, but it will never be smooth. Sparingly sprinkle over some flaky salt, if you'd like.

*Baking with Dorie*

Bake the brownies for 28 to 30 minutes, or until a tester inserted into the center comes out clean; the brownies will have just begun to shrink from the sides of the pan. Transfer the pan to a rack and let rest for 15 minutes, then run a table knife around the edges of the pan, if needed. Turn the pan over and peel away the paper, then re-invert the brownies onto the rack and allow them to cool to room temperature before cutting into bars.

Because of the raisins, the brownies don't always cut neatly, but you have a better chance of getting a good slice if you wait for them to cool. Also, it's only when they're at room temperature that you can really appreciate the olive oil. In fact, I think that these are more flavorful after they've been wrapped and held overnight.

STORING: Wrapped well, the brownies will keep for 3 or 4 days at room temperature or for up to 2 months in the freezer; thaw in the wrapper.

## Playing Around

Dried cherries are excellent here instead of the raisins, as are figs or apricots—chop or snip the fruit into small pieces before incorporating it. The dried fruit should be very soft: Be sure to give it a quick soak in very hot water to start. (Drain and dry well before adding them to the batter.) Snippets of oil-cured black or pitted Niçoise olives are a wonderful match with chocolate and a natural, of course, with the olive oil.

# Brown-Sugar Oat Squares

*Makes 16 squares*

1 cup (136 grams) all-purpose flour

½ cup (40 grams) oats (*not* instant), plus 2 tablespoons for topping

½ teaspoon fine sea salt

½ teaspoon ground cinnamon

¼ teaspoon ground allspice

½ cup (100 grams) packed brown sugar

1 stick plus 1 tablespoon (9 tablespoons; 4½ ounces; 127 grams) unsalted butter, cut into chunks, at cool room temperature,

2 teaspoons turbinado or granulated sugar for sprinkling

THESE ARE QUICKLY AND EASILY made—just whir all the ingredients together in a food processor and press into the pan. The squares may look prim and proper, but their munchability is as high as a chocolate-chipper's. They're caramelish because they've got brown sugar; chewy because of the oats buzzed into the dough; and quite pretty in their golden plainness. That they've got a bit of spice—allspice and cinnamon—is one of their quiet lures. Depending on how you're offering these—lunch box or pretty plate—you can cut them into ample squares, as I usually do, or into daintier triangles.

Center a rack in the oven and preheat it to 350 degrees F. Butter an 8-inch square baking pan, or use baker's spray.

Put the flour, oats, salt, cinnamon and allspice in a food processor and whir to reduce the oats to a powder. You might have a few larger pieces of oats here and there, and that's fine—nice, actually. Add the brown sugar and process to blend. Drop in the butter and pulse, scraping the bowl as needed, until you've got moist curds and clumps that hold together when pressed. It's better to under- than overprocess, so stop before the dough comes together in a ball.

Turn the curds into the pan and use your fingertips to press them down. To compress and smooth them, roll a spice jar over them or tamp them down with the bottom of a glass or measuring cup. Don't strong-arm them, though—you just want to bind the dough. Sprinkle the oats over the dough, followed by the turbinado or granulated sugar.

Bake the bars for 23 to 25 minutes, or until the top is golden—they will feel softish to the touch, but they'll get a little firmer as they cool. (At 23 minutes, you get soft and chewy squares; at 25 minutes they're a tad crisper.)

Transfer the pan to a rack and let sit for 3 minutes, then run a table knife around the edges of the pan. Invert the bars onto the rack (you'll lose some oats—it's unavoidable), then invert onto a cutting board—these need to be cut while they're warm. Using a long slicing knife, cut the cookie into 16 squares. (If you want smaller cookies, cut the squares on the diagonal to make diamonds or cut them in half to make rectangles.) Return the bars to the rack and let cool to room temperature.

STORING: Well wrapped, the bars will keep for about a week at room temperature or for up to 2 months in the freezer; thaw in the wrapper.

# Glenorchy Flapjacks

*Makes 16 bars*

3 cups (240 grams) oats (*not* instant)

1 cup (120 grams) shredded sweetened coconut

⅓ cup (73 grams) crystallized ginger or well-drained stem ginger in syrup (see below), finely chopped

⅓ cup (53 grams) moist, plump raisins or dried cranberries

½ teaspoon fine sea salt

1 stick (8 tablespoons; 4 ounces; 113 grams) unsalted butter, cut into chunks

½ cup (100 grams) packed brown sugar

¼ cup (60 ml) Lyle's Golden Syrup or brown rice syrup

About 2 tablespoons sesame seeds for topping (optional)

**A WORD ON THE GINGER:**
You can use stem ginger (ginger that has been cooked in sugar syrup) or crystallized ginger. If your crystallized ginger is hard—a common problem—run it under hot water in a sieve, then dry it well. The sugar coating will wash off, but that's okay.

**PEOPLE FLOCK TO GLENORCHY** on the South Island of New Zealand to see the landscapes that amazed them in *Lord of the Rings*. I went and came home with a cookie. We'd stopped at Mrs. Woolly's General Store for ice cream and it was there that I spotted what I thought was a granola bar. Turned out it was the traditional British treat called "flapjacks," which have nothing to do with pancakes and everything to do with oats: Think of your favorite chewy oatmeal cookie and then imagine it as the energy bar of your dreams. Eleonora Kramer, the store's baker, gave me the recipe, and as we traveled around, I saw flapjacks everywhere, from convenience stores to hip restaurants, and they were all different.

When I got home, I started with Eleonora's recipe (which calls for Lyle's Golden Syrup—brown rice syrup works perfectly too) and then, inspired by all the flapjacks I'd tasted on that trip, added ginger, dried fruit, coconut and seeds. Add or subtract as you'd like—the cookies will always be irresistible.

Center a rack in the oven and preheat it to 350 degrees F. Butter a 9-inch square baking pan, or use baker's spray. Line the bottom and two opposite sides with parchment paper, leaving an overhang on the two opposite sides—the overhang will serve as handles when you unmold the bars.

Stir the oats, coconut, ginger, raisins and salt together in a large bowl.

Put the butter, brown sugar and syrup in a medium saucepan and bring to a boil, stirring occasionally. When bubbles cover the entire surface, remove the pan from the heat and pour the mixture over the dry ingredients, stirring so that every oat is coated. Scrape the mixture into the prepared pan and use a spatula to press it down evenly and smooth the top. If you're using the sesame seeds, sprinkle them over the surface. ⟶

Bake the bars for 24 to 27 minutes, until they're golden brown—they'll still feel fairly soft when poked. The temptation is to bake them longer, so that they feel set, but that's a mistake: The bars will firm as they cool. Transfer the pan to a rack and let rest for 5 minutes, then run a table knife around the edges of the bars. Using a dough scraper or a chef's knife, score 16 bars—I first score a cross that divides the slab into quarters and then score 4 bars in each quarter. Let cool to room temperature.

Grab the parchment handles and carefully lift the slab onto a cutting board. Using the dough scraper or chef's knife, cut through the marks you scored to make 16 bars.

STORING: The bars will keep in a tightly sealed container—I put wax or parchment paper between the layers—for at least 5 days at room temperature.

CREAM PUFFS

# TWO PERFECT
# LITTLE PASTRIES

AND MERINGUES

# A CREAM PUFF DOUGH HOW-TO

It's thanks to the French pastry chef Pierre Hermé that I fell in love with cream puff dough. We were working together on our first book, when he mentioned, rather casually, that once cream puff dough is shaped into whatever it's destined to be, it can be frozen and baked straight from the freezer. This piece of information was transformative, because it moved something I'd thought of as fancy into the realm of the everyday.

That cream puff dough, aka pâte à choux, is equally good for things sweet and salty is another of its marvels. The most basic pâte à choux, a recipe that might be five centuries old, contains neither sugar nor salt, and it is the building block for sweet éclairs or savory cheese puffs, my favorite cocktail go-along. I use the dough for cream puffs filled and topped with a crackly cookie dough (page 217) or studded with crunchy sugar (page 220). It's the dough I pipe into short, chubby lengths for éclairs (page 227) and long, skinny strips for my newest pastry, cream-puff Pocky sticks (page 223). As though it weren't versatile enough, there's more—it can be flavored with spice; dusted with nuts; frosted, iced or glazed; and, maybe best of all, made with cocoa (page 226).

Cream puff dough is the only dough I know that is both cooked and baked. For the cooked part, you heat milk, water, butter, sugar (optional) and salt together until the butter melts, then add the flour all at once and cook that. Next you beat in eggs. That's the dough:

basic! It is shaped and then baked (or frozen and then baked). There's nothing difficult about making it, but there are a few things to keep in mind while you're working on it.

• It's important that the milk-water mixture be very hot—I like to bring it just to a boil—but what's most important is that the butter melts.

• Once you've added the flour and incorporated it into the hot liquid, keep cooking and stirring. In some ways, this is the most important step in the process, because you must dry the dough—it's what will make it puff in the oven. Continue cooking and stirring for another 4 minutes or so to get it right.

• The eggs need to be beaten into the dough with conviction—don't add another egg until the previous one is fully incorporated. I use a stand mixer with a paddle attachment when I've got three or more eggs to add, and I make the dough by hand when there are only two eggs, but do whatever's easiest for you.

• It's best to shape the dough as soon as it's made. Whether you're piping or spooning or scooping, and whether you're baking the dough immediately or sliding it into the freezer, you should use the dough while it's still warm—it's when it's easiest to handle and will give you the greatest puff and the freshest flavor.

• Anything you make with cream puff dough can be frozen as soon as it's shaped. Freeze whatever you've made uncovered and then, when frozen solid, pack airtight. When you're ready to bake, arrange the frozen pastries on a lined baking sheet and let them sit on the counter while you preheat the oven.

# Cream Puffs with Crackle and Cream

*Makes 12 large puffs*

## FOR THE TOPPING

½ cup plus 2 tablespoons (85 grams) all-purpose flour

½ cup (100 grams) packed brown sugar

4½ tablespoons (2¼ ounces; 64 grams) cool unsalted butter, cut into small pieces

Pinch of fine sea salt

¾ teaspoon pure vanilla extract

## FOR THE PUFFS

½ cup (120 ml) milk

½ cup (120 ml) water

1 stick (8 tablespoons; 4 ounces; 113 grams) unsalted butter, cut into 4 pieces

1 tablespoon sugar (optional)

½ teaspoon fine sea salt

1 cup (136 grams) all-purpose flour

4 large eggs

1 large egg white

## FOR THE CREAM FILLING

3 cups (720 ml) very cold heavy cream

⅓ cup (67 grams) sugar

2 to 3 teaspoons pure vanilla extract

I THINK OF THESE as the gold standard of cream puffs. They're both light enough to merit the name puff and sturdy enough to hold—and hold up to—a filling. They're made with a dough I'd fiddled with for years—I stopped tweaking it after I discovered that the addition of an egg white was the secret to baking in the firmness you need for the puffs to hold their shape when you cut and fill them. The filling is vanilla whipped cream and the crown is a cloak of cookie crackle. Called *craquelin*, it seems like a trick: You make a brown-sugar cookie dough, roll it very thin, cut it out and then balance it on top of the unbaked puffs. As the puffs grow in the oven, so does the cookie dough—it spreads over the tops, speckling the puffs with crunch and giving them a distinctive look, some sweetness and another terrific texture.

The two classic fillings for cream puffs are whipped cream and pastry cream, but lemon or another curd or curd mixed with whipped cream is good too. Fill the puffs with ice cream, and you can call the dessert profiteroles (see Playing Around)—just add hot fudge sauce.

*For a quick how-to on cream puff dough, see the sidebar on the page opposite*

TO MAKE THE TOPPING: Put all of the ingredients *except* the extract in the bowl of a stand mixer fitted with the paddle attachment, or a large bowl you can use with a hand mixer, and mix on low speed until you have very moist clumps and curds—squeeze some of the dough, and it should hold together. (You can also do this by hand.) Beat in the vanilla. Turn the dough out onto a work surface, knead it into a cohesive ball and shape it into a disk.

Working between sheets of parchment, roll out the dough until it's between 1/16 and 1/8 inch thick. Slide the dough, still between the parchment, onto a baking sheet and put in the freezer until needed. (*The dough can be frozen, wrapped airtight, for up to 2 months. Use it directly from the freezer.*)

TO MAKE THE PUFFS: If you're going to bake the puffs as soon as they're made, center a rack in the oven and preheat it to

*Two Perfect Little Pastries*

425 degrees F. Using a cookie cutter or a drinking glass as a template, draw 12 circles, 2¼ to 2½ inches in diameter, on a piece of parchment paper, leaving a couple of inches between the circles. Flip the paper over and use it to line a baking sheet. (Or shape the puffs freehand, if you'd like.)

Have a pastry bag fitted with a plain ¾-inch-diameter tip at hand. Or cut a ¾-inch slit in the tip of a disposable pastry bag or a bottom corner of a large ziplock bag. (If piping isn't for you, you can spoon out the dough.)

Put the milk, water, butter, sugar, if using, and salt in a medium saucepan and bring to a boil over medium heat. When the butter has melted, add the flour all at once, grab a sturdy flexible spatula and begin beating. Beat until you've got a dough that pulls away from the pan and leaves a film on the bottom (you might not get a film if your pan is nonstick), about 4 minutes.

Turn the dough out into the bowl of a stand mixer fitted with the paddle attachment, or into a large bowl that you can use with a hand mixer (or the spatula). Add the eggs one at a time, beating for a minute after each goes in; beat in the white. You'll have a smooth, shiny dough.

Scrape the dough into the pastry or ziplock bag and dab a bit of it onto the corners of the baking sheet to anchor the parchment. Using the circles as your guide, pipe (or spoon) out a dozen puffs: Hold the tip an inch or two above the center of each circle and, keeping the bag upright and steady, squeeze out enough dough to fill the circle. Moisten your finger and smooth down any pointy tops. (*The unbaked puffs can be frozen, uncovered, on the baking sheet until solid, then packed airtight and kept in the freezer for up to 2 months.*)

Remove the topping from the freezer, peel the paper away from both sides of the dough and, using a 2¼- to 2½-inch-diameter cookie cutter, cut out a dozen rounds. Balance a circle of topping on each puff.

Bake the puffs for 5 minutes, then turn the oven temperature down to 350 degrees F and bake for another 35 minutes. Turn the oven off, slip a wooden spoon into the oven door to keep it slightly ajar and let the puffs dry for 15 to 20 minutes. The puffs should be firm and you should be able to peel them away from the paper easily.

Cool the puffs completely on the baking sheet or a rack.

TO MAKE THE CREAM FILLING: Working in the bowl of a stand mixer fitted with the whisk attachment, or in a large bowl with a hand mixer, beat the cream on medium speed until it holds soft peaks. Beat in the sugar a tablespoon or two at a time, followed by the vanilla. Continue beating just until the cream holds its shape.

TO FILL THE PUFFS: Cut each puff in two around or near its middle—you can divide the puffs in half or cut off the top third. If you want to pipe the cream into the puffs, scrape it into a pastry bag fitted with a large, fluted star tip (or use a snipped ziplock bag); alternatively, you can spoon the cream into the puffs—I use a ½-cup-capacity ice cream scoop for this. Fill each puff with cream and finish with the top cap.

You can serve the puffs now or refrigerate briefly.

STORING: The baked puffs are best eaten the day they are made, although they can be refreshed in a 350-degree-F oven for a few minutes if kept longer. If you've filled the puffs, it's best to serve them within 3 hours (keep them in the fridge until you need them).

## *Playing Around*

### PROFITEROLES

Cut the puffs as described above and fill each one with a generous scoop of ice cream (a ½-cup scoop is good here). Serve the puffs in bowls with spoons and pass a pitcher of Hot Fudge Sauce (page 371).

# One-Bite Cinnamon Puffs

*Makes about 100 mini puffs*

½ cup (120 ml) water

½ cup (120 ml) milk

1 stick (8 tablespoons; 4 ounces; 113 grams) unsalted butter, cut into 4 pieces

2 tablespoons sugar

½ teaspoon fine sea salt

½ teaspoon ground cinnamon

1 cup (136 grams) all-purpose flour

4 large eggs

1 large egg white

Pearl or sanding sugar for sprinkling (see below)

**A WORD ON THE SPRINKLING SUGAR:** The traditional topping for these is pearl sugar, sometimes called Swedish sugar (I use Lars brand). Crunchy pearl sugar grains are matte white and the size of teensy pebbles—they are both sweet and decorative. You can also sprinkle the tops of the puffs with shimmery sanding sugar, which has a much finer texture. Whatever you use, be generous.

**AND A WORD ON QUANTITY:** You can halve the recipe (use 1 tablespoon egg white—lightly beat the white to measure it—or omit it), but I prefer to make the entire recipe and then freeze the unbaked puffs, ready for my next party.

CINNAMON-SCENTED PUFFS are my play on *chouqettes*, mini cream puffs topped with crunchy sugar that are a favorite at French pâtisseries. You often find them piled high in a big bowl on the counter, ready to be scooped into a bag and nibbled on the way home. They're a snack beloved as much by kids as by their grandparents; an after-school treat; a go-along with tea; or a last bite before bedtime.

Cinnamon is not a spice that's used often in France, but I love it in these—there's just a smidge, but it adds mystery to the baby-size nibbles. I think of them as the popcorn of the sweet world. And, because they are eaten with popcorn gusto, this recipe makes lots of puffs.

*For a quick how-to on cream puff dough, see page 216.*

Position the racks to divide the oven into thirds and preheat it to 350 degrees F. Line two baking sheets with parchment or baking mats.

Have a pastry bag fitted with a plain ¼-inch-diameter tip at hand. Or cut a ¼-inch opening in the tip of a disposable pastry bag or a bottom corner of a large ziplock bag. Alternatively, you can form the puffs using a ½-teaspoon measuring spoon.

Put the water, milk, butter, sugar, salt and cinnamon in a medium saucepan and bring to a boil over medium heat. When the butter is melted, add the flour all at once, grab a sturdy flexible spatula and begin beating. Beat until you've got a dough that pulls away from the pan and leaves a film on the bottom (you might not get a film if your pan is nonstick), about 4 minutes.

Turn the dough out into the bowl of a stand mixer fitted with the paddle attachment, or into a large bowl that you can use with a hand mixer (or the spatula). Add the eggs one at a time, beating for a minute after each goes in; beat in the white. You'll have a smooth, shiny dough.

Scrape the dough into the pastry or ziplock bag and pipe out little buttons of dough about ½ to ¾ inch in diameter, or spoon out the dough; leave a scant inch between the mounds. (*You can*

*freeze the puffs, uncovered, on the baking sheets until solid, then pack airtight and keep in the freezer for up to 2 months.)*

Just before baking, sprinkle each puff generously with pearl sugar.

Bake the puffs for about 25 minutes, quickly rotating the sheets from top to bottom and front to back after 12 minutes. Turn off the oven, open the door a crack—hold it open with a wooden spoon—and let the puffs dry for about 15 minutes, at which point they should feel firm and you should be able to peel them off the paper easily. Then cool on the baking sheet or a rack until they are only just warm or at room temperature.

STORING: These are best the day they're made. If you've got leftovers, or if they soften—as they will with time and/or humidity—pop them into a 350-degree-F oven for 5 to 10 minutes.

## *Playing Around*

### TWO-BITE CINNAMON PUFFS

If you'd like to make bigger puffs, use a small cookie scoop (one with a capacity of 2 teaspoons) or a spoon to form them. You'll get about 50 puffs. Increase the baking time to 30 to 35 minutes and bake until the puffs are golden and almost firm, then leave them in the turned-off oven with the door slightly ajar for 15 minutes, or until firm.

*Baking with Dorie*

# Chocolate-Tipped Cream-Puff Pocky Sticks

*Makes about 25 long or 50 short sticks*

¼ cup (60 ml) water

¼ cup (60 ml) milk

½ stick (4 tablespoons; 2 ounces; 57 grams) unsalted butter, cut into pieces

1 teaspoon sugar

¼ teaspoon fine sea salt

½ cup (68 grams) all-purpose flour

2 large eggs

### FOR THE GLAZE

Milk or Dark Chocolate Glaze

3 ounces (85 grams) milk, semisweet or bittersweet chocolate, finely chopped

1 teaspoon flavorless oil, such as canola

*or*

White Chocolate–Matcha Glaze

3 ounces (85 grams) good-quality white chocolate, finely chopped

1 teaspoon flavorless oil, such as canola

½ teaspoon culinary-grade matcha powder

Sanding or pearl sugar or sprinkles for decorating (optional)

**A WORD ON QUANTITIES:**
If you decide to make shorter sticks, you'll need to make more glaze. The glaze recipes are easily doubled; or make one recipe of each glaze.

**INSPIRED BY THE JAPANESE CHOCOLATE-CAPPED BISCUITS** called Pocky sticks, these crisp cookies are piped as long as grissini and as slender as swizzle sticks. Baked until they're break-with-a-snap crisp, glazed with chocolate and finished with a sprinkling of sugar, they're nifty served alongside ice cream, as an after-dessert nibble or a snack. I think these are most stylish—and the most fun—when they're piped a foot long, but they're also attractive at half the length.

*For a quick how-to on cream puff dough, see page 216.*

Position the racks to divide the oven into thirds and preheat it to 350 degrees F. Using a ruler and pencil, draw 12-inch-long lines, separated by ¾ to 1 inch, on two sheets of parchment, 13 to 15 per sheet. Or, if you want shorter sticks, draw lines that are about 6 inches long. Flip the paper over and line the baking sheets with it.

Have a pastry bag fitted with a plain ¼-inch-diameter tip at hand. Or cut a ¼-inch opening in the tip of a disposable pastry bag or a bottom corner of a large ziplock bag.

Put the water, milk, butter, sugar and salt in a medium saucepan and bring to a boil over medium heat. When the butter is melted, add the flour all at once, grab a sturdy flexible spatula and begin beating. Beat until you've got a dough that pulls away from the pan and leaves a film on the bottom (you might not get a film if your pan is nonstick), about 4 minutes.

Turn the dough out into the bowl of a stand mixer fitted with the paddle attachment, or into a large bowl that you can use with a hand mixer (or the sturdy spatula). Add the eggs one by one, beating for a minute after each goes in. You'll have a smooth, shiny dough.

Scrape the dough into the pastry or ziplock bag and dab a bit of dough onto the corners of the baking sheets to anchor the parchment. Using steady pressure and holding the tip of the pastry bag at a 45-degree angle close to the parchment, pipe the dough from the top of each line to the bottom.

Bake the sticks for 25 minutes, quickly rotating the sheets from top to bottom and front to back after 12 minutes. Turn off the oven, open the door a crack—hold it open with a wooden spoon—and let the sticks dry for about 15 minutes, at which point they should feel firm and you should be able to peel them off the paper easily.

Cool the sticks on the baking sheets or on racks.

**TO GLAZE THE STICKS:** To make either or both glazes, combine the ingredients in a small microwave-safe bowl or a small heatproof bowl. Melt the chocolate in the microwave or over a pan of simmering water, stirring to blend.

The easiest way to glaze the fragile sticks is to lay them out on a lined baking sheet and spoon some of the glaze over one end of each stick. Alternatively, you can dip the sticks into the glaze. Scatter the sugar or sprinkles over the chocolate while it's still wet. Slide the sticks into the refrigerator to let the glaze set, about 30 minutes.

**STORING:** The sticks are best the day they're made. If you've got leftovers, or if they soften—and if you haven't glazed them—pop them into a 350-degree-F oven for 5 to 10 minutes.

# Chocolate Eclairs

*Makes 8 éclairs*

## FOR THE ÉCLAIRS

½ cup (68 grams) all-purpose flour

1½ tablespoons unsweetened cocoa powder

¼ cup (60 ml) milk

⅓ cup (80 ml) water

½ stick (4 tablespoons; 2 ounces; 56 grams) unsalted butter, cut into pieces

1 tablespoon sugar

¼ teaspoon fine sea salt

2 large eggs

## FOR THE GLAZE

3 ounces (85 grams) semisweet or bittersweet chocolate, finely chopped

1 teaspoon flavorless oil, such as canola

## FOR THE FILLING

Chocolate Pastry Cream (page 361) or another filling of your choice (see headnote)

**A WORD ON QUANTITY:** Piped-out eclairs can be frozen and baked whenever they're needed, so you might want to double the recipe.

I GUESS YOU could think of éclairs as elongated cream puffs, but that would deprive them of their singularity. They are believed to have been invented by the renowned eighteenth-century French pastry chef Carême, and the name *éclair* means "flash of lightning." Did Carême know how quickly people would eat his invention? Or did he name them that because they were so startling? And does it make a difference? Pastry cream is the traditional filling, but whipped cream works nicely; ice cream is good too. Here, I make the shells with chocolate cream puff dough, fill them with chocolate pastry cream and glaze the éclairs with chocolate. You can use the classic dough if you prefer (see Playing Around).

*For a quick how-to on cream puff dough, see page 216.*

**TO MAKE THE ÉCLAIRS:** If you're going to bake the éclairs as soon as they're made, center a rack in the oven and preheat it to 425 degrees F. Using a pencil, draw 8 lines, each 5 inches long, on a piece of parchment paper, leaving about 1½ inches between them. Flip the paper over and use it to line a baking sheet.

Have a pastry bag with an opening of about 1 inch (you don't need a tip) at hand. Or cut a 1-inch opening in the tip of a disposable pastry bag or a bottom corner of a large ziplock bag.

Whisk together the flour and cocoa powder. Put the milk, water, butter, sugar and salt in a medium saucepan and bring to a boil over medium heat. When the butter is melted, add the flour mixture all at once, grab a sturdy flexible spatula and begin beating. Beat until you've got a dough that pulls away from the pan and leaves a film on the bottom (you might not get a film if your pan is nonstick), about 4 minutes.

Turn the dough out into the bowl of a stand mixer fitted with the paddle attachment, or into a large bowl that you can use with a hand mixer or the spatula. Add the eggs one by one, beating for a minute after each goes in. You'll have a smooth, shiny dough.

Scrape the dough into the pastry or ziplock bag and dab a bit of dough onto the corners of the baking sheet to anchor the parchment. Using the lines as your guide, pipe the éclairs: Hold the tip close to the paper and squeeze with steady pressure; use a small knife or a pair of scissors to cut the dough when you get to the end of each one. (*You can freeze the unbaked éclairs at this point, uncovered, until solid, then pack airtight and keep in the freezer for up to 2 months.*)

Slide the baking sheet into the oven and immediately lower the temperature to 375 degrees F. Bake the éclairs for 30 minutes, then turn off the oven and slip a wooden spoon into the oven door to keep it slightly ajar. Allow the éclairs to dry in the turned-off oven for 10 minutes. Then transfer the baking sheet to a rack and let the éclairs cool to room temperature. (*You can cover the baked éclairs lightly and hold them overnight at room temperature. If they're a little spongy when you're ready for them, refresh them briefly in a 350-degree-F oven.*)

**TO MAKE THE GLAZE AND COAT THE TOPS OF THE ÉCLAIRS:** Split the éclairs lengthwise in half using a serrated knife and set the bottoms aside. Have a large plate or a tray at hand.

Melt the chocolate and oil together in a microwave-safe bowl in the microwave—do this in short spurts, and stir a few times—or in a heatproof bowl set over a pan of simmering water (don't let the bowl touch the water). If the bowl isn't wide enough to hold an éclair top, transfer the glaze to one that is. Working with one éclair top at a time, dip the tops into the glaze, lift them up, letting the excess fall back into the bowl, and set on the plate or tray. When all the tops are glazed,

put them in the refrigerator for at least 30 minutes (or up to a couple of hours) to set the chocolate, which will remain a tad soft even when chilled.

**TO FILL THE ÉCLAIRS:** You can pipe the pastry cream into the bottom halves of the éclairs using a pastry bag with or without a tip, or cut an opening in the tip of a disposable pastry bag or a bottom corner of a ziplock bag to do this. (Or use a spoon to fill the éclairs.) Cap the filled éclairs with the glazed tops.

You can serve the eclairs now or keep them refrigerated for up to 8 hours before serving.

**STORING:** Eclairs are best eaten soon (or no longer than 8 hours) after assembling.

## Playing Around

### CHOCOLATE SHORTCAKE ECLAIRS

One of my favorite éclairs is filled with whipped cream and fresh strawberries. Make 1½ recipes Whipped Cream (page 362), beating it until it is firm. If you've got a large star tip for a pastry bag, use it to pipe a generous amount of cream into the bottom half of each éclair; or use a spoon. Top the cream with thinly sliced fresh strawberries and finish with the glazed tops. Serve right away or refrigerate for a few hours.

### CLASSIC ECLAIRS

Make a half recipe of the dough for Cream Puffs with Crackle and Cream (page 217), using 2 eggs and omitting the white. Proceed as above.

# Gouda Gougères

*Makes about 55 puffs*

½ cup (120 ml) water

½ cup (120 ml) milk

1 stick (8 tablespoons; 4 ounces; 113 grams) unsalted butter, cut into 4 pieces

½ teaspoon fine sea salt

½ teaspoon ground cumin

1 cup (136 grams) all-purpose flour

4 large eggs

3 ounces (85 grams) Gouda, preferably one with a little age (see headnote), shredded or grated

A few tablespoons cumin seeds for sprinkling

Maldon or other flaky sea salt for sprinkling

**A WORD ON WORKING AHEAD:** The easiest way to have fresh puffs when you need them is to scoop out the freshly made dough and freeze the puffs on the baking sheets until solid, then pack airtight and freeze for up to 2 months. When you're ready to bake, arrange the frozen puffs on a lined baking sheet and let them sit on the counter while you preheat the oven. Sprinkle with the cumin and salt right before.

*GOUGÈRES* IS THE FRENCH NAME for cheese puffs, the nibble that's become my signature. Visit me, and I'll greet you at the door with a glass of cold white wine and a bowl of hot-from-the-oven gougères. Because I love them so much and bake them so often, I've made them with dozens of different cheeses (see Playing Around), yet it's only recently that I discovered how good gougères are made with Gouda. Gouda can range from softish, mild, pale and creamy to hard-enough-to grate, caramel-colored and sharp. As the cheese ages, its texture firms and its flavor intensifies. The color of its wax coating changes too—young cheeses are covered in red wax, more mature cheeses are wrapped in black wax. Since I love strong flavors, I prefer older Goudas, but this recipe will work with any Gouda you like, even smoked. (If you want to use smoked cheese, use it as an accent, swapping just one quarter to half the amount of regular cheese for smoked.)

When I began making gougères with Gouda, I started seasoning the dough with ground cumin and sprinkling the puffs with cumin seeds and flaky salt just before baking. Like more traditional gougères, these are great with white wine, especially a sparkling one, but when there's Gouda and cumin in the mix, beer's a good choice too.

*For a quick how-to on cream puff dough, see page 216.*

Preheat the oven to 350 degrees F. If you want to bake all of the puffs at once, position the racks to divide the oven into thirds and line two baking sheets with parchment paper or baking mats. If you're going to freeze half or more of the batch, center a rack in the oven and line just one baking sheet.

Put the water, milk, butter, salt and cumin in a medium saucepan and bring to a boil over medium heat. When the butter is melted, add the flour all at once, grab a sturdy flexible spatula and begin beating. Beat until you've got a dough that pulls away from the pan and leaves a film on the bottom (you might not get a film if your pan is nonstick), about 4 minutes.

*Two Perfect Little Pastries*

Turn the dough out into the bowl of a stand mixer fitted with the paddle attachment, or into a large bowl that you can use with a hand mixer (or the spatula). Add the eggs one by one, beating for a minute after each goes in. You'll have a smooth, shiny dough. Beat or stir in the cheese.

Scoop out balls of dough with a small cookie scoop (one with a capacity of 2 teaspoons) and arrange on the baking sheet(s), leaving a scant 2 inches between them, or use a teaspoon to portion out rounded spoonfuls of dough. (*You can make the puffs ahead and freeze them on the baking sheets until solid, then pack airtight and freeze for up to 2 months.*)

Sprinkle the tops of the puffs with cumin seeds and top each with a few flakes of sea salt. Bake the puffs for 30 minutes; if you're baking two sheets, quickly rotate the sheets from top to bottom and front to back after 15 minutes.

Turn off the oven, open the door a crack—prop it slightly ajar with a wooden spoon—and let the puffs dry for about 10 minutes; they should feel firm and you should be able to peel them off the paper easily. Serve immediately— although these are delicious warm or at room temperature, they are really at their best when they're hot.

STORING: Please try to serve these as soon after they're baked as possible. If you must hold them, you can give them a few minutes in a 350-degree-F oven to refresh them before serving.

## *Playing Around*

### CHEESE STICKS

Pipe the dough out into long sticks. You can use a pastry bag or a disposable pastry bag with a ½-inch opening cut in the tip for this; or cut an opening in a bottom corner of a ziplock bag. For directions on piping, see the Pocky Sticks recipe, page 223.

Bake the sticks for 25 minutes, rotating the sheets from top to bottom and front to back after 12 minutes, then dry the sticks in the turned-off oven with the door propped slightly ajar for 15 minutes. While the puffs are good hot, these are best at room temperature.

### CLASSIC GOUGÈRES

The classic cheese for gougères is Gruyère or Comté. You can add a couple of pinches of herbes de Provence or 2 to 3 teaspoons chopped fresh rosemary to the dough and sprinkle some finely chopped walnuts on top of the puffs (or sticks) before baking them, if you like. Parmesan is also good with rosemary and walnuts. Cheddar is always a fine idea: Pair it with about ¼ teaspoon mustard powder or smoked paprika (a little of either can go a long way) and finely chopped almonds for the sprinkle—smoked almonds, if you've got them. Sesame seeds go with just about everything.

# A MERINGUE HOW-TO

Meringue is the miracle of egg whites—maybe it's what egg whites were put in this world to become. An amalgam of whites, sugar, air and heat, meringue is the radical transformation of egg whites from a viscous liquid to an airy, shatter-at-a-touch solid. Although making meringue doesn't take talent, it does take patience. But it's easy to get a textbook-perfect meringue—just follow these pointers:

• It's easiest to separate eggs when they're cold. Be careful when you separate them: Even a little bit of yolk or other fat can impede the egg whites' astonishing rise. The safest way is to use three bowls. Crack the egg and put the white in one bowl and the yolk in another. If the white is yolkless, transfer it to the bowl you'll be using to make the meringue. Continue this one-by-one process until you've separated all the eggs. If you don't need the yolks for the recipe, you can cover and refrigerate them for up to 1 day.

• Egg whites beat to greatest volume when they're at room temperature. If you don't have time to let them sit, put your whites in a small bowl set inside a larger bowl filled with hot water and warm them for a few minutes, stirring a couple of times.

• Make sure the bowl and beater(s) that you're using to make the meringue are clean, free of any grease and dry.

• Recipes for meringue vary, but most are based on a ratio of about ¼ cup (50 grams) sugar to 1 large egg white. The sugar needs to go into the whites at a specific point: Start adding it when the whites have just turned opaque and are starting to hold a shape. Add the sugar 1 tablespoon at a time and wait a few beats each time before adding the next. It's a slow process, but it's this gradual incorporation of sugar that builds structure and strength.

• The sign of a perfect meringue is shiny peaks. And, unlike whites beaten without sugar, which can go from perky peaks to puffs and clouds, a sign of overbeating and a fatal turn of events, you have to work hard to overdo it with meringue.

• Meringue is best used as soon as it's made, but it's got a little staying power. If you have to set it aside for a very short time while you're working on other parts of a recipe, do it. Give it a few snappy turns with the whisk before proceeding, and it should be as good as new.

• Plan ahead: Follow the individual recipe for shaping and baking, but remember that the meringues will be in the oven for a long while. They don't bake so much as they dry. For most recipes, you'll bake them at a low temperature, then turn off the heat and let them dry for a while in the turned-off oven.

• Meringues will keep almost forever if they're stored in a dry place. A tin, a cardboard box, a cookie jar—anywhere that protects them from humidity, meringue's nemesis.

# Meringue Snackers

*Makes 6 meringues*

1 cup (200 grams) sugar,
  plus 1 tablespoon

2½ tablespoons confectioners' sugar

4 large egg whites, at room temperature

¾ teaspoon distilled white vinegar

1½ teaspoons pure vanilla extract
  (optional)

**PLAN AHEAD:** To get the volume that you need, the whites must be at room temperature, so leave them out, covered, for at least 1 hour before setting to work. Also, plan on dedicating your oven to the meringues for at least 4 hours.

**A WORD ON SIZE:** This recipe makes 6 big puffs, but the meringue can be spooned or scooped out into smaller mounds (such as snowballs; see Playing Around). It's also lovely piped into spirals or kisses or used to make layers for cakes or other desserts, such as beautiful individual Pavlovas (see photo and page 235).

**THERE ARE A ZILLION REASONS** to love meringues, but top of the list are looks, texture and taste. Whether they're higgledy-piggledy because you scooped them out with a big kitchen spoon, snowballish because you used an ice cream scoop or sleek and smooth, having been swished into shape with an icing spatula, they're attention grabbers. And their texture is as playful as their looks—they're crunchy here, marshmallowy there. But it's their taste that's most surprising. Because they're baked slowly for a long time, the flavor is mostly caramelish.

This is the meringue recipe from which just about all things meringue spring, but I'm guessing that, like me, you'll use it most often for these simple, snackable puffs, great on their own, alongside ice cream or broken up and scattered over anything that needs a touch of sweetness and crunch.

*For a quick how-to on meringues, see the opposite page.*

**TO MAKE THE MERINGUES:** Center a rack in the oven and preheat it to 250 degrees F. Line a baking sheet with parchment paper or a baking mat.

Strain the 1 tablespoon granulated sugar and the confectioners' sugar through a fine-mesh sieve; set aside.

Working in the (clean, dry, grease-free) bowl of a stand mixer fitted with the whisk attachment, or in a large bowl using a hand mixer, beat the whites and vinegar on medium-high speed until they form soft peaks, about 3 minutes. With the mixer running, add the remaining 1 cup (200 grams) granulated sugar 1 tablespoon at a time, waiting a few seconds after each addition. It will take about 5 minutes, maybe even longer, to get all the sugar into the whites, but it's this slow process that makes pristine meringue. Once all the sugar is in, beat for 2 minutes or so, until you have stiff, glossy, beautifully white peaks. If you want to add the vanilla, beat it in now. Switch to a flexible spatula and fold in the reserved sugar mix.

**TO SHAPE THE MERINGUES:** Use a big spoon (I use a serving spoon) to scoop 6 heaping portions of meringue out onto the baking sheet, leaving about 2 inches between them.

*Two Perfect Little Pastries*

Bake the meringues—undisturbed, don't open the oven—for 1 hour and 45 minutes. The puffs will have cracked and colored lightly. Turn off the heat, open the oven door a little to let out whatever steam may have developed, then close the door and let the meringues finish baking (actually, they're not so much baking as drying) for another 2 hours. When you take them out, you should be able to easily peel them off the paper or mat.

STORING: Kept away from humidity, meringues will be fine for days (if not weeks). Store them in a box or just put them on a plate and leave them uncovered.

## Playing Around

### SNOWBALLS

Use a large cookie scoop—one with a capacity of 3 tablespoons—to scoop out the meringue. You'll get about a dozen, maybe a few more. Bake for 1 hour and 15 minutes, then leave them in the turned-off oven for at least 2 hours.

### TINTED MERINGUES

If you'd like to color the meringue, scoop some of the finished meringue into a bowl and add a little food coloring, drop by drop and stirring after each addition, until you have a color that's a shade or two darker than you'd like. Then fold the tinted meringue into the rest of the meringue in your mixing bowl. If you want streaky color, don't be thorough when you fold.

### PAVLOVAS

The three components of a Pavlova, the dessert created to honor the Russian ballerina Anna Pavlova, are meringue, whipped cream and fresh fruit. While you can build the Pavlovas on the Snackers, it's more traditional (and I think nicer) to press down the center of each puff before baking to make a little nest for the filling. After you've scooped the meringue onto the baking sheet (or piped it), use the back of a spoon to make a small bowl in the center of each puff. Bake as directed. When the meringues are cool, spoon or pipe whipped cream (page 362) into the indentations and top with lightly sugared berries or soft fruit cut into small pieces. Or, if you'd like to make one large Pavlova, use all of the meringue to form a 7- to 8-inch-diameter mound; create a bowl for the whipped cream. Bake for 2½ hours and cool in the turned-off oven for at least 2 hours.

Once filled with cream and topped with fruit, Pavlovas are best served immediately or refrigerated for only an hour or two.

### ETON MESS

A messy Pavlova can be an Eton mess. To make a "mess," break up some meringues and put the pieces in a bowl—you can make a big mess, like a trifle, or individual desserts—then top with cream and berries. or soft fruit Serve with spoons.

# Little Marvels

*Makes 10 cakes*

**FOR THE MERINGUES**

1 recipe batter for Meringue Snackers (page 233), ready to shape

**FOR THE CREAM**

2 cups (480 ml) very cold heavy cream

¼ cup (30 grams) confectioners' sugar

1 teaspoon ground cinnamon (optional)

1 teaspoon pure vanilla extract (optional)

**FOR THE SPREAD (OPTIONAL; SEE HEADNOTE), CHOOSE ONE:**

Cookie spread, such as Lotus Biscoff

Peanut butter

Melted chocolate

Thick jam

**FOR THE OUTER COATING (FIGURE ABOUT 2 CUPS [3 OR 4 GENEROUS HANDFULS] OF WHICHEVER ONE YOU CHOOSE)**

Chocolate shavings (any kind of chocolate)

Chopped cookies

Coconut, shredded or flaked, sweetened or unsweetened, toasted or not

Chopped toasted nuts

Chopped meringue

Sprinkles

**THESE ADORABLE SMALL CAKES** are inspired by the famous *merveilleux*, or "marvelous" cakes, that Fred Vaucamps bakes in his shops across Paris. Their name makes them sound as though they came out of a fairy tale and, delightfully, they look and taste that way too. They're created with rounds of meringue, sandwiched with whipped cream, covered with more whipped cream and rolled in something pretty and crunchy, like chocolate shavings, caramelized nuts or crumbled meringue. The cream is luxurious, the meringue just a little soft and chewy and the rocky little bits on the outside of the confections are light, sometimes a little crisp and always flavorful.

I'm giving you options here, including the opportunity to add another flavor to the little cakes by spreading the bottom round of meringue with cookie spread, peanut butter, melted chocolate or jam. You can also put a little spice in the whipped cream. My favorite combination is a swish of cookie spread, cinnamon whipped cream and chocolate shavings.

**TO MAKE THE MERINGUES:** Position the racks to divide the oven into thirds and preheat it to 250 degrees F. Using a pencil, draw ten 3-inch circles on each of two sheets of parchment paper; leaving about 2 inches between the circles. Turn the sheets over and use them to line two baking sheets.

You can spoon the meringues out or shape them with a small icing spatula, but it's faster and easier to pipe them. Use a pastry bag without a tip, or cut a ½-to-¾-inch-wide opening in the tip of a disposable piping bag or a bottom corner of a large ziplock bag. Fill the bag with the meringue and dab a little of it on the four corners of each baking sheet to secure the parchment. Using the circles as your guide, aim to pipe disks that are between ¼ and ½ inch high, but don't get nutty about it—the diameter is more important than the height.

*Two Perfect Little Pastries*

Bake the meringues for about 50 minutes. You don't want the meringues to take on (much) color; they're properly baked when they peel off the paper easily. Turn off the oven and open the oven door a crack to let out whatever steam may have developed, then close the door and leave the meringues in the turned-off oven for another hour. (*You can make the meringues at least a week ahead; just keep them covered and dry.*)

TO MAKE THE WHIPPED CREAM: Working in the bowl of a stand mixer fitted with the whisk attachment, or in a large bowl with a hand mixer, beat the cream just until it begins to thicken a bit. Gradually add the sugar and then the cinnamon, if you're using it, and beat until the cream is thick enough to use as a frosting. If you're using vanilla, whip it in now. (*The cream can be covered and refrigerated for up to an hour or so. If you need to hold it longer, see page 362.*)

TO ASSEMBLE THE CAKES: If you want to add a spread, coat the top side of half of the meringues with whatever you've chosen. Top with whipped cream—you can use a spoon or a cookie scoop to portion out the cream—see what you like, but 2 tablespoons of cream should do it for each cake— then cap each cake with another disk of meringue,

flat side up. Using a small icing spatula, frost the tops and sides of the cakes with the remaining whipped cream. The layer doesn't have to be very thick, just generous enough to capture the crunchies you'll cover it with. Pop the cakes into the freezer for 10 minutes or the refrigerator for about 1 hour before coating them. (*The cakes can stay in the refrigerator for about 5 hours; cover them lightly and keep them away from anything with a strong odor.*)

TO COAT THE CAKES: Put whatever you've chosen as your coating in a shallow bowl or a small tray. One by one, roll the cakes in the coating, getting some of the crunchies around the sides and on the tops. If it's easier for you, use a spoon—I roll them and use a spoon to help me get a good coating. Refill the bowl as needed. Refrigerate the cakes for an hour, or until you need them. (*The cakes can also be frozen for up to 2 months; see Storing.*)

STORING: The cakes should be eaten cold, straight from the refrigerator, and preferably on the day that they're made. However, you can freeze them: Freeze on a tray until solid, then wrap each one well and store in the freezer for up to 2 months. You can put them in the refrigerator for an hour to defrost, but I think they're wonderfully delicious—like mini ice cream cakes—still frozen.

# Parfait-Layered Vacherin

*Makes 6 to 8 servings*

1¼ cups (300 ml) very cold heavy cream

3 large eggs, preferably organic (see below), at room temperature

3 tablespoons sugar

2 teaspoons pure vanilla extract

4 cups (100 grams) broken pieces of Meringue Snackers (page 233; or use store-bought meringues)—you want pieces of all sizes, from small chips to pebbles and peanuts

Caramel Sauce, homemade (page 370) or store-bought, warmed

About ½ cup (about 50 grams) sliced almonds, toasted

**A WORD ON THE EGGS IN THE PARFAIT:** They're raw. If you feel uncomfortable eating raw eggs, replace the parfait filling with ice cream; see Playing Around. If you do make the parfait, use the freshest eggs you can find. Local eggs are good; organic eggs are good; local organic eggs are best.

**PLAN AHEAD:** The dessert needs to freeze for at least 6 hours.

**THIS GETS MY VOTE** for entry into the pantheon of great frozen desserts. There are layers of chunky meringue and layers of parfait, a mixture of beaten egg whites, yolks and whipped cream, lithe, luscious and, when frozen, reminiscent of the richest ice cream you've ever had. The cake is built in a soufflé dish or springform and stowed in the freezer until it's ready for its star turn. Then, just before serving—or at the table, if you want to share the drama—you pour on warm caramel sauce, allowing it to cover the top and slip over the edges before you finish the cake with a flourish of toasted almonds. It's stunning, but not fussy to make. This recipe was given to me by my Parisian friend Thibault Lafarie, who told me it had been a favorite in his family for generations—one spoonful, and I understood why.

You need to build the vacherin in a 2-quart mold. If you have a soufflé dish, that would be very French. Alternatively, make it in an 8-inch springform pan or a 2-quart bowl.

Working in the bowl of a stand mixer fitted with the whisk attachment, or in a large bowl with a hand mixer, whip the cream until it holds medium peaks. If you're using a stand mixer, scrape the cream into another bowl (unless you have a second mixer bowl). Cover the cream and refrigerate. Wash and dry the mixer bowl and whisk, if you used them, or the beaters.

Working in a large bowl, whisk the egg yolks and 2½ tablespoons of the sugar together until slightly thickened and pale. Beat in the vanilla.

Put the whites in the clean bowl of the stand mixer fitted with the whisk attachment, or in a large bowl that you can use with the hand mixer and beat until they turn opaque. Still beating, sprinkle in the remaining ½ tablespoon sugar, then continue to beat until the whites form medium-firm peaks; you don't want the whites to be too stiff.

Working with a large flexible spatula, carefully fold the whipped cream into the yolks. It's okay if you have a few streaks of yolks at this point. Turn the whites into the bowl and very delicately fold them in. Try to be as light-handed but thorough as you can. The mixture will deflate—it's unavoidable; just be quick and gentle.

Sprinkle one-third of the meringues over the bottom of the soufflé dish (or pan or bowl) and cover with half the parfait mixture, then repeat, ending with meringue, so you have 3 layers of meringue and 2 of parfait. Press a piece of plastic against the top surface and freeze the vacherin for at least 6 hours. (*The vacherin can be frozen, tightly covered, for up to 1 month.*)

Shortly before serving, unmold the vacherin by dipping the dish or bowl (not the springform) into warm water, wiping it dry and inverting it onto a platter. Or, better yet, warm the sides with a hairdryer and then turn out the vacherin. If you've used a springform pan, you can just run a table knife around the edges of the pan, remove the sides and leave the vacherin on the base. Pretty up the sides, if necessary, with a small offset spatula or a table knife. Pop the vacherin back into the freezer until you need it.

When ready to serve, pour the caramel over the vacherin, letting some of it run down the sides and sprinkle with the toasted almonds. Serve immediately.

STORING: Leftover vacherin will keep for up to 1 month, well covered, in the freezer.

## *Playing Around*

### CLASSIC ICE CREAM VACHERIN

Replace the parfait filling with whatever flavor—or flavors—of ice cream you like. Just before you're ready to serve, unmold the vacherin, cover the top (and the sides, if you'd like) with whipped cream (page 362) and scatter over the toasted almonds. Pass a pitcher of the caramel sauce at the table.

THROUGH

# PIES, TARTS, COBBLERS AND CRISPS

THE SEASONS

# APPLES, APPLES, APPLES

If it's fall, winter or spring, no matter if I'm in America or in France, I always have a stock of apples at hand. To me, they're Mother Nature's most accommodating fruit. They're as good in something savory (take a look at the Custardy Apple and Kale Cake, page 334, and the Apple-Parm Tart, page 307) as they are in sweets, traditional or new. Whenever I've got a few apples, I know I can make something good.

My go-to apples are Fuji and Gala, but recently I've been reaching for sweet-tart Mutsus, which I like in a tarte Tatin. If you can get heirloom apples or old varieties at your farmers' market,

grab them—it's always exciting to have new flavors to play with.

For most things you bake with apples, it's good to have a mix—some sharp apples and some sweet ones, some juicy apples along with some firmer and drier ones. Sometimes when you've got slim apple slices, it's nice to leave the peel on some of them, just to add a spot of color and a different texture.

And while you can always use store-bought crusts to make pies, I hope that if you've got the time, you'll make a stand-out crust to go with your apple desserts.

# Mulled-Butter Apple Pie

*Makes 6 to 8 servings*

3 tablespoons unsalted butter

1 short cinnamon stick

1 star anise

1 cardamom pod, bruised

1 slice fresh ginger (optional)

10 black peppercorns

1 wide strip orange or tangerine zest, any remaining pith removed

1 recipe All-Butter Pie Dough (page 347), divided in two, each piece rolled out into an 11- to 12-inch round and chilled (or use store-bought pie dough; see below)

About 3 pounds (about 1.3 kilos) apples (5 or 6 large)—one kind or a mix

¼ cup (50 grams) sugar, or more to taste

2 tablespoons all-purpose flour

¾ teaspoon pure vanilla extract

½ teaspoon fine sea salt

Squeeze of lemon or orange juice, or more to taste

Cream or milk for brushing

Turbinado, sanding or granulated sugar for sprinkling

Ice cream for serving (optional)

**A WORD ON THE CRUST:** If you don't have time to make the All-Butter Pie Dough, you can use store-bought. Look for pie dough that's already rolled out and buy two: one to press into the pie pan and one to use as the top crust.

BROWN BUTTER, butter cooked until it colors lightly and wafts out the aroma of toasted nuts, is always a good idea and perhaps the best idea for an apple pie. The mulled spices? They're a good idea too. The spices—left whole—are steeped in the butter along with a strip of orange zest and then strained out, leaving behind their lovely scents and flavors. Choose whatever apples you like most for pie (if you've got a mix, that's nice) and have some ice cream in the freezer—this one's good à la mode. For a more classic apple pie, see Playing Around.

Put the butter, spices and strip of zest in a medium saucepan, turn the heat to medium and melt the butter. Once the butter has melted, stay close and let it cook until it turns golden brown and smells like hazelnuts. There may be dark specks on the bottom of the pan, and that's fine. Take the pan off the heat and let the butter steep while you work on the crust and apples.

Butter a 9-inch pie pan and fit one round of dough into it, allowing the excess to drape over the sides of the pan. Cover and refrigerate until needed.

Center a rack in the oven and preheat it to 400 degrees F. Have a baking sheet lined with parchment paper or a baking mat at hand.

Peel the apples, cut them in half and remove the cores. Slice the apples ¼ to ½ inch thick or cut them into ½- to 1-inch chunks. Toss the slices or chunks into a large bowl, add the sugar, flour, vanilla and salt and stir everything together. Add the butter, pouring it through a strainer (discard the spices and zest), stir again and then stir in the lemon or orange juice. Taste a piece of apple and see if you want more sugar or juice.

Turn the apples out into the chilled piecrust, poking them into the corners and mounding them in the center. Moisten the rim of the crust with water. Peel away the paper from the top crust and drape the crust over the apples, cupping your hands and pressing the crust against the filling to get a nice fit, then press the top and bottom crusts together with your fingers. Trim the excess dough away,

cutting it even with the edges of the pan, and finish the pie by pressing the border with the tines of a fork. (If you want to flute the border, don't trim the dough that hangs over the edges of the pan—use it for the fluting.) Cut a small circle out of the center of the crust (I use a piping tip or a teensy cookie cutter to do this) and make a few long cuts radiating out from the center. (*The unbaked pie can be frozen for up to 2 months; wrap airtight when it's solid. Let it sit out on the counter while you preheat the oven.*)

Brush the crust with cream or milk and sprinkle with sugar. Put the pie pan on the lined baking sheet.

Bake the pie for 40 minutes. Tent the pie loosely with a piece of foil or parchment and/or shield the edges of the pie. Bake for another 15 to 25 minutes (total time is about 55 to 65 minutes, but it may be longer), or until the crust is deeply golden and, most important, the filling is bubbling—if it bubbles through the circle and slits, so much the better. Transfer the pie to a rack and let rest until the pie is just warm or reaches room temperature.

Serve with ice cream, if you like.

STORING: Although it's best the day it's made, the pie will hold for another day, covered, at room temperature or in the fridge. If you like cold pie, have at it straight from the refrigerator; if you'd prefer, warm the chilled pie in a 350-degree-F oven.

## Playing Around

CLASSIC APPLE PIE

I make this double-crusted pie in a 9-inch deep-dish pie pan. Toss 4 pounds (1.8 kg) apples (about 6 very large) with ¾ cup (150 grams) sugar, the grated zest of 1 lemon, 2 tablespoons all-purpose flour or quick-cooking tapioca, ½ teaspoon ground cinnamon, ¼ teaspoon freshly grated nutmeg and ¼ teaspoon fine sea salt. After you've piled the apples into the crust, dot them with 2 tablespoons cold unsalted butter, cut into pieces. Bake the pie—tenting it and/or shielding the edges after 30 minutes—for a total of 65 to 75 minutes, or until the juices are bubbling.

# Apple Galette

*Makes 6 to 8 servings*

About 1¼ pounds (565 grams) sweet apples, such as Golden Delicious, Fuji, Gala or Mutsu (3 to 4 medium), peeled, halved and cored

Juice of ½ lemon (more or less)

1 tablespoon sugar, or more to taste

¼ teaspoon ground cinnamon

¼ teaspoon ground ginger

1 recipe Galette Dough (page 353), rolled into an 11- to 12-inch round and chilled (or use store-bought pie dough; see below)

½ cup (120 ml) Caramel Applesauce (page 365) or other thick applesauce

Turbinado, sanding or granulated sugar for sprinkling

2 tablespoons or so honey or apple jelly for glazing (optional)

**A WORD ON THE CRUST:** If you don't have time to make the Galette Dough (page 353), you can use store-bought pie dough. Look for dough that's already rolled out.

GALETTES, THE SIMPLEST OF ALL TARTS, take very little time to put together but are always alluring. You bend the dough, pleat it and let it go this way and that: That's the fun of a galette. This one has a sweet crust with crackle and flake, tasty apples and homemade applesauce that holds a small surprise: the sharp, bittersweet depth of dark caramel.

If the crust is rolled out and ready to go (or if you've got a store-bought one) and the applesauce is made (or you're using a jar from the market), you can get this into the oven in about fifteen minutes.

Center a rack in the oven and preheat it to 400 degrees F.

Working with one half apple at a time, lay the halves cut side down on a cutting board and slice crosswise into pieces that are about ¼ inch thick (a little thinner is fine). Toss the slices into a large bowl and sprinkle over some lemon juice. Add the sugar, cinnamon and ginger and stir everything around until the apples are coated. Taste a slice to see if you want more lemon juice or sugar. Let the apples sit while you work on the dough. (*You can keep the apples at room temperature for up to 1 hour.*)

If the dough isn't already on a piece of parchment, slip it onto one now (or onto a baking mat) and then slide onto a baking sheet; if necessary, peel away the top piece of paper. Spoon the applesauce onto the center of the dough and spread it out evenly, leaving a band of about 2 inches bare all around. Using a slotted spoon (or your hands), lift the apples out of the bowl and onto the applesauce, mounding them in the middle. Pick up the edges of the dough and fold them up against the apples. As you fold, the dough will bend, ruffle and pleat on itself, and that's what you want. Don't worry about being neat or about getting everything even. If you see any cracks, fix them by smoothing them with a little water on your finger. If there's any liquid left in the bowl, pour it over the apples. (You shouldn't have a lot, but if you do, just pour over 1 to 2 tablespoons of it.) Brush the dough lightly with water and then sprinkle with some sugar.

Bake the galette for 45 to 50 minutes, or until the apples are tender—poke them with a skewer or the tip of paring knife to test. (Check at 30 minutes and loosely tent the galette if you think the crust is browning too quickly.) Slide the baking sheet onto a rack.

If you want to glaze the apples, warm the honey or jelly (add a splash of water to the jelly) until it liquefies (you can do this in the microwave or on the stovetop), then brush a thin layer over the apples. Wait until the galette is just warm or reaches room temperature to serve.

STORING: You can keep any leftovers at room temperature overnight and munch on a slice for breakfast, or reheat briefly in a 350-degree-F oven before serving.

# Caramel-Apple Crisp

*Makes 6 to 8 servings*

## FOR THE TOPPING

½ cup (68 grams) all-purpose flour

¼ cup (34 grams) whole wheat flour

¼ cup (50 grams) packed brown sugar

2 tablespoons sugar

½ teaspoon ground cinnamon

¼ teaspoon fine sea salt

1 stick (8 tablespoons; 4 ounces; 113 grams) cold unsalted butter, cut into small pieces

1 teaspoon pure vanilla extract

½ cup (40 grams) oats (*not* instant)

## FOR THE CARAMEL SAUCE

1 cup (200 grams) sugar

3 tablespoons water

1 tablespoon light corn syrup

¾ (180 ml) heavy cream, warmed or at room temperature

½ teaspoon sea salt, preferably fleur de sel

2 tablespoons unsalted butter, at room temperature

1½ teaspoons pure vanilla extract

About 2½ pounds (a generous kilo) apples (4 or 5 large), peeled (see right), cored and cut into 1-inch chunks

Ice cream for serving (optional)

**WHEN YOU BAKE APPLES** with caramel sauce, you get a juicy mixture—juicier than a traditional apple pie filling, because there are no thickeners. You also get one that's less sweet—"burning" the sugar to caramelize it gives it pleasantly bitter undertones. These are the characteristics that make this filling a good match for a topping that's sweet, earthy and crunchy. It's a topping that began life as streusel and ended by welcoming whole wheat flour (the earthy element) and oatmeal.

You can swap the apples for pears or make this with quinces or, better yet, a combination of quinces, apples and/or pears. While you're fiddling, think about adding toasted nuts (walnuts or pecans) to the mix.

**A WORD ON THE APPLES:** Just about any apple can be used except McIntosh, which would get too soft. I like to use an assortment. For example, think about a mix of Fuji, Gala and Golden Delicious, and maybe throw in a Granny Smith. If you'd like, leave the peel on some of the apples.

**AND A WORD ABOUT WORKING AHEAD:** You can make the caramel sauce and topping well in advance. Even better, you can assemble the crisp, slide it into the freezer and wait for it to freeze solid, then cover it tightly and store it there for up to 2 months. Let it sit at room temperature while you preheat the oven. It may need a few more minutes in the oven.

*steps continue* —————➤

**TO MAKE THE TOPPING:** Whisk both flours, both sugars, the cinnamon and salt together in a large bowl. Drop in the pieces of butter and press, mash and schmoosh the ingredients together until you've got moist clumps that hold together when pressed. Sprinkle over the vanilla, then add the oats and use a flexible spatula—or your hands—to mix them in. (Alternatively, you can do this in a mixer fitted with the paddle attachment—after the mixture comes together, break it into clumps with your fingers.) Cover the bowl and refrigerate the topping for at least 1 hour, or freeze it while you make the caramel sauce and prepare the apples. (*The topping can be refrigerated, covered, for up to 3 days.*)

**TO MAKE THE CARAMEL SAUCE:** Pour the sugar, water and corn syrup into a medium heavy-bottomed saucepan, put the pan over medium-high heat and cook without stirring. Once the sugar melts and starts coloring, swirl the pan. Then cook until the caramel, which will boil and may even smoke, turns a medium amber color. You can check the color by dropping some on a white plate. As the caramel cooks, it might spatter onto the sides of the pan—wash down the spatters with a silicone pastry brush dipped in cold water.

Turn off the heat, stand back and add the cream, salt and butter. The mixture will sputter dramatically, but it will quickly calm down, and when it does, stir it until it is smooth and creamy. If, as you're stirring, you feel as though there are lumps (or something not melted at the bottom of the pan), return the pan to medium heat and stir for another minute or two to smooth things out. Stir in the vanilla extract. Pour the sauce into a heatproof bowl or container and cover when cool. (*The sauce can be refrigerated for up to 1 month. Reheat gently, thinning with a little cream if necessary before using.*)

**TO PREPARE THE APPLES AND ASSEMBLE THE CRISP:** Center a rack in the oven and preheat it to 400 degrees F. Line a baking sheet with parchment paper or a baking mat—you'll need the liner to catch drips. Butter a 9-inch deep-dish pie pan.

Put the apple chunks in a large bowl and pour over ⅔ cup of the caramel sauce. (You'll have caramel sauce left over; save it for another use.) Turn the apples around until they're evenly coated with sauce and then scrape them into the pie pan, mounding them in the center.

Cover the apples with the topping, pinching off pieces as you drop them on top of the fruit—the topping may look precarious, but once it's in the oven, the heat will secure the clumps. (*The assembled crisp can be frozen for up to 2 months; see headnote.*)

Bake the crisp for 40 to 45 minutes, or until the topping is golden brown and the juices are bubbling. (Check it after 30 minutes, and if it looks as though it's browning too quickly, tent it loosely with parchment or foil.) The bubbling's important—when the juices are bubbling in the center, you know the crisp is done. Transfer to a rack and let the crisp sit until it's just warm or has come to room temperature before serving.

If you're serving a scoop of ice cream with each portion of crisp, think about drizzling a little of the leftover caramel sauce over it.

STORING: Like pie, this is best the day it's made. If you've got leftovers, cover, refrigerate and serve them cold the next day.

## *Playing Around*

### CARAMEL PANDOWDY OR COBBLER

The caramel apples make a fine base for either a pandowdy (page 257) or cobbler (page 263), two other desserts that are best when they're saucy.

# *Szarlotka*

*Makes 8 to 10 servings*

## FOR THE CRUST

2¼ cups (306 grams) all-purpose flour

¾ cup (150 grams) sugar

2 teaspoons baking powder

½ teaspoon fine sea salt

1 stick plus 3 tablespoons (11 tablespoons; 5½ ounces; 155 grams) cold unsalted butter, cut into small pieces

1 cold large egg

1 cold large egg white

## FOR THE FILLING

About 3 pounds (1.3 kilos) sweet apples, such as Fuji or Gala (about 5 large), peeled, cored and cut into ½-inch pieces

⅓ cup (67 grams) packed brown sugar, or more to taste

1½ tablespoons all-purpose flour

1 cup (160 grams) moist, plump raisins, preferably golden

Freshly squeezed lemon juice to taste

Confectioners' sugar for dusting

Ice cream or whipped cream for serving (optional)

A COUPLE OF YEARS AGO, a woman I met at a book signing told me that her favorite apple dessert was Polish and that it was called *szarlotka*. I'd never heard of it, but once I'd baked it, I felt as though I had been reunited with a beloved dessert my grandmother used to make for us.

Made in a springform pan, the szarlotka stands tall and announces its presence as something out of the ordinary. Not quite a pie, it's like a combination of a cake, a crumble and a torte. The filling is a mix of apples, raisins and brown sugar that tips toward classic. But the most fascinating part of the dessert is the crust, which is softer than a classic crust and used in two ways: Part of it lines the pan and the remainder is frozen and then grated over the top, so that it bakes up ripply and rough, like a crumble or a crisp.

Butter a 9- to 9½-inch springform pan.

TO MAKE THE CRUST: Put the flour, sugar, baking powder and salt in a food processor and pulse to blend. Drop in the pieces of butter and pulse about 15 times—you want the mixture to pass from the looks-like-sand stage to the discernible-crumbs stage; scrape the bottom of the bowl a couple of times (don't allow a hard layer of ingredients to form under the blade and around the edges).

Lightly beat the egg and white together and add to the flour mixture in 3 additions, pulsing after each, and then pulse (and scrape the bowl, if needed) until the dough forms moist clumps and curds.

Turn the dough out, gather it together and cut off one third of it. Wrap the smaller chunk and tuck it into the freezer. Shape the remaining dough into a ball, flatten it and sandwich it between sheets of parchment paper.

Roll the dough into a round that's about 14 inches in diameter (peel back the paper occasionally to make sure that it's not creasing the dough, and roll both sides of the dough). If the dough's still cold, you can fit it into the pan now; if not, slide the dough, still between the sheets of paper, into the refrigerator for about 20 minutes.

Remove the parchment, transfer the dough to the springform and press it gently against the bottom and up the sides of the pan, then trim the top, if necessary, even with the rim of the pan. If your dough doesn't come all the way up to the top, that's fine—just go as far up as you can. Patch the dough if it tears (press the edges together), and don't be concerned if you have to pleat the sides here and there. Pop the pan into the refrigerator or freezer while you preheat the oven and make the filling.

Center a rack in the oven and preheat it to 375 degrees F. Line a baking sheet with parchment paper or a baking mat.

TO MAKE THE FILLING: Toss all of the ingredients *except* the lemon juice into a large bowl and mix to coat the apple pieces with sugar and flour—I find it most efficient to use my hands here. Mix in a splash of lemon juice and taste a chunk of apple. Do you want a bit more brown sugar? A little more juice? Adjust the sugar and juice to your liking, give the apples another toss and leave the mix on the counter for 5 minutes, then stir again.

Place the dough-lined pan on the baking sheet and spoon in the filling, including any liquid that has accumulated. The apples may or may not mound above the pan's rim; it's good either way. Remove the chunk of dough from the freezer and, using the large holes of a box grater (or a similar tool, such as a Microplane), grate the frozen dough over the filling. (I find it's actually easiest to grate some of the dough onto a board, lift it up and sprinkle it over the filling and then grate some more, but you'll find your own best method.) You probably won't be able to grate the entire piece—it might become too soft to grate or you might be getting dangerously close to your fingers, but that's okay: you'll have enough to cover the apples and it's nice to have some spaces for the fruit to peek through.

Bake the pie for 40 minutes. Tent it loosely with foil or parchment and bake for another 25 minutes or so (the total baking time is about 65 minutes), until the top is a lovely golden brown and, most important, the fruit juices are bubbling up through the top crust.

Transfer the szarlotka, on the baking sheet, to a rack and let rest for 20 minutes. Gently run a table knife between the pie and the sides of the pan and remove the sides of the springform. Let the pie cool until it's just warm or reaches room temperature.

Dust the pie with confectioners' sugar before serving. It's easiest to use a serrated knife and a gentle sawing motion to cut it. It's also easiest to cut thick slices. Scoop some ice cream or whipped cream alongside or on top of the slices of pie, if you'd like.

STORING: The szarlotka is best the day it is made, but it is still good the day after. You can cover it and keep it at room temperature or refrigerate it. If it turns out that you like it cold, you can keep it for another day. It can also be wrapped well and frozen for a month or so—it'll be fine when it defrosts (thaw it in its wrapper), though not as good as freshly made.

## *Playing Around*

Have some fun with the filling: Swap the apples for pears or use a combination of apples and pears. As for the raisins, they're up for grabs. You can use dried cherries or cranberries, small cubes of dried pineapple or apricot or slivers of dried mango. A bit of candied ginger is good too. The filling would welcome nuts—give them a quick toasting. Other spices, such as cinnamon, nutmeg or allspice, are another option.

# Apple Pandowdy

*Makes 6 servings*

## FOR THE FILLING

⅓ cup (67 grams) sugar

2 medium or 1 large lemon

About 2½ pounds (about 1 kilo;) sweet, juicy apples, such as Golden Delicious, Fuji or Gala (4 to 6 large)

2 tablespoons cold unsalted butter, cut into 8 pieces

## FOR THE CRUST

One 11- to 12-inch round All-Butter Pie Dough (page 347), frozen or well chilled (or use store-bought pie dough; look for dough that's already rolled out)

Milk for brushing

Sanding or granulated sugar for dusting

Ice cream or whipped cream for serving (optional)

## A WORD ON THE CRUST:

Instead of cutting out shapes from the dough, you can just lay the whole crust over the fruit, moistening the rim of the pie pan first, pressing the dough against the rim and then tucking the overhang under the rim or against the sides of the pan. Cut slits in the crust and at serving time, crack the crust into the fruit.

**A PANDOWDY'S A PIE** that's got only a top crust, often one made of odd-shaped pieces of dough—the dessert was probably created to put pastry scraps to good use. My favorite way to make it is to cut triangles of pie dough and arrange them in a mishmash over the fruit. Neatness is never the point with a pandowdy—it's the haphazardness, the dowdiness of the pie, that makes it beautiful. When you bring it to the table, break up the crust, let it fall into the filling and then spoon out into bowls.

You can put spices in the filling, but I hope you'll try this spare lemon-up-front version first. Having apple pie without cinnamon may seem un-American; in fact, it's unassailably good. I make this dessert throughout the year with whatever fruits are plentiful; see Playing Around.

**TO MAKE THE FILLING:** Put the sugar in a large bowl and grate the zest from the lemon(s) over it. Reach into the bowl and use your fingers to rub the zest into the sugar until the sugar is moist and fragrant.

Peel and core the apples and cut them into chunks about ½ inch on a side or into slices that are about ¼ inch thick. Add the apples to the bowl with the sugar and squeeze over the juice from the lemon(s). Toss everything around in the bowl until the apples are coated with sugar and juice. Set the bowl aside, stirring now and then, while you preheat the oven.

Center a rack in the oven and preheat it to 425 degrees F. Butter a 9-inch pie pan and put it on a baking sheet lined with parchment paper or a baking mat.

Give the apples a last turn and then pile them into the pie pan—don't forget the juices in the bowl. Dot the top of the apples with the butter.

**TO PREPARE THE CRUST:** Lay the chilled round of pie dough on a cutting board and, using a pizza wheel or a knife, cut it into pieces. I usually opt for triangles of various sizes and shapes, but long strips and squares work, as do rounds made with cookie cutters. Place the pieces of dough over the apples in whatever pattern pleases

you—I usually go for haphazard. It's nice if you leave a little space between the pieces so the juices can bubble over. Lightly brush the dough with milk and sprinkle with sanding or granulated sugar.

Bake the pandowdy for 20 minutes—the crust might get a little color and the juices may just begin to bubble. Turn the heat down to 375 degrees F and continue to bake until you can see juices bubbling all the way to the middle of the pan, 25 to 35 minutes more. If the crust seems to be getting too dark too fast, loosely tent the pandowdy with foil or parchment.

Place the baking sheet on a rack and let the pandowdy cool for at least 30 minutes before serving. The pandowdy is good warm or at room temperature and very good with either ice cream or whipped cream.

STORING: Like most pies, this is meant to be eaten soon after it's made. However, if you have pandowdy left over, you can keep it covered at room temperature for up to 1 day and rewarm it in a 350-degree-F oven before serving.

## Playing Around

In fall and winter, I make pandowdy with apples and pears (traditional and my favorite), sometimes with dried fruit tossed in. In the spring, I make it with rhubarb, with or without strawberries. And in summer, I turn to blueberries or mixed berries, peaches, nectarines, even plums. Use your favorite fruit pie filling recipe, but don't use any thickeners.

# Tarte Tatin

*Makes 6 to 8 servings*

⅔ cup (133 grams) sugar

3 tablespoons water (optional)

3 tablespoons unsalted butter, cut into 6 pieces

5 to 7 large apples (about 2¾ pounds; 1½ kilos) apples—see below

One 11- to 12-inch round Galette Dough (page 353), All-Butter Pie Dough (page 347) or All-Purpose Tart Dough (page 355), chilled (or use store-bought dough; see below)

Sugar for dusting

Crème fraiche, whipped cream or vanilla ice cream for serving (optional)

**A WORD ON THE APPLES:** In France, the apple of choice for a Tatin is Golden Delicious. Lately, my favorite apple for this recipe is the Mutsu—very like Golden Delicious in its balance between sweet and tart, but firmer. Fuji apples are also nice here. The larger the apples, the better. That said, don't let searching for a particular size or type of apple stand in the way of making this—in the end, most apples (oh, except maybe McIntoshes or other soft, mealy apples) Tatinize deliciously.

**A WORD ON THE CRUST:** Almost any crust that you like will work for a Tatin. If you don't have time to make your own, use store-bought pie dough (look for dough that is already rolled out) or puff pastry (depending on the brand, you might have to roll it to size).

**TARTE TATIN IS A TART BUILT** to be turned over. You create a layer of caramel, arrange large pieces of apple over the caramel, cover with the dough, bake and then . . . ta-da: Turn it all upside down, lift off the pan, admire your work and settle in for a treat. Whether the apples are too deeply caramelized or not caramelized enough, it never matters: The tart is always delicious. If you get a case of nerves while making it, remember that the original tarte Tatin was itself a mistake—according to what might be a legend, the Tatin sisters, who ran a hotel near Paris, intended to make a classic apple tart but cooked the apples in the sugar for too long and, to save appearances, upended it to serve.

Many versions of the recipe make the tart in a skillet. But these days I'm doing things in new ways. For starters, I bake the tart in a cake pan, which is much easier to handle. The pan makes turning out the tart simple and safe. (Caramel is so hot and so sticky that safety is an issue.) And because I let the tart rest in the pan before unmolding it, the caramel has time to find its way deeper into the apples. Small changes, big differences.

Center a rack in the oven and preheat it to 300 degrees F. Put a 9-inch cake pan, one that's 2 inches tall and preferably nonstick, in the oven to warm. (You can turn the oven off after it heats—you're not going to bake the tart soon, you're just heating the pan now to make lining it with caramel easier.)

**TO MAKE THE CARAMEL:** Choose a skillet that's about 9 inches in diameter (again, nonstick is good), pour in the sugar and spread it evenly over the bottom of the pan. If you're new to carameling, you might want to moisten the sugar with the 3 tablespoons water. Adding water slows the process, giving you a bit more time to judge the color. Have a silicone or wooden spatula at hand, along with a small white plate (or piece of parchment paper). Turn the heat under the pan to medium-high and stay close. As soon as you see the sugar changing color around the edges of the pan, swirl the pan or use the spatula to stir small circles around the pan's circumference, drawing the unmelted sugar to the edges little by little. When all the sugar has melted (if there's smoke, don't be alarmed, but do move the pan away from the heat for a moment) and the caramel is a light amber color (check the color by putting a drop on the plate or parchment) take the pan off the heat, stand away and add the butter piece by piece. It might seethe and spatter—just stand clear.

Remove the cake pan from the oven and pour in the caramel, carefully tilting the hot pan so that the caramel covers the bottom. Set the pan aside to let the caramel cool to room temperature and harden, an hour or so. (*You can leave the pan at room temperature for up to a day. Set a plate over the pan once the caramel has hardened.*)

WHEN YOU'RE READY TO BAKE: Center a rack in the oven and preheat it to 375 degrees F. Line a baking sheet with parchment or a baking mat.

Peel 5 of the apples (leave the others until you know whether or not you'll need them), cut them in half from top to bottom and remove the cores. Leave one apple half whole and place it, cut side up, in the center of the pan. Remember, you'll later be turning the cake pan upside down to unmold the tart, so you want to place the pretty sides of all the apples against the bottom of the pan. You have a choice now: You can fill the pan with apple halves or you can cut the rest of the peeled apples in half from top to bottom and fill the pan with apple quarters. No matter which cut you choose, you want to lay the apples as close to one another as you can get them, arranging the pieces so that their rounded sides are on the bottom. Peel, core and cut as many more apples as you need to get the tightest arrangement (depending on the size of your apples, how you cut them and how you design your tart, you might

have one or two circles around the half apple in the center). Then cut some of the remaining apples into wedges or pieces to fill in any gaps.

Using the bottom of the pan as a guide, trim the round of dough so that you've got just an extra inch all around. Lift the pan away and drape the dough over the top. Do the best that you can to tuck the dough in around the apples. Dust the top of the dough with sugar and put the pan on the lined baking sheet.

Bake the tart for about 45 minutes, until the dough is nicely golden. Peek, and you'll see that the caramel is bubbling around the apples. Transfer the pan to a rack and let the tart rest and settle for up to 30 minutes. The apples will have absorbed most of the caramel after 30 minutes. If you'd like to have some runny syrup, let the tart rest for just 10 minutes or so.

Place a large flat plate, preferably one with a rim that can hold any syrup, over the pan, carefully flip the setup over and remove the pan. If any of the apples have stuck to the pan, use a table knife to gently pry them off and return them to their spot in the tart. If there's more than a little syrup on the plate, wipe it away.

The tart is ready to serve, with or without cream or ice cream.

STORING: Tarte Tatin is meant to be served the day it is made, preferably soon after it is baked. However, it will hold for a day lightly covered at room temperature. If you'd like, you can reheat it in a 350-degree-F oven or give it a few seconds in the microwave.

# Cottage Berry Cobbler

*Makes 8 servings*

## FOR THE BERRIES

About 6 cups (about 1 kilo) mixed berries (see headnote)

3 tablespoons sugar, or to taste

¼ cup (34 grams) all-purpose flour, plus more if desired (see headnote)

1 tablespoon finely chopped fresh herbs or 1 teaspoon spice (see headnote)

Juice of ½ lime or lemon, or to taste

## FOR THE BISCUITS

2 cups (172 grams) all-purpose flour

1 tablespoon baking powder

¼ teaspoon baking soda

½ teaspoon fine sea salt

¾ stick (6 tablespoons; 3 ounces; 85 grams) cold unsalted butter, cut into small chunks

½ cup (120 ml) cold milk, plus more for brushing

½ cup (125 grams) cold cottage cheese, preferably full-fat, drained if necessary

Sanding or granulated sugar for dusting

Strained Yogurt (see page 379), whipped cream or ice cream for serving (optional)

**A WORD ON THE BISCUITS:**
The cobbler will work with any kind of biscuit, so if there's a recipe that you particularly like, use it. No matter which recipe you choose, you'll get the prettiest cobbler if you follow the directions to shape the dough into a square and then cut biscuits from the square.

**A COBBLER IS** a combination of fruit and biscuits, an old-fashioned dessert that slips happily into any time of the day, even breakfast. It's also a dessert that accommodates fruits of all seasons, although juicy fruits are best. For this cobbler, I like using blackberries, blueberries, raspberries and halved strawberries. How much of each is up to you. Whereas with a pie you want to limit the amount of juice the fruit gives off, with a cobbler, abundant juice is a plus—it's nice to have "gravy" for the biscuits. (Add more flour if you'd prefer thicker juices.) If I've got herbs, I add them. The berries are good with mint, basil, lemon verbena and even a little lemon thyme; I do a mix. If you don't have herbs, use a little spice, perhaps ginger, cinnamon or coriander.

The constants in all this are the biscuits, and the ones I like best are made simply and spotlight cottage cheese. The dough comes together with fingers and a fork—no special equipment, no special skills. It's the perfect recipe for biscuit beginners.

**TO PREPARE THE BERRIES:** Mix all the ingredients together. Set aside while you make the biscuits, coming back from time to time to give the berries a stir.

Center a rack in the oven and preheat it to 375 degrees F. Lightly butter a 9-inch pie pan or round baking dish and put it on a baking sheet lined with parchment paper or a baking mat.

**TO MAKE THE BISCUITS:** Whisk the flour, baking powder, baking soda and salt together in a large bowl. Drop in the pieces of butter and use your fingers to toss and coat them with flour. Then rub, squeeze, squish, mash and cut in the butter until you've got a bowl full of pieces of every size from oatmeal flakes to baby peas. (If you prefer, you can do this with a pastry blender.) Pour over the cold milk and using a fork, gently toss, turn and stir. Stop before the dough comes together, add the cottage cheese and continue to mix—use a light hand—until you've got a soft, moist, lumpy dough that holds together when pinched. If there's a little flour at the bottom of the bowl, just leave it. ⟶

Lightly flour a work surface and scrape the dough onto it. Dust your hands with flour and pat the dough into a 5-inch square (don't worry about being exact). With a bench scraper or a long knife, cut the dough into 16 pieces (again, don't fuss over precision).

Stir the berries a couple of times, taste and see if there's anything you want to add, then turn them into the pie pan (or dish).

Arrange the squares of biscuit dough over the berries (if you find you don't want to use all of them, you can freeze the leftovers; see page 41). Try to leave a little space between the biscuits, but if some of them touch, that's fine. Brush the biscuits with milk and sprinkle them lightly with sanding or granulated sugar.

Bake the cobbler for 10 minutes, then lower the oven temperature to 350 degrees F. Bake for another 30 minutes or so—you'll know the cobbler is done when the biscuits are golden and the fruit is bubbling up around them. Transfer the baking sheet to a rack and cool the cobbler for at least 15 minutes before serving.

Serve warm (my choice) or at room temperature, with or without yogurt, whipped cream or ice cream on top.

STORING: The cobbler is at its best shortly after it comes from the oven—that's when the biscuits are most tender. However, there are fans of room-temperature cobblers too. If you've got leftovers, cover and keep in the refrigerator overnight. The biscuits won't be great, but the fruit will be good. I often just scoop out the fruit and have it with some yogurt.

## Playing Around

### NECTARINE-BERRY COBBLER

You will need about 2 pounds (about 900 grams) nectarines. (You can use peaches, but if you do, peel them.) Cut the fruit into chunks about 1 to 2 inches on a side. Add about 1 cup (150 grams) of blueberries and if you'd like, ½ to 1 teaspoon ground ginger or cardamom.

# Double-Pear Picnic Pie

*Makes 8 to 12 servings*

## FOR THE CRUST

1 recipe Sour Cream Pie Dough
(page 350), divided in two, shaped
into rectangles and chilled for at least
3 hours

## FOR THE FILLING

About 2 pounds (about 900 grams)
pears, such as Bartlett or Anjou (4 to
5 medium), peeled or not

5 moist, plump dried pears, finely
chopped, snipped or slivered

A few pieces moist, plump candied
ginger, finely chopped or snipped
(optional but delicious)

3 tablespoons apricot jam or orange
marmalade

2 tablespoons sugar

Grated zest and juice of ½ lemon

Cream or milk for brushing

Sanding, turbinado or granulated sugar
for sprinkling

**A WORD ON THE PAN:** I like
to bake this in a quarter sheet
pan, a rimmed baking sheet
that's 9 × 12 inches. You can use
a similar-sized baking pan. If all
you've got is a large rimmed
baking sheet, run a double
thickness of foil across the middle
of it to serve as a divider and build
the pie in half of the pan.

**AND A WORD ON WORKING
AHEAD:** You can assemble the pie,
freeze it unbaked and then, when
you're ready for it, brush the crust
with cream, sprinkle with sugar and
slide it into the oven. It might need
a few more minutes in the oven, so
watch the color of the crust.

**A PICNIC PIE** sets me thinking of easy-going family meals,
of coffee and conversation and of course, of picnics, whether
indoors or out. There's something generous and inviting about
these large, slim, fruit-filled pastries, built in low-rimmed
pans, baked to bubbling and cut into squares. My filling's a
mix of fresh and dried pears, with some candied ginger and a
good hit of lemon zest and juice. As for the crust, it's a tender
sour-cream dough that's easy to work with and bakes to a
beautiful golden brown.

A picnic pie is more idea than edict, so fill it with
whatever you'd like. Feel free to swap the crust as well (see
Playing Around).

**TO ROLL THE CRUST:** Line the bottom of a quarter sheet pan
or 9-x-12-inch baking pan with parchment paper (see at left).
Alternatively, you can butter the pan and bake the pie without the
paper (it may or may not stick, but most of the time it doesn't) and
serve the pie straight from the pan.

Dust a work surface with flour, put one of the dough rectangles on
it and dust the top, then roll until you have a sheet that's 11 inches
wide and 16 inches long. Turn the dough over from time to time
and keep the work space floured just enough so you can move the
dough around.

Roll the dough up on your pin and then unroll it into the pan, letting
the excess drape over the sides. Fit the dough into the pan, gently
pressing it against the bottom and sides; if it splits or breaks, press
it together with a moistened finger. If you've got a bare patch, cut
some of the excess dough and glue it where you need it. Slide
the pan into the refrigerator while you roll out the second piece of
dough and make the filling.

Roll the second piece of dough into an 11-x-16-inch rectangle,
sandwich it between pieces of parchment, slide it onto a baking
sheet or cutting board and refrigerate until needed. (*The rolled-out
crusts can be frozen, well wrapped, for up to 2 months.*)

**TO MAKE THE FILLING:** The fresh pears should be cut into thin slices, but the slices shouldn't be so thin that they bend. I like to use a mandoline or food processor, but you can cut the fruit easily by hand. Toss the pears into a large bowl, add the rest of the ingredients and stir to blend, a job best done with your hands. Set the filling aside for 10 minutes, then toss again.

**TO ASSEMBLE THE PIE:** Remove the lined pan from the fridge and scoop the filling into the crust. If you've got a lot of liquid in the bowl, just drizzle a little of it over the filling—you don't need much, since the pears will release some liquid as they bake. Spread the filling evenly over the crust, nudging the fruit into the corners. Moisten the edges of the dough with a little water.

Arrange the second piece of dough over the filling; if the top crust is too cold to be pliable, wait a couple of minutes. Working your way around the pan, press the two layers of dough together. If you're using a quarter sheet pan, which has low sides, use a knife to cut the double layer of dough even with the top of the pan, press the layers together and flute them or fold them inward. If you're using a taller pan, cut the dough to a height of ½ to 1 inch and fold it over—flute it if you'd like. No matter how you've finished the edges, moisten your finger and seal them. Refrigerate the pie while you preheat the oven. (*The pie can be frozen, well wrapped, for up to 2 months; see headnote.*)

Center a rack in the oven and preheat it to 375 degrees F. Line a baking sheet with parchment or a baking mat.

When the oven is hot, put the pie on the baking sheet. Brush the top of the pie with cream or milk, sprinkle with sugar and cut at least 6 slits in the top crust—if you want, you can cut more slits in any design that pleases you.

Bake the pie for 50 to 55 minutes—if it looks like it's getting too brown, tent it loosely with foil or parchment—or until you see some juice bubbling through the slits. It's possible that you'll have juices bubbling around the side of the pie—it seems to happen even when you've sealed the edges meticulously; it also never seems to spoil the enjoyment of the pie.

Transfer the pie to a rack and leave for 5 minutes. If you want to turn the pie out of the pan, put a piece of parchment or a baking mat on the work surface (or don't, the drips are only syrup) and top with a rack, then run a table knife around the edges of the pie if you think they might be stuck and turn the pan over onto the rack. Peel away the paper, if you used it, and turn the pie right side up onto another rack. (If you didn't use paper and the pie has stuck, turn the pan back over again and just cut the pie in the pan when you're ready.) Cool for at least 20 minutes, or until the pie comes to room temperature.

**STORING:** Most pies are meant to be eaten the day they are made. This one's okay the day after, but the crust will soften overnight.

## Playing Around

You can make this with All-Butter Pie Dough (page 347; make 1½ recipes) and it will be great, but I hope you'll try it with the sour cream dough first.

You can substitute apples for the pears. Leave the peel on some of the apples and swap dried apple rings for the dried pears. Or, in summer, try this with berries (leave out the dried fruit or add dried cherries or cranberries, which are nice with all kinds of berries), nectarines or peeled peaches. In fall, try plums, maybe with some prunes, which, after all, are dried plums. And in winter, make it with fresh pineapple.

# Father's Day Blueberry-Cherry Pie

*Makes 8 servings*

1 recipe All-Butter Pie Dough (page 347), divided in two, each piece rolled into an 11- to 12-inch round and chilled (or use store-bought dough; see below)

## FOR THE FILLING

1½ pounds (680 grams) sweet cherries, pitted and halved

1 quart (600 grams) blueberries

3 tablespoons water

4 to 6 tablespoons sugar

¼ to ½ teaspoon fine sea salt

Finely grated zest and juice of 1 lime or lemon (or half of each)

2½ to 3 tablespoons all-purpose flour

About ½ teaspoon ground cinnamon or coriander (optional)

2 tablespoons almond flour or dry bread crumbs

Milk for brushing

## FOR THE GLAZE (OPTIONAL)

About 2 teaspoons water

¼ cup (30 grams) confectioners' sugar

**A WORD ON THE CRUST:** If you don't have time to make the All-Butter Pie Dough, you can use store-bought. Look for pie dough that's already rolled out and buy two: one to press into the pie pan and one to use as a top crust.

**A WORD ON WORKING AHEAD:** The unbaked pie can be frozen for up to 2 months; wrap airtight once it's frozen solid. Bake directly from the freezer if using a metal pie pan; if Pyrex, let it sit at room temperature while you preheat the oven.

**FATHER'S DAY 2020** was particularly special, since it fell about five weeks before my son, Joshua, was to become a father. I made a pie that I thought would make both Michael and Joshua happy. They both love blueberries, but Michael's got a nostalgic spot in his heart for the cherry pie of his college days—that packaged snack pie glazed with a confectioners' sugar icing. And so, on that landmark day, I made a pie with equal parts blueberries and sweet cherries and gave it a sugar glaze (which you can consider optional). You could go with all blueberries or all cherries, but if you make an all-cherry pie, I'd suggest you add lime juice—sweet cherries are delicious eaten out of hand, but they can bake up bland.

It's not too much to think about serving the pie with Berry Ice Cream (page 376) made with blueberries. Ice cream or whipped cream would be good too.

Butter a 9-inch pie pan and fit one piece of the dough into it. Don't trim away the excess dough; just let it drape over the sides of the pan. Put the pan and the top round of dough in the refrigerator until you're ready for them.

Center a rack in the oven and preheat it to 425 degrees F. Line a baking sheet with parchment or a baking mat.

**TO MAKE THE FILLING:** Put half of the cherries and half of the blueberries in a medium saucepan. Stir in the water, ¼ cup (50 grams) of the sugar, ¼ teaspoon of the salt and the zest. Cook over medium-high heat, staying close and stirring often, until the mixture boils and thickens into a jam; this will take at least 6 minutes and maybe as many as 10.

Stir in 2½ tablespoons flour and cook for another minute or two. The mixture should be thick, as in gloppy. If it's not, stir in another ½ tablespoon flour and cook for another minute. Remove the pan from the heat.  ⟶

*Pies, Tarts, Cobblers and Crisps*

If the pan is large enough to hold the rest of the fruit, keep working in it; if not, scrape the jam into a large bowl. Stir the remaining blueberries and cherries into the jam, along with the citrus juice. Taste and see if you'd like more sugar. If you want to add spice, stir it in now.

Take the crusts out of the fridge and sprinkle the almond flour or bread crumbs over the bottom crust. Scrape the filling into the crust, nudging it into the corners. Peel away the paper from the top crust and check to see if it's pliable—if it's not, wait a couple of minutes. (The crust needs to be just bendable enough that it won't crack when you fit it over the fruit.) Moisten the rim of the bottom crust and lift the top crust onto the pie, draping it over the filling. Very gently press the top crust against the fruit and then use your fingers to press the top and bottom crusts together.

Trim the excess dough away, cutting it even with the edges of the pan, and finish the pie by pressing the border with the tines of a fork. (If you want to flute the border, don't trim the dough that hangs over the edge of the pan—use it for the fluting.) Cut out a small circle from the center of the crust (I use a piping tip or a cookie cutter). (*At this point, the pie can be frozen for up to 2 months; see headnote.*)

Brush the crust with milk and put the pie on the lined baking sheet. Bake for 25 minutes, then cover the edges of the crust with foil to protect them. Lower the oven temperature to 375 degrees F and bake for another 40 minutes or so (total time is about 65 minutes), until the crust is golden and, most important, the filling is bubbling. Check the filling's progress by peeking through the center opening. If the filling bubbles up and over the crust, your pie will be even more beautiful. Transfer the pie to a rack.

**IMMEDIATELY MAKE THE OPTIONAL GLAZE IF USING:** Working in a small bowl, stir a teaspoon of cold water into the sugar. Continue to add water by the droplet until you've got a glaze that you can easily brush across the pie. Using a pastry or silicone brush, coat the top of the warm pie with the glaze.

The pie is ready to serve when it's just warm or at room temperature.

**STORING:** Pie is always at its most delectable the day it is made. However, this one will hold for a day lightly covered at room temperature or in the fridge. If you want to warm the pie, pop it into a 350-degree-F oven (the glaze may get wonky, but the pie will still be good).

# My Favorite Pumpkin Pie

*Makes 8 servings*

One 9-inch piecrust made with All-Butter Pie Dough (page 347) or Sour Cream Pie Dough (page 350), partially baked and cooled (or use a store-bought piecrust; see below)

FOR THE FILLING

1 can (15 ounces; 425 grams) pumpkin puree (*not* pumpkin pie filling)

1 cup (240 ml) heavy cream

½ cup (120 ml) sour cream

3 large eggs

⅔ cup (133 grams) packed brown sugar

1½ teaspoons ground ginger

1 teaspoon star anise powder (see below)

½ teaspoon fine sea salt

2 tablespoons dark rum

2 teaspoons pure vanilla extract

Lightly sweetened whipped cream for topping or serving

A WORD ON STAR ANISE POWDER: If you can't find ground star anise, you can do what I do and grind the whole spice in a small coffee grinder. Or you can instead go with just cinnamon or ¼ teaspoon cinnamon and ¼ teaspoon Chinese five-spice powder, which contains star anise. It's a bit more savory, but nice with the pumpkin, ginger and cinnamon.

A WORD ON THE CRUST: If you don't have time to make the All-Butter or Sour Cream Pie Dough, you can use a store-bought piecrust or even a graham cracker crust. If you decide on a graham cracker, make sure to buy a large crust; one that says it serves 10 should be the right size.

FOR YEARS, I fiddled with pumpkin pie, sure that there was another mix of ingredients that would make it even creamier or another blend of spices that would send it into another orbit. This is the filling that ended my fiddling. It's as silky as a French custard, and the spices, while sparer than usual, are enchanting. There's no cinnamon, nutmeg or allspice, pumpkin pie's usual spices. Instead, there's ginger and star anise, a match that sparks pumpkin's one-dimensional flavor. The bit of dark rum is a booster as well.

Center a rack in the oven and preheat it to 350 degrees F. Put the pie pan with the partially baked crust on a baking sheet lined with parchment paper or a baking mat.

TO MAKE THE FILLING: Put all the ingredients in a blender or a food processor and whir, scraping the container as needed, until you've got a smooth mixture. (Or you can just whisk the ingredients together.) Rap the container against the counter a few times to try to pop as many bubbles as possible. Pour the filling into the crust—you may have a little more filling than the crust can hold (especially if your crust shrank a bit when it was baked)—it's hard to calculate this.

BAKE THE PIE FOR 35 MINUTES AND THEN CHECK IT: You want to bake it until the filling is puffed and set around the edges but just set at the center. You'll probably need another 5 minutes or even another 10, but it's always good to check early. When the pie is done, carefully transfer the baking sheet to a rack and let the pie cool until it's only just warm or at room temperature. (The pie can also be served chilled.)

When you're ready to serve, cover the top of the pie with whipped cream or slice the pie and serve the cream on the side.

STORING: Without a whipped cream topping, the pie can stand at room temperature for up to 8 hours. You can keep it refrigerated for another day, but its texture won't be as luxurious.

## Playing Around

### MARSHMALLOW-TOPPED PUMPKIN PIE

Like more classic pumpkin pies, this one's good with marshmallows. When the filling is at room temperature, or after it's chilled, cover the edges of the crust with foil. Set a rack about 10 inches below the broiler and preheat the broiler. Cover the entire surface of the pie with mini marshmallows (or with halved full-size marshmallows) and toast until golden, 1 to 3 minutes. Or, if you've got a kitchen torch, use it. Serve the pie immediately, or within the hour.

# Maple-Walnut Pie

*Makes 8 servings*

One 9-inch piecrust made with All-Butter Pie Dough (page 347) or Sour Cream Pie Dough (page 350), partially baked and cooled (or use a store-bought piecrust)

### FOR THE FILLING

¾ cup (180 ml) pure maple syrup

½ cup (100 grams) packed brown sugar

3 large eggs, at room temperature

1½ teaspoons pure vanilla extract

½ teaspoon fine sea salt

½ teaspoon ground cinnamon, or more to taste

3 tablespoons (1½ ounces; 42 grams) unsalted butter, melted and cooled

1½ cups (200 grams) walnuts (halves or pieces)

Lightly sweetened whipped cream or ice cream for serving (optional)

**A WORD ON THE CRUST:** You can finish the edge of the crust any way you'd like, including with flutes. Often I just press the dough against the rim of the pie pan and then trim it even all around. Sometimes I decorate it by pressing the tines of a fork against the edges.

## Playing Around

### PECAN PIE

You can swap the maple syrup for light (my preference) or dark corn syrup, and pecans for the walnuts. If you want to serve pecan pie to my husband, please add some chopped dark chocolate or chocolate chips; ½ cup (85 grams) should do it.

I DIDN'T REALLY mean to shake up a holiday classic, but when the sack I had in the freezer turned out to have walnuts, not pecans, I made the swap. I made another change too: I replaced the traditional pecan-pie sweetener, corn syrup, with maple syrup, a natural with walnuts. The pie has the bumpy, lightly crusty top that I love in pecan pie. And the filling's got that characteristic softness broken up by pieces of nuts. But the pie has additional pleasures: a slight, welcome touch of bitterness, since walnuts aren't as sweet as pecans, and a little crunch, since the meaty nuts retain their bite, such a delightful surprise. Of course you can make this pie with pecans and/or with corn syrup, if you'd like (see Playing Around), but I hope you'll give this new combination a try.

Center a rack in the oven and preheat it to 400 degrees F. Put the pan with the partially baked crust on a baking sheet lined with parchment paper or a baking mat.

TO MAKE THE FILLING: Whisk the syrup and brown sugar together in a large bowl. One by one, whisk in the eggs, making sure each is blended in before adding the next. Whisk in the vanilla, salt and cinnamon, followed by the butter. Switch to a flexible spatula, add the walnuts and stir until they're coated. Turn the filling into the crust and poke the nuts down with the spatula.

Slide the pie into the oven and bake for 5 minutes. Reduce the oven temperature to 350 degrees F and bake the pie for another 30 to 35 minutes, but take a look at the crust after 10 minutes—if it looks brown, cover it with foil. You want to bake the pie until it has puffed all the way to the center. It will rise high and crack, and that's fine—it will settle itself down within minutes as it cools. Transfer the pie to a rack and cool to room temperature.

Serve the pie with whipped cream or ice cream, if you'd like.

STORING: The pie is best the day it is made. If you've got leftovers, you can leave them covered at room temperature or chill them—they're good, but different each way.

# Lick-the-Pot Chocolate Pudding Pie

*Makes 8 servings*

## FOR THE CRUMB CRUST

2½ cups (about 250 grams) cookie crumbs, made from Bastagone, Lotus Biscoff or other spice cookies (about 1 box)

½ stick (4 tablespoons; 2 ounces; 57 grams) unsalted butter, melted

## FOR THE PUDDING

7 ounces (200 grams) bittersweet chocolate (see Playing Around), finely chopped

2¼ cups (540 ml) milk, preferably whole

⅓ cup (67 grams) sugar

4 large egg yolks

3 tablespoons cornstarch

½ teaspoon fine sea salt

2 tablespoons unsalted butter

1½ teaspoons pure vanilla extract

## FOR THE TOPPING

¼ cup (56 grams) mascarpone

½ cup (120 ml) very cold heavy cream

2 tablespoons confectioners' sugar, sifted

1 teaspoon pure vanilla extract

**PLAN AHEAD:** The pudding needs to be cold, so plan to refrigerate it for at least 3 hours.

MY HUSBAND CAN WALK into the kitchen a dozen times, see me baking, smile and walk out. But if I'm at the stove stirring this chocolate pudding, he's there, looking over my shoulder, waiting to grab the pot before I spoon out the last of the thick, shiny pudding. That he loves the pudding in this pie, which has a spice cookie crumb crust and is finished with a generous layer of mascarpone whipped cream, is clear—there's never a sliver left over.

TO MAKE THE CRUST: Put the crumbs and melted butter in a 9- to 9½-inch pie pan and use your hands to toss them together until the crumbs are thoroughly moistened. Press the crumbs firmly over the bottom and up the sides of the pan. If you're using a 9-inch pan, the crust will be thickish, and that's nice. Refrigerate for at least 30 minutes.

Center a rack in the oven and preheat it to 350 degrees F.

Place the pie pan on a baking sheet and bake the crust for 10 minutes. Let cool while you make the filling. (*The crust can be cooled, covered and refrigerated for up to 3 days or frozen, well wrapped, for up to 2 months.*)

TO MAKE THE PUDDING: Melt the chocolate—you can do this in a microwave or in a heatproof bowl set over a pan of gently simmering water (don't let the water touch the bowl). Set aside.

Rinse out a medium saucepan with cold water, but don't dry it (this helps keep the milk from scorching), pour in the milk and add half the sugar. Stir, then bring the milk just to a boil.

While the milk is heating, whisk the remaining sugar, the yolks, cornstarch and salt together in a large bowl. Place the bowl on a dish towel or a silicone pot holder to anchor it. Whisking the yolk mixture without stopping, slowly drizzle in about ½ cup (120 ml) of the hot milk. (Adding it slowly keeps the yolks from scrambling.) Still whisking, add the remainder of the milk in a slow, steady stream.

Rinse out the saucepan with cold water and pour in the pudding. Put the pan over medium heat and, whisking nonstop and taking care to get into the corners of the pan, cook until the pudding thickens and a bubble or two pops on the surface. Lower the heat and—whisking, whisking, whisking—simmer the pudding for another 2 minutes. Off the heat, whisk in the melted chocolate, followed by the butter and vanilla.

Give the pudding one last, grand whisk, then pour it into the crust. (If you've got some leftover, pour it into a cup to enjoy later.) Gently swivel the pie pan to even the pudding, then press a piece of plastic wrap against the surface and refrigerate the pie for at least 3 hours. (*The pie can be refrigerated for up to 2 days.*)

TO MAKE THE TOPPING: Put the mascarpone in the bowl of a stand mixer or a bowl that you can use with a hand mixer. Stir the mascarpone with a spatula or fork, just to break it up. Attach the mixer bowl to the mixer stand, if using, and fit it with the whisk attachment. Pour the cream and confectioners' sugar into the bowl and beat on medium-high until the cream holds medium peaks. With the mixer on low, add the vanilla. (*If you have to make the topping ahead, line a strainer with damp cheesecloth, spoon in the topping, cover with damp cheesecloth, put the strainer over a bowl and keep refrigerated until needed, up to 5 hours.*)

TO FINISH: Spread the topping over the pie; you can do this up to 2 hours ahead and keep the pie refrigerated until you are ready for it.

STORING: The pie is best served soon after it's finished with the topping.

## Playing Around

I prefer the pudding made with bittersweet chocolate, but it will also take to semisweet or milk chocolate. If you use a sweeter chocolate, you might want to cut down the sugar by a tablespoon or two.

You can make the pie in a fully baked traditional piecrust (like the all-butter crust; page 347) or a store-bought graham cracker crust. Or skip the crust and ladle the pudding into cups—you'll get 6 servings.

# Strawberry Cheesecake–Chocolate No-Bake Pie

*Makes 8 servings*

## FOR THE GANACHE

½ cup (120 ml) heavy cream

4 ounces (113 grams) semisweet or bittersweet chocolate, finely chopped

2 tablespoons unsalted butter, cut into 4 pieces

1 Graham Cracker Crust (page 358), baked and cooled (buy the larger size), or a store-bought piecrust, or a 9- to 9½-inch tart crust made with Chocolate Tart Dough (page 349), fully baked and cooled

## FOR THE CHEESECAKE

4 ounces (113 grams) finest-quality white chocolate, finely chopped

8 ounces (226 grams) cream cheese, softened

¼ cup (50 grams) sugar

2 teaspoons pure vanilla extract

⅓ cup (80 ml) sour cream or ricotta

½ cup (120 ml) very cold heavy cream

About 10 strawberries, hulled and halved lengthwise

## TO FINISH (OPTIONAL)

About 10 strawberries, hulled

Chocolate shavings

HERE'S A PIE that harbors secrets. Tucked away at the bottom is a thin layer of dark chocolate ganache with a lush texture and full-on chocolate flavor. Next come strawberries, fresh, juicy, sweet and brilliantly red, which are then hidden under a layer of a light cheesecake, subtly flavored with white chocolate and ever so slightly sharpened by cream cheese and sour cream. You can leave the pie plain—its pristine white top is lovely—but I add more strawberries and a dusting of shaved dark chocolate.

To make this a truly no-bake dessert, use a store-bought graham cracker crust. To make it more elegant, use the chocolate crust.

TO MAKE THE GANACHE: Rinse a small saucepan with cold water, but don't dry it (this helps prevent the cream from scorching). Pour in the cream and, working over medium heat, bring it just to a boil. Turn off the heat and add the chocolate to the pan. Wait for 30 seconds and then, working with a small flexible spatula and starting in the center of the pan, stir the chocolate and cream together. Keep stirring in ever-widening concentric circles until you have a thick, shiny, smooth mixture. Piece by piece, blend in the butter.

Pour the ganache into the crust, leveling it with the spatula. Slide the crust into the refrigerator or freezer while you make the cheesecake layer.

TO MAKE THE CHEESECAKE: Put the white chocolate in a small microwave-safe bowl, set the microwave to 50-percent power and work in short spurts, stirring the chocolate often and gently, to melt it. You can also do this in a heatproof bowl set over a pan of simmering water (don't let the water touch the bowl).

Working in a large bowl with a flexible spatula, beat the cream cheese and sugar together until smooth and creamy. Stir in the vanilla, followed by the melted white chocolate and the sour cream or ricotta. Beat until the mixture is fully blended.

Whip the cream to firm peaks with a mixer or by hand, then fold it into the cheesecake mixture.

TO ASSEMBLE THE PIE: Remove the crust from the refrigerator or freezer. Arrange the halved strawberries cut side down over the chilled ganache. You may or may not use all the berries, but you want to be generous and to keep the berries in a single layer—they'll look prettier when you cut the pie. Cover the berries with the cheesecake mixture.

TO FINISH THE PIE (OPTIONAL): If you'd like (and I always do), decorate the top of the pie with strawberries—they can be sliced, halved or, if they're tiny, left whole—and then, if you'd like, finish the pie with a shower of shaved chocolate.

Serve now, or refrigerate the pie until needed. I think it's best after it's had a little time in the fridge.

STORING: The pie can be kept covered in the refrigerator overnight.

## Playing Around

This combination of layers is fun to play with. Instead of the strawberries, try soft fruits, such as raspberries or blackberries, sliced bananas, small pieces of pineapple, thin slices of apricots, figs or pitted cherries (think Black Forest Cake). You could also consider nixing the fruit for a thin layer of jam or marmalade (4 or 5 tablespoons should do it) between the ganache and the cheesecake (freeze the jam layer for 10 minutes to set it before topping with the cheesecake); finish with chocolate shavings.

# French Riviera Lemon Tart

*Makes 6 to 8 servings*

## FOR THE CRUST

1 cup (136 grams) all-purpose flour

¼ cup (30 grams) confectioners' sugar

¼ teaspoon fine sea salt

½ stick (4 tablespoons; 2 ounces; 57 grams) unsalted butter, at room temperature

3½ tablespoons mild olive oil

1 large egg yolk

## FOR THE FILLING

¾ cup (150 grams) sugar

2 teaspoons cornstarch

Finely grated zest of 1 lemon

⅔ cup (160 ml) freshly squeezed lemon juice (from 4 to 5 large lemons)

2 large eggs

2 large egg yolks

½ stick (4 tablespoons; 2 ounces; 57 grams) unsalted butter, cut into small pieces

2 tablespoons mild olive oil

Whipped cream, crème fraîche or ice cream for serving (optional)

THIS RECIPE SHOULD BE filed under "magic trick": You make the crust with just a fork and your fingers, press it into the pan and bake it—no machines, no chilling and only ten minutes in a very hot oven. Then, while the crust is cooling on a rack, you prepare the lemon filling, another ten minutes' worth of work. Fill the crust, slide it into the fridge for an hour and, abracadabra, it's done! The crust is sweet and crumbly, cookie-like but tender. And the filling manages to be smack-your-lips puckery and refined at the same time. Thin, satiny smooth, lithe and seductive, it sets to a shine that I was certain only pâtissiers could achieve. Both the crust and the filling use olive oil—not surprisingly, since the tart comes from one of the richest olive-growing regions in France.

The tart is the creation of my friend Rosa Jackson, who taught it as part of a class in her sunny atelier, Les Petits Farcis, in Nice. It's simple and luscious.

Center a rack in the oven and preheat it to 425 degrees F. Place a 9- to 9-½-inch tart pan (one with fluted sides and a removable bottom) on a baking sheet lined with parchment paper or a baking mat.

TO MAKE THE CRUST: Whisk 2 tablespoons of the flour, the confectioners' sugar and salt together in a large bowl. Drop in the pieces of butter and, using your fingers, squeeze, mash and press everything together until the butter is fairly well blended into the dry ingredients. Add the rest of the flour and stir the mixture with your hand—there's too much flour to fully incorporate now, so just get it started. Stir the olive oil and yolk together, pour the mixture into the bowl and, still working by hand, mix and press and even knead a bit to draw all the ingredients together into a smooth ball. It takes a very short time, and when the dough comes together, it's very satisfying.

Press the dough evenly over the bottom and up the sides of the pan. If the dough runs up above the rim of the pan, trim it with a small knife. ⟶

Bake the crust for 10 to 12 minutes, or until it's lightly golden all over. Transfer the crust, still on the baking sheet, to a rack and let it rest while you make the filling. (*The crust can be kept at room temperature for up to 1 day or wrapped airtight once cooled and frozen for up to 2 months.*)

TO MAKE THE FILLING: Whisk the sugar, cornstarch, lemon zest and juice together in a medium saucepan. Drop in the eggs and yolks and whisk to blend. Place the pan over medium heat and whisk, whisk, whisk. You needn't be vigorous, but you must be vigilant—you want to make sure that the whisk is covering the entire bottom of the pan and that the mixture never boils. After 7 to 10 minutes (the amount of time depends on your pan and how much heat you've got under it), you'll notice that the mixture has lightened a bit in color, has thickened just a tad and has a layer of bubbles on top—you're there. (If you've got an instant-read thermometer, you're looking to reach about 160 degrees F.)

Pull the pan from the heat and whisk for a minute or so, then add the butter piece by piece, whisking until each one is incorporated before adding the next. Whisk in the olive oil. Pour the filling into the crust.

Refrigerate the tart for at least 1 hour, or until the filling is set. (*Once the tart has set, you can cover the top and keep it in the fridge for up to 1 day.*)

Serve the tart cold or just cool, with or without whipped cream, crème fraîche or vanilla ice cream on the side.

STORING: The tart is best eaten the day or the day after it's made.

# *Rhubarb-Bottom, Strawberry-Top Tart*

*Makes 6 to 8 servings*

### FOR THE BERRY PASTRY CREAM

2 cups (225 grams) chopped
    strawberries

1¼ cups (300 ml) milk

3 large egg yolks

⅓ cup (67 grams) sugar

3½ tablespoons (28 grams) cornstarch

Pinch of fine sea salt

1½ teaspoons pure vanilla extract

Red food coloring (optional)

### FOR THE RHUBARB

¼ cup (60 ml) water

¼ cup (50 grams) sugar

Slice of lime

2 to 3 slender stalks rhubarb, trimmed and
    cut crosswise into ¼-inch-wide slices

One 9- to 9½-inch tart shell made with
    Sweet Tart Dough (page 348), baked
    and cooled

About 1 quart (about 680 grams)
    strawberries

1 lime

**PLAN AHEAD:** The pastry cream
needs to be chilled for 2 hours.

I LOVE A DESSERT that looks like it follows all the rules, then turns out to be a rebel. This has all the components of a classic fruit tart: a sweet crust, a pastry cream filling and a fruit topping. But it's also got a hidden layer of quickly poached rhubarb—it's cooked for only a minute, so it retains its striking personality. Even the fruit topping has a surprise: Fresh strawberries are brushed with a little of the poaching syrup and then, at the very last minute, get a perk-up squirt of lime juice and a shower of zest. But it's the pastry cream that's the least expected element here—it's made with pureed strawberries. Replacing part of the milk in the traditional recipe with fruit is a neat way to pack in more flavor. Always a good thing. (Of course the tart can be made with traditional Vanilla Pastry Cream, page 360, and it will be lovely.)

You can prepare everything but the cut-up fruit for the top ahead of time, but try to put the tart together as close to serving time as possible, so the crust will be crisp, the cream cold and the fruit bright.

TO MAKE THE PASTRY CREAM: Puree the strawberries using an immersion or regular blender or a food processor. You should have ¾ cup.

Rinse a medium saucepan with cold water, but don't dry it (this will help keep the milk from scorching), pour in the milk and bring almost to a boil.

Meanwhile, whisk the yolks, sugar, cornstarch and salt together in a medium bowl until blended. Place the bowl on a dish towel or a silicone pot holder to anchor it. Whisking constantly, drizzle in one quarter of the hot milk, then add the remaining milk in a steadier stream. Return the mixture to the saucepan, put it over medium heat and, whisking vigorously—make sure to get into the corners of the pan—bring to a boil. Whisk in the strawberry puree and, whisking without stopping, let the cream boil for 1 to 2 minutes.

Scrape the pastry cream into a clean bowl and add the vanilla. If you'd like, stir in a few drops of food coloring. Press a piece of plastic wrap against the surface of the cream and refrigerate until it's thoroughly chilled, at least 2 hours. (*The cream can be refrigerated for up to 3 days.*)

TO POACH THE RHUBARB: Bring the water, sugar and lime slice to a boil in a small saucepan. Drop in the rhubarb and poach for 1 minute. Drain in a strainer set over a bowl; hold on to both the fruit and the syrup. (*You can poach the rhubarb a day ahead. Let the fruit and syrup cool separately and then combine them in a jar; refrigerate.*)

TO ASSEMBLE THE TART: If you combined the rhubarb and syrup, drain the rhubarb (save the syrup). Scatter the pieces of rhubarb over the bottom of the tart shell. Give the pastry cream a few brisk turns with a spatula to get it to spreadable and then fill the tart with it, smoothing the top. Decide how you'd like to cut the strawberries—I usually cut them in half the long way—and cover the cream with them, pressing them gently into the cream. Stir a squirt of lime juice into the rhubarb syrup and lightly brush the syrup over the berries. You could serve the tart now, but if you've got time, refrigerate it for at least 1 hour to firm up the cream. (*The tart can be refrigerated for up to 8 hours.*)

When you're ready to serve the tart, finely grate the zest from about half the lime. Sparingly sprinkle some lime juice over the berries and finish with the zest.

STORING: The tart is best served the day it is made, but you can refrigerate leftovers, covered, for up to a day.

## *Playing Around*

This is a recipe to have fun with: The technique of replacing some of the milk in the pastry cream with strawberry puree works with other soft fruits—think mango or berries.

BERRY PUDDING

The pastry cream filling makes a lovely pudding on its own; if you'd like, you can double the recipe. Spoon it into small bowls and top with fresh berries and grated lime zest.

# Cocoa-Cranberry Linzer Tart

*Makes 8 servings*

## FOR THE CRUST

1¾ cups (6¼ ounces; 175 grams) almond flour, or an equal weight of almonds, finely ground in a food processor

1⅓ cups (181 grams) all-purpose flour

2 tablespoons unsweetened cocoa powder

1¼ teaspoons ground cinnamon

¾ teaspoons ground ginger

½ teaspoon fine sea salt

1 stick (8 tablespoons; 4 ounces; 113 grams) cool unsalted butter, cut into chunks

⅔ cup (132 grams) sugar

1 large egg, at room temperature

½ teaspoon pure vanilla extract

2 ounces (57 grams) semisweet or bittersweet chocolate, finely chopped

## FOR THE FILLING

About 2 cups (255 grams) cranberries, fresh or frozen (no need to thaw)

½ cup (120 ml) raspberry jam (with or without seeds)

¼ cup (60 ml) water

3 tablespoons sugar

½ to 1 teaspoon pink peppercorns, finely chopped (optional)

About 20 raspberries (optional)

Sanding or granulated sugar for sprinkling

**I'VE BEEN A FAN** of Linzer tarts since childhood. I love the crumbly nut dough with its hint of spice, and the jam filling, traditionally raspberry. There was a bakery near our house that made Linzer cookies and tarts, but not all the time, so that when my mom did bring them home, they were always a surprise and a treat. In my Linzer, the nuts in the crust are almonds; the spices include cinnamon, which is usual, and ginger, which is not; and I add both cocoa and chopped chocolate. Although the filling has raspberry jam, along with a few fresh raspberries, if you want them, the primary flavor comes from sharp cranberries—perfect with the chocolate and spice. Instead of making a lattice tart, I sandwich the cranberry jam between two rounds of the cookie-like crust.

**TO MAKE THE CRUST:** Whir both flours, the cocoa, cinnamon, ginger and salt together in a food processor just to blend. Turn the ingredients out onto a large piece of parchment (you'll use the paper again to roll out the dough).

Put the butter and sugar in the processor and process until smooth, scraping the bowl as needed. Add the egg and vanilla and process to incorporate. Use the parchment to funnel the dry ingredients into the processor and pulse until you have a bowl of moist curds (set the parchment aside). Scatter over the chocolate and pulse just to combine.

Turn the dough out and knead it gently into a ball, then cut it in half and flatten each piece into a disk.

Working with one half at a time, roll each piece of dough between sheets of parchment until you've got a circle that's just large enough to allow you to cut a 9-inch round from it (you'll do this later). Keeping them between the parchment, stack the rounds on a baking sheet and refrigerate or freeze until you need them. (*Once they are firm, you can wrap the rounds airtight and freeze for up to 2 months.*)

TO MAKE THE FILLING: Place all the ingredients *except* the fresh raspberries in a medium saucepan and bring to a boil over medium heat, stirring frequently. Lower the temperature to a simmer and cook, stirring, until the cranberries start to pop, then continue to cook on low, stirring, for 3 minutes more. Scrape the jam into a bowl, cover and cool to room temperature. (*You can pack the jam into a tightly covered jar and refrigerate it for up to 1 week.*)

TO ASSEMBLE AND BAKE THE TART: Center a rack in the oven and preheat it to 375 degrees F. Butter a 9-inch cake pan, preferably one that's 2 inches high, and have a baking sheet lined with parchment paper or a baking mat at hand.

Using the bottom of the cake pan as a guide, trim each round of dough to the size of the pan. Fit one piece into the pan and spread the cranberry jam evenly over it; dot with the fresh raspberries, if you're using them. Cut a small steam circle in the center of the second round of dough and set it over the filling, gently pressing the dough into place. (You aren't sealing the tart—the jam layer is meant to be exposed on the sides.) Put the pan on the lined baking sheet and sprinkle the top with sanding or granulated sugar.

Bake the tart for 45 to 50 minutes, or until the filling is bubbling; loosely tent the top with a piece of foil or parchment if you think it's getting too dark, too fast. Transfer the pan to a rack and let rest for 20 minutes, then run a table knife around the sides. Unmold the tart onto the rack and then turn it over onto another rack or a serving plate. (*Once cooled, the tart can be frozen, well wrapped, for up to 2 months.*)

Serve the tart warm or at room temperature.

STORING: Any leftover tart can be covered and kept in the refrigerator for up to 2 days. Enjoy it cold, or let it come to room temperature.

# Alsatian-Style Blueberry Tart

*Makes 6 servings*

One 9- to 9½- inch tart shell made with Sweet Tart Dough (page 348), partially baked and cooled

2 tablespoons almond flour or dry bread crumbs

¼ cup (50 grams) sugar

¼ teaspoon ground cinnamon

About 3½ cups (about 525 grams) blueberries

1 large egg

½ cup (120 ml) heavy cream

½ teaspoon pure vanilla extract

Pinch of fine sea salt

Confectioners' sugar for dusting (optional)

WHILE THIS RICH, beautiful tart is a native of Alsace, a region in the east of France, it might as easily have come from America's Down East—berries and cream are beloved the world over. Here blueberries are baked on a cushion of sugar, cinnamon and almond flour (or dry bread crumbs) that preserves the crust's crispness and then covered with a creamy custard flavored with a splash of vanilla (although there's nothing to stop you from adding a bit of eau-de-vie or brandy, so nice in this kind of dessert). Under heat, the berries pop and speckle the thin layer of custard—the look is lovely in its simplicity and homeliness, the taste comforting.

Center a rack in the oven and preheat it to 375 degrees F. Put the tart pan on a baking sheet lined with parchment paper or a baking mat.

Stir the almond flour or bread crumbs, 1 tablespoon of the sugar and the cinnamon together and sprinkle over the bottom of the crust. Fill the crust with the blueberries—they should come to the rim of the crust; no need to pack them in.

Bake the tart for 30 minutes. As soon as you slide the tart into the oven, make the custard.

Whisk together the egg, the remaining 3 tablespoons sugar, the cream, vanilla and salt in a bowl. Rap the bowl against the counter to break the surface bubbles. You won't be completely successful, but that's fine.

After the tart has baked for 30 minutes, remove it from the oven, keeping it on the baking sheet. Give the custard a gentle stir and one more debubbling rap against the counter, then pour it evenly over the berries. Take a look at the crust—if it's already quite brown, cover the edges with foil.

Bake the tart for another 25 minutes or so, until the custard is set (a tester should come out clean) and slightly puffed. Transfer it to a rack and let it cool to room temperature before removing the tart ring.

If you'd like, dust the top of the tart with confectioners' sugar before serving.

STORING: Eat this the day you make it, when the custard's best. If you have leftovers, cover, refrigerate and have them cold the next day.

## Playing Around

You can use raspberries in place of the blueberries, or a mix of berries, but the recipe will also work with rhubarb or sweet cherries. If you use cherries, pit them and then halve them if you'd like.

# Double-Chocolate Rhubarb Tart

*Makes 6 servings*

½ cup (120 ml) jam (see headnote)

1 to 2 teaspoons water

One 9- to 9½ -inch tart shell made with Chocolate Tart Dough (page 349), partially baked and cooled

About ½ recipe Chocolate Frangipane (page 359); see below

3 to 4 slender stalks fresh rhubarb, trimmed

**A WORD ON THE CHOCOLATE FRANGIPANE:** You won't need the full recipe. However, it's tricky to make a half recipe because of the egg. I make the whole recipe, use what I need and freeze the rest. Think about using the rest in a banana tart; see Playing Around.

WHEN MY DAUGHTER-IN-LAW, Linling Tao, tasted this tart, she said, "Does anyone give awards for best dessert?" I was delighted, especially because it was the first time I'd put rhubarb and chocolate together and I wasn't sure the combo would conjure deliciousness. But it did! The tart crust is chocolate, very dark and appealingly sandy, like shortbread. The main filling is frangipane, an almond cream made here with the addition of dark chocolate; once baked, it's like a fudge brownie. The crust is spread with jam before the frangipane is added—cherry, raspberry, strawberry or black currant jam would all be luscious, as would rhubarb. The top of the tart is paved with chunks of fresh rhubarb, which softens in the oven but retains its beloved acidity.

Bring the jam and water to a boil in a microwave-safe bowl in the microwave or in a small pan over medium heat, stirring occasionally. Pour into the crust and spread evenly over the bottom. Pop the pan into the freezer and chill while you preheat the oven.

Center a rack in the oven and preheat it to 375 degrees F. Line a baking sheet with parchment paper or a baking mat.

Give the frangipane a few good beats with a flexible spatula to soften it. Remove the jam-lined crust from the freezer and spread the frangipane evenly over the jam. Be gentle—the jam will be cold but not fully frozen, so it will shimmy as you try to cover it. The frangipane will come up just below the rim of the crust. Use an offset icing spatula or a knife to smooth the surface.

Peel the rhubarb, if it needs it—older rhubarb or fat stalks can be stringy, so it's best to pull off the strings, either by hand or with a small knife. Cut the rhubarb into pieces about 1½ inches long and arrange them over the top of the tart, lightly pressing them into the frangipane. It's hard to say how much rhubarb you'll need, but it's good to be generous. Put the pan on the lined baking sheet.

Bake the tart for 55 to 60 minutes—shield the edges of the tart with foil if you think the crust is getting a bit too dark (it's usually fine, but check on it)—or until the frangipane has puffed all the way to the center and a tester inserted into it comes out clean. As the frangipane bakes, it will rise around the rhubarb and develop a beautiful crackly surface. Transfer the tart to a rack and allow it to cool to room temperature before removing the tart ring.

Serve the tart at room temperature or, if you'd like, chilled.

STORING: Enjoy the tart the day it's made or up to 1 day later. I keep the tart lightly covered on the counter, but it can be refrigerated and enjoyed cold.

## Playing Around

### CHOCOLATE BANANA TART

Make the crust and frangipane. Instead of the jam, use Nutella—or even Lotus Biscoff Cookie Butter. Use 2 bananas instead of the rhubarb. Cut them in half the long way and then into chunklets. Because banana darkens, you might want to finish the baked tart with a very thin layer of warm apple jelly.

# Parisian Custard Tart

*Makes about 12 servings*

### FOR THE FILLING

3 cups (720 ml) milk

½ cup (120 ml) water

½ cup (100 grams) sugar

¼ cup (50 grams) packed brown sugar

⅓ cup (43 grams) cornstarch

4 large eggs

2 tablespoons dark rum (or an additional 1½ teaspoons pure vanilla extract)

1 tablespoon pure vanilla extract

### FOR THE PASTRY

1 sheet puff pastry (at least 8½ ounces; 240 grams), preferably all-butter, defrosted if necessary, or 1 recipe All-Purpose Tart Dough (page 355), rolled into a 12- to 13-inch round and chilled if necessary

**A WORD ON ROLLING OUT PUFF PASTRY:** Depending on what brand of puff pastry you buy, you may find yourself faced with a geometry problem: How do you roll a rectangular sheet of pastry into a round? The easiest way to deal with it is to roll the dough into a large square and then cut the dough into a circle. If you can find puff pastry that's already rolled into a round, you'll be on easy street.

**PLAN AHEAD:** The custard needs to chill before filling and baking the tart. Once baked, the tart has to cool and then be refrigerated for another hour or more. It's ideal if you make it the day before—it really benefits from an overnight stay in the fridge.

THE MACARON MAY BE synonymous with Paris, but there's another, less well-known dessert that's beloved in the city—this tart. It's basic and plain, distinctive but not at all dainty, decorative or attention-grabbing. It's simply a crust, often puff pastry, filled with pastry cream and baked until the custard is set and the top is browned to a mahogany char. The darker the top, the more authentic the tart.

In Paris, this dessert is called a flan—I know you might be tempted to think of crème caramel, but the two desserts are very different. The tart can be tall, like a torte (or a New York cheesecake), or short, like a typical tart; it can be rich or lean, and the filling flavored or not. Mine is less than 2 inches tall; creamy but not rich or heavy; set but still jiggly; and full of warm flavor—I use lots of vanilla and also dark rum, vanilla's good pal. And because I use store-bought puff pastry for the crust (although you could make it with tart dough, if you prefer), this tart can be an everyday dessert, a snack or a take-a-break-from-work treat, as it is for Parisians.

TO MAKE THE FILLING: Give a medium heavy-bottomed saucepan a quick rinse with cold water, but don't dry the pan (this will help prevent the milk from scorching), then pour in the milk and water. Stir in half of the granulated sugar and bring just to a boil—keep an eye on it: Once the milk boils, it's just a nanosecond before it bubbles over the pot and makes a mess. Remove the pan from the heat.

While the liquids are heating, whisk together the rest of the granulated sugar, the brown sugar and cornstarch in a large bowl. Add the eggs and whisk energetically to blend well. Put the bowl on a folded kitchen towel or a silicone pot holder to anchor it. Whisking the sugar-egg mixture nonstop, drizzle in about one quarter of the hot liquid. Then, still whisking, pour in the rest in a steadier stream.

Rinse the saucepan (no need to be thorough) and pour the custard mixture into it. Set the pan over medium heat and, whisking

without stopping and making sure that the whisk reaches every part of the pan, including the corners, cook the custard until the first bubble rises to the top and pops, at which point the custard will be noticeably thicker and your whisk will leave tracks. Lower the heat a bit and cook and stir for another minute or two, your insurance that the custard is sufficiently cooked and that the cornstarch won't taste raw.

Scrape the custard into a clean bowl and stir in the rum, if you're using it, and vanilla. Press a piece of plastic wrap against the surface and let the custard sit at room temperature for about 30 minutes; stir now and then if you're around.

Put the bowl in the refrigerator and chill the custard for at least 1 hour. Better yet, let it get thoroughly cold. You can speed the process by placing the custard bowl in a larger bowl filled with ice cubes and cold water—come back to the bowl now and then to stir until it's cold. (*The custard can be refrigerated in an airtight container overnight*.)

TO MAKE THE CRUST: Butter a 9-inch springform pan (if your pan is 9½ inches, that's fine).

If you're using puff pastry, roll it out into a round that's 12 to 13 inches in diameter (see headnote); if you're using tart dough, you're all set. Using your hands or rolling the pastry up around your pin to make it easier, position the pastry over the pan. Gently ease it into the pan and press it against the bottom and up the sides. You're aiming for the dough to come about 1½ inches up the sides. If the edges are ragged and uneven, just leave them—they'll get trimmed later. Put the pan in the refrigerator until ready to use; when the crust is firm, cover it tightly.

WHEN YOU'RE READY TO BAKE: Center a rack in the oven and preheat it to 425 degrees F.

Remove the custard from the fridge and whisk it a bit to loosen it, then scrape it into the pastry-lined springform pan and smooth the top. Using a table knife, trim the dough so that it reaches just about ½ inch above the custard.

Bake the tart for 50 to 55 minutes, or until the top of the custard is dark, dark brown—if it looks black in places, that's great and most authentic. It won't be brown all over, though, and it might bubble and mound in places. If you get bubbles, you can prick them with the tip of a knife or just leave them.

Transfer the pan to a rack and wait for 5 minutes, then, if some of the custard has risen above the crust and stuck to the sides of the pan, run a table knife gently between the pan and the custard. Let the flan cool to room temperature, then cover it lightly and refrigerate it. It's best if you can chill it overnight, but that's not always convenient—give it as much time as you can.

When you're ready to serve, remove the sides of the springform and if you'd like, lift the tart off the base and onto a serving platter (if it's easier, leave it on the base). You can serve it cold, at room temperature or at any temp in between. Cut into wedges and serve with a fork . . . or don't. When you're having the tart as a snack, do as Parisians do: Eat it out of hand.

STORING: Covered tightly, the tart will keep for about 3 days in the fridge. Make sure to keep it away from foods with strong odors.

# Candied Almond Tart

*Makes 12 servings*

## FOR THE CRUST

⅓ cup (40 grams) confectioners' sugar

½ teaspoon fine sea salt

½ teaspoon ground cinnamon

1 large egg yolk, lightly beaten

½ teaspoon pure vanilla extract

1 stick plus 2 tablespoons (10 tablespoons; 5 ounces; 141 grams) unsalted butter, melted and cooled for a few minutes

1⅔ cups (227 grams) all-purpose flour

## FOR THE FILLING

1 stick (8 tablespoons; 4 ounces; 113 grams) unsalted butter, cut into chunks

⅔ cup (134 grams) sugar

¾ teaspoon ground cinnamon

½ teaspoon fine sea salt

3 tablespoons milk

2 cups (200 grams) sliced almonds

**A WORD ON SERVING SIZE:** Usually, I'd say that a tart this size serves 6 to 8, but because this one is particularly rich and deliberately sweet, it's best served in thin slices.

THIS RECIPE WAS INSPIRED BY a stunning tart I saw in a Lisbon bakery. It was filled with sliced almonds, and each almond seemed to have been polished with a gloss of caramel. The caramel was darker in some spots than in others and the almonds, looking like so many shiny petals, formed a jagged mosaic. I wanted to go back and get the tart, but I never managed it, so instead I created one with the same look and a texture somewhere between crunchy and chewy. The taste—very almond and almost butterscotch—is one I imagined the original had. While I was at it, I gave it a cookie crust flavored with cinnamon and vanilla. It's not authentically anything, but it is decidedly delectable.

Center a rack in the oven and preheat it to 350 degrees F. Butter a 9-inch fluted tart pan with a removable bottom and have a baking sheet lined with parchment paper or a baking mat at hand.

**TO MAKE THE CRUST:** Working in a large bowl, whisk together the confectioners' sugar, salt and cinnamon. Add the yolk and vanilla and whisk to blend. It will take a bit of whisking to draw in all the dry ingredients, but you'll get it done in a minute or so. Pour the melted butter into the bowl in a steady stream, whisking all the while. Then switch to a flexible spatula and stir in half of the flour. Once it's incorporated, add the rest of the flour and keep stirring until it's fully blended into the butter mixture. The dough will be a bit like Play-Doh.

Press the dough evenly over the bottom and up the sides of the pan. Prick the bottom well and place the pan on the lined baking sheet. (*If you'd like, you can freeze the crust, well covered, for up to 2 months; bake it directly from the freezer.*)

Bake the crust for 18 to 20 minutes, until it's lightly golden. Check the crust after 10 minutes. Even though you've pricked it, it will puff: Poke the puff with the point of a knife and if necessary, press the dough down with the back of a fork or a spatula. Check again periodically and poke and press if needed. Transfer to a rack and cool until just warm or at room temperature. (*You can make*

*the crust a day ahead and keep it, covered, at room temperature.*) Increase the oven temperature to 400 degrees F.

TO MAKE THE FILLING: Have the prebaked crust on a lined baking sheet.

Put the butter and sugar in a medium saucepan, preferably one with a heavy bottom, and cook over medium-low heat, stirring to melt and blend the ingredients. Turn the heat up to medium and boil until the mixture is a pale- to medium-amber color, 3 to 4 minutes. Stir in the cinnamon and salt. Take the pan off the heat, stand away and add the milk—the caramel may sputter and it might seize, but it'll be fine. Return the pan to medium heat and stir until the mixture is smooth again. Add the almonds and cook, stirring nonstop, for another 2 to 3 minutes—you want to be certain that the almonds are coated with caramel.

Immediately scrape the mixture into the crust, pressing and pushing to get the nuts into the edges and to even the top. Don't wait—the filling firms quickly.

Bake the tart for about 15 minutes, or until the caramel is bubbling and, most important, the top is a deep golden brown. The tart is tastiest when the caramel flavor is at its deepest. Transfer the tart to a rack and cool to room temperature.

To cut the tart into thin slices, it's easiest to use a sharp chef's knife—put the tip of the knife in the center of the tart, rest the blade against the filling and cut in one crisp motion. The crust is sturdy and the filling firm, so be definitive.

STORING: The tart is best the day it is made, but it will hold for another day at room temperature as long as the room isn't humid.

*Pies, Tarts, Cobblers and Crisps*

# Steph's Bakewell Tart

*Makes 8 servings*

One 9- to 9½-inch tart shell made with All-Purpose Tart Dough (page 355), partially baked and cooled

## FOR THE CAKE

1¼ cups (4½ ounces; 125 grams) almond flour, or an equal weight of almonds, finely ground in a food processor

½ cup (68 grams) all-purpose flour

1 teaspoon baking powder

Pinch of fine sea salt

1 stick (8 tablespoons; 4 ounces; 113 grams) unsalted butter, very soft

½ cup (100 grams) sugar

2 large eggs, at room temperature, lightly beaten

½ teaspoon almond extract

1 slightly rounded cup (about 240 ml) raspberry jam

⅓ cup (33 grams) sliced almonds (optional)

## FOR THE ICING (OPTIONAL)

½ cup (60 grams) confectioners' sugar

½ to 1 tablespoon water

Clotted cream, crème fraîche or whipped cream for serving (optional)

I'D NEVER TASTED a Bakewell tart, a British specialty, until my friend Stephanie Johnston came to dinner carrying one on a plate. When her daughters arrived, there were cheers all around: "Mum's brought the Bakewell!" For the Johnstons, the tart holds generations of memories. Steph's mom, Granny Annie, was the original Bakeweller, and although she did all the cooking for her pub and restaurant in England, she'd make this tart only for her family—it was that special.

Most British bakers agree that three of the Bakewell tart's elements are nonnegotiable: a crust, of course; a layer of jam, often raspberry; and a layer of almond sponge cake on top. Whether or not the tart is finished with a sprinkling of sliced almonds seems to be a matter of family preference: Steph's recipe included them, and a drizzle of icing too. Her Bakewell has the perfect mix of textures—firm and flaky (the crust), almost gooey (the jam) and slightly chewy (the cake)—and a lovely combination of sweet and tart flavors.

Center a rack in the oven and preheat it to 350 degrees F. Place the crust on a baking sheet lined with parchment paper or a baking mat.

TO MAKE THE CAKE: Whisk both flours, the baking powder and salt together.

Working in the bowl of a stand mixer fitted with the paddle attachment, or in a large bowl with a hand mixer, beat the butter and sugar together on medium speed for about 3 minutes, until pale, creamy and light. Gradually add the eggs, beating all the while and scraping the bowl with a flexible spatula as needed. Ignore the inevitable curdling—the batter will even out when the dry ingredients go in. Beat in the almond extract.

Turn the mixer off, add half of the dry ingredients and mix them in on low speed. When they're incorporated, stop the mixer, add the rest of the flour mixture and beat only until it disappears into the batter. Give the batter a few last turns by hand with the spatula.

Spread the jam evenly over the bottom of the crust. Spread the batter over the jam, covering it as thoroughly as you can. (The batter needs to be cajoled into spreading, but if it's not perfect, it'll still be fine.) If you'd like, sprinkle the top with the sliced almonds.

Bake the tart for 40 to 50 minutes, or until the top feels firm to the touch and is puffed all the way to the center. Check after about 25 minutes, and if the tart is browning quickly, tent it loosely with foil or parchment. Transfer the tart to a rack and let cool to room temperature.

**TO MAKE THE OPTIONAL ICING:** Stir the sugar and ½ tablespoon water together in a small bowl. If the icing doesn't run off the spoon slowly and

steadily, add more water drop by drop until it does. Drizzle the icing over the tart and let dry at room temperature.

Serve the tart with cream, if desired.

**STORING:** The Bakewell, like all tarts, is best the day it's made, but you'll still be happy with it the next day; keep it covered at room temperature.

# SALTY SIDE UP

## SIDES AND MORE

# Blue Cheese Bites

*Makes 24 bites*

¾ cup (102 grams) all-purpose flour

¾ teaspoon baking powder

½ teaspoon fine sea salt

½ teaspoon freshly ground black pepper

2 large eggs, at room temperature

1½ tablespoons honey

1 tablespoon sugar

⅓ cup plus 2 tablespoons (scant 110 ml) olive oil

4 small fresh figs (or other fresh or dried fruit; see below), cut into small bits

2 ounces (57 grams) blue cheese (see headnote), cut into small bits

**A WORD ON THE FRUIT:** Figs are a treat, but not always easy to find and the good ones come around only in the fall. Use them if you can, but know that small cubes of fresh pears or moist, plump dried apricots, cherries or prunes will be equally delicious with the olive oil and cheese.

**THESE TWO-BITE MORSELS** deliver two flavors: the soft tang of blue cheese and the sweet lusciousness of fresh figs (or ripe pears or dried fruit, when figs are out of season or out of reach). The cheese and fruit are cut into very small pieces and folded into a batter that gets its richness from olive oil. It's an extremely simple batter that you make by hand, and it's a convenient one too—you can store it in the refrigerator (it benefits from a chill) and bake it just before you're ready to serve these for brunch or cocktails.

Use whatever blue cheese you like best or, if you're not wild about blue, choose a soft goat or a flavorful cow's-milk cheese—a ripe, runny Brie works really well. My preference here is for the tender, mellow French blue Fourme d'Ambert, or a spoonable Gorgonzola dolce.

**PLAN AHEAD:** The batter should be refrigerated for at least 2 hours.

You'll need two mini muffin tins (with 12 cups each) to make the full batch. If you'd like, you can bake in batches or bake only as many as you need. Before you spoon the batter into the pan(s), butter and flour the cups, or use baker's spray.

Whisk the flour, baking powder, salt and pepper together.

Working in a medium bowl, whisk together the eggs, honey and sugar. Give it a little oomph—you want the ingredients to be fully blended. Add the dry ingredients all at once and, using the whisk or a flexible spatula, stir and fold until you've got a homogeneous batter. Add the olive oil in a few additions, using a light touch and a stir-and-fold

motion. The batter will be thick and shiny. Gently fold in the figs (or whatever fruit you're using) and cheese.

You can either spoon the batter into the muffin tins and cover them with plastic wrap or leave the batter in the bowl and press a piece of plastic wrap against the surface to create an airtight seal. Refrigerate for at least 2 hours. (*The batter can be refrigerated for up to 2 days.*)

**WHEN YOU'RE READY TO BAKE:** Center a rack in the oven and preheat it to 375 degrees F. If you need to prep and fill the muffin tins, do it now.

Bake the bites for 10 to 13 minutes, or until they are puffed and golden; a tester inserted into the center of one should come out clean. As soon as the bites

are baked, unmold them. Either carefully pry them out with a table knife or grab a corner of the muffin tin and rap the tin against the counter to release them. Let them rest on a rack for about 10 minutes, or until they are just warm or at room temperature—they're good at any temperature.

STORING: These are best the day they're made.

# Goat Cheese–Black Pepper Quick Bread

*Makes 10 servings*

1¾ cups (238 grams) all-purpose flour

1 tablespoon baking powder

½ teaspoon fine sea salt

½ teaspoon freshly ground black pepper, or more to taste

3 large eggs, at room temperature

⅓ cup (80 ml) milk, at room temperature

⅓ cup (80 ml) extra-virgin olive oil, preferably fruity

1 tablespoon honey

Grated zest of 1 lemon

4 ounces (113 grams) soft goat cheese, cut into small pieces (see below)

3 tablespoons chopped fresh mint

**A WORD ON THE CHEESE:**
Choose a soft goat cheese with a flavor you like. Because soft goat cheese is hard to wrangle into pieces—it's sticky—give yourself the advantage by working with the cheese when it's cold. (I cut the cheese when it's cold and return the pieces to the fridge until I need them.) Size and neatness don't matter here, so just slice away the rind (if there's one), cut the cheese into bits (try to get them about a half inch or so on a side, if you can even get sides) and stir the bits into the dough as evenly as you can.

NO MATTER WHEN I SERVE this easy nibble with its bits of goat cheese, a fair bit of mint and more than a dash of freshly ground black pepper, I imagine myself outdoors, at a garden party or on a café terrace, with a glass of cold wine—it's often rosé—and a bunch of good friends. Kind of like a muffin and kind of like a sponge cake, the loaf rises and browns beautifully and has a crumb with a little give.

Center a rack in the oven and preheat it to 350 degrees F. Butter an 8- to 8½-inch loaf pan, or use baker's spray.

Whisk the flour, baking powder, salt and pepper together in a large bowl. Whisk together the eggs, milk, oil, honey and lemon zest in a small bowl. Pour the wet ingredients over the dry and, using a flexible spatula, lightly stir the mixtures together; you don't need to be thorough. Add the cheese and mint and, using as few strokes as possible, mix until almost uniformly incorporated—it's better to be fast than thorough here. You'll have a heavy, sticky dough. Turn the dough out into the pan and use the spatula to poke it into the corners and to even the bumpy top.

Bake the loaf for 34 to 38 minutes, or until it's golden, tall and crowned (perhaps cracked) and a tester inserted into the center comes out clean. Transfer the pan to a rack and leave the loaf in the pan for 3 minutes, then unmold it onto the rack. Turn it right side up and let cool to room temperature. You can eat the loaf when it's warm, but I think its texture is better when it's allowed to cool.

The loaf cuts beautifully if you use a serrated knife and don't make the slices too thin. Slice the bread about ½ inch thick.

STORING: Wrapped well, the loaf will keep for about 2 days at room temperature or for up to 2 months in the freezer; defrost in its wrapper.

# Potato-Parm Tart

*Makes 8 servings*

One 11-inch round Savory Galette Dough (page 354; see below), chilled

### FOR THE FILLING

3 ounces (85 grams) cream cheese, softened

2 tablespoons milk

⅓ cup (33 grams) finely grated Parmesan

2 to 4 tablespoons finely sliced scallions, snipped fresh chives or minced shallots (optional)

Fine sea salt and freshly ground black pepper

### FOR THE TOPPING

1 medium potato (red, yellow or russet), scrubbed but not peeled

Olive oil for brushing

About 2 tablespoons finely grated Parmesan

Fleur de sel or flaky sea salt

Freshly ground black pepper

Small fresh thyme or rosemary sprigs (optional)

**A WORD ON THE CRUST:** You can use any other not-sweet dough instead of the Galette Dough, a round of store-bought pie dough or ready-made puff pastry.

THERE ARE THREE THINGS I know about this not-baked-in-a-pan tart: It is fun to make, it looks beautiful and it delights everyone. The buttery crust, a favorite, is flat and round, like a pizza crust (or a platter) and prebaked so it shows off its best qualities. The filling is a thin, satiny layer of cream cheese and Parmesan—add scallions, chives or shallots, if you've got them. And the topping is simply a potato sliced as thin as chips, so that the slices bake quickly and curl just a bit under heat. I leave the peel on the potato because I like the way it rims each slice with color. Use a mandoline, Benriner or the slicing blade on your food processor for the potato, lay the petals out in overlapping circles and you'll have a tart any pastry pro would be proud of.

I like to serve this as a starter or, cut into small pieces, as a warm nibble with drinks. I also like to switch things up now and then and add an apple to the mix; see Playing Around.

Center a rack in the oven and preheat it to 400 degrees F. Line a baking sheet with parchment paper or a baking mat.

Place the rolled-out dough on the lined baking sheet and prick it all over with the tines of a fork. Cover it with a sheet of parchment and put another baking sheet on top of it. Or, If you don't have a second baking sheet, put a baking pan or tart pan over it—you want to weight it down.

Bake the crust for 15 minutes. Remove the baking sheet and the top sheet of parchment and bake for another 5 to 8 minutes, or until lightly golden. Transfer to a rack and let the crust cool somewhat before you fill and top it—it can be slightly warm, but it shouldn't be hot. (Leave the oven on.)

TO MAKE THE FILLING: Working in a small bowl with a flexible spatula, beat the cream cheese and milk together until the milk is mostly absorbed; the mixture will be lumpy. Stir in the grated Parmesan and scallions, chives or shallots, if you're using them. Taste and season with salt and pepper. (*The filling can be made up to 2 days ahead and kept covered in the refrigerator.*)

**TO MAKE THE TOPPING AND BAKE THE TART:** Working with a mandoline, a Benriner or other slicer or the slicing blade of a food processor, cut the potato into very thin rounds. (Or use a sharp knife to cut the thinnest slices you can.)

Spread the filling evenly over the crust, leaving a ½-inch border bare. Starting on the bare edge of the crust (or, if you prefer, just where the filling starts), arrange the potato slices in concentric circles, slightly overlapping them, to cover the entire surface. Brush the potatoes with a little oil and sprinkle with the cheese. Season lightly with salt and pepper and if you've got herbs, scatter some of them over the tart; set the rest aside.

Bake the tart for 20 to 25 minutes, or until the filling is bubbling (it may bubble over the edges, but that's fine) and the potatoes are cooked through and lightly browned. (If you've left some crust exposed and it looks as though it's coloring too deeply, shield the edges with foil after about 10 minutes.) Transfer the tart to a serving platter and, if you have fresh herbs, sprinkle the rest over the tart. Wait for about 10 minutes before cutting the tart into wedges.

**STORING:** While you can make the crust and filling ahead, the tart is really a make-it-and-eat-it affair. It's still fine at room temperature an hour or so after baking, but it's so much better just out of the oven.

## *Playing Around*

### APPLE-PARM TART

Replace the potato with an apple, preferably one with red skin. Or, for fun, make the tart with alternating slices of potato and apple, my favorite variation.

# Pear-Comté Tart

*Makes 6 servings*

## FOR THE CRUST

One 9- to 9½-inch tart shell made with All-Purpose Tart Dough (page 355), partially baked and cooled (or use store-bought pie dough)

About 2 tablespoons Dijon mustard, preferably French (optional)

## FOR THE FILLING

2 large eggs

⅔ cup (160 ml) heavy cream

Fine sea salt and freshly ground black pepper

A little freshly grated nutmeg (optional)

3 ounces (85 grams) Comté (or Gruyère or sharp cheddar), shredded (about 1 cup)

## FOR THE TOPPING

1 to 2 ripe, juicy pears

2 ounces (56 grams) Comté (or Gruyère or sharp cheddar), cut into small cubes (about ½ cup; optional)

3 tablespoons walnut pieces or coarsely chopped walnuts (optional)

**FRESH PEARS AND CHEESE** are a combination that only gets better when baked—heat deepens both of their flavors and binds them more closely to one another. My choice for this tart, which I serve as a starter at dinner or for lunch with a small salad, is a nutty cheese like Comté or Gruyère. If I can find older Comté or Gruyère, I grab it—the cheeses get a little more assertive as they age, and I like that. But younger cheeses, as well as sturdy American or English cheddars, make fine companions to the pears. (For a few other cheese-and-pear matches, take a look at Playing Around.) The tart is mild by nature, but you can build stronger flavors into it by coating the base with sharp mustard and/or dotting the surface with small chunks of the cheese. Scattering over chopped walnuts is also nice. The filling base is a custard from the quiche family.

Center a rack in the oven and preheat it to 375 degrees F. Put the tart pan on a baking sheet lined with parchment paper or a baking mat.

Lightly coat the bottom of the crust with the mustard, if you're using it.

**TO MAKE THE FILLING:** Whisk the eggs and cream together in a bowl. Season lightly with salt and pretty generously with pepper. If you like nutmeg, add a few scrapings. Stir in the shredded cheese.

**TO ASSEMBLE THE TART:** I like to leave the skin on the pears—it browns nicely in the oven and looks pretty. Since pears can be all different sizes and weights, start with one pear. Cut it in half from top to bottom, remove the core and cut each half into 8 pieces.

Give the filling a last whisk and pour half of it into the tart shell. Arrange the pear slices in the crust—try to slant the slices skin side up. If you're happy with how they fill the tart, you're set; if you'd like more, slice into the second pear and add to the tart. Pour in the rest of the filling—you might not need it all. If you're using them, scatter over the cubes of cheese. ⟶

If you want to add walnuts, after the tart has baked for 15 minutes, top with the nuts. Continue to bake the tart for another 10 to 15 minutes (total bake time is 25 to 30 minutes), or until the custard is puffed all the way to the center, golden brown and set. A tester inserted into the center should come out clean, and if you tap the pan, the custard shouldn't jiggle. Transfer the tart to a rack and wait for 5 minutes before removing the tart ring.

You can serve the tart hot, warm or at room temperature. It's even tasty (but not as elegant) chilled.

STORING: Like most tarts, this one's best soon after it's made. If you have any left over, cover and refrigerate for up to 1 day.

## Playing Around

### MUENSTER-PEAR TART

Try the tart with a true Alsatian Muenster, cutting the cheese into cubes (avoid the rind) rather than shredding it. Omit the nutmeg and swap the walnuts for cumin seeds. Just don't overdo it—cumin is powerful, and a few seeds go a long way.

### CHÈVRE-PEAR TART

Instead of the shredded cheese, use cubes of creamy chèvre (cubing chèvre is easiest if you start with a log of cold cheese). Omit the nutmeg, and don't brush the crust with mustard. If you'd like, sprinkle the pears with some fresh thyme leaves. And do use the walnuts, so good with goat cheese.

### BLUE CHEESE–PEAR TART

Pears are often paired with soft blue cheeses like Gorgonzola dolce and Fourme d'Ambert, and just as often with firmer, sharper and saltier blues, like Roquefort or Stilton. Find a blue that you like and cut it into small cubes. Omit the mustard and nutmeg but include the walnuts—they're good with blue cheeses. If you'd like, add a tablespoon of honey to the custard or drizzle a little honey over the bottom of the crust before you pour the custard into it. Honey is particularly good with strong, crumbly blues.

# Fig and Goat Cheese Tart

*Makes 8 servings*

## FOR THE FILLING

About 10½ ounces (300 grams) soft goat cheese, to equal about 1½ cups

1 cup (240 ml) plain Greek yogurt (drained if there's liquid in the container)

1 lime

Fine sea salt and freshly ground black pepper

2 teaspoons honey, or more to taste

1 to 2 teaspoons finely chopped fresh mint and/or oregano (optional)

## FOR THE FRUIT

8 to 12 figs, depending on size, quartered

2 tablespoons brown sugar

1 to 2 teaspoons sherry vinegar or balsamic vinegar

Freshly ground black pepper

One 9- to 9½-inch tart shell made with All-Purpose Tart Dough (page 355), fully baked and cooled (or use store-bought pie dough)

Arugula, honey and black pepper for topping the tart (optional)

**A WORD ON FRUITS THROUGH THE SEASONS:** In the fall, you can swap the figs for pieces of plums or pluots, or even black grapes (choose a seedless variety). In the winter, use small cubes of pear or pieces of firm persimmon. In the spring and summer, rhubarb is interesting (slice the raw portion super-thin); peaches, apricots or melon would be good too. Depending on the fruit, you might want to bake the pieces with honey or maple syrup instead of brown sugar.

I SPOTTED A RECIPE like this one tacked onto an advertisement for Champagne in a French magazine, made my own version of it that night and have been riffing on it ever since. Each part of the tart is straightforward—a crust, a no-bake cheese filling, a topping of cut-up fruit—but together, they're fascinating. The filling is definitely savory, but it's also a touch tangy, a bit herby and a smidge sweet. Half of the fruit—in this case, fresh figs—is sweetened and baked; the other half is left raw and spiked with a splash of vinegar; and all of it is seasoned with black pepper. As the seasons change, so can the fruit (see note below) and the cheese (see Playing Around; the tart in the photograph is made with cream cheese and ricotta).

**TO MAKE THE FILLING:** Beat the goat cheese and yogurt together in a bowl until smooth and well blended—it will look like icing for a cupcake. You can do this by hand, but I think you get a better consistency with an electric mixer. Grate the lime zest over the mixture, then squeeze in the juice and mix. Season with salt and pepper and drizzle in the honey; taste and decide if you'd like some more. Stir in the mint and/or oregano, if you're using it (if you'll be keeping the filling for several hours or overnight, hold off on stirring in the herbs until you need it). Scrape the filling into a bowl, cover and refrigerate while you prepare the fruit. (*The filling can be made up to 1 day ahead and kept covered in the fridge.*)

**TO PREPARE THE FIGS:** Center a rack in the oven and preheat it to 350 degrees F.

Cut each fig into 4 wedges. Put half of the wedges in a bowl, cover and set aside. Put the remaining wedges in a small baking dish, sprinkle over the brown sugar, season with pepper and toss well. Bake for about 10 minutes, or until the sugar is melted and bubbling. Set aside to cool.

**TO ASSEMBLE THE TART (DO THIS AS CLOSE TO SERVING TIME AS POSSIBLE):** Toss the raw figs with the vinegar in a small bowl, using the larger amount if you have more than 4 raw figs. If the sugar has set around the baked figs, put them in the microwave (or otherwise heat them) just until the sugar melts.

Fill the tart crust with the cheese mixture, smoothing or swirling the top. Arrange the baked figs over the filling—you can be neat or haphazard—and then fill in the spaces with the vinegared figs. If you're using arugula—you just need a few leaves—combine the melted sugar and vinegar that's left in the bowls and dip the arugula in this "vinaigrette." Scatter the arugula over the top of the tart and, if you'd like, drizzle over a bit more honey and sprinkle with black pepper. Serve immediately.

STORING: Once the tart is put together, it's best to enjoy it as soon as possible.

## Playing Around

### FRUIT AND RICOTTA TART

For the filling, use 8 ounces (226 grams) cream cheese, softened, 1½ cups (374 grams) ricotta, the grated zest and juice of 1 lime, 1 scallion, trimmed and thinly sliced, and fine sea salt and freshly ground black pepper to taste. Follow the directions for the goat cheese filling.

# Free-Style Mushroom, Herb and Ricotta Tart

*Makes about 6 servings*

## FOR THE RICOTTA SPREAD

1 cup (212 grams) ricotta

¼ cup (60 ml) plain yogurt, preferably Greek

½ shallot, finely chopped, rinsed in cold water and patted dry

2 scallions, trimmed and finely sliced

1 to 2 tablespoons minced fresh herbs (see headnote)

Fine sea salt and freshly ground black pepper to taste

## FOR THE MUSHROOM TOPPING

1 tablespoon unsalted butter

1 tablespoon olive oil

1½ pounds (680 grams) mushrooms (a mix is good; see headnote), cleaned, trimmed and sliced

1 to 2 garlic cloves, germ removed and minced (to taste)

3 tablespoons white wine

Fine sea salt and freshly ground black pepper

3 scallions, trimmed and finely sliced

2 tablespoons minced fresh herbs (see headnote)

1 Raggedy-Edged Almond-Herb Crust (page 356), cooled

## TO FINISH (OPTIONAL)

Extra-virgin olive oil, walnut oil or toasted sesame oil

A handful of micro-greens tossed with oil, lemon juice, salt and pepper

**WORD ON WORKING AHEAD:**
That the crust, ricotta spread and even the mushrooms can be prepared ahead of time makes this tart a kind of marvel.

LIKE SO MANY DISHES that I've come to depend on, this one grew out of a spur-of-the-moment idea. It started in Paris, on a day I'd invited friends to come for dinner. When I got to the market in the morning, the stalls were brimming with autumn mushrooms and I bought a big bagful, thinking I'd sauté them, toss them with fresh herbs, maybe serve them on toast as a starter. But when I got home, the idea took a turn tartward. Instead of toast, I made a ragged-edged, free-form crust with some almond flour and herbs in it, and if I hadn't needed it as a platter for the mushrooms, I might have nibbled through it like one big cracker. What I brought to the table that night was the terrific crust topped with a mixture of ricotta and yogurt (with more herbs, and shallots and scallions too), then a layer of those inspiration mushrooms and on top of that, a little salad. It was nothing I'd originally expected and everything that my guests and I loved.

Since that evening, I've made the tart many times, but it's always had a spur-of-the-moment quality to it, even when I've planned to make it. The herbs end up being what's on hand—I count myself lucky when I've got chives, tarragon and dill, but still find the tart lovely when all I've got is parsley. The mushrooms can be a mix of light and dark, meaty and delicate, or just white ones from the supermarket. The salad, which is an option, not a requirement, is prettiest when it's small— micro-greens and sprouts are ideal—but a toss of anything, including spinach, does the trick.

TO MAKE THE SPREAD: Drain the ricotta and yogurt if there's liquid in the containers. (If you'd like, you can spoon the ricotta and/or yogurt into a strainer and drain for 30 minutes.) Put the ricotta in a large bowl and whisk until smooth. Add the remaining ingredients and whisk to blend well, then taste and add more salt and pepper if needed. Cover and refrigerate until you're ready to serve the tart; pour off any accumulated liquid before using. (*The spread can be refrigerated for up to 2 days.*)

*Salty Side Up*

**TO MAKE THE MUSHROOM TOPPING:** Warm the butter and oil in a large skillet (nonstick is good here) over medium-high heat. When the bubbles have subsided, toss in the mushrooms and garlic and cook, stirring, until the mushrooms are brown and tender—at this point, the pan will be almost dry, and that's what you want. Pour in the wine, stir and cook until it's almost evaporated. Season with salt and pepper and remove the pan from the heat. (*You can leave the mushrooms at room temperature for up to 3 hours, or pack into a covered container and refrigerate for up to 2 days; reheat in a skillet with a little water before using.*)

**TO ASSEMBLE AND SERVE THE TART:** Place the crust on a cutting board or serving plate and cover with the ricotta-yogurt spread. Stir the scallions and herbs into the mushroom topping and spoon it over the spread. If you'd like, drizzle the tart with some oil—olive, walnut or sesame—and/or scatter over the micro-greens.

Cut the tart at the table using a pizza wheel—not very elegant, but very effective—or a long chef's knife.

**STORING:** The tart is best served as soon as it's assembled.

# Vegetable Ribbon Tart

*Makes 4 to 6 servings*

**FOR THE PASTRY**

1 sheet puff pastry (about 8 ounces; 227 grams), preferably all-butter, defrosted if necessary (see right)

**FOR THE VINAIGRETTE**

1½ tablespoons fresh lemon juice (grate the zest for the topping before juicing the lemon)

1½ teaspoons white balsamic vinegar

¼ teaspoon honey, or more to taste

¼ teaspoon za'atar, herbes de Provence or dried oregano

Pinch of fine sea salt, or to taste

¼ teaspoon grated fresh ginger or a pinch of ground ginger

1 tablespoon olive oil

¼ teaspoon toasted sesame oil

**FOR THE TOPPING**

About 2 cups (3 or 4 generous handfuls) shaved and/or thinly sliced vegetables (see right)

A handful of cherry or grape tomatoes, halved, quartered or sliced

2 scallions, trimmed and finely sliced

2 tablespoons finely chopped mixed fresh herbs, such as parsley, dill, cilantro and/or tarragon

Finely grated lemon zest of ½ to 1 lemon (reserved from above)

Fine sea salt and freshly ground black pepper

½ cup (113 grams) hummus (see headnote)

2 hard-boiled eggs, halved or quartered, or more if you'd like

**I THINK I MUST HAVE BEEN** channeling my inner French host when I first made this tart—it's so like something my Parisian friends would make. It's naturally pretty and a little fancy, even though the important ingredients are store-bought. The filling is hummus from the supermarket—it can be plain or roasted pepper or beet or whatever's your favorite. It's topped with colorful raw vegetables and herbs tossed with vinaigrette. If you've got a little vegetable patch, this is the recipe to show it off. If you're going out shopping, get carrots, fennel, peppers, beets and cucumbers. I slice in some scallions and tomatoes too and finish it all with hard-boiled eggs. As for the crust, I use frozen puff pastry, scoring it so that it rises around the edges, like a frame. And if you want to make this a little more substantial and a lot more herbaceous, it's easy to do; see Playing Around.

**A WORD ON THE PUFF PASTRY:** This recipe is based on a piece of pastry that weighs about 8 ounces and can be rolled out into a square about 11 inches on a side or a rectangle that's 8 to 9 inches by 11 to 13 inches. (Pepperidge Farm puff pastry fits this description.) But if you've got pastry that rolls out to a different size, you can increase or decrease the amounts for the filling and topping as necessary. Precision is not important here. As recipes go, this one's more idea than formula.

**AND A WORD ON WORKING AHEAD:** Each component of the tart can be prepared ahead. Even the vegetables, minus the tomatoes, can be done ahead—toss them into a large bowl, crumple a couple of damp paper towels over the top, cover and refrigerate for up to 4 hours.

**TO ROLL AND BAKE THE PASTRY:** Center a rack in the oven and preheat it to 425 degrees F, or the temperature recommended on the package of puff pastry.

Unroll or unfold the puff pastry onto a work space; keep it on the paper it came with or use a fresh sheet of parchment. You want a square or rectangle that's ⅛ inch thick (see above), so roll it →

out if needed. Mark off a 1-inch border on all sides of the dough by nicking it with the tip of a knife—think of it as a frame. Then, using the nicks as your guide, run the knife tip against the edge of a ruler to score the border, taking care not to cut all the way through the dough. Prick the inner rectangle or square of dough—leave the "frame" as is—and slide the paper and dough onto a baking sheet.

Bake the pastry for about 15 minutes (or follow the package directions). Let color and puff be your guide: You want the sheet to be golden brown (pale puff pastry isn't tasty) and puffed all over. Transfer the baking sheet to a rack and let the pastry cool to room temperature. (*As long as your kitchen isn't humid, you can keep the pastry uncovered at room temperature for up to 8 hours. If it needs a crisping, reheat it for a few minutes and cool before topping.*)

Just before you're ready to construct the tart, use a fork or your fingers to crush and flatten the pastry in the inner rectangle or square. Don't discard the crumbs and pieces—leave them on the tart; they'll add more texture.

TO MAKE THE VINAIGRETTE: Put all of the ingredients *except* the olive and sesame oils in a small jar with a tight-fitting lid and shake to blend. Add the oils and shake again. Taste, and if you think it needs a little more of something, add it now. Set aside until needed. (*You can make the vinaigrette a few hours ahead and let it sit at room temperature or refrigerate it. Shake well before using.*)

TO MAKE THE TOPPING AND ASSEMBLE THE TART: Put the shaved and/or sliced vegetables, the tomatoes and scallions in a large bowl. (*The vegetables, without the tomatoes, can be refrigerated for up to 4 hours ahead; see headnote. Add the tomatoes when ready to assemble the tart.*) Add most of the herbs and the lemon zest, season well with salt and pepper and toss together. Give the vinaigrette a good shake, pour it over the vegetables and toss again. Taste and add more salt or pepper if needed.

Place the pastry on a serving plate or a nice cutting board. Spread the hummus over the flattened portion of the pastry (leave the puffed border bare). Top the hummus with the vegetables—some will probably get away and tumble over the edges, and that's fine and pretty—followed by the eggs. Season the eggs with salt and pepper, sprinkle the tart with the remaining herbs and serve immediately.

You can cut the tart with a chef's knife—snap the blade down as you cut, don't saw—or a pizza wheel. Whatever you use, there will be flying shards of pastry—they're part of the tart's charm.

STORING: While you can prepare much of this ahead of time, the tart is not meant to be kept.

## Playing Around

Instead of hummus, the filling can be guacamole, tzatziki, tapenade, Herbed Ricotta (page 380) or even scallion cream cheese.

HERB-CRUSTED VEGETABLE-RIBBON TART

Instead of light and flaky puff pastry, try the tart with the Raggedy-Edged Almond-Herb Crust (page 356). The crust will go with any spread you decide to use. It will also make a more substantial tart, so you can either serve it in smaller portions or call it a light meal.

# Ricotta-Tomato Tart

*Makes 6 servings*

2 large eggs

½ teaspoon fine sea salt

¼ teaspoon freshly ground black pepper, or more to taste

1⅓ cups (333 grams) ricotta, drained if there's liquid in the container

1 lemon

2 teaspoons olive oil, plus more for finishing if desired

⅓ cup (13 grams) minced mixed fresh herbs, such as dill, parsley, tarragon, thyme, cilantro and/or basil

2 scallions, trimmed and finely sliced

One 9- to 9½-inch tart shell made with All-Purpose Tart Dough (page 355), partially baked and cooled (or use store-bought pie dough)

1 to 2 tomatoes, cut into chunks (1 to 1½ inches) and patted dry

THE BEDROCK OF THIS TART IS RICOTTA, with its soft texture and mild, milky flavor. It's the perfect base for a filling that includes abundant fresh herbs and sharp lemon zest. When I made the mixture, I was thinking of it as a dip or a spread for vegetables, but I added an egg on a hunch, smoothed it into a crust and baked it, creating a filling that I turn to often. The texture is creamy and light, but the flavors are substantial—just the kind of balance I like. It could go out into the world as it is and be topped with a salad at the table, but it's splendid when you scatter over some chunks of tomatoes and let them bake into the filling, highlighting the tomatoes' sweetness and mellowing their acidity. The recipe is easy to put together and easy to play with—both the filling and the topping will bend to take in what you've got on hand; see Playing Around.

Center a rack in the oven and preheat it to 350 degrees F. Line a baking sheet with parchment or a baking mat.

Working in a large bowl, whisk the eggs, salt and pepper together until foamy. Add the ricotta, switch to a flexible spatula and beat to blend. Grate the zest of the lemon over the cheese and squeeze in a couple of teaspoonfuls of juice, then add the oil and give everything a good stir. Blend in the herbs and scallions. (*The filling can be made to this point, covered and refrigerated overnight. If any liquid has accumulated, discard it.*)

Turn the filling into the crust and smooth the top. Arrange the tomato chunks over the filling (be neat or haphazard) and put the tart on the lined baking sheet.

Bake for 45 to 50 minutes, or until the filling has puffed all the way to the center; a tester inserted into the center of the tart should come out clean. Transfer the pan to a rack, brush the top very lightly with oil, if you'd like, and cool to room temperature.

STORING: Once the tart is baked, it's best served that day. If you've got leftovers, cover and keep them overnight at room temperature or in the fridge.

## Playing Around

The herbs in the filling are up for grabs, and so are the vegetables for the topping. The tart is beautiful and delicious finished with very thin slices of zucchini (arrange them like petals in circles over the top), rounds of red onion (you can mix them with the zucchini or the tomatoes) or lightly steamed vegetables, such as asparagus, strips of leeks or slivers of snow peas.

# Tomato Tart

*Makes 8 servings*

5 medium tomatoes, cut into ¼-inch-thick slices

Fine sea salt

One 8-x-11 inch tart crust made with 1 recipe Savory Galette Dough (page 354) or ½ recipe All-Butter Pie Dough (page 347), partially baked and cooled (or use store-bought pie dough)

2 tablespoons grainy mustard, preferably French, or more to taste

1 tablespoon Dijon mustard, preferably French, or more to taste

4 teaspoons honey

3 or 4 fresh basil leaves (optional)

About ⅓ cup (about 30 grams) grated cheese, such as Gruyère, Comté, or cheddar

Freshly ground black pepper

About 1 tablespoon olive oil for drizzling

A few sprigs of fresh thyme and/or rosemary (optional)

Finely chopped fresh parsley, basil or cilantro, for finishing (optional)

**A WORD ON SIZE AND AMOUNTS:** You can make this tart in any size or shape tart pan you like. If you use a standard 9-inch fluted tart pan, you'll need fewer tomatoes—4 should do the trick. And if you do make it in the smaller pan, use 1½ tablespoons grainy mustard, ½ tablespoon Dijon and 1 tablespoon honey.

I MAKE THIS RECIPE all during tomato season and often on the margins of the season too. Miraculously, it turns even not-so-flavorful tomatoes tasty. And it does this simply and easily. You swish the bottom of the crust with mustard and honey and add some grated cheese. Once the tomatoes are laid into the crust and seasoned, you send them into the oven to roast, where their juices concentrate, their natural sweetness intensifies and their edges crinkle appealingly.

Place a double thickness of paper towels on a large plate or cutting board. Arrange a layer of tomato slices on the towels and sprinkle with salt. Cover with another double layer of towels and the remaining tomatoes, salt these tomatoes and cover with more towels. Allow the tomatoes to drain for at least 20 minutes. (*If it's more convenient, you can do this up to a day ahead; keep the set-up in the refrigerator.*)

WHEN YOU'RE READY TO BAKE: Center a rack in the oven and preheat it to 400 degrees F. Place the crust on a baking sheet lined with parchment paper or a baking mat.

Whisk together the two mustards and the honey in a small bowl, taste and see if you want more of either mustard and then spread the mixture evenly over the bottom of the crust. If you've got the basil, tear a leaf and sprinkle over the pieces. Top with about ¼ cup (20 grams) of the cheese. Arrange the tomato slices in the pan, overlapping them slightly. It's hard to know how many slices you'll need, so you might have some left over (for salad or a sandwich). Tear the remaining basil leaves, if you have them. and tuck the pieces between the tomatoes. Season the tomatoes with pepper and drizzle with about 1 tablespoon olive oil. Toss on the fresh herb sprigs, if you've got them.

Bake the tart for about 30 minutes, or until the tomatoes can be easily pierced with the tip of a knife—it's nice if they're a bit curled and maybe browned around the edges. The mustard might be bubbling—a good thing. Remove the sprigs of herbs (they'll have

burned) and sprinkle over the rest of the cheese. You can slide the pan back into the oven to melt the cheese—leave it in the oven for about 3 minutes—or just let the tart's heat do the job. If you'd like to give the tomatoes a little shine, drizzle over a tiny bit more oil. Scatter over the fresh herbs, if you're using them.

The tart can be served hot, just warm or at room temperature. If it's not piping hot, you might want to brush a little more oil over the tomatoes to polish them up.

STORING: The tart is meant to be enjoyed the day it's made.

## Playing Around

I've made this recipe with slices of Swiss from the deli counter, with sheep's-milk cheese from the Basque Country and with expensive aged Comté, and it's always been great, so use what you've got.

# Spinach-Mozzarella Pie with Parm Crumble

*Makes 6 to 8 servings*

About 3 tablespoons olive oil

1 medium onion, finely chopped, rinsed in cold water and patted dry

1 large shallot, finely chopped, rinsed in cold water and patted dry

3 garlic cloves, germ removed and finely chopped

Pinch of sugar

4 cups (200 grams) baby spinach (or other greens; see below)

Fine sea salt and freshly ground black pepper

One 9-inch deep-dish piecrust made from Savory Galette Dough (page 354) or All-Butter Pie Dough (page 347), partially baked and cooled (or use store-bought pie dough)

½ cup (120 ml) heavy cream

½ cup (120 ml) milk

2 large eggs

1 large egg yolk

¼ cup (21 grams) finely grated Parmesan

2 scallions, trimmed and thinly sliced

½ cup (87 grams) finely cubed mozzarella

Parm Crumble (page 377), chilled

**A WORD ON THE SPINACH:**
I usually buy a bag of washed, ready-to-eat baby spinach to use here, but you can choose other greens if you'd like. Baby kale is great, as is any other kind of kale as long as you cut the leaves away from the thick stems and slice them thin. Ditto chard, or even broccoli rabe.

**IT'S ALWAYS FUN** when ingredients you know will be good together turn out to be even better than you expected. That was the case with this pie. The spinach, cooked with onions and garlic, and the mix of mozzarella and Parmesan could only be great together, but they become the best they can be in the custard filling. The pie is tastier at room temperature than it is warm, making it an easy do-ahead, perfect for a picnic or potluck.

Working in a large skillet, warm 2 tablespoons of the oil over medium heat. Drop in the onion, shallot and garlic and cook, stirring, until softened but not colored, 3 to 5 minutes. Stir in the pinch of sugar, add the spinach and turn up the heat. Toss the spinach around, adding a little more oil if you think you need it, until it wilts, about 2 minutes. Season with salt and pepper and spoon into a strainer set over a bowl. Press against the mixture to dry it as best as you can and let cool. (*You can refrigerate the spinach mixture, covered, for up to 1 day.*)

Center a rack in the oven and preheat it to 375 degrees F. Put the crust on a baking sheet lined with parchment paper or a baking mat.

Working in a medium bowl, whisk together the cream, milk, eggs, yolk and Parmesan. Season lightly with salt and generously with pepper, then stir in the scallions.

Press the spinach mixture against the strainer again, and if there's still liquid coming out, ball up the spinach and squeeze to dry it. Spread the spinach in the bottom of the crust. Pour the filling into the crust and scatter over the mozzarella cubes. Break the Parm crumble into small nuggets and cover the top of the pie with them.

Bake the pie for about 45 minutes, or until it's golden brown and puffed all the way to the center; a tester inserted into the center should come out clean. Transfer the pie to a rack and allow to cool for at least 45 minutes, or until it reaches room temperature.

**STORING:** You can keep the pie at room temperature for up to 8 hours before serving. Leftovers will keep covered in the fridge for about 2 days.

*Salty Side Up*

# Clam Chowder Pie

*Makes 6 to 8 servings*

One 11- to 12-inch round Savory Galette Dough (page 354), fitted into a 9-inch pie pan and ready to bake (or use store-bought pie dough)

## FOR THE FILLING

About 1⅓ cups (about 10 ounces; 300 grams drained weight) chopped canned clams (three 6½-ounce/ 184 gram cans); see right

3 strips bacon

2 celery stalks, trimmed and chopped into ¼- to ½-inch pieces

1 small red bell pepper, cored, seeded and chopped into ¼- to ½-inch pieces

Fine sea salt and freshly ground black pepper

1 to 2 garlic cloves, germ removed and finely chopped

About 1½ cups (about 200 grams) frozen peas and/or corn kernels, defrosted and patted dry

2 scallions, trimmed and cut into ¼-inch-thick slices

1 to 2 tablespoons chopped fresh herbs, such as parsley, cilantro and/or dill

1 cup (240 ml) heavy cream

2 teaspoons Old Bay Seasoning, or more to taste

2 teaspoons Worcestershire sauce, or more to taste

Tabasco or other hot pepper sauce

2 large eggs

1 large egg yolk

## FOR THE TOPPING

1 tablespoon unsalted butter, melted

1 cup (57 grams) oyster crackers, preferably Oysterettes, if you can find them

Fine sea salt

IT'S HARD TO SAY when or how I had the idea to turn one of my favorite dishes, clam chowder, into a pie. But once it was done, it seemed just right. The clams, the warm herbs and the hits of heat and umami that you get from Old Bay, Worcestershire and Tabasco—they're as good together when you eat them with a knife and fork as they are when you sip them in a Bloody Mary. The creamy pie is topped with crunchy Oysterettes, those taste-of-New-England crackers that are often served in little packets alongside chowder. Oddly, the potatoes that are so sublime in chowder don't work well in pie, but peas and corn do. I use frozen, because I always keep them on hand. If you've got fresh, use them.

A WORD ON THE CLAMS: I often use canned chopped clams because they're always readily available. Of course, minced fresh (or frozen) clams would be delicious.

Center a rack in the oven and preheat it to 400 degrees F. Place the crust on a baking sheet lined with parchment paper or a baking mat.

Put the clams in a strainer and shake out as much liquid as you can; set the strainer over a bowl and let drain while you work on the bacon.

Starting in a cold skillet, cook the bacon over medium heat until crisp. Pat the bacon dry between paper towels and once it cools, chop it into bits. Keep the fat in the skillet.

Remove the clams from the strainer and pat them as dry as you can get them; set aside. Rinse the strainer and set it over a large bowl—you'll use it for the vegetables.

Set the skillet over medium heat, toss in the celery and bell pepper, season with salt and cook, stirring, just until the vegetables soften, about 4 minutes. Mix in the garlic and cook for 1 minute more, then season with pepper and turn everything into the strainer to drain.

Gently mix the cooked vegetables, bacon bits, clams, peas and/or corn, scallions and herbs together in a bowl. Season with salt and pepper. Although the bacon and clams are naturally salty, the filling will still need salt. (*The filling can be covered and refrigerated for up to 8 hours. Let it sit on the counter while you preheat the oven.*)

Scrape the filling into the crust; use a spatula to even it. Pour the cream into a large measuring cup with a spout or a bowl and season with the Old Bay, Worcestershire, Tabasco, salt and pepper. Taste and decide what you'd like more of—it's good when it's just a bit hot and peppery. Add the eggs and yolk and whisk to blend.

Slowly pour the cream over the filling, waiting a few seconds for the cream to find its way into and around the filling before pouring in more. You may or may not use all of the cream mixture.

Slide the pie into the oven and bake for 15 minutes.

MEANWHILE, MAKE THE TOPPING: Toss the butter and crackers together in a bowl and season with salt. Set aside for the moment.

Once the pie has baked for 15 minutes, scatter over the crackers. Bake the pie for 30 to 35 minutes longer (a total of 45 to 50 minutes), until it's puffed and set all the way to the center and a tester inserted into the middle of the pie comes out clean. After the pie has been in the oven for about 25 minutes, you'll probably want to tent it loosely with foil or parchment if the crackers or crust are browning too quickly. Transfer the pie to a rack and let sit for at least 15 minutes before slicing and serving.

The pie is good warm or at room temperature.

STORING: The pie is best the day it is made. Because it is so nicely seasoned, its flavor isn't bad after a night in the fridge, but the texture of the filling will be quite firm and the topping won't be as appealing as it is freshly baked.

# Double-Corn Tomato Crisp

*Makes 6 servings*

## FOR THE FILLING

2 pounds (907 grams) ripe tomatoes, any kind and any size, cored and cut into 1- to 2-inch chunks

Kernels from 2 ears corn (about 2 cups; 280 grams)

1 small onion, finely chopped, rinsed in cold water and patted dry

1 tablespoon olive oil

1 tablespoon sherry vinegar or balsamic vinegar

1 tablespoon honey

1 teaspoon fine sea salt, or more to taste

½ teaspoon freshly ground black pepper, or more to taste

Pinch of cayenne pepper or squirt of hot sauce (optional)

3 tablespoons finely chopped fresh herbs, such as basil, coriander, parsley and/ or thyme

## FOR THE TOPPING

1 cup (176 grams) yellow cornmeal

½ cup (68 grams) all-purpose flour

1 tablespoon sugar, or more to taste

1 teaspoon fine sea salt

¾ stick (6 tablespoons; 3 ounces; 85 grams) cold unsalted butter, cut into small chunks

THERE'S A TIME, usually in August, when the markets are so full of wonderful tomatoes that I stock up as though they won't be available the next day. It was after such a spree that I made my first tomato crisp. That I kept making it beyond the summer, and that it was still good, is a testament to the crisp—even average tomatoes are appealing once baked into this dish. And, yes, frozen corn can be used too.

Serve as part of a brunch, put it next to grilled fish—I love it with swordfish—or spoon out alongside burgers, steaks or any kind of chicken. And while you might think it would be at its best straight out of the oven, the flavors are actually best when the crisp is just warm and still good at room temperature.

TO MAKE THE FILLING: Put all of the ingredients *except* the herbs in a large bowl and stir to mix. Set aside, stirring occasionally, while you preheat the oven and make the topping.

Center a rack in the oven and preheat it to 375 degrees F. Line a baking sheet with parchment paper or a baking mat and put a 2-quart baking dish, round, square or rectangular, on it; Pyrex, enamel or pottery is good here,.

TO MAKE THE TOPPING: Put all the ingredients *except* the butter in the bowl of a stand mixer or a medium bowl and stir them together. Drop in the butter and toss to coat the pieces with cornmeal and flour. Attach the bowl to the mixer stand, if using, fit it with the paddle attachment and, working on medium-low speed, beat until you've got a bowl full of fine nubbins. Or, if you're working by hand, rub everything together to break down the butter. When you squeeze some of the mixture between your fingers, it should hold together.

TO ASSEMBLE AND BAKE THE CRISP: Using a slotted spoon, lift the tomato and corn mixture out of the bowl and into the baking dish. Scoop out ¼ cup (60 ml) of the delicious liquid from the bowl and pour it over the vegetables, add the herbs and mix to blend well. (If you've got leftover juices, hold onto them!

Pour into a jar and refrigerate—they'll make a good drink over ice—think gazpacho—or the base for a nice vinaigrette.) Taste and see if you want more salt, pepper and/or cayenne or hot sauce.

To cover the vegetables with the topping, grab small amounts of the topping, squeeze into clumps and drop onto the vegetables; even it with your fingers.

Bake the crisp for 40 to 45 minutes, or until the topping is browned and the filling is bubbling madly. Transfer the baking dish to a rack and let the crisp rest. You can dig in after about 20 minutes, but the flavors and textures are better when the crisp is warm rather than hot or at room temperature.

The crisp can be kept at room temperature for about 8 hours.

STORING: Leftover crisp can be refrigerated and reheated in a 350-degree-F oven before serving.

# Asparagus-Lemon Quiche

*Makes 6 servings*

One 9- to 9½-inch tart shell made with All-Purpose Tart Dough (page 355), partially baked and cooled (or use store-bought pie dough)

6 medium-to-thick stalks asparagus, trimmed

1½ teaspoons unsalted butter

2 small shallots or 1 small onion, finely minced

Fine sea salt and freshly ground black pepper

One ¼-inch-thick slice lemon (including rind), cut into slivers

2 large eggs

½ cup (120 ml) heavy cream

⅓ cup (80 ml) sour cream

¼ cup (10 grams) minced mixed fresh herbs (see headnote)

2 tablespoons finely grated Parmesan (optional)

Olive oil for brushing (optional)

EVERYONE'S GOT THEIR OWN IDEA of what declares the true arrival of spring. The traditional harbinger may be the robin, but for me, it's asparagus. When the stalks appear in bundles at the farmers' market or are ready to be cut in the garden, it's time to pull out your sunglasses and put on extra sunblock. And time to bake. The two surprising ingredients in this quiche are chopped fresh lemon and sour cream. The sour cream wakes up the custard, adding sharpness and cutting richness. And the lemon, sliced into slivers, peel and all, and scattered over the bottom of the crust, turns up intermittently, delivering pucker.

If you've got peas, fresh or frozen, you can add them to the tart (blanch fresh peas with the asparagus; don't defrost frozen ones). And mix up the herbs—chives and tarragon are great with asparagus (the peas too) and it's nice to include some mint and if you have it, a bit of oregano, too. Scallion greens are always welcome.

Center a rack in the oven and preheat it to 400 degrees F. Place the tart pan on a baking sheet lined with parchment paper or a baking mat.

Bring a large skillet of salted water to a boil. Drop in the asparagus and blanch for 3 minutes (the asparagus shouldn't be completely cooked), then drain in a colander, run under cold water and pat dry.

Cut off the asparagus tips—make them about 3 inches long, then slice them lengthwise in half. Cut the remaining stalks on the bias into slices about ¼ to ½ wide. Wipe out the skillet.

Put the skillet over medium heat and add the butter. When it's melted, toss in the shallots or onion and cook, stirring, just until softened, about 3 minutes. Season with salt and pepper and scrape into the crust, spreading them evenly. Scatter over the lemon and sliced asparagus stalks.

Whisk the eggs, cream, sour cream and herbs together in a bowl just until blended. Season with salt (about ¼ teaspoon) and pepper, then pour the mixture into the crust. Arrange the asparagus tips, cut side down, any way you'd like on top of the filling.

Bake the quiche for 25 to 30 minutes, sprinkling on the Parm, if using, after it has been in the oven for 20 minutes. The quiche is done when the custard is set—a tester will come out clean—and puffed. Transfer to a rack and, if you like, brush some olive oil over the top, using only enough to give it a gloss.

Serve the quiche when it's just warm or has come to room temperature.

STORING: The quiche is at its peak the day it is made—best within a few hours of being baked. If you've got leftovers, refrigerate them and have them as a snack the next day.

# *Custardy Apple and Kale Cake*

*Makes 6 to 8 servings*

¾ cup (102 grams) all-purpose flour

1 teaspoon baking powder

1 teaspoon fine sea salt, plus more to taste

½ teaspoon freshly ground black pepper, plus more to taste

4½ tablespoons olive oil

1 small onion or 1 large shallot, finely chopped, rinsed in cold water and patted dry

2 loosely packed cups (175 grams) shredded or chopped kale

2 large eggs

⅓ cup (80 ml) milk

2 large or 3 medium apples, peeled or not, halved, cored and cut into 1- to 2-inch chunks

1 cup (85 grams) shredded cheese, such as cheddar or Monterey Jack (can be spicy or a mix of regular and smoked)

THIS CAKE, which is almost like a pudding, ping-pongs between sweet and savory, between familiar and startingly new. The ingredients are everyday—there are chunks of apple and shreds of kale, slices of onion and a handful of shredded cheese, mild, spicy or smoked. But when they're folded into the custardy batter and baked, they emerge transformed, still beloved and comforting, but now original. The cake is at its creamiest served warm; it becomes a little denser at room temperature. Marbled with kale and paved with chunks of soft, sweet apple, it can be a star at brunch or become a light supper—it does everything an omelet does, but it does it with more style

Center a rack in the oven and preheat it to 350 degrees F. Generously butter an 8-inch springform pan, or use baker's spray, and put it on a baking sheet lined with parchment paper or a baking mat.

Whisk the flour, baking powder, salt and pepper together; set aside.

Warm 1 tablespoon of the olive oil in a medium skillet over medium heat. Add the onion or shallot and cook, stirring, until softened, about 2 minutes. Drop in the kale, turn it around a few times and then pour in a spoonful or so of water. Cook, stirring, until the water evaporates and the greens are wilted. (If I'm using curly kale, I stop cooking it when it's still got a little chew.) Season with salt and pepper and scrape the mixture into a strainer set over a bowl; let drain.

Working in a medium bowl, whisk the eggs until they're foamy. Whisk in the milk. Add half of the flour mixture and, still working with the whisk, stir to blend it into the eggs; you may see a few small lumps—don't worry. Whisk in the remaining 3½ tablespoons oil, and when it's incorporated, blend in the rest of the flour. At this point, you can whisk more energetically for a minute to even out the batter. Switch to a flexible spatula and stir in the apples, stirring to coat them with batter, followed by the kale and then the cheese. You'll have a thick, bumpy mix.

Scrape the batter into the pan and jab at it with the spatula to get it into the corners, then even the top. The batter won't come close to filling the pan.

Slide the pan into the oven and bake for about 45 minutes, or until the top is lightly golden (it will be browner around the edges) and a tester inserted deep into the center comes out clean; the cake may pull away from the sides of the pan. Transfer to a rack and let rest for 10 minutes.

Carefully run a table knife around the edges of the cake and remove the sides of the springform pan (open the springform slowly and make sure nothing is stuck to the sides before fully opening it). Allow the cake to cool until it is just slightly warm or at room temperature. If you want to remove the cake from the bottom of the springform pan, wait until the cake is almost cooled, then turn it over onto a rack, remove the bottom of the pan and invert the cake onto a serving plate.

While the cake is nice just after it's baked, I think it tastes best just slightly warm or at room temperature.

STORING: Lightly covered, the cake can be kept at room temperature overnight. If you'd like to keep it for another day, wrap it and refrigerate.

# Smoked Salmon Roll-Up

*Makes 8 to 10 servings*

## FOR THE CAKE

2 teaspoons poppy seeds

¼ teaspoon garlic powder, or more to taste

¼ teaspoon onion powder, or more to taste

½ cup (68 grams) all-purpose flour

¼ cup (32 grams) cornstarch, plus more for dusting

6 large eggs, separated, at room temperature

½ teaspoon fine sea salt

Finely grated zest and juice of ½ lemon

## FOR THE FILLING

8 ounces (226 grams; generous 1 cup) whipped cream cheese

4 ounces (113 grams) smoked salmon, finely chopped

2 scallions, trimmed and thinly sliced

About 2 tablespoons finely chopped fresh dill, or to taste

About 2 tablespoons snipped fresh chives, or to taste

About 2 teaspoons capers, rinsed, patted dry and chopped

Freshly squeezed lemon juice to taste

Fine sea salt and freshly ground black pepper

## TO FINISH (OPTIONAL)

Finely sliced cucumber (peeled or not)

Finely sliced radishes

Freshly squeezed lemon juice

Fine sea salt and freshly ground black pepper

A handful of arugula if serving the cukes and radishes as a salad

## A WORD ON WORKING AHEAD:

As fancy as this looks, it can easily be made ahead. You can prepare both the cake and the filling the day before.

---

**THIS IS THE BAKER'S ANSWER** to the corner deli's bagels and lox special. It's a sponge cake—there's no sugar in the batter, but there's salt, lemon and poppy seeds to give it good flavor—rolled up around a few brunch favorites: cream cheese, silky smoked salmon, scallions, capers and chives. It makes a chic dinner starter served with a ruffle of green salad or some diced and dressed tomatoes. It's also a wonderful brunch dish.

**TO MAKE THE CAKE:** Center a rack in the oven and preheat the oven to 400 degrees F. Coat a rimmed baking sheet that's about 12 × 17 inches with baker's spray, line it with parchment paper and spray the paper. Have a clean kitchen towel and a strainer at hand.

Stir the poppy seeds and garlic and onion powder together in a small bowl.

Sift the flour and cornstarch together onto a sheet of parchment paper (easy to use later as a funnel) or into a medium bowl.

Put the egg whites in the bowl of a stand mixer fitted with the whisk attachment, or in a large bowl you can use with a hand mixer, and put the yolks in another large bowl. Whisk the yolks with the salt and lemon zest.

Beat the whites at medium-high speed until they hold firm peaks, taking care to stop before they separate into puffs. Spoon about a quarter of the whites over the yolks, add the lemon juice and whisk to blend—you're using the whites here to lighten the yolks, so there's no need to be gentle. Sprinkle the poppy seed mixture over the yolks, scrape the remainder of the whites into the bowl and top with the dry ingredients. Working with a flexible spatula, gingerly fold everything together, turning the bowl as you fold and being on the lookout for pockets of flour—they have a habit of hiding at the bottom of the bowl. The mixture will deflate—it's inevitable—so just carry on.

Scrape the batter out onto the parchment-lined baking sheet and spread it evenly across the entire surface.

Bake for 6 to 8 minutes, or until the cake has puffed (it will puff unevenly) and the top feels dry to the touch. Transfer the baking sheet to a rack and immediately, while the cake is still hot, lay the kitchen towel out on a work surface and dust it with cornstarch—shake the cornstarch through the strainer onto the towel. Run a table knife around the edges of the baking sheet to loosen the cake and turn it out onto the towel. Lift off the baking sheet and very carefully peel away the parchment. If necessary, turn the towel so that a short side of the cake is parallel to you (if you prefer a longer, more slender cake, you can roll it up starting from a long side), and roll the cake up as tightly as possible in the towel. Twist the ends of the towel to compress the cake, then allow to cool to room temperature. (*The cake can be made up to 1 day ahead and left, rolled up, at room temperature.*)

TO MAKE THE FILLING: Stir all of the ingredients *except* the lemon juice, salt and pepper together in a bowl until well blended. Taste and add as much juice, salt and pepper as you'd like. (*The filling can be refrigerated, covered, overnight.*)

TO ASSEMBLE THE ROLL-UP: Unroll the cake—you can leave it on the towel—and spread the filling evenly over it, leaving just a thin strip bare at the far end. Using the towel and your hands, roll the cake up as neatly and carefully as you can, finishing with the seam on the bottom (or as close to the bottom as you can manage). Slice off—and nibble on—the ragged ends.

TO FINISH THE ROLL-UP (OPTIONAL): If you'd like to top the roll-up, toss the cucumber and radish slices with a squirt of lemon juice, season with a little salt and pepper and arrange in an attractive pattern down the length of the roll. Alternatively, add some arugula to the mix and serve as a salad alongside the roll-up.

The roll-up is ready to serve now, or you can refrigerate it and serve chilled—it's good both ways.

STORING: The roll-up can be wrapped in plastic and kept in the refrigerator for up to 1 day.

# Whip-It-Up-Quick Cornbread

*Makes 8 to 10 servings*

1 stick (8 tablespoons; 4 ounces; 113 grams) unsalted butter (see below)

1¾ cups (306 grams) fine-grain cornmeal (see headnote)

¼ cup (34 grams) all-purpose flour

1 to 2 tablespoons sugar (optional)

1½ teaspoons baking powder

1 teaspoon fine sea salt

½ teaspoon baking soda

¼ teaspoon freshly ground black pepper, or more to taste

Pinch or more of cayenne pepper, to taste

2 large eggs

1¾ cups (420 ml) buttermilk (well shaken before measuring)

## OPTIONAL ADD-INS

4 to 6 strips cooked bacon, finely chopped

1 cup (140 grams) corn kernels, frozen or canned, drained if necessary and patted dry

1 small jalapeño pepper, trimmed, seeded and finely chopped

4 scallions, trimmed and finely sliced

3 or 4 tablespoons minced fresh herbs, such as parsley, cilantro, dill and/or rosemary

About ½ cup (about 45 grams) shredded cheddar or Monterey Jack cheese for topping (optional)

**A WORD ON FAT:** You need ½ cup (120 ml) of fat for this recipe, but you can switch up what you use. If you'd like, you can make the recipe with vegetable oil instead of the butter; you'll get a springier texture. Or, for a slightly smoky flavor, try using a blend of 3 tablespoons bacon fat and 5 tablespoons butter.

CORNBREAD BELONGS TO the quick-bread family, a clan of breads and muffins leavened with baking powder, but its name might just as well mean quick to mix and quick to bake. This bread, which I love alongside roast chicken, anything slow-simmered and saucy and almost everything grilled, particularly fish, is delicious, good-looking, made with ingredients I always have on hand and put together in minutes.

The bread is moist yet still showcases cornmeal's crumbliness (a virtue). I use a fine-grain yellow cornmeal, but if you like gritty, you can try this with a slightly coarser grind. (Anything rougher is better for polenta or mush, where the cornmeal is cooked in liquid.) You can also add spices, herbs, corn kernels, crisp bacon and/or chopped scallions and, if you like, top the bread with grated cheese; see the suggestions below. My favorite pan for this is a cast-iron skillet, but you'll still get a satisfying bread if you use a baking pan or a pie pan. Whether you serve the cornbread straight from the oven or at room temperature, slathered with butter (and maybe a drizzle of honey) or plain as can be, you'll find yourself marveling at how little effort it takes to make something so good.

Center a rack in the oven and preheat it to 400 degrees F. If you've got a 9- to 10-inch cast-iron or other oven-going skillet, place it on the stovetop. If you're using a 9-inch deep-dish pie pan or a 9-inch square baking pan, set it on the counter.

If you're baking in the skillet, put the butter in the pan, turn the heat under the skillet to medium and melt the butter. Otherwise, melt the butter and pour it into your baking pan.

Working in a large bowl, whisk the cornmeal, flour, sugar, if using, baking powder, salt, baking soda and both peppers together. Beat the eggs in a medium bowl and whisk in the buttermilk. Switch to a flexible spatula, pour the eggs and buttermilk over the dry ingredients and stir, stopping before the batter is fully blended. Grab the skillet or baking pan and carefully swirl the melted butter around so that it coats the sides of the pan (or do this with a pastry brush). Pour the butter into the bowl with the batter and mix it in. If you want add-ins, stir them in now. Turn the batter into the skillet or baking pan and sprinkle the top with the cheese, if you're using it.

Bake for 20 to 22 minutes, or until a tester inserted in the center of the bread comes out clean. Transfer the pan to a rack (or trivet) and serve now or later. The bread is good steaming-hot or at room temperature.

STORING: As with most quick breads, this one's best the day it is made, although you can wrap it and keep it at room temperature overnight. You might want to reheat it or slice and toast it before serving. You can also wrap it airtight and freeze for up to 2 months; defrost in its wrapper and reheat or toast it.

# Cheese Puffers

*Makes 12 puffers*

3 tablespoons unsalted butter, cut into 12 pieces

1¼ cups (170 grams) all-purpose flour

2 teaspoons baking powder

½ teaspoon fine sea salt

A few grinds of black pepper

Pinch of cayenne pepper

3 large eggs

1 cup (240 ml) milk, at room temperature

4 ounces (113 grams) cheddar cheese (see headnote), shredded

3 scallions, trimmed and finely sliced or chopped

**A WORD ON THE MUFFIN TIN:**
If you have a cast-iron muffin tin, put it in the oven when you start to preheat it and melt the butter in the cups a minute before you're ready to add the batter. Check puffers after 15 minutes in the oven.

THESE ARE A CROSS between a muffin and a popover. They look like muffins (they're baked in a muffin tin) but are made like popovers (the butter is heated in the tin, so the batter gets a quick boost as soon as it goes into the oven). And when the puffers are hot, they're stretchy and custardy—and really only like themselves.

They're good as a go-along with soup, stew or chili, and they're also terrific with anything you'd serve at brunch. Not surprisingly, these are best soon after they come out of the oven, so gather your people.

I usually make these with shredded cheddar and chopped scallions, because I always have these ingredients in the fridge. But you can use a different cheese that melts easily—Gruyère is delicious in these as is Monterey Jack, Havarti or even Swiss—and add other flavors and textures as well. These can take a little spice (consider paprika or mustard powder, for instance) some herbs (like thyme, rosemary or parsley) or some chopped nuts.

Center a rack in the oven and position another rack just below it. Preheat the oven to 425 degrees F. Have a baking sheet lined with foil or a baking mat and a muffin tin at hand. (If you're using a cast-iron pan, put it into the oven now; see above.) Put the baking sheet on the lower rack—it will be your drip-catcher.

Drop one piece of the butter into each muffin cup; set aside (see above if using a cast-iron pan).

Working in a large bowl, whisk together the flour, baking powder, salt, black pepper and cayenne.

In another bowl or a large measuring cup, whisk the eggs and milk together. Using a flexible spatula, stir the liquid ingredients into the dry, then blend in the cheese and scallions. Be thorough, but don't be overzealous.

Put the muffin tin into the oven and as soon as the butter has melted, remove it and brush the butter around the sides of each cup with a silicone or other pastry brush. Using a big cookie scoop or a spoon, divide the batter among the cups and immediately return the tin to the oven.

Bake for 20 to 23 minutes, or until the puffers are tall and golden. The butter will be bubbling around them and a tester inserted into the center of one will come out clean. Transfer the tin to a rack, run a table knife around the edges of each cup and pop the puffers out. Serve immediately.

**STORING:** These are meant to be eaten as soon as they're baked, but if they must wait for a few hours, quickly reheat them in a hot oven.

BASICS,
MUST-KNOWS
AND FILLIPS

# DOUGHS AND CRUSTS: A HOW-TO

I collect crust recipes with the same enthusiasm that I collect scarves and for almost the same reason: Just as a beautiful scarf can make a simple tee look good, so a well-made crust can tip the scales on a pie or tart, pushing it from satisfactory to very special.

Once I figured out crusts—I was afraid of tackling them for a long time—I took both pleasure and pride in making them. I also became practical: I've always got a few rolled-out rounds of dough in the freezer— usually some crusts too—ready for a haul from the farm stand or a spur-of-the-moment urge to bake. But if you're not already at the point where you can jump up and bake a pie on a whim, here are some tips to get you there.

•   I'm convinced that the food processor is the best tool for making dough. Make sure your butter is very cold—almost frozen is the kind of cold you want—and cut it into small chunks. When the dry ingredients have been amply whirred, remove the top, scatter over the butter and then start pulsing. Pulse in long— 10-second—spurts and stop often to scrape the bottom of the work bowl; the dough has a habit of getting under the blade and packing down there. Keep pulsing until you've got moist clumps and curds. Don't be surprised if it takes you 10, 15 or 20 pulses to get a clumpy dough that holds together when you pinch it. Whatever liquid you're using for the crust, most often eggs or water, pulse it in gradually. Stop mixing before the dough forms a ball on the blade.

•   Dough is easiest to roll when it's just made. Put it between two sheets of parchment and roll to size. If it's still cold, you can fit it into the pan now; if not, chill or freeze until it's cool but workable.

•   If your rolled-out dough is coming out of the fridge or freezer, let it rest just until it's pliable before fitting it into the pan or using it to make a galette or other free-form pastry. Cold dough cracks easily, but it's also fixed easily: Smooth and seal the cracks with your fingers and a little water.

•   As for freezing the dough, you've got options. For the freshest flavor, I prefer to freeze the unbaked dough. Freeze rolled-out dough sandwiched between sheets of parchment on a baking sheet or cutting board (so it will stay flat). When it's frozen, remove it from the sheet or board and wrap it in foil or plastic (I use foil). If you've got a few rounds, stack them. Or, you can fit the rolled-out dough into the pan and wrap it well. Bake it straight from the freezer if your pan isn't Pyrex; Pyrex pans should be allowed to sit at room temperature while you preheat the oven. You can also freeze a fully baked crust in the pan, well wrapped. Unbaked or baked, crusts can be frozen for up to 2 months.

•   Here's a tip for keeping the edges of your crusts from getting too brown: Make a pie shield. Fold a 12-inch piece of foil or parchment into quarters and then in half again. Holding the point, cut out a 4-inch quarter-moon, then open up the foil or parchment. When the edges of your crust are golden (or just shy of the color you want—even with the shield, the crust might take on a bit of color), drop the shield into place. After you've used the shield, hold on to it—you'll be able to use it several more times.

# All-Butter Pie Dough

*Makes two 9- to 9½- inch crusts*

3 cups (408 grams) all-purpose flour

¼ cup (50 grams) sugar

1½ teaspoons fine sea salt

2 sticks (8 ounces; 226 grams) unsalted butter, frozen or very cold, cut into small pieces

Up to ½ cup (120 ml) ice water

**PLAN AHEAD:** The crust needs to be refrigerated for at least 1 hour.

**THIS IS MY PIE DOUGH.** Period. It's both flaky and a bit firm, and it's got a lot of flavor. It can be used with all kinds of fillings. It rolls without fuss. It holds a crimped edge. If you've never made a piecrust before, you can make this one and pin a blue ribbon on your apron.

The recipe makes two crusts. You can cut it in half if you want to, but it's nice to have an extra crust on hand. Roll it out, wrap and freeze it or, if you've got an extra pie pan, fit it into the pan and freeze it.

*For a quick how-to on doughs and crusts, see the page opposite.*

Put the flour, sugar and salt in a food processor and pulse to blend. Scatter the pieces of butter over the flour and pulse the machine in long spurts until the butter is well incorporated. This could take more than a dozen blitzes. Add the ice water a little at time, processing after each addition. Stop when you have moist clumps and curds (you may not need all of the water)—don't process until the dough forms a ball; pinch a bit of the dough, and it should hold together easily. Turn the dough out, divide it in half and shape each half into a disk.

Working with one disk at a time, flour a sheet of parchment paper, center the dough on it, flour the dough and cover with a second sheet. Roll the dough into a round that's between 11 and 12 inches in diameter.

If the dough is cold enough, fit it into a buttered pie pan (or the pan you're using); leave whatever dough hangs over the edge. If it's not cold, chill it until it's workable, then fit it into the pan. Keep the second round between the sheets of paper and slide it onto a baking sheet. Freeze or refrigerate for at least 1 hour.

Follow the directions in the recipe you're using for filling and finishing the crusts. If you're making an open-faced pie and need a partially or fully baked bottom crust, either crimp the dough that's hanging over the pan to make a decorative edge or trim the excess dough even with the rim of the pan and press the tines of a fork against the dough.

**GETTING READY TO BAKE:** Center a rack in the oven and preheat it to 375 degrees F. Place the pie pan on a baking sheet and fit a piece of parchment or foil against the crust; fill with dried beans or rice.

**TO PARTIALLY BAKE:** Bake for 20 minutes, then carefully remove the paper or foil and weights and bake for another 3 to 4 minutes—you want the crust to be firm, but it doesn't need to take on much color.

**TO FULLY BAKE:** Bake for 20 minutes, then carefully remove the paper or foil and weights and bake for about 8 minutes more, or until the crust is beautifully golden.

Transfer the crust to a rack and let cool.

**STORING:** The rolled-out crusts or the unbaked pie shells can be wrapped well and refrigerated for up to 3 days or frozen for up to 2 months. You can also freeze baked crusts (in the pans) for up to 2 months.

# Sweet Tart Dough

*Makes one 9- to 9½-inch tart crust or piecrust*

1½ cups (204 grams) all-purpose flour

⅓ cup (40 grams) confectioners' sugar

2 tablespoons sugar

¼ teaspoon fine sea salt

Grated zest of 1 lemon (optional)

1 stick plus 1 tablespoon (9 tablespoons; 4½ ounces; 128 grams) very cold unsalted butter, cut into small pieces

1 large egg yolk

½ teaspoon pure vanilla extract (optional)

**PLAN AHEAD:** The crust needs to be refrigerated for at least 1 hour.

**AT ITS HEART,** this is a shortbread cookie standing in as a crust. The dough is sweet and full of character—it won't go unnoticed no matter how flashy the filling. I think of its texture as crisp-tender—it will cut with a snap and melt in your mouth. Bake it until it's deeply golden, and you'll increase the rich flavors of butter and caramelized sugar. If you'd like even more flavor, you can treat the dough the way you would a shortbread cookie—add lemon zest and vanilla. (For a more classic tart dough, see Playing Around.)

*For a quick how-to on doughs and crusts, see page 346.*

Put the flour, both of the sugars, the salt and lemon zest, if using, in a food processor and pulse to blend. Scatter over the pieces of butter. Cut the butter into the dry ingredients until you've got some pieces the size of oatmeal flakes and others the size of peas. Work in long pulses and scrape the bowl often.

Stir the yolk and vanilla, if you're using it, together and add in 3 additions, pulsing after each. Then pulse until the dough just starts to come together and clumps and holds together when pinched. Turn it out onto a work surface, knead into a compact ball, flatten into a disk and sandwich between two sheets of parchment paper.

Roll the dough into an 11- to 12-inch round. If it's cold enough, fit it into a 9- to 9½-inch fluted tart pan with a removable bottom or a pie pan, prick the bottom with a fork and trim the top even with the pan's rim. If it's not cold, chill it until it's workable and then proceed. Refrigerate for at least 1 hour.

**GETTING READY TO BAKE:** Center a rack in the oven and preheat it to 375 degrees F.

Place the pan on a baking sheet, fit a piece of parchment or foil against the crust and fill with dried beans or rice.

**TO PARTIALLY BAKE:** Bake for 20 minutes, then carefully remove the paper or foil and weights and bake for 4 more minutes—you want the crust to be firm but it doesn't need to take on much color.

**TO FULLY BAKE:** Bake for 20 minutes, then carefully remove the paper or foil and weights and bake for 7 to 10 minutes more, or until it is firm and golden brown.

Transfer the crust to a rack and let cool.

**STORING:** The rolled-out crust or the unbaked tart shell can be wrapped well and refrigerated for up to 3 days or frozen for up to 2 months. You can also freeze the baked crust (in the pan) for up to 2 months.

## Playing Around

**CLASSIC SWEET TART DOUGH**

For a tad more tender crust, use ½ cup confectioners' sugar and no granulated sugar. For a plain crust, omit the lemon zest and vanilla extract.

# Chocolate Tart Dough

*Makes one 9- to 9½-inch tart crust*

1¼ cups (170 grams) all-purpose flour

¼ cup (30 grams) confectioners' sugar

¼ cup (21 grams) unsweetened cocoa powder

¼ teaspoon fine sea salt

1 stick plus 1 tablespoon (9 tablespoons; 4½ ounces; 128 grams) cold unsalted butter, cut into bits

1 large egg yolk, lightly beaten

**A WORD ON THE YIELD:** This recipe makes a generous amount of dough. If you're using it to line a 9- to 9½-inch tart pan, you'll have extra dough left over to roll out, dust with sugar and bake as cookies.

**THIS IS MY TOP CHOICE** for chocolate tart dough, one that never disappoints. I like it filled with Chocolate Frangipane (page 359), a luscious almond filling, or fruit (try the Chocolate Banana Tart, page 291, or Double-Chocolate Rhubarb Tart, page 290). Or pile it high with berries or ice cream or spoon it full of Cranberry Curd (page 364). If you're making any tart that you think would be good with chocolate, swap this for Sweet Tart Dough (page 348).

*For a quick how-to on doughs and crusts, see page 346.*

Put the flour, confectioners' sugar, cocoa and salt in a food processor and whir to blend. Scatter over the pieces of butter and work them in using long pulses. You might have to pulse as many as two dozen times to get a mixture that's coarse and crumbly. Use a knife to break up any dough that settles and packs at the bottom of the bowl. Add the yolk a little at a time, pulsing after each bit goes in, until you've got a bowl full of moist clumps and curds; squeeze some, and they should hold together. Turn the dough out onto a work surface and knead to bring it together into a ball. Pat the dough into a disk.

Put the dough between two sheets of parchment paper and roll it into an 11- to 12-inch round. If it's cold enough, fit it into a 9- to 9½-inch fluted tart pan with a removable bottom or a pie pan, prick the bottom with a fork and trim the top even with the pan's rim. If it's not cold, chill it until it's workable and then proceed. Refrigerate for at least 1 hour.

**GETTING READY TO BAKE:** Center a rack in the oven and preheat it to 375 degrees F.

Place the pan on a baking sheet, fit a piece of parchment or foil against the crust and fill with dried beans or rice.

**TO PARTIALLY BAKE:** Bake for 20 minutes, then carefully remove the paper or foil and weights and bake for another 3 to 4 minutes, until the crust no longer looks raw. Color is hard to judge with chocolate, but the crust should feel as though it's starting to firm.

**TO FULLY BAKE:** Bake for 20 minutes, then carefully remove the paper or foil and weights and bake for about 8 minutes more—the crust will feel firm.

Transfer the crust to a rack and let cool.

**STORING:** The rolled-out crust or the unbaked tart shell can be wrapped well and refrigerated for up to 3 days or frozen for up to 2 months. You can also freeze the baked crust (in the pan) for up to 2 months.

# Sour Cream Pie Dough

*Makes enough dough for 1 picnic pie or two 9-inch piecrusts*

4 cups (544 grams) all-purpose flour

½ cup (100 grams) sugar

1½ teaspoons fine sea salt

3 sticks (12 ounces; 339 grams) very cold unsalted butter, cut into bits

1 cup (240 ml) cold sour cream

**PLAN AHEAD:** The dough needs to be refrigerated for at least 3 hours.

**THAT THIS DOUGH IS EASY TO ROLL** is reason enough to love it, but there's also its terrific taste and texture. Because it's made with sour cream, it has a full, somewhat tangy flavor. The sour cream also makes it tender, a little flaky and a bit cakey. You can make this by hand or in a food processor.

Unlike most of my other doughs, this one is best chilled *before* rolling and fitting it into the pan. You can substitute the dough for pie dough; follow the baking instructions in the recipe.

*For a quick how-to on doughs and crusts, see page 346.*

**TO MAKE THE DOUGH IN A FOOD PROCESSOR:** Put the flour, sugar and salt in the processor and pulse to blend. Drop in the bits of butter and pulse until you've got moist clumps. This can take a minute or more—be sure to scrape the sides and bottom of the bowl from time to time. When you've got crumbs that hold together when pinched, add the sour cream and pulse until it's incorporated and you've got a moist dough. Turn it out onto a work surface and gently knead it a couple of times to bring it together.

**TO MAKE THE DOUGH BY HAND:** Whisk the flour, sugar and salt together in a large bowl. Drop in the bits of cold butter, toss to coat them with flour and then, working with your fingertips or a pastry blender, mash and rub the butter into the flour until you've got moist crumbs and pieces of stretched and smashed butter—be patient, it's a lot of ingredients, and it can take a few minutes to reach this stage. Add the sour cream and, working with a fork and your hand, toss and stir everything together as though you were mixing a salad. Then, working either in the bowl or on a work surface, knead the dough a few times to bring it together.

Shape the dough into a chubby log, cut it in half and pat each half into a rectangle (for a picnic pie) or a round (for a pie). Wrap in plastic and refrigerate for at least 3 hours.

The dough rolls easily when chilled. Roll out one piece on a floured work surface, turning it over so that you roll on both sides, and dusting the surface with more flour as you need it. Roll the dough up on your rolling pin and place it over your pan. Let it fall into the pan and then use your fingers to fit it into place. If you get a crack or tear, mend it by joining the pieces with a moistened finger. If there's a bare spot, cut off a piece of excess dough, moisten it and the borders of the spot, and patch it. Cover and refrigerate until chilled. If you're making a top crust with the second piece of dough, roll the dough to size between sheets of parchment paper. Refrigerate or freeze until cold.

**GETTING READY TO BAKE:** Center a rack in the oven and preheat it to 375 degrees F.

Place the pan on a baking sheet and fit a piece of parchment or foil against the crust; fill with dried beans or rice.

**TO PARTIALLY BAKE THE BOTTOM CRUST:** Bake for 20 minutes, then carefully remove the paper or foil and weights and bake the crust for another 3 to 4 minutes, until just firm; it shouldn't take on much color.

**TO FULLY BAKE THE BOTTOM CRUST:** Bake for 20 minutes, then carefully remove the paper or foil and weights and bake the crust for about 8 minutes more, until firm and golden.

Transfer the crust to a rack and let cool.

**STORING:** The dough—rolled out or not, or fitted into the pan—can be wrapped well and frozen for up to 2 months. You can also freeze the baked crust (in the pan) for up to 2 months.

# Cream Cheese Dough

*Makes enough dough for about 40 cookies*

4 ounces (113 grams) cold cream cheese

1 stick (8 tablespoons; 4 ounces; 113 grams) cold unsalted butter

1 cup (136 grams) all-purpose flour

¼ teaspoon baking powder

¼ teaspoon fine sea salt

**PLAN AHEAD:** The dough needs to chill for at least 2 hours.

THIS DOUGH, the classic one used to make rugelach (page 189), is a mix of cream cheese and butter, with less flour than you'd think and no sugar.

*For a quick how-to on doughs and crusts, see page 346.*

Take the cream cheese and butter out of the refrigerator 10 minutes before you're ready to start and cut into 4 chunks each. (You want these ingredients to be slightly softened but still cool.)

Put the flour, baking powder and salt in a food processor and pulse to blend, then scatter over the pieces of cream cheese and butter and pulse the machine 6 to 10 times, so that the flour coats the chunks. Process, scraping down the sides of the bowl often, until the dough forms large curds—stop at the curd stage, you don't want the dough to form a ball.

Turn the dough out, gather it into a ball and divide it in half. Shape each half into a square or round, wrap in plastic wrap and refrigerate for at least 2 hours.

Follow the Rugelach recipe (page 189) for working with the dough. If you want to use the dough for another recipe, roll the dough out on a floured work surface, reflouring it as needed so that the dough moves easily, or between sheets of parchment.

STORING: Tightly wrapped, the dough will keep in the refrigerator for up to 3 days and in the freezer for up to 2 months; thaw overnight in the refrigerator.

# Galette Dough

*Makes 1 galette crust or 1 tart crust or piecrust*

1½ (204 grams) cups all-purpose flour

2 tablespoons sugar

½ teaspoon fine sea salt

1 stick (8 tablespoons; 4 ounces:
   113 grams) very cold unsalted butter,
   cut into 16 pieces

¼ cup (60 ml) ice water

**PLAN AHEAD:** The dough needs
to be chilled for at least 2 hours.

THIS MIGHT COME AS CLOSE to an all-purpose use-it-for-everything dough as any I know. It's got pie dough's flakiness and tart dough's crisper texture and butter-rich flavor. It's supremely easy to roll. It's ideal for all kinds of free-form rustic tarts—it holds its shape beautifully—and it can also be used for traditional tarts and pies. Make it sweet, or leave out the sugar and make it savory (see Playing Around). I like this dough so much that I always have two rolled-out rounds—one sweet, one savory—in the freezer. It's nice to know that a galette is only a few apples (page 248) or potatoes (page 306) away.

*For a quick how-to on doughs and crusts, see page 346.*

Put the flour, sugar, and salt in a food processor and pulse a couple of times to blend. Scatter the pieces of butter over the dry ingredients and pulse until the butter is cut into the flour. At first you'll have a mixture that looks like coarse meal and then, as you pulse more, you'll get small flake-size pieces and some larger pea-size pieces too. Add a little of the ice water and pulse, add some more and pulse and continue until all of the water is in. Then work in longer pulses, stopping to scrape the sides and bottom of the bowl if needed, until you have a dough that forms nice, bumpy curds that hold together when you pinch them.

Turn the dough out onto a work surface and knead it gently to bring it together. Gather the dough into a ball, flatten it into a disk and put it between two large pieces of parchment paper. Immediately roll the dough into an 11- to 12-inch round (or the size the recipe you're making calls for). If you're making a galette, don't worry too much about getting the exact size or about having the edges of the round be perfect—ragged is pretty for a galette or other rustic tart. The dough will be thicker than you think it should be, and that's fine—it's what you need for a free-form pastry.

Slide the rolled-out dough, still between the sheets of paper, onto a baking sheet or cutting board and refrigerate for at least 2 hours.

When you're ready to use the dough, let it sit at room temperature for a few minutes, just so that it's pliable enough to lift and fold without cracking.

If you're making a tart or pie rather than a galette, fit the dough into the pan and trim it (or do as the recipe suggests).

GETTING READY TO BAKE A TART CRUST OR PIECRUST: Center a rack in the oven and preheat it to 375 degrees F.

Place the pan on a baking sheet, fit the chilled crust with a piece of parchment or foil and fill with dried beans or rice.

TO PARTIALLY BAKE: Bake for 20 minutes, then carefully remove the paper or foil and weights and bake for another 3 to 4 minutes, until only just firm; it shouldn't take on color.

TO FULLY BAKE: Bake for 20 minutes, then carefully remove the paper or foil and weights and bake for another 8 minutes, until firm and golden.

Transfer to a rack and let cool.

STORING: The rolled-out crust or the unbaked crust can be wrapped well and refrigerated for up to 3 days or frozen for up to 2 months. You can also freeze the baked crust (in the pan) for up to 2 months.

## Playing Around

SAVORY GALETTE DOUGH

Reduce the sugar to 1½ teaspoons, or omit it, and, if you'd like, increase the salt to ¾ teaspoon.

# All-Purpose Tart Dough

*Makes one 9- to 9½-inch tart crust or piecrust*

1¼ cups (170 grams) all-purpose flour

1 teaspoon sugar

½ teaspoon fine sea salt

¾ stick (6 tablespoons; 3 ounces; 85 grams) very cold unsalted butter, cut into bits

1 large egg

1 teaspoon ice water

**PLAN AHEAD:** The dough needs to be refrigerated for at least an hour.

THIS RECIPE IS FOR FRENCH *pâte brisée,* or short crust. In Paris, my friends think of this dough as all-purpose—they'll use it for an apple tart as often as they'll roll it out for a quiche—and so that's what I've dubbed it. Like its American cousin, All-Butter Pie Dough (page 347), it's easy to work with and can switch-hit sweet or savory. However, it bakes up firmer than pie dough—the better to hold the flutes of a tart pan—and more golden, because it's got plenty of butter. It also tastes richer—that's the butter again.

*For a quick how-to on doughs and crusts, see page 346.*

Put the flour, sugar and salt in a food processor and pulse to blend. Scatter over the pieces of butter. You want to cut the butter into the dry ingredients until you've got some pieces the size of oatmeal flakes and others the size of peas. Work in long pulses—you might need as many as 20—and scrape the bowl often. Stir the egg and water together and add in 3 additions, pulsing after each. Then pulse until the dough just starts to come together, forms moist curds and clumps and holds together when pinched.

Turn the dough out onto a work surface, knead into a compact ball and flatten into a disk, then sandwich between sheets of parchment. Roll the dough into an 11-inch round. If it's cold enough, fit it into a 9- to 9½-inch fluted tart pan with a removable bottom or into a pie pan, prick the bottom with a fork and trim the top even with the pan's rim. If it's not cold, chill it until it's workable and then proceed. Refrigerate the crust in the pan for at least 1 hour.

**GETTING READY TO BAKE:** Center a rack in the oven and preheat it to 375 degrees F.

Place the pan on a baking sheet, fit a piece of parchment or foil against the crust and fill with dried beans or rice.

**TO PARTIALLY BAKE:** Bake the crust for 20 minutes, then carefully remove the paper or foil and weights and bake for another 4 minutes, until just firm; it shouldn't take on much color.

**TO FULLY BAKE:** Bake the crust for 20 minutes, then carefully remove the paper or foil and the weights and bake for 7 to 10 minutes more, or until it is firm and golden brown.

Transfer to a rack and let cool.

**STORING:** The rolled-out crust or unbaked tart shell can be wrapped well and refrigerated for up to 3 days or frozen for up to 2 months. You can also freeze the baked crust (in the pan) for up to 2 months.

# Raggedy-Edged Almond-Herb Crust

*Makes 1 free-form crust*

1½ cups (204 grams) all-purpose flour

½ cup (¾ ounce; 50 grams) almond flour or an equal weight of almonds, finely ground in a food processor (or an additional ⅓ cup/45 grams all-purpose flour)

½ teaspoon fine sea salt

1 stick (8 tablespoons; 4 ounces; 113 grams) cold unsalted butter, cut into bits

2 to 3 tablespoons minced fresh herbs (see headnote)

1 cold large egg, lightly beaten

THIS CRUST IS LIKE a kind of platter, a delicious base for savory spreads and toppings. It's the crust for the Free-Style Mushroom, Herb and Ricotta Tart (page 313), and it can be used for the Vegetable Ribbon Tart too (page 319). Turn to it whenever you want to pile on a mix of vegetables and herbs or a hearty salad, maybe one that includes chunks of cheese or some grilled vegetables. It's also good with anything you might put on a cracker—try it with a swipe of cream cheese and slices of smoked salmon, and a glass of rosé.

Although I love the texture you get when you use some almond flour, you'll still get a great crust using only all-purpose flour. Similarly, a mix of herbs, maybe chives, dill, rosemary and thyme, is always a good idea, but if all you've got is a bunch of parsley or some scallion greens, don't let that stop you.

*For a quick how-to on doughs and crusts, see page 346.*

Put both flours and the salt in a food processor and pulse to blend. Drop in the pieces of butter and pulse about 15 times—you want the mixture to pass from the looks-like-sand stage into the discernible-crumbs stage—scraping the bottom of the bowl a couple of times (don't allow a hard layer of ingredients to form under the blade and around the edges).

Drop in the herbs and pulse only to blend. Add the egg in 3 additions, pulsing after each, and then pulse (and scrape if needed) until the dough forms clumps and curds; it should hold together when pinched. If the dough seems dry, pulse a few times more and if it still seems dry, add a splash of cold water and pulse again.

Turn the dough out, gather it into a ball and then, working with a bit of it at a time, rub the dough across the counter with the heel of your hand (this finishes the blending). Gather the dough together again and flatten it into a disk.

Place the dough between two sheets of parchment and roll to a thickness of ⅛ inch, peeling back the paper occasionally to make sure that it's not creasing the dough and flipping the dough so you roll both sides. Don't worry about the shape—it can be any shape you want—it's the thickness that counts. And don't worry about the edges—you want them ragged. Prick the dough all over with a fork and slide it, still between the paper, onto a baking sheet. Refrigerate for at least 2 hours or freeze for at least 1 hour.

WHEN YOU'RE READY TO BAKE: Center a rack in the oven and preheat it to 400 degrees F.

Peel away both sheets of parchment. Put the bottom piece of paper on the baking sheet, replace the dough on it and cover it loosely with the top sheet to keep it from coloring too much. Bake for 18 to 20 minutes, or until the crust is golden around the edges. Remove the top sheet of paper and bake for another 2 to 3 minutes, to give the crust more color and firmness. Transfer the baking sheet to a rack and let the crust cool to room temperature.

STORING: The rolled-out dough can be wrapped well and refrigerated for up to 3 days or frozen for up to 2 months. Once the crust is baked, it's best to use it within 8 hours. If you need to hold the baked crust overnight, and if it doesn't seem firm enough when you are ready to use it, refresh it in a 350-degree-F oven for 5 to 10 minutes.

# Graham Cracker Crust

*Makes one 9-inch crust*

1½ cups (168 grams) graham cracker crumbs (from about 9 crackers)

2 tablespoons sugar

¼ teaspoon fine sea salt

1 stick (8 tablespoons; 4 ounces; 113 grams) unsalted butter, melted

A GRAHAM CRACKER CRUST IS an indispensable part of the baker's kit. It's easy to make the crust at home, but in a pinch, store-bought crusts are good. If you buy a store-bought crust, make sure to choose one that's a full 9 inches—these are the ones that say they serve 10.

Butter a 9-inch pie pan.

Put all the ingredients in a large bowl and stir until the crumbs are thoroughly moistened with butter. I like to do this with my fingers.

Press the crumbs evenly over the bottom and up the sides of the pan. Pop it into the freezer while you preheat the oven. (*The crust can be frozen, well wrapped, for up to 2 months; see page 346.*)

Center a rack in the oven and preheat it to 350 degrees F.

Put the pie pan on a baking sheet and bake the crust for 10 minutes. Cool completely before filling.

STORING: Wrapped well, the crust, baked or unbaked, will keep in the freezer for up to 2 months. The baked crust can be kept, covered, at room temperature overnight or in the refrigerator for a few days.

# Chocolate Frangipane

*Makes about 1½ cups*

¾ stick (6 tablespoons; 3 ounces; 85 grams) unsalted butter, at room temperature

⅔ cup (132 grams) sugar

¾ cup (about 2½ ounces/75 grams) almond flour, or an equal weight of almonds, finely ground in a food processor

2 teaspoons all-purpose flour (or omit the flour and use 1 more teaspoon cornstarch to make the frangipane gluten-free)

1 teaspoon cornstarch

¼ teaspoon fine sea salt

1 large egg, at room temperature

2 teaspoons dark rum or 1 teaspoon pure vanilla extract

2 ounces (56 grams) semisweet or bittersweet chocolate, melted

PLAN AHEAD: The frangipane is best if chilled for at least an hour before using.

## Playing Around

To make classic frangipane, omit the chocolate. For either chocolate or classic, you can replace the almonds with an equal weight of other nuts, such as hazelnuts, pistachio, or walnuts.

FRANGIPANE IS TRADITIONALLY A MIXTURE of ground almonds (although you can use other nuts), sugar, egg and butter (see Playing Around); this version, which includes chocolate, is the filling for Double-Chocolate Rhubarb Tart (page 290) and Chocolate Banana Tart (page 291). You can omit the chocolate in the recipe to make classic frangipane. Frangipane is always baked, and it usually chilled before baking.

TO MAKE THE FRANGIPANE IN A FOOD PROCESSOR: Put the butter and sugar in the processor and process until the mixture is smooth and creamy. Add the almond flour, all-purpose flour, if using, cornstarch and salt and process to blend. Add the egg and process for 1 minute, or until the frangipane is homogenous. Add the rum or vanilla and pulse to mix, then add the melted chocolate, pulsing and processing only until the chocolate is evenly incorporated.

TO MAKE THE FRANGIPANE WITH AN ELECTRIC MIXER: If you're using a stand mixer, fit it with the paddle attachment; if you're using a hand mixer, work in a medium bowl. Beat the butter on medium speed for about 3 minutes, until smooth and creamy. Add the sugar and beat for another 2 minutes. Add the almond flour, all-purpose flour, if using, cornstarch and salt and beat until well blended. Drop in the egg and beat for another 2 minutes. Add the rum or vanilla, then beat in the melted chocolate.

You can use the frangipane as soon as it's made, but it's really best if you chill it, covered, for at least 1 hour.

STORING: Tightly covered, the frangipane will keep in the refrigerator for 3 to 5 days. Give it a good stir before using—you want it to be spreadable. You can also freeze it for up to 2 months; defrost in the refrigerator overnight.

# Vanilla Pastry Cream

*Makes about 2 cups*

2 cups (480 ml) milk

6 large egg yolks

½ cup (100 grams) sugar

⅓ cup (43 grams) cornstarch, sifted

1 tablespoon pure vanilla extract

3½ tablespoons (1¾ ounces; 50 grams) unsalted butter, softened

THINK OF PASTRY CREAM, *crème pâtissière,* as pudding with a French accent. It's the traditional filling for a fruit tart, cream puffs (page 217) or éclairs (page 228) and is often used as a filling for layer cakes. For a chocolate version, see the page opposite.

Rinse a medium saucepan with cold water, but don't dry it (this helps prevent the milk from scorching). Pour the milk into the pan and heat until you see bubbles around the perimeter of the pan.

Meanwhile, working in a medium bowl (put it on a folded dish towel or a silicone pot holder to anchor it), whisk the yolks, sugar and cornstarch together until blended. Whisking constantly, drizzle in about one quarter of the hot milk. When the yolks are warm, add the rest of the liquid in a steadier stream. Pour the mixture into the saucepan, set it over medium heat and, whisking vigorously, bring to a boil. Keep at a boil—never stop whisking, and make sure to get into the corners of the pan—for 1 to 2 minutes. Remove from the heat and if the cream isn't smooth, press it through a sieve into a clean bowl. Stir in the vanilla.

Let the pastry cream sit at room temperature for 10 minutes, then stir in the butter bit by bit.

Press a piece of plastic wrap against the surface of the cream and refrigerate it until it's thoroughly chilled, at least 2 hours; or fill a large bowl with ice cubes and cold water, set the bowl of pastry cream in it and stir occasionally until it's cold. Cover and refrigerate until needed.

STORING: Well covered, pastry cream will keep in the refrigerator for up to 3 days. Whisk it well to loosen it before using.

# Chocolate Pastry Cream

*Makes about 2½ cups*

2 cups (480 ml) milk

4 large egg yolks

6 tablespoons (72 grams) sugar

3 tablespoons cornstarch, sifted

¼ teaspoon fine sea salt

7 ounces (200 grams) bittersweet chocolate, melted and still warm

2½ tablespoons unsalted butter, at room temperature

IF YOU'D LIKE to add a little more flavor to this cream, you can steep the milk with whole spices (think cinnamon stick, cardamom pods, star anise or pepper, for instance). Steep for about 15 minutes, then drain and discard the spices.

Rinse a medium saucepan with cold water, but don't dry it (this helps prevent the milk from scorching). Pour the milk into the pan and heat until you see bubbles around the perimeter of the pan.

Meanwhile, working in a medium bowl (put it on a folded dish towel or a silicone pot holder to anchor it), whisk the yolks, sugar and cornstarch together until blended. Whisking constantly, drizzle in about one quarter of the hot milk. When the yolks are warm, add the rest of the liquid in a steadier stream. Pour the mixture into the saucepan, set it over medium heat and, whisking vigorously, bring to a boil. Keep at a boil—never stop whisking. and don't miss the corners of the pan—for 1 to 2 minutes. Remove the pan from the heat and if the cream isn't smooth, push it through a sieve into a clean bowl.

Whisk in the melted chocolate and let the mixture sit for 5 minutes, then whisk in the butter bit by bit, stirring until the butter is fully incorporated and the cream is smooth.

Press a piece of plastic wrap against the surface of the cream and refrigerate it until it's thoroughly chilled, at least 2 hours; or fill a large bowl with ice cubes and cold water, set the bowl of pastry cream in it and stir occasionally. until it is cold. Cover and refrigerate until needed.

STORING: Well covered, pastry cream will keep in the refrigerator for up to 3 days. Whisk it well to loosen it before using.

# Whipped Cream

*Makes about 2 cups*

1 cup (240 ml) very cold heavy cream

2 tablespoons confectioners' sugar (or more to taste), sifted

1 teaspoon pure vanilla extract (optional)

IT'S EASY TO TAKE whipped cream for granted. But perfectly whipped cream is a singular pleasure.

Working in the bowl of a stand mixer fitted with the whisk attachment, or in a large bowl with a hand mixer, beat the cream with the confectioners' sugar on low speed just until it starts to thicken. Taste, and if you want more sugar, add it now. Then continue to beat until you get the thickness you'd like. I start off on low-medium speed with my stand mixer, up the speed to medium/medium-high and beat until the cream is almost the texture I want. I finish it by hand with a whisk, just so I can be in control. When the cream is ready, whip in the vanilla, if you're using it.

STORING: Whipped cream is best used soon after it's made, but you can keep it covered in the refrigerator for a few hours. If you want to store it for up to 24 hours (or if you've got leftover cream that you want to save), line a strainer with a piece of damp cheesecloth, fit the strainer over a bowl, scrape in the cream, cover and refrigerate.

# Lemon Curd

*Makes about 2 cups*

1¼ cups (250 grams) sugar

4 large eggs

1 tablespoon light corn syrup

¾ cup (180 ml) freshly squeezed lemon juice (from 4 to 6 lemons)

1 stick (8 tablespoons; 4 ounces; 113 grams) unsalted butter, cut into chunks

USE THIS CURD in a tart or as the filling for a jelly roll or a layer cake or just spread it over a toasted English muffin. It's very easy to make, quick too, and always better than store-bought. If you'd like, use a combination of lemon and lime juice.

Whisk the sugar, eggs and corn syrup together in a medium saucepan. Whisk in the lemon juice and then drop in the butter. Place the pan over medium heat and, whisking all the while—make sure to get into the corners—cook for 6 to 8 minutes. You're looking for the curd to thicken enough for the whisk to leave tracks and, most of all, for a bubble or two to come to the surface and pop.

Scrape the curd into a heatproof bowl or jar and press a piece of plastic wrap against the top to seal it. Cool to room temperature and then chill in the refrigerator before using.

STORING: Kept in an airtight container, the curd will hold in the fridge for about 3 weeks.

# Chocolate Ganache

*Makes about 2 cups*

1 cup (240 ml) plus 2 tablespoons heavy cream

8 ounces (227 grams) semisweet or bittersweet chocolate, finely chopped

½ stick (4 tablespoons; 2 ounces; 57 grams) unsalted butter, cut into 4 pieces, at room temperature

I KNOW THAT there's science explaining why ganache works, but really it's magic. You stir three rich ingredients together—chocolate, cream and butter—and they form a silken emulsion. You can use ganache as a tart filling (pour it into a prebaked crust and chill it) or as a glaze. For a glaze, use it as soon as it's made: Pour it over whatever you're glazing or use it as dip for decorating cookies. Chill ganache, and it becomes a frosting or a spread to use between cake layers or to sandwich cookies.

Rinse a small saucepan with cold water, but don't dry it (this helps prevent the cream from scorching). Pour in the cream, set the pan over medium heat and bring just to a boil.

Remove from the heat and add the chocolate. Wait 30 seconds and then, working with a small flexible spatula and beginning in the center of the pan, start stirring the chocolate and cream together. Stir in ever-widening concentric circles until you have a thick, shiny, smooth mixture. Piece by piece, blend in the butter until melted and smooth.

If you're using the ganache as a filling or glaze, use it immediately. If you're using it to frost a cake, you'll have to wait for it to thicken. You can leave it on the counter, stirring occasionally (it thickens slowly), or you can put the bowl in a larger bowl of cold water and ice cubes, in which case, stir often and stay close—it can thicken in a flash in the ice bath. Alternatively, chill it in the refrigerator, checking on it and stirring frequently. If you miss the moment, you can always reheat the ganache gently.

STORING: Tightly covered, ganache will keep in the refrigerator for up to 5 days or in the freezer for up to 2 months. Let it come to room temperature before using. You can also bring the ganache to temperature in a microwave oven—work in very short spurts, and don't forget to stir—or you can put the bowl over a saucepan of simmering water and stir until you get the consistency you want. Whatever method you use to warm the ganache, be gentle—too much heat, and it can separate.

# Cranberry Curd

*Makes about 2 cups*

One 12-ounce (340 gram) bag cranberries (don't defrost if frozen)

1¼ cups (250 grams) sugar

⅓ cup (80 ml) freshly squeezed lemon juice (from 2 to 3 lemons)

¼ cup (60 ml) freshly squeezed orange or tangerine juice

1 tablespoon light corn syrup

3 large eggs

1 large egg white

1 stick (8 tablespoons; 4 ounces; 113 grams) unsalted butter, cut into chunks

I COULD EAT THIS off a spoon and call it dessert. It's a soft, smooth curd with the sharpness that's cranberry's signature. But because cranberries have skins, this curd takes just a few minutes more to make than citrus curds do—you've got to puree it midway through the cooking. It's worth the effort.

Put the cranberries, sugar, lemon juice, orange juice and corn syrup in a medium saucepan and set over medium heat. Stirring almost constantly—and lowering the heat if there are spatters—cook until the cranberries have popped and the mixture becomes a not-too-thick jam; it'll take about 5 minutes. Scrape the jam into a blender or processor—or use a stick blender—and whir until it's as smooth as you can get it. If you'd like, you can strain it to get rid of any stubborn skins.

Return the jam to the saucepan, beat in the eggs and egg white, drop in the butter and put the pan back over medium heat. Cook, stirring nonstop, until the curd thickens and a bubble or two comes to the surface and pops.

Scrape the curd into a heatproof bowl or jar and press a piece of plastic wrap against the top to seal it. Cool to room temperature and then chill in the refrigerator before using.

STORING: Kept in an airtight container, the curd will hold in the fridge for about 3 weeks.

# Caramel Applesauce

*Makes about 1¾ cups*

⅔ cup (133 grams) sugar

2 to 2½ pounds (about 1 kilo) apples (3 large or 5 medium), peeled, halved, cored and quartered

IF AN APPLESAUCE could qualify as complex, this one would. First you make a caramel, then lay the apples in it. They cook until they're so tender that they qualify as mushy, and that's it. Run them through a food mill or simply beat them into sauciness with a wooden spoon. I use this in the Apple Galette (page 248), but it's good for a bunch of other things, including spreading on biscuits or scones; serving alongside a simple cake, like Miso-Maple Loaf (page 69) or Buttermilk-Molasses Quick Bread (page 82); or just enjoying by the spoonful, with or without yogurt or vanilla ice cream.

TO MAKE THE CARAMEL: Choose a skillet that's about 9 inches in diameter (I prefer nonstick), pour in the sugar and spread it evenly over the bottom of the pan. (If you're new to carameling, you might want to moisten the sugar with a tablespoon or 2 of water. Adding water slows the process, giving you a bit more time to judge the color.) Turn the heat under the pan to medium-high and stay close. As soon as you see the sugar changing color around the edges of the pan, either swirl the pan or use a silicone spatula or wooden spoon to stir small circles around the pan's circumference, drawing the unmelted sugar to the edges little by little. When all the sugar has melted and turned a light amber color—if it's smoking, don't be alarmed—take the pan off the heat.

Arrange the apples snugly in the pan. Put the pan over medium-high heat and bring the caramel to a boil. Lower the heat to medium and cook for about 20 minutes—no need to do anything but keep an eye on the pan and turn the heat down if there's spattering. When you can easily pierce the apples with a knife, use a spoon to turn them over (don't worry if they break) and cook for 5 more minutes.

The apples are scalding hot, so you might want to let them cool a bit before pureeing them. Scrape the apples into a food mill and puree them into a bowl, beat them with a spoon until they're saucy or blend them with a stand or immersion blender. It's unlikely, but if the applesauce isn't as thick as you'd like it now, scrape it into a saucepan and cook it down a bit.

Spoon the applesauce into a heatproof container and once it cools, cover it tightly—or serve.

STORING: Kept covered in the refrigerator, the applesauce will be delicious for at least 3 weeks.

# Streusel

*Makes about 1½ cups*

¾ cup (102 grams) all-purpose flour

3 tablespoons sugar

1 tablespoon brown sugar

¼ teaspoon ground cinnamon

¼ teaspoon fine sea salt

5½ tablespoons (2¾ ounces; 78 grams) cold unsalted butter, cut into small cubes

½ teaspoon pure vanilla extract

STREUSEL MAKES a great topping for coffee cakes or muffins, fruit pies and crisps. And if you bake it (see Playing Around), you'll have delicious crunchy bits to scatter over soft sweets like ice cream and mousse. You can make the streusel by hand or with a mixer.

PLAN AHEAD: The streusel should be chilled for at least an hour; 3 hours is better (a longer chill means that the streusel will hold its shape better under heat).

Whisk the flour, both sugars, the cinnamon and salt together in a medium bowl or the bowl of a stand mixer. Drop in the cubes of cold butter and toss the ingredients together with your fingers until the butter is coated.

TO MIX THE STREUSEL BY HAND: Squeeze, mush or otherwise mash, rub and press everything together until you have a bowl of moist clumps and curds. You know it's ready if you can pinch the streusel and it holds together. Sprinkle over the vanilla and toss to blend.

TO MAKE THE STREUSEL WITH A STAND MIXER: Attach the bowl to the mixer stand, fit it with the paddle attachment and mix on medium-low speed until the ingredients form moist, clumpy crumbs. Pinch the streusel, and it should hold together. Reaching this stage may take longer than you'd expect, so hold on. Sprinkle over the vanilla and mix until blended.

Pack the streusel into a covered container and refrigerate for at least 1 hour (3 hours are better) before using. To use the streusel for a topping, pinch off pieces of varying sizes.

STORING: Stored in a ziplock bag (squeeze out as much of the air as you can) or a sealed container, the streusel will keep in the refrigerator for up to 2 weeks. Packed airtight, it can be frozen for up to 2 months; thaw in the refrigerator.

## Playing Around

BAKED STREUSEL CRUNCH

Make the streusel and chill it for 2 hours or more. When you're ready to bake, center a rack in the oven and preheat it to 350 degrees F. Line a baking sheet with parchment paper or a baking mat. Spread the streusel over the sheet, using your fingers to either loosen clumps or make them, depending on what you want to use the streusel for. Bake for 15 minutes or so, stirring often, until the streusel is golden brown. Transfer the baking sheet to a rack and let cool to room temperature. You can keep the crunch in a container at room temperature for up to 1 week; freeze for longer storage.

# Cocoa Streusel

*Makes about 2 cups*

1 cup (136 grams) all-purpose flour

⅓ cup (67 grams) packed brown sugar

¼ cup (21 grams) unsweetened cocoa powder

2 tablespoons sugar

½ teaspoon fine sea salt

5½ tablespoons (2¾ ounces; 78 grams) cold unsalted butter, cut into small cubes

**PLAN AHEAD:** The streusel should be chilled for at least 2 hours.

**VERY DARK AND DEEPLY CHOCOLATY,** this streusel can be used in two ways. You can sprinkle it over the tops of cakes and cookies before you slide them into the oven, or you can bake the streusel and use it to add crunch to tarts, puddings, ice cream or even your morning yogurt.

Put all of the ingredients *except* the butter in a medium bowl and toss them together with your fingers—you want to make sure that neither the brown sugar nor the cocoa is lumpy. Drop in the pieces of butter and rub and squeeze everything together until you've got moist clumps and curds.

Cover and refrigerate for at least 2 hours before using or baking. (*The streusel can be refrigerated for up to a week.*)

**TO BAKE THE STREUSEL:** Center a rack in the oven and preheat it to 300 degrees F. Line a baking sheet with parchment paper or a baking mat.

Spread the streusel over the baking sheet, using your fingers to either loosen clumps or make them, depending on what you want to use the streusel for. Bake for 15 to 18 minutes, or until the crumbs have separated into grains or small clusters. Let the crumbs cool to room temperature on the baking sheet before using or packing for storage.

**STORING:** The unbaked streusel will keep for up to a week in the refrigerator. The baked crumbs will keep in a sealed container at room temperature for at least 1 week or in the freezer for up to 2 months. Break up any big crumbs with your fingers before using.

# Praline Sprinkle and Spread

*Makes about 3 cups sprinkle or 1½ cups spread*

1 cup (200 grams) sugar

1½ cups (200 grams) roasted peanuts or other nuts (see headnote), warm or at room temperature

A WORD ON QUANTITY:
You can use all of the brittle to make the sprinkle or spread, or use some of it to make sprinkle and some to make spread—the recipe's flexible. If you make both sprinkle and spread, you'll obviously have less of each than indicated in the yield.

THIS PRALINE IS SIMPLY A BRITTLE made from turning nuts in caramelized sugar. Two ingredients, about 4 minutes of work and endless pleasure. While you might want to eat the brittle as soon as it cools, I beg you to leave enough of it to make both the sprinkle and spread. A little whir in a food processor and you'll have praline sprinkle, flavorful bits and dust for topping Peanut-Butter Chocolate Chip Cookies, Paris Style (page 156) or One Big Break-Apart Chipper (page 152) or for sprinkling over pudding, ice cream, custard or yogurt. Continue to whir the sprinkle in the processor, and you'll get a paste—think cookie spread, like Nutella or peanut butter.

You can make the praline with pretty much any kind of nut—almonds, pecans, pistachios, peanuts or a mix—but you need to use an equal weight (*weight,* not volume) of sugar and nuts. And don't start with less than 3½ ounces (100 grams) nuts unless you've got a mini food processor (less won't spin around in the work bowl).

Have a nonstick baking sheet or one lined with a baking mat at hand. Also have a silicone spatula or wooden spoon at the ready.

Put the sugar in a heavy-bottomed pan—you can use a skillet or a medium saucepan. Turn the heat under the pan to medium-high and stay close. As soon as you see the sugar changing color around the edges of the pan, either swirl the pan or use the spatula or wooden spoon to stir small circles around the pan's circumference, drawing the unmelted sugar to the edges little by little. When all the sugar has melted and turned a light amber color—if it's smoking, don't be alarmed, but do move the pan away from the heat for a moment—take the pan off the heat and add the nuts.

Put the pan back on the burner, lower the heat to medium and stir to coat the nuts with caramel, another minute or so. Scrape the nuts and caramel onto the baking sheet, spreading the brittle out if you can (don't worry if you can't). Set aside until the brittle has cooled to room temperature, then crack it into shards.

**TO MAKE THE SPRINKLE:** Toss the pieces of brittle into a food processor and pulse until you've got a powder—I think it's nice when there are a few discernible bits of brittle here and there, but feel free to opt for homogeneity. If all you want is sprinkle, you're done, but I usually remove some of the sprinkle and turn the rest into spread. (FYI: 1 cup sprinkle will make ½ cup spread.)

**TO MAKE THE SPREAD:** Toss the pieces of brittle (or the sprinkle) into the food processor and whir in long pulses, stopping often to scrape the sides and bottom of the bowl, until you've got a mixture that resembles peanut butter. You might be tempted to stop early—don't. You want to keep processing until the caramel is broken down (the heat from the machine helps here) and the nuts have released their oil.

**STORING:** Packed airtight and stored in a cool, dry place, the sprinkle will keep for a couple of weeks; don't refrigerate it. If the sprinkle gets moist, spread it out on a baking sheet and dry it for a couple of minutes in a moderate oven. Kept in a tightly covered container at room temperature, the spread will be good for about 2 weeks; stir before using.

# Caramel Sauce

*Makes about 1½ cups*

1 cup (200 grams) sugar

3 tablespoons water

1 tablespoon light corn syrup

¾ (180 ml) heavy cream, warmed or at room temperature

½ teaspoon sea salt, preferably fleur de sel

2 tablespoons unsalted butter, at room temperature

1½ teaspoons pure vanilla extract

THE FIRST TIME I paid attention to caramel sauce was at a dressy restaurant, where it was brought to the table by a waiter, who lifted the small pitcher with a sense of ceremony and poured thick ribbons of the sauce over a thin slice of tart. At that time, I didn't know that you could make the sauce in minutes. Even though I make it often at home now, I still think it's fancy, mostly because of what it's capable of doing: A spoonful of it turns a scoop of vanilla ice cream into a celebration. It's part of what makes the Parfait-Layered Vacherin (page 239) so good, and it's wondrous with just about anything chocolate.

Put the sugar, water and corn syrup in a medium heavy-bottomed saucepan, set the pan over medium-high heat and cook—don't stir the ingredients, but once they melt and start coloring, swirl the pan—until the caramel, which will boil and may even smoke, turns a medium amber color. (You can check the color by dropping some on a white plate.) As the caramel cooks, it might spatter onto the sides of the pan—wash down the spatters with a silicone or other pastry brush dipped in cold water.

Turn off the heat, stand back and add the cream, salt and butter. The mixture will sputter dramatically, but it will quickly calm down, and when it does, stir until it is smooth and creamy. If there are lumps of caramel or some not melted at the bottom of the pan, return the pan to medium heat and stir for another minute or two to smooth things out. Stir in the vanilla extract.

Pour the sauce into a heatproof jar or container and leave uncovered until it reaches room temperature.

STORING: You can keep the sauce tightly covered in the refrigerator for up to 1 month. Warm it gently so that it's pourable (you can do this in the microwave) and thin it with a little cream, if you'd like.

# Hot Fudge Sauce

*Makes a generous cup*

6 ounces (170 grams) semisweet or bittersweet chocolate (not chips), finely chopped

¾ cup (180 ml) heavy cream

3 tablespoons light corn syrup

2 tablespoons sugar

THE ICE-CREAM–PARLOR PERENNIAL, but better than anything you can buy, because you get to make it with your favorite chocolate. It's great with either semisweet or bittersweet chocolate, but not really right with chocolate chips—they just don't melt properly.

Put all the ingredients in a medium saucepan and cook over medium-low heat, stirring constantly, until the chocolate melts and the mixture comes to a light simmer, about 5 minutes. Still stirring, let it simmer for a minute or two, then scrape it into a heatproof container.

You can use the sauce now, or cover and refrigerate until needed. Reheat gently before using.

STORING: You can keep the sauce tightly covered in the refrigerator for up to 2 weeks.

# Coffee Extract

*Makes about 2 tablespoons*

1½ tablespoons instant espresso

¼ teaspoon sugar (optional)

1 tablespoon boiling water

THINK OF THIS AS COFFEE CONCENTRATE, a way to add coffee's full flavor and aroma to a recipe without adding a lot of liquid. I rely on it for the Mochaccino Muffins (page 68), and use it when I want to flavor a frosting, an icing or a plain batter. The recipe produces just a couple of spoonfuls, which is all you usually need for one baking session—it's strong stuff!—but it multiplies endlessly and keeps a long time.

Stir the espresso and sugar, if you're using it, into the boiling water, mixing to dissolve the powder. Cool before using.

STORING: The extract will keep in a tightly covered jar for months at room temperature or in the fridge.

# Confectioners' Sugar Icing

*Makes about ½ cup*

1 cup (120 grams) confectioners' sugar (or more or less, depending on what you want), sifted

About 1 tablespoon milk, water, lemon juice or other liquid (or more or less, depending on what you want)

¼ teaspoon pure vanilla extract (optional)

**A WORD ON QUANTITY:** Figure that you'll end up with half as much icing by volume than the amount of sugar you start with. You'll get slightly more if you want a thinner, more translucent glaze.

CONFECTIONERS' SUGAR ICING is the most versatile decoration in a baker's kit. It can be made translucent or opaque, flavored or not, colored or not, and drizzled or brushed. It's nothing more than a lot of sugar and a little liquid. The sugar is always confectioners,' but the liquid can be water or milk, lemon juice or even something alcoholic. And the recipe—well, you kind of make it up as you go along: It depends on what you're using it for. Less liquid for opaque drizzles, more for thinner, clearer glazes. Add cocoa for a chocolate finish (see Playing Around).

Put the confectioners' sugar in a medium bowl and little by little, work in the milk or other liquid with a flexible spatula. At first it will seem impossible that such a small amount of liquid could moisten all that sugar—just keep stirring. Add the vanilla, if you're using it, and then, if you'd like a thinner icing, add more liquid by the drop. If the icing is too thin, add a little more sugar. For most jobs, an icing that falls slowly and steadily from the tip of a spoon is just right.

**STORING:** It's best to use this icing as soon as it's made.

## Playing Around

### CHOCOLATE ICING

Mix 1 cup (120 grams) confectioners' sugar and 3 tablespoons unsweetened cocoa powder together. Stir in 4 to 5 tablespoons water, depending on the thickness you want.

# Chocolate Glaze or Dip

*Makes about ¼ cup*

3 ounces (85 grams) milk chocolate, semisweet or bittersweet chocolate or good-quality white chocolate

1 teaspoon flavorless oil, such as canola

Food coloring (optional)

THIS IS THE EASIEST WAY I know to add pizazz to plain sweets. The two-ingredient blend allows you to glaze cookies and small cakes by simply dipping them into it; you can cover larger surfaces by pouring it. By adding a small amount of flavorless oil to chocolate, you can create a glaze that firms nicely in the refrigerator. The recipe works for all kinds of chocolate, and if you use white chocolate, you can add food coloring, if you'd like (add it immediately after you've made the glaze). If you want to add sprinkles or crunchies or any kind of other decoration to whatever you've glazed, do it before the glaze sets.

This recipe multiplies easily.

Melt the chocolate and oil together in the microwave—do this in short spurts and stir a few times—or in a heatproof bowl over a pan of simmering water (don't let the bowl touch the water). The mixture is ready to use as soon as it's blended.

If you want to color the glaze, do it as soon as it's made.

Refrigerate whatever you dip or glaze for about 30 minutes to set the chocolate.

STORING: You can keep leftover glaze tightly covered in the refrigerator for 4 days or so; gently reheat before using.

# Vanilla Ice Cream

*Makes about 1½ pints*

2 cups (480 ml) heavy cream

1 cup (240 ml) milk

½ cup (100 grams) sugar

2 tablespoons honey

2 tablespoons powdered milk

2 tablespoons vodka

½ teaspoon fine sea salt

1 tablespoon pure vanilla extract

PLAN AHEAD: The ice cream needs to freeze for at least 6 hours.

THIS IS MY HOUSE ICE CREAM. It's Philadelphia-style, which means that it doesn't have egg yolks. It's a fresh, bright ice cream with a lovely texture and easy scoopability—that's the vodka at work. If you'd like to use a different alcohol, one with flavor, do it. If you want to add chips or nuts, coconut, brittle, cookie bits or anything else, do it just a couple of minutes before you're ready to stop churning.

Working in a blender (first choice) or a food processor, blend all of the ingredients together, scraping the container occasionally, until smooth. Pay attention to the powdered milk—it has a pesky way of clumping. (*The ice cream mixture can be refrigerated, covered, for up to 1 day.*)

When you're ready, pour the mixture into an ice cream maker and churn according to the manufacturer's directions. Pack the ice cream into a freezer container, cover and freeze for at least 6 hours before serving.

The ice cream's texture is best after it's had a few minutes at room temperature, so either take the container out 5 minutes before scooping or scoop and let it stand for a couple of minutes before serving.

STORING: The ice cream will keep in the freezer for at least 1 week. After that, its texture may be a little less velvety.

# Chocolate Ice Cream

*Makes a generous pint*

2 cups (480 ml) heavy cream

1 cup (240 ml) milk

⅔ cup (134 grams) sugar

⅓ cup (28 grams) unsweetened cocoa powder

3 tablespoons powdered milk

½ teaspoon fine sea salt

5 ounces (142 grams) semisweet or bittersweet chocolate, coarsely chopped

2 tablespoons vodka

PLAN AHEAD: The ice cream needs to freeze for at least 6 hours.

LIKE MY VANILLA ICE CREAM (page 374), this mixture is Philadelphia-style, meaning it has no eggs. The flavor is chocolate times two: There's cocoa and semisweet or bittersweet chocolate. As with all homemade ice cream, this one's yours to play with. Add whatever chips or crunchies you'd like, just at the last minute, right before the ice cream is fully churned.

Working in a medium saucepan, whisk together the cream, milk, sugar, cocoa, powdered milk and salt. Try to ignore how ugly it looks—it won't be smooth. Add the chopped chocolate. Set over medium heat and, whisking almost constantly, cook until the chocolate melts and the mixture comes to a boil. Still whisking, boil for 3 minutes, then remove the pan from the heat.

The mixture has to cool before you can churn it, so either leave it on the counter and stir frequently or pour it into a heatproof bowl and set the bowl in a larger bowl filled with water and ice cubes. (*The ice cream mixture can be refrigerated, covered, for up to 1 day.*)

When you're ready, pour the mixture into an ice cream maker and churn according to the manufacturer's directions. Pack the ice cream into a freezer container, cover and freeze for at least 6 hours before serving.

The ice cream's texture is best after it's had a few minutes at room temperature, so either take the container out 5 minutes before scooping or scoop and let it stand for a couple of minutes before serving.

STORING: The ice cream will keep in the freezer for at 1 week. After that, its texture may be a little less velvety.

# Berry Ice Cream

*Makes a generous quart*

8 ounces (226 grams) berries (see headnote), fresh or frozen, hulled if necessary

2 cups (480 ml) heavy cream

1 cup (240 ml) buttermilk (shaken well before measuring) or milk

½ cup (100 grams) sugar

3 tablespoons honey

3 tablespoons powdered milk

3 tablespoons vodka

½ teaspoon fine sea salt

1 teaspoon pure vanilla extract

**PLAN AHEAD:** The ice cream needs to freeze for at least 6 hours.

I MAKE THIS SMOOTH, creamy, easy-to-scoop berry ice cream all the time, using fresh berries in season and frozen berries off-season (don't defrost before using). The recipe works for any kind of berry, so have some fun. The buttermilk amplifies the berries' natural edge, but you can use whole milk, if you prefer.

Working in a blender (first choice) or a food processor, blend all of the ingredients together, scraping the container occasionally, until smooth. Pay attention to the powdered milk—it has a tendency to clump. If the texture of the berry seeds or skins seems too present, press the mixture through a strainer before churning. (*The ice cream mixture can be covered and refrigerated for up to 1 day.*)

When you're ready, pour the mixture into an ice cream maker and churn according to the manufacturer's directions. Pack the ice cream into a freezer container, cover and freeze for at least 6 hours before serving.

The ice cream's texture is best after it's had a few minutes at room temperature, so either take the container out 5 minutes before scooping or scoop and let it stand for a couple of minutes before serving.

**STORING:** The ice cream will keep in the freezer for 1 week. After that, its texture may be a little less velvety.

# Parm Crumble

*Makes about 1⅔ cups*

¾ cup (102 grams) all-purpose flour

7 tablespoons (3½ ounces; 100 grams) cold unsalted butter, cut into 14 pieces

1 loosely packed cup (3 ounces; 85 grams) finely grated Parmesan (see below)

Fine sea salt if needed

**A WORD ON THE CHEESE:** The volume measurement for the Parmesan (1 cup, *not* packed) is based on fine, powdery Parmesan, the texture you get when you buy it ready-grated. If you want to grate your own cheese, do, but please weigh it: you want 3 ounces (85 grams). Also, it's best if you stick to Parmesan or Grana Padano. You won't get the right texture if you use moister, chewier, stretchier cheeses.

**PLAN AHEAD:** The crumble needs to chill for at least 2 hours.

**IF STREUSEL WERE SALTY AND SAVORY AND SHARP,** this is what it would be. You can scatter this over pies like Spinach-Mozzarella Pie with Parm Crumble (page 325), and you might want to use it to top a not-too-sweet muffin. Sometimes I'll scrunch the mixture up to make popcorn-size pieces, bake them and eat them like, well, popcorn, with cocktails; see Playing Around.

Put the flour and cold butter in the food processor and pulse about 5 times, just to coat the butter pieces with flour. Add the Parm and work in long bursts until you have a moist curds-and-clumps dough. Taste the dough and add a little salt if you think it needs it. Pack the dough into a covered container and chill for at least 2 hours before baking as directed in whatever recipe you're using.

**STORING:** Refrigerated, the crumble will keep for about a week. It can be frozen for up to 2 months and used without thawing.

## Playing Around

**PARM CRUMBLE NIBBLES**

Form the dough into nuggets about the size of popcorn and chill. Spread the pieces out on a lined baking sheet and bake in a 350-degree-F oven for 15 to 20 minutes, or until golden. Check a couple of times during the bake, and if the nuggets have spread and are sticking together, break them up. Cool on the baking sheet.

# Cheddar Streusel

*Makes about 1½ cups*

¾ cup (102 grams) all-purpose flour

2 teaspoons sugar

½ teaspoon fine sea salt

5½ tablespoons (2½ ounces; 78 grams) very cold unsalted butter, cut into small pieces

¼ cup (20 grams) shredded sharp cheddar (see below)

**A WORD ON THE CHEESE:** If you use store-bought shredded cheddar, as I often do, coarsely chop it before you add it to the streusel.

**PLAN AHEAD:** The streusel needs to be refrigerated for at least an hour before using.

SCATTER THIS STREUSEL OVER Cheese-Swirl Babka Buns (page 38), Tomato Tart (page 322), Pear-Comté Tart (page 309) or a quiche. It's a great make-something-better recipe.

Whisk together the flour, sugar and salt in a medium bowl or the bowl of a stand mixer. Drop in the cubes of cold butter and toss the ingredients together with your fingers until the butter is coated.

**TO MIX THE STREUSEL BY HAND:** Squeeze, mush or otherwise mash, rub and press everything together until you have a bowl of moist clumps and curds. You'll know it's ready when you can pinch the streusel and it holds together. Stir in the cheese.

**TO MAKE THE STREUSEL WITH A STAND MIXER:** Attach the bowl to the mixer stand, fit it with the paddle attachment and mix on medium-low speed until the ingredients form moist, clumpy crumbs. Pinch the streusel, and it should hold together. Reaching this stage may take longer than you'd expect, so hold on. Add the cheese.

Pack the streusel into a covered container and refrigerate for at least 1 hour. When you're ready to use the streusel for a topping, pinch off pieces of varying sizes.

**STORING:** Stored in a ziplock bag (squeeze out as much of the air as you can) or a sealed container, the streusel will keep in the refrigerator for up to 2 weeks. Packed airtight, it can be frozen for up to 2 months; thaw in the refrigerator.

## Playing Around

If you'd like, add a pinch or two of chile powder or herbs (fresh or dried) to the mix. Whisk them together with the flour. The streusel can also take nuts—try it with pumpkin seeds, say ¼ cup's (a small handful) worth. Add them after the cheese.

# Strained Yogurt

Plain yogurt, preferably Greek

**A WORD ON QUANTITY:**
Depending on how much liquid your yogurt has to begin with, you might lose half its volume in straining, so plan accordingly.

STRAINED YOGURT CAN BE A NICE STAND-IN for whipped cream alongside a slice of pie or atop a wedge of cake—even better if you're looking for a touch of acidity. It's good plain, mixed with a little sugar, drizzled with honey or topped with jam. To tilt it in a savory direction for serving alongside a savory tart or galette, add a little salt and any herbs or spices you'd like after it's strained.

You'll need a strainer, a large bowl to set it over—you want a few inches between the bottom of the bowl and the bottom of the strainer—and some cheesecloth. Cut two large pieces of cheesecloth, dampen them, wring them out and lay them in the strainer to form a double layer. You may have to crisscross them.

Put the yogurt in the cheesecloth, draw up the edges to make a bundle and squeeze to release as much liquid as you can. (Don't tighten the top so much that when you squeeze, you risk tearing the cheesecloth.) Place the cheesecloth bundle in the strainer, put a weight on top of it and stow the setup in the fridge. Let the yogurt drain for at least 3 hours, or as long as overnight.

**STORING:** Kept in a covered container in the refrigerator, the strained yogurt will hold for about 3 days.

# Herbed Ricotta

*Makes about 2 cups*

2 cups whole-milk ricotta, drained if necessary (see below)

1 large lemon

3 tablespoons minced shallots, rinsed in cold water and patted dry

2 scallions, trimmed and thinly sliced

1 tablespoon extra-virgin olive oil

About ½ teaspoon fleur de sel or ¼ teaspoon fine sea salt, or more to taste

Freshly ground black pepper

⅓ cup minced mixed fresh herbs, such as dill, parsley, tarragon, thyme, cilantro and/or basil

**A WORD ON THE RICOTTA:** If there's liquid in the container, it's best to drain it. Line a strainer with a double thickness of damp cheesecloth, place it over a bowl, spoon in the ricotta and pull the edges of the cheesecloth up around the cheese; weight it with a plate or a can of something. Put it in the refrigerator and let drain for from 30 minutes to up to 1 day.

**PLAN AHEAD:** The ricotta should be chilled for at least an hour before serving.

**THIS RECIPE IS A STANDARD FOR ME.** I usually have some in the fridge, and while it's good just piled on a piece of toast (try it on a thick slice of The Daily Bread, page 000), I like to serve it with Tomato Tart (page 322) or alongside Double-Corn Tomato Crisp or make it the base of the Vegetable Ribbon Tart (page 319).

Put the ricotta in a medium bowl. Finely grate the lemon zest over the cheese, then juice the lemon and blend the juice into the ricotta. Stir in the shallots, scallions, olive oil, salt and a healthy pinch of pepper. Taste for salt and pepper, then stir in the herbs. Cover and chill for at least 1 hour.

Taste and adjust for salt, pepper and lemon juice if necessary before serving.

**STORING:** Tightly covered, the ricotta will keep in the refrigerator for up to 2 days. Stir well before using.

# Index

Note: Page references in *italics* indicate photographs.